DEMISE OF THE BRITISH EMPIRE IN THE MIDDLE EAST

To the memory of our parents

DEMISE OF THE BRITISH EMPIRE IN THE MIDDLE EAST

Britain's Responses to Nationalist Movements 1943–55

Edited by

MICHAEL J. COHEN and
MARTIN KOLINSKY

LONDON AND NEW YORK

First Published in 1998 in Great Britain by
Routledge
2 Park Square, Milton Park, Abingdon, Oxon, OX14 4RN
270 Madison Ave, New York NY 10016

Transferred to Digital Printing 2011

Website http://www.routledge.com

Copyright of collection © 1998 Routledge & Co. Ltd.
Copyright of articles © 1998 contributors

British Library Cataloguing in Publication Data

Demise of the British Empire in the Middle East: Britain's responses to
nationalist movements, 1943–55
1. National liberation movements – Middle East – History
2. Great Britain – Colonies – Asia   3. Great Britain –
Politics and government – 1945–1964
I. Cohen, Michael J. (Michael Joseph), 1940–   II. Kolinsky,
Martin
322.4'2'0956'09044

ISBN 0-7146-4804-3 (cloth)
ISBN 0-7146-4477-3 (paper)

Library of Congress Cataloging-in-Publication Data

Demise of the British Empire in the Middle East: Britain's responses to
nationalist movements, 1943–55 / edited by Michael J. Cohen and Martin
Kolinsky.
   p.   cm.
Includes bibliographical references (p.   ) and index.
ISBN 0-7146-4804-3 (cloth)   0-7146-4477-3 (paper)
1. Great Britain–Foreign relations–Middle East. 2. Middle East–
Foreign relations–Great Britain. 3. Great Britain–Politics and
government–1945– 4. Middle East–Politics and government–1945–
5. Nationalism–Middle East. I. Cohen, Michael Joseph, 1940–
II. Kolinsky, Martin.
DS63.2.G7D46   1998
327.41056–dc21   98-14415
                                                                                   CIP

*All rights reserved. No part of this publication may be reproduced, stored in or introduced
into a retrieval system, or transmitted, in any form or by any means, electronic,
mechanical, photocopying, recording or otherwise, without the prior written permission of
the publisher of this book.*

Typeset by Vitaset, Paddock Wood, Kent

Publisher's Note
The publisher has gone to great lengths to ensure the quality of this reprint
but points out that some imperfections in the original may be apparent.

Contents

Notes on the contributors	vii
Preface	ix
List of abbreviations	xi
Map of the Mediterranean and Middle East theatre of war	xii
Introduction	xiii

PART 1: THE EFFECT OF WAR ON THE MIDDLE EAST

1 Britain and decolonization: The Labour governments
and the Middle East, 1945–51
NICHOLAS OWEN … 3

2 The strategic role of the Middle East after the war
MICHAEL J. COHEN … 23

PART 2: ASPECTS OF ARAB NATIONALISM

3 Britain and the politics of the Arab League, 1943–50
MICHAEL THORNHILL … 41

4 Economic aspects of Arab nationalism
RODNEY WILSON … 64

5 A new Middle East? The crystallization of the Arab state
system after the Second World War
BRUCE MADDY-WEITZMAN … 79

vi *Demise of the British Empire in the Middle East*

PART 3: EGYPT IN CONFLICT WITH BRITAIN

6 Lampson and the wartime control of Egypt
MARTIN KOLINSKY   95

7 Egypt 1945–52: The uses of disorder
CHARLES TRIPP   112

8 Britain and the Egyptian problem, 1945–48
JOHN KENT   142

9 Discord or partnership? British and American policy
  toward Egypt, 1942–56
PETER L. HAHN   162

PART 4: DEGREES OF ACCOMMODATION WITH BRITAIN

10 The decline of British influence and the ruling elite in Iraq
MICHAEL EPPEL   185

11 British rule in Jordan, 1943–55
ILAN PAPPÉ   198

12 Britain and the Palestine question, 1945–48: The dialectic
   of regional and international constraints
AVRAHAM SELA   220

Index   247

Notes on the contributors

Michael J. Cohen holds the Lazarus Philips Chair in History at Bar-Ilan University, Israel. In 1998 he was appointed a Member of the Institute for Advanced Study, Princeton. His latest books are *Truman and Israel* (1990), and *Fighting World War Three from the Middle East: Allied Contingency Plans, 1945–54* (1997). He also co-edited a volume with Martin Kolinsky, *Britain and the Middle East in the 1930s* (1992).

Michael Eppel is Lecturer in the Department of Middle Eastern History at the University of Haifa, Israel. His publications include *The Palestine Conflict in the History of Modern Iraq* (1994).

Peter L. Hahn is Associate Professor of History at Ohio State University, and associate editor of *Diplomatic History*. He is author of *The United States, Great Britain and Egypt, 1945–1956* (1991) and several articles on Anglo–American relations and US policy in the Middle East. He is currently writing a major monograph on US policy toward the Arab–Israeli conflict through 1967.

John Kent is Reader in International History at the London School of Economics and Political Science. His publications include *The Internationalization of Colonialism: Britain, France and Black Africa, 1939–1956* (1992), and *British Imperial Strategy and the Origins of the Cold War, 1944–1949* (1993). He has recently completed a three-volume study of Egypt and the Defence of the Middle East 1945–56 as part of the British Documents on the End of Empire project, to be published by the Stationery Office in 1998.

Martin Kolinsky is Senior Lecturer in the Department of Political Science and International Studies, University of Birmingham. His latest books are *Law, Order and Riots in Mandatory Palestine, 1928–1935* (1993), and, co-edited with Michael J. Cohen, *Britain and the Middle East in the 1930s* (1992). His next book is on British Policy towards the Middle East during the Second World War.

Bruce Maddy-Weitzman is Senior Research Associate at the Moshe Dayan Center for Middle Eastern and African Studies, Tel Aviv University. His publications include *The Crystallization of the Arab State System, 1945–1954* (1993), and he edited, with Efraim Inbar, *Religious Radicalism in the Greater Middle East* (1997). He is editor of *Middle East Contemporary Survey* (annual).

Nicholas Owen is Praelector in Politics and University Lecturer at Queen's College, Oxford. He is author of several articles on aspects of decolonization in British politics and his book on the Labour Party and Indian Independence is to be published by the Clarendon Press.

Ilan Pappé is Senior Lecturer in the Department of Political Science, Haifa University, and the academic head of the Institute for Peace Research at Givat Haviva, Israel. He is author of *Britain and the Arab–Israeli Conflict, 1948–1951* (1988) and *The Making of the Arab–Israeli Conflict, 1947–1951* (1992). He is co-editor, with J. Nevo, of *Jordan: The Making of a Pivotal State* (1995), and, with M. Maoz, of *Ideas and Politics in the Middle East* (1997).

Avraham Sela is Senior Lecturer in Middle Eastern Studies at the Department of International Relations, the Hebrew University of Jerusalem. He is author of *Unity within Conflict: The Arab Summit Conferences 1964–1982* (1982), and *The Palestinian Ba'th: The Arab Ba'th Socialist Party in the West Bank under Jordan 1948–1967* (1984), both in Hebrew. His forthcoming books are *The Decline of the Arab–Israeli Conflict*, and, as co-editor with Moshe Ma'oz, *The PLO and Israel: From Armed Struggle to Political Settlement*.

Michael Thornhill completed a DPhil in Modern History at the University of Oxford in 1995. His thesis on *Britain and the Egyptian Question, 1950–54* is being published by Macmillan. In 1995–96, he held a Lectureship at Keble College, Oxford, and is currently Research Coordinator on the *New Dictionary of National Biography*.

Charles Tripp is Senior Lecturer in Politics with reference to the Near and Middle East at the School of Oriental and African Studies, University of London. He is co-author (with Shahram Chubin) of *Iran and Iraq at War* (1988) and *Iran–Saudi Arabia Relations and Regional Order* (1996), the co-editor (with Roger Owen) of *Egypt under Mubarak* (1988) and the editor of *Contemporary Egypt: Through Egyptian Eyes* (1993).

Rodney Wilson is Professor of Economics at the University of Durham, and former Pro-Director of the Centre for Middle East and Islamic Studies. Recent publications include: *Economic Development in the Middle East* (1995), and *Economics, Ethics and Religion: Jewish, Christian and Muslim Economic Thought* (1997).

Preface

Compared with the work of a single author, an edited volume provides a variety of perspectives on a subject and draws on a wider range of sources. The task of the editors is to try to find the balance between editorial guidance in the given thematic direction to attain coherence, while respecting the academic freedom of the individual contributors. Clearly an identity of views cannot be imposed, as that would be merely artificial and would drain interest from the material. Rather, the balance has to be achieved through a mutual learning process conducted in good faith. The editors are grateful to the contributors for their co-operation towards this goal. Therefore, it will be clear that the views expressed by the contributors are not necessarily shared by the editors.

We also wish to thank Robert Easton, the former managing editor at Frank Cass, and Andrew Humphrys for their help and encouragement.

The chapters are based on original research, which is documented in the Notes. The most frequently used source was the Public Record Office, Kew, Richmond, Surrey (PRO). Unless otherwise indicated, references are to PRO documents.

The map is reproduced with the kind permission of the Controller of Her Majesty's Stationery Office. It was published originally in *The Mediterranean and the Middle East*, Vol. 1, by Major-General I. S. O. Playfair (London: HMSO, 1954) (United Kingdom Military Series on the History of the Second World War).

Abbreviations

AACE	Anglo–American Committee of Enquiry [on Palestine]
ABC	American, British, Canadian Planners
ACAS	Assistant Chief of Air Staff
AIR	Records of Air Ministry
BDCC(ME)	British Defence Coordinating Committee (Middle East)
BDEEP	British Documents on the End of Empire Project
Cs-in-C	Commanders in Chief
Cab	Records of Cabinet
CCs	Cabinet Conclusions
CM	Cabinet Meeting Minutes
COS	Chiefs of Staff
CP	Cabinet Paper
DCC	Defence Coordination Committee
DEFE	Records of Defence Ministry
DO	Records of Defence Committee
FRUS	*Foreign Relations of the United States*
GOC	General Officer Commanding
HAC	[Palestinian] Higher Arab Committee
IPC	Iraq Petroleum Company
JCS	Joint Chiefs of Staff
JP	Joint Planning Staff Papers
JPS	Joint Planning Staff
JSPC	Joint Strategic Plans Committee (American)
JWPC	Joint War Plans Committee (American)
MEC	Middle East Command
MEDO	Middle East Defence Organization
NA	National Archives, Washington DC
NARA	National Archives and Records Administration
NATO	North Atlantic Treaty Organization
NEA	Office of Near East and African Affairs, State Department
NSC	National Security Council
PHP	Post Hostilities Planning
PREM	Records of the PM's Office
PRO	Public Record Office
PSF	President's Secretary's Files
RG	Record Group, National Archives, Washington, DC
SAC	Strategic Air Command
UN	United Nations
UNSCOP	UN Special Committee on Palestine
WHCF	White House Central File
WP	War Cabinet Paper

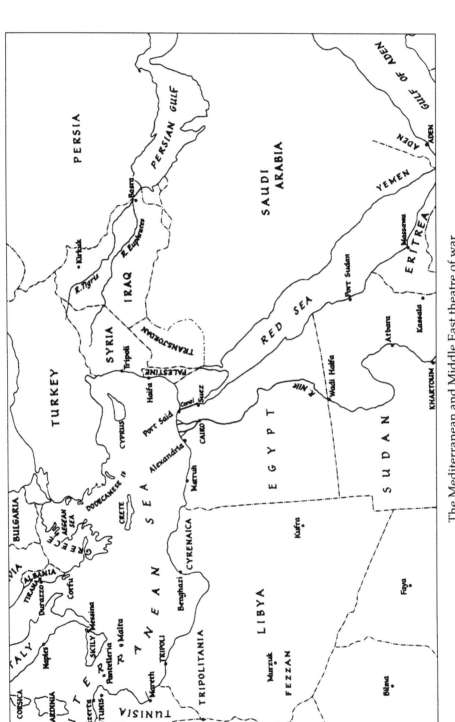

The Mediterranean and Middle East theatre of war

Introduction

The erosion and collapse of British power in the Middle East began during the Second World War and reached its nadir in 1954, with the Anglo–Egyptian agreement to evacuate Egypt. The process of erosion was due both to Britain's decline from Great Power status to junior partner in the Atlantic alliance, and to indigenous developments in the Middle East itself.

During this period of transition, however, Britain remained a serious force in Middle Eastern affairs, with a considerable military presence. Although dependent on America, Britain never forgot her own interests in the Middle East, even in the darkest hours of the war. Hence the ambiguities of the Anglo–American relationship, vacillating between discord and partnership, which are discussed in Peter Hahn's chapter on Egypt. The ambiguities, never resolved, reached boiling point with the Suez Crisis.

The Labour government elected in July 1945 sought to adjust Britain's role to the changing currents of Middle Eastern politics, as the contribution by Nicholas Owen shows. Foreign Secretary Ernest Bevin wanted to restore the legitimacy of the empire in the region by holding out the promise of an economic and social partnership with the masses rather than, as traditionally, with the pashas. But the effort lacked both political and financial credibility. Rodney Wilson's chapter explores the economic aspects further, specifying the extent of Britain's financial debt to Middle Eastern governments, particularly to Egypt, and the unwelcome constraints imposed by the Treasury on holders of sterling assets.

These factors weakened Britain's diplomatic position, but did not bring about a sudden collapse. On the contrary, Britain's unrivalled experience and oversight of Middle Eastern affairs meant that it attempted to influence the very expression of Arab nationalism. Britain's role in the formation and early policies of the Arab League are considered in the chapter by Michael Thornhill. Closely related matters in the politics of the region are discussed by Bruce Maddy-Weitzman, and with specific reference to Jordan and to Israel and the Palestinians in the chapters by Ilan Pappé and Avraham Sela.

The cornerstone of British interests in the Middle East was Egypt, and several chapters are devoted to this subject. Martin Kolinsky focuses on the long-term deleterious effects of the 'Abdin incident', in which the British ambassador forced King Faruq to appoint a government amenable to British interests. This occurred in February 1942, as British forces were retreating before the Rommel offensive in the Western Desert.

After the war, as Michael J. Cohen shows, Britain's strategic interest in Egypt had by 1947 changed from ensuring the security of the Suez Canal, as the main imperial artery to India, to building up the Suez Base in order to defend the region against the Soviets, in the event of a new global conflict. By some contrast, John Kent suggests that the British presence in Egypt after the war became mostly a matter of preserving 'face', in an age when its prestige in the region was very much on the wane. Although divergent, the two approaches are not necessarily in contradiction; rather, they emphasize different aspects of a complex transitional period.

Egyptian politics from 1945 to the Free Officers' *coup d'état* in July 1952 are analyzed by Charles Tripp. He examines the way in which the Wafd party staged and manipulated street demonstrations against the British occupiers, in order to maintain some vestige of nationalist credibility. However, the growing inability of the political parties to control what Tripp calls 'the theatre of mass politics', and the increasing perception that the monarchy was corrupt beyond redemption, led eventually to the overthrow of the established political order. A crucial turning point in the long political crisis was the unsuccessful intervention of Egypt in the 1948 war against the new state of Israel. The defeat brought the Egyptian army into politics.

The coup by the Free Officers was symptomatic of a wider social revolution in the Middle East after the Second World War. As noted by Michael Eppel in his chapter on Iraq, the status of the ruling traditional elites was threatened by a new Westernized middle strata, the *effendiyya*. The old conservative ruling elites had no solutions for the economic and social distress of the masses, or for the aspirations of emergent educated groups. In Iraq the old regime fell in 1958, six years after the coup in Egypt, two years after the Suez Crisis, when al-Nasir's prestige was at its height.

Across the Middle East, the old guard tried to divert the *effendiyya's* frustrations towards the British, a process facilitated by the latter's decline and by their evident incapacity to defend the area against outside threats. The older elites could not escape the censure of the Arab masses for their alleged complicity with outside imperial interests. Thus a new strand of Arab nationalism emerged, and became entangled with the crisis in Palestine.

Introduction   xv

The British decision to relinquish their mandate in Palestine in 1947, and the subsequent vote in the United Nations to partition the country, created a new surge of nationalist emotion. The first Arab–Israeli war in 1948 was a traumatic event, and the standing of the conservative Arab elites was reduced further by the humiliation suffered by the Arabs in the fighting. The Egyptian Army placed the blame for their defeat on King Faruq, who was accused of having exploited the war for his own financial benefit. King Abdallah of Jordan, widely considered in the Arab world to be a 'poodle' of the British, was assassinated in July 1951, when he was believed to be about to sign a peace treaty with Israel.

The various chapters on Britain's turbulent relations with Egypt, Jordan, Iraq and with the Arab League, and her inability to control events in Palestine, all illustrate the final eclipse of British imperial power, despite the efforts of the Labour government to retain dominance and legitimacy in this area of the world.

In conclusion, it should be noted that Saudi Arabia, not surveyed in this volume, was perhaps an exception to the general course of post-1945 history in the region. The demise of British influence and power in the Saudi kingdom may be dated to President Roosevelt's February 1943 decision to grant Lend-Lease aid to Al 'Saud. Thus the British were ousted not by the burgeoning local nationalist agitation that characterized most of her other Middle Eastern holdings, but by the superior economic power of the Americans, which they could neither match nor resist.

PART 1

THE EFFECT OF WAR ON THE MIDDLE EAST

1

Britain and decolonization: The Labour governments and the Middle East, 1945–51

NICHOLAS OWEN

'The benefits of partnership between Britain and the countries of the Middle East have never reached the ordinary people', Bevin wrote to Halifax in October 1945, 'and so our foreign policy has rested on too narrow a footing, mainly on the personalities of kings, princes or pashas. There is thus no vested interest among the peoples to remain with us because of benefits obtained. Hence it is easy for Great Britain to be blamed when difficulties arise.'[1] Bevin's unsuccessful attempt to raise the standard of living of 'peasants not pashas' through economic and social development in the Middle East has usually been mocked as sentimental and ignorant. For John Saville, it amounted to little more than an old man's vanity, which the career diplomats of the Foreign Office were prepared to indulge, provided it did not disturb the familiar rhythms of Britain's traditional alliances in the region.[2] From a very different perspective, Correlli Barnett has pilloried Bevin as a deluded 'world fantasist' obsessed by the fallacy that the Soviet Union was itching to acquire the marginal and poverty-stricken states of the Middle East and that, as a consequence, Britain should pour scarce national resources into a fruitless attempt to develop them.[3]

However, between the lines of Wm Roger Louis and Michael J. Cohen's accounts of British policy in the Middle East and in detailed studies by Wesley K. Wark of the diplomat Sir John Troutbeck, by Paul Kingston of the Development Division of the British Middle East Office, and by Robert Vitalis of Anglo–American competition in Egypt, a more nuanced reading of Bevin's policy can be found.[4] The experiment repays study, not least for the intriguing light it casts both upon Labour perceptions of empire and upon the severe constraints under which any new departure in imperial policy operated.

I

The origins of Labour's distinctive Middle Eastern policy are to be found in several developments. The first was the belief – new found in Labour circles – that the British Empire–Commonwealth, if suitably reformed, might serve as a vehicle for the strengthening of socialism and prosperity at home, and peace abroad.[5] This view had been far from dominant in the Labour Party of the interwar years, when, under the influence of Liberal refugees such as H. N. Brailsford, Leonard Woolf and J. A. Hobson, imperial policy had been dominated by the internationalist conviction that, since competition for colonial raw materials and markets had been a prime cause of the recent global conflict, only the establishment of open diplomacy, regulated by democratic checks and controls, and the placing of colonies under international supervision might prevent a future war. Radical critics on the left had felt from the start that, in the absence of socialist victories at other metropoles, internationalizing the empire would simply collapse into a form of collective colonialism. By 1940, with the failure of the League of Nations to fulfil the internationalists' expectations and the apparent resilience of European colonial systems in the face of internal and external criticism, it now appeared even to Labour's pragmatists that internationalists had placed too much faith in the benevolence of other nations and the power of international organizations. Most important of all, it was hard to see how the principles of the 'open door' and minimal interference under which League mandates operated might be reconciled with the desire of colonial critics such as W. M. Macmillan and the Fabian Colonial Bureau, founded by Arthur Creech Jones and Rita Hinden in 1940, to see colonial governments introduce schemes for strong, centralized, state-led development. In 1943, even such a sceptic as Stafford Cripps, who in the 1930s had regularly denounced the empire as a capitalist conspiracy held together by exploitation, force and fraud, was to be found insisting that it should be seen 'not as a relic of a past era in our history', but as 'a new and powerful weapon', and 'a living, developing organism, full of hope and promise if wisely nurtured, and soundly directed'.[6] For Bevin too, extending wartime planning to the empire provided a means to 'remedy some Nineteenth Century wrongs'.[7] Our crime, he remarked to Francis Williams, 'isn't exploitation. It's neglect.'[8]

Of course, Labour's attachment to developing the empire was not merely a matter of ideological preference; it seemed to follow from the cold logic of Britain's post-war economic and strategic position. By its participation in wartime government, Labour had clearly demonstrated its recognition of a national interest which transcended the domestic

Britain and decolonization 5

political battle and the demands of internationalism. Moreover, the experience of global war ensured that, among Labour's leaders at least, the national interest would be defined imperially, for it seemed to them to prove that the Empire–Commonwealth was a vital support for British pretensions to world-power status. 'If we are to carry our full weight in the post-war world with the US and the USSR', wrote Attlee in 1943, 'it can only be as a united British Commonwealth'.[9] Bevin's famous speech to the 1945 Party Conference made the point effectively:

> You will have to form a Government which is at the centre of a great Empire and Commonwealth of Nations, which touches all parts of the world, and which will have to deal ... with every race and every difficulty.

Domestic matters might be 'fought out on our own soil', but foreign and imperial policy was 'an entirely different situation'. 'Revolutions', Bevin asserted, 'do not change geography'.[10]

In these calculations, the Middle East, delicately poised between the emerging superpowers and their conflicting post-war interests, was to play a central role. For Bevin, indeed, the recent war had proved it was an area of 'cardinal importance ... second only to the United Kingdom itself'.[11] With the loss of the Indian Army, bases in the Middle East were essential bulwarks in Britain's global defences. Airfields in Iraq offered a means of striking at the Soviet Union's oil interests in Grozny and Baku.[12] The Suez base provided Britain with unrivalled military installations in the region and the ability to control the vital artery to the east, through which dollar-free oil supplies and Egyptian cotton, each in their way important for Britain's industrial recovery, were brought. It lay at the heart of Britain's system of global communications to India, the Far East and Australia, and its loss would force costly excursions around the Cape or across central Africa.

Were Britain to weaken her presence, Soviet influence, already pressing hard at the northern tier of the region (Greece, Turkey, Iraq and, above all, Iran, where they remained in occupation until mid-1946) would swiftly move in, with exactly the same hideous consequences for British interests as had occurred in eastern Europe. Indeed, Soviet success in the Middle East would provide communism with an eastern entrée to India, Burma and Malaya, and southern and western doors into Africa. For Bevin no less than Eden, therefore, the Middle East was Britain's jugular vein, to be protected at almost any cost. It was with these arguments and the aid of the Foreign Office and the Chiefs of Staff that Bevin was able by the summer of 1947 to crush Attlee's attempt to question Britain's place in the Middle East.[13] For Attlee, modern air power and decolonization in Asia had rendered the historic role of the region as the gateway to the Indian Ocean redundant. It might be left as a huge and desolate buffer zone – a 'wide glacis of desert and Arabs'[14] – between areas of British and Soviet influence. His arguments, however, most notably in their insistence that the Middle East empire could be defended better by the United Nations than by British forces, were less a prescient view of Britain's declining power than a late flowering of the pre-war internationalist ethos. It was for this reason that they were fatally weakened by the onset of the cold war.

If the region was to play this part well, however, it had to be developed. 'My whole aim', Bevin wrote to Attlee in January 1947, 'has been to develop the Middle East as a producing area to help our own economy and take the place of India.' True, its economies were still weak and vulnerable, lacking the trained manpower necessary for high productivity in peacetime and effective defence in wartime; its states were divided by ethnic and dynastic rivalries; but with measures to promote economic growth and regional defence reorganization under British auspices, Bevin hoped, this could all change. 'This was once a rich region', he told Attlee, 'and could be so again with good government and modern methods'. 'If we help it to build itself up', he insisted, 'it can become economically prosperous and a valuable market for us.'[15] Besides its military and economic benefits, development would bring political stability to the region. Schemes of economic modernization, in offering a better standard of living to the peasants and workers who worked in them and political experience and authority to the educated classes who would be trained to administer them, would strengthen the case for future partnership with Britain. They would also undermine the arguments of radicals and communists both in the Middle East and in the Soviet bloc that imperial ties were inherently exploitative. The sensitivity Britain showed in handling the nationalist demands of her colonies, after all, was a significant measure of her international moral reputation, and as such an important weapon in the propaganda of the cold war. To meet the Soviet challenge required an effective partnership with the United States and acquiring a reputation for liberalism at the United Nations and other international forums by replacing the language and practice of colonialism with that of partnership and development.

So much, of course, was common ground across the party system. Given the severe post-war limits on Britain's resources, pressure for demobilization and economies, and the unwillingness of the British electorate to sanction colonial war or even prolonged suppression of resistance, it clearly made sense for Britain to seek to maintain its primacy by converting systems of formal rule and alliances into an informal system based on ties of mutual interest and regard. Indeed, in essence this was nothing very new, for ever since 1917, formal rule had rarely been regarded as an indispensable means of securing British

Britain and decolonization 7

interests. Even before Labour ministers produced their own proposals, Foreign Office officials had clearly recognized that it would no longer be possible to hold the Middle East with the methods of Cromer, but that moderate nationalists should be strengthened against the radicals through quiet and unobtrusive support.[16] It is likely therefore that any party would have had to reduce the massive costs of military occupation of the Middle East through soliciting co-operation with local nationalist politicians. Exactly such a process of retraction and redeployment had been carried out after the First World War.[17]

Labour's distinctiveness thus lay neither in the ends of imperial policy, nor wholly in the means devised to attain them, but more in the route by which it had reached them. Labour's schemes of social and economic development were the product neither of unthinking imperialist attitudes inherited from wartime association with its political opponents, nor of its supposedly craven dependence upon traditionally minded civil servants and military advisers. Rather, their true origins lie in Bevin's – and Labour's – long-standing concern about the unhealthy turn that nationalism had taken in the colonized world, and its desire to remould it into shapes with which British socialists could work.

In the evolution of these views, Labour's unhappy encounter with Indian nationalism was formative.[18] While the party had long held that India should achieve political freedom, it had been periodically troubled with the prospect that it would do so under the leadership of the Congress Party, which, dominated by lawyers and businessmen, seemed an unlikely vehicle for the advancement of working-class interests or for genuine industrial and economic change, and which employed strategies of non-co-operation and civil disobedience strongly at odds with Labour's own ideas of responsible political action. During the war, irritated by the unwillingness of Congress to support the British war effort, Bevin and Cripps had therefore called for a more progressive social and industrial policy aimed at making the 'struggle in India ... no longer ... between Indian and British on the nationalist basis, but between the classes in India upon an economic basis', thereby 'splitting Congress' and diverting nationalists from sterile oppositionism into the more profitable channels of 'nation-building'. The plan, Bevin had argued, 'offered a first rate opportunity of turning the minds of the people of India from political agitation towards economic progress'.[19]

II

These Indian experiments were rendered irrelevant by the success of the Congress Party in the elections of October 1945. But many of the same ideas found their way into Labour's plans for remaining parts of the Empire–Commonweath, such as Cyprus and west and central Africa.[20] In the Middle East, it took the form of Bevin's attempt to harness the energies of Arab nationalism for new purposes. There were three main elements to his policy. First, Bevin repeatedly ruled out the use of force to repress nationalist political activity, except where this itself took the form of violence or terrorism. Like Attlee, Bevin held that, unless there was a clear threat to public order, the deployment of British bayonets against nationalists would simply alienate precisely those elements whose support it was necessary to win, while also discrediting Britain with her American ally. It was in part this reasoning that deterred the cabinet from deploying force against Mussadeq at Abadan in 1951, a telling contrast to the attempt by their Conservative successors to topple al-Nasir in 1956.

The same thinking made Bevin chary of the old methods of backstairs cabinet-making that had hitherto been among the most effective tools for manipulating nationalist factions to British advantage.[21] In Egypt, it was Bevin who turned down an official proposal to unseat Prime Minister al-Nuqrashi (despite his evident lack of sympathy with the turn of nationalist politics) on the grounds that anti-British sentiment was too well established to be quelled in such a fashion. He also ruled out intervention in the Egyptian elections of 1950 to assist the Wafd against their more radical rivals. In Iran, he refused to accept Foreign Office plans to put pressure on the Shah to pick a strong prime minister capable of introducing reforms, and vetoed plans to encourage secessionist tendencies in south-west Iran to act as a counter to communist influence in Teheran. He was no less anxious to curb the electoral engineering of Rex Leeper, British Ambassador in Athens, on the grounds that it made it much easier for Greek nationalists to shrug off the blame for the slow rate of post-war recovery on to British military 'advisers'. Of course, Bevin was not alone in doubting the efficacy of such interventions, but on several occasions his weight seems to have been thrown decisively against the wilder schemes of his officials.[22] Nationalist leaders were the symptoms, not the causes, of unrest and the problem they represented could not be cured simply by arresting them, but by forcing them to take responsibility for the solutions they advocated.

Bevin wanted to be as helpful as possible about removing the main thorns of nationalist discontent, taking equality and partnership to be the secret of imperial unity in defence matters. The Russians, as Bevin commented, 'treated all the different races of the Soviet Union ... on exactly the same footing ... and the result was one vast and homogenous force. We should do the same'.[23] Thus the treaties which governed the British military presence in the region were to be renegotiated and bases

Britain and decolonization 9

relocated to lessen the tensions that had grown up around them. In 1946, Labour ministers were prepared – against the advice of the Chiefs of Staff – to countenance the complete withdrawal of British troops from Egypt by September 1949, and the preservation of British interests not by occupation but by a treaty that committed its parties to little more than mutual goodwill in the event of war. Bevin was adamant that he would 'far rather have properly and technically trained Egyptians at our disposal in the event of war than 10,000 British troops occupying an unwilling country'.[24] If Suez had to be evacuated to appease nationalist opinion, Bevin optimistically assumed, then a fresh start might be made in whatever was retained of the Palestine mandate, or perhaps in the friendlier surroundings of Cyrenaica, Cyprus, Transjordan, or even in the Sudan or Kenya. To this end, the existing agreement with Abdallah of Transjordan, by which Britain subsidized the Jordanian Army in return for defence co-operation and the preservation of British bases, was strengthened in 1946. In 1948, in the Treaty of Portsmouth, Bevin was prepared to place British air bases in Iraq under the joint control of both governments.

But Bevin recognized that new bargains with unelected and unaccountable pashas and palace go-betweens, however important they might be for securing the support of the powerful, were not sufficient to meet the nationalist challenge unless they were combined with policies designed to break the unnatural coalition of classes and interests that underpinned anti-imperial agitation and to force its leaders to answer to those whom they claimed to represent. Economic modernization was the lever that Bevin proposed to employ. 'My experience of 30 years of international trade', he insisted, 'is that if you get men talking together about the same occupation, the same trade, the same machines, nationalism ceases, and occupation and life interest takes its place.'[25]

Within a few weeks of taking office, Bevin told his officials that he wished the forthcoming conference of Middle East diplomats to discuss 'measures of social advancement' and a policy 'which would benefit the common people' to improve trade and forestall Soviet criticism of British rule.[26] Addressing the inaugural meeting, he announced that he wanted to broaden the basis of Britain's influence in the Middle East, which had hitherto rested too heavily upon British troops and on a narrow range of economic interests such as oil and cotton. A Middle East Development Board should be established, financed by UK and Middle Eastern capital and operating under the rules governing public utilities, to harness the resources of the whole region and turn it from a 'defence area' into a 'development area'.[27] By 'holding out hopes of economic betterment and a raising of the standard of living', Bevin told officials, '[development]

10 *Demise of the British Empire in the Middle East*

would help to counteract the nationalist tendencies which must be expected after the war'. To cope with the difficulties of economic adjustment in the wake of demobilization and wartime inflation, Middle Eastern officials were told by Bevin's deputy, Philip Noel-Baker, that it was vital 'to divert ... the Arab world from politics to the solution of raising standards of life'.[28] Over the coming years, Bevin pushed this line with a remarkable and undaunted consistency. In Egypt, he rejected official advice that social reform should be realized through co-operation with King Faruq and a political class that had distanced itself from the people.[29] 'I can well believe', he told the British Ambassador in Egypt, 'that the Rulers and Pashas of Egypt are made to feel uncomfortable when the rotten conditions of the working people of their country are published to the world'.

> I doubt, however, whether the people themselves feel similar resentment. Pashadom is jealous of its power and frightened of any exposure of its shortcomings. But I do not believe that the Pashas will maintain for ever undisputed sway over Egypt. As Foreign Secretary of a Labour Government I look beyond the present Egyptian rulers, who deflect towards us the social discontent that should really be directed against them.[30]

In Bevin's view, the ruling classes of the Middle East had failed to distribute the new wealth they had made from the war and from oil production to the poorer members of their societies. It was necessary for Britain to make it clear that it stood ready to meet the demand for post-war social progress. In Iraq, fearful that British intentions were discredited by association with the 'old gang' surrounding the Regent, Bevin pressed for free elections and for the diversion of oil revenues into capital projects to improve education, land use and agriculture, on the lines of the Tennessee Valley Authority.[31] In Iran, Bevin noted, the unwillingness of the oil industry to share its profits more widely threatened to destabilize local economies and provoke a dangerous reaction against Western capitalism, which would strengthen the hands of local communists and risk Soviet intervention from the north. In July 1946, he pressed the Anglo-Iranian Oil Company (which, though largely owned by the British Government was, as Bevin noted sourly, 'virtually a private company') to introduce more progressive welfare benefits and higher pay for its workers. When the Soviet Union successfully negotiated a deal with the Iranians to exploit Azerbaijani oil, he considered going further still to appease anti-foreign sentiment in Iran, proposing the replacement of Anglo-Iranian with a 'mutually advantageous' joint company based on profit-sharing rather than royalties.[32] 'I am not going to have the Russians stealing our wind [sic]', Bevin insisted, 'by appearing as the sole supporters of the people'.[33]

Britain and decolonization 11

III

Bevin's plans failed almost wholly to achieve their objectives. When Churchill brought the Conservatives back to office in 1951, British power in the region rested largely on the old foundations. Negotiations to renew the treaties had either collapsed, as in Egypt, or had resulted in agreements that were almost immediately repudiated, as in Iraq. Britain's presence in the region remained heavily dependent on privileges secured under the old regimes, above all for the increasingly vulnerable soldiers in the costly and resented Suez base. Worse still, Bevin's cherished development plans were only implemented in the most limited way and never proved sufficient to win Britain popularity, let alone reshape Arab nationalism. Neither in India nor even in West Africa did Labour's new imperial policy stem the tide of political agitation against British rule to any appreciable degree. But nowhere did it fail as spectacularly as in the Middle East.

This was largely because in several ways the Middle East constituted a much less satisfactory arena than other parts of Britain's world system for Bevin's plans for development. In the first place, the constitutional structures through which the reforms were to be proposed, debated and implemented were unwieldy. Since the 1920s, only Palestine had been under direct British rule. Especially before the development of the region's oil resources, Britain's economic penetration had been quite shallow and its cultural influences had never succeeded in making much impact on established patterns of belief and social practice. British control was sustained much more through military and diplomatic supremacy than through the imposition of an administrative structure and the construction of networks of local collaborators, as was the case in Asia and Africa. The emerging party structures of the legislatures of Cairo and Baghdad lay largely outside the reach of British influence. Few credible intermediaries thus existed to publicize and argue for the worth of British socio-economic reforms. Lacking sufficient popular support to call for sacrifices on the part of the colonized themselves, the British found themselves able neither to explain the lure of development to those who might benefit from it nor to anticipate likely objections.

Acceptance of British views, especially on questions of socio-economic reform, thus had to be won indirectly, through the careful courting of clients and the promotion of local initiative. This dictated a cautious and slow approach right from the start. 'It is no good thrusting experts upon the Egyptian government', insisted the Cairo Embassy. 'Any suggestion that we want to run their country for them will make them turn elsewhere for assistance.'[34] Arab governments, it was reported by officials, were 'genuinely anxious to receive technical advice and help

12 *Demise of the British Empire in the Middle East*

but are suspicious of anything which might be represented as savouring of administrative interference'.[35] However grandiloquent his plans in private, Bevin was careful in public always to stress the technical and apolitical nature of British development aid.[36] Indeed, there was a certain irony in the fact that Bevin's commitment to the principle of 'non-interference' debarred him from more energetic attempts to push reforms on reluctant pashas and governments. But as Michael Wright, chosen by Bevin to lead the campaign for development, pointed out as delicately as possible to his political master, given the granting of formal independence after the First World War before Ottoman corruption had been replaced by traditions of public service, 'we have tied our own hands'. 'If we intervened, we should be blamed for interference in internal affairs: if we did not, reaction would remain.'[37] All that Britain could do was 'to push the case for social reform very hard when necessary, and … to give considerable backing to the best elements', and even this 'may at times bring us very near to the border of internal interference or even across it'.[38]

Such a potentially abrasive process inevitably required copious supplies of lubrication. Unfortunately, these were in lamentably short supply. Proffering development aid to such allies was difficult to justify to British taxpayers, who were believed to be even less sympathetic to the claims of the Middle East – and especially the supposedly 'treacherous' Faruq regime[39] – than to those of the colonial empire. Without the ability to levy local taxes themselves, which – especially now that Egypt and Iraq were sterling creditors – would in any case have made British-led development look somewhat like vicarious generosity, Bevin found his schemes lay at the mercy of the Treasury, which treated requests for overseas development with miserly parsimony, especially when they involved spending outside the dependent empire. Thus although Bevin had hoped for at least a 20-year commitment, the Middle East Office was funded grudgingly only on a year-by-year basis.[40] 'I am not sure that we are thinking on a big enough scale', he complained in 1946.[41] But, in sum, the reserves were insufficient to fund much more than 'a dozen teachers for Egypt, a labour adviser for the Iraqi government, an agricultural project for Jordan'[42] – each proposal fought long and hard against Treasury limits, especially after the devaluation of September 1949.

But the real problem, as the Board of Trade and the Treasury noted at the start, was 'not to find sterling for the Middle Eastern countries, but to find goods for their sterling, of which they had plenty.'[43] Although Bevin had promised the cabinet that the plan would provide a 'golden opportunity for the British exporter',[44] it was one that they were unable to take up. It was no use suggesting plans for economic development

Britain and decolonization 13

to Middle Eastern governments until British factories were able to supply them with the necessary imports, or the Treasury with the dollars to buy them elsewhere. British officials working for the supply missions in the region had already found that shortage of materials and tonnage made it hard for them to retain the confidence of Arab governments after the relaxation of official controls.[45] But in the short run, British capital goods were required for domestic reconstruction and for export to dollar-earning markets. The Middle East failed to meet this condition, and attempts by the Foreign Office to persuade the Treasury of its potential as a source of cheap food production were dismissed as unrealistic and out of keeping with Bevin's desire to build up the region's own standard of living.[46] When these problems of supply were combined with Britain's refusal to permit Iraq and Egypt to convert their sterling balances into dollars and hence to purchase their capital goods elsewhere, it was unsurprising to find that their governments regarded Bevin's commitment to development with cynicism. All in all, it was unlikely that such inadequate resources would serve to smooth Anglo–Arab relations to any significant degree.

Extracting the financial resources for development was not helped by official rivalries within Whitehall and its legations and embassies in the Middle East. In the first place, the evolution of plans for these types of development had hitherto been largely a matter for the Colonial Office, while Middle Eastern policy came under the auspices of the Foreign Office. The development secretariat in London thus suffered badly from staffing problems and bureaucratic isolation. Although, in deference to Bevin's views, a dedicated Middle East Office based in Cairo was given a degree of autonomy and direct links to London, it was distrusted by the embassies, fearful of its encroachment on sensitive political questions, which made it hard for it to establish contact with Middle Eastern politicians.[47] There was also great difficulty in finding sufficient British experts willing to go to the Middle East.[48] Bevin hoped to attract high-flyers from the armed services and universities for the Cairo field office, whose staff, employed on career-long contracts, would rove the whole region. 'It was not possible to treat the question piecemeal', he insisted.[49] However, an interim report in January 1946 made dismal reading. Progress had been 'slow and somewhat disappointing': the Middle East Office had inherited the offices of the Middle East Supply Centre, but very few of its personnel, and suffered from limited staffing right from the start. 'Are we casting our net wide enough?', Bevin wondered.[50] The real problem, however, lay in the conflicting needs of the respective governments. Middle East governments, especially that of Iraq, almost invariably wanted to recruit British experts for their own service, rather than have them seconded from the imperial power, with the implications of foreign domination that this entailed. It proved hard to attract candidates for posts which offered so little security of tenure, and several Arab governments found it preferable to attract assistance with development from American or Swedish advisers. Nor did the British schemes ever generate the local employment that Bevin had hoped to see. In Egypt, British officials were engaged not in recruiting staff but in laying them off in advance of the running down of the service installations.[51] Local staff could not be paid sufficient to keep them from the effects of post-war inflation, and hence, much to the horror of Stafford Cripps, turned to informal methods of supplementing their incomes.[52]

Of course, American assistance in the plans and financing of development might have made a substantial difference to this problem. But US officials, in breaking up the Middle East Supply Centre at the war's end, had already demonstrated their desire for a swift return to free and private international trade. Thus, although Bevin had shown some early enthusiasm for the idea of co-operating with the United States, and an informal mission was sent to Washington in 1947, it was ruled out on the grounds that American firms would then win the bulk of the contracts that resulted. In Egypt, British hopes of dominating post-war development had already been seriously undermined by the emergence of a 'new deal' coalition between American multinationals and Egyptian business leaders and investors.[53] Indeed, without the unpopular dollar restrictions Britain imposed on countries in the sterling area, officials privately admitted, there would be a 'flood of orders to the United States for goods which we are not in a position to supply'.[54] The problem with American development experts, one British diplomat commented loftily, was that they 'would inevitably turn themselves into commercial travellers'.[55] Indeed, fear that Britain would prove unable to supply the needs of Arab governments even discouraged development officials from 'sound[ing] the market'.[56]

Worse still, Bevin had not clearly identified the class of collaborators with which he wished to build new bridges. Doubtless he was correct to believe that the Egyptian *fellahin* (peasants) would be grateful to 'anyone who helped them out of their miserably unhealthy and pauperous plight'.[57] But such a task, though admirable in its way, could never have succeeded in cracking the shell of Arab nationalism. The rural peasantry whom such policies were designed to help did not form its main body of support. The struggle within the nationalist camp was between the old class of notables, government servants and landowners, who had gained security from their links with the monarchies and the British, and the younger, more radical urban movements, dominated by students and progressive teachers. Bevin's policies had little appeal to either group.

Britain and decolonization 15

For the 'old gang', shaken and discredited by the reassertion of imperial power during the war, public association with the British was a dangerous gamble that threatened to expose them to their political rivals at their most vulnerable point: their inability to resist foreign domination. As Bevin's officials began their work, the Egyptian parliament, far from welcoming the prospect of partnership and co-operation, was engaged on a new company law aimed at pushing British capital and personnel out of Egyptian companies. Indeed, it had been the proliferation of oppressive controls and alien bureaucracy, which accompanied the use of the Middle East as a transit base and conduit for wartime supplies, that had done most to swell anti-British feeling in recent years.[58] Those fearful that price controls would hold down their profits or restrictive shipping quotas depress their standard of living could hardly be expected to look favourably upon proposals for greater economic planning and intervention, particularly under British auspices. It was unclear at the start how Bevin's schemes were to be implemented without the imposition of an army of British technicians, experts and advisers in the much-resented tradition of the Middle East Supply Centre. It was perhaps partly for this reason that the plans of American officials for the fostering of capitalist free trade as the best means of defending the region against communism, often won a more sympathetic hearing among the Arab political elite than Bevin's socialist remedies.

Of course, Bevin's hope was that a programme of social reform would serve to win the support of the younger and hitherto-excluded elements of nationalist movements for a British connection, not least because it would promote political changes and the devolution of power to precisely these groups. But until such political changes were achieved, it was rightly feared among such nationalists that resources for development from the British would simply drain away into the old gutters of palace corruption and be used to consolidate the power of existing elites. Proposals for development posed tricky questions of the allocation of land and resources between regions and classes, which threatened to deflate and distract nationalist energies. Such groups, moreover, were frequently engaged in attempting to broaden the scope of their respective territorial and isolationist nationalisms to make them less dependent upon western traditions of thought and more open to region-wide exchanges.[59] For the young urban nationalist, therefore, Bevin's offer of development and a settlement of Anglo–Arab differences threatened the prospect not of partnership, but of a more permanent exclusion from power.

It was small wonder, therefore, that nationalists preferred to resist the erosion of their common front against the British and their allies by

16   *Demise of the British Empire in the Middle East*

focusing less on divisive issues of economic development than on issues which united them more readily, such as the presence of British troops and the perfidy of Labour's betrayal of the Arabs in Palestine. Bevin's difficulty was that satisfying these regional demands conflicted painfully with the demands of his grand strategy. For in no other region did strategic demands and external pressure interlock as powerfully as they did in the Middle East to restrict the ability of British policy-makers to follow the logic of concessions to nationalism. As the cabinet discussions on the renegotiation of the Anglo–Egyptian Treaty make clear, Labour ministers were fully aware that the presence of British troops was the main sticking-point with the Egyptian negotiators, and that resting on the 1936 treaty provisions was morally and legally shaky.[60] But even so, they felt that the strategic imperatives of the cold war left them almost no flexibility to deal with the situation as they wished. No matter how feverishly Bevin and the Chiefs of Staff searched the map, Egypt's location, if not its political instability, suited British strategic needs better than any alternative. Without an agreement on the evacuation of combatant troops, proposals for defence co-operation proved to be stillborn.

Above all, of course, there was the question of Palestine.[61] It is sufficient here to note its baleful effects on Bevin's plans for regional defence co-operation and development. In 1945, Bevin had hoped that the rising standards of living that development would bring might even ease the Palestinian situation, by softening the conflict for land and resources in the area and thereby allowing rates of Jewish immigration to be stepped up.[62] Such optimism did not last for long. Broken promises on the questions of Jewish immigration and the Palestinian homeland, and Britain's supposed acquiescence in the creation of the state of Israel inevitably suggested to Arab leaders that British promises of security – and hence the military alliances of which they were part – were not worth having. This certainly made it harder for the Iraqi leaders to persuade their nationalist supporters that the Soviet threat called for the ratification of a British military treaty they had signed at Portsmouth in January 1948. Bevin was undoubtedly desperate that the resolution of the Palestinian problem should not be allowed to disrupt his attempts to build new alliances in the Arab world. But American pressure from without and the Zionist ties of the Labour Party within made it impossible for him to go further in meeting Arab demands for the suppression of Israel.[63]

In the poisonous atmosphere this created, plans to create a new Anglo–Arab understanding based on economic development were bound to be seen at best as an irrelevance. As Bevin acknowledged in 1949, Arab governments '[will] refuse to respond to our guidance on

Britain and decolonization 17

social and economic matters if they find us differing too widely from them over Palestine'.[64] Britain's traditional allies were forced to disavow any connection with those who had supposedly sponsored the emergence of Israel, while the Arab League, which officials had hoped to use as a means of promoting development, was too preoccupied with political affairs to do more than pass resolutions of a general nature and set up a largely dormant sub-committee.[65] While Arab states remained divided and uncertain about the regional ambitions of the new Jewish state, there was little chance of British-led economic development being successful unless it was directed primarily towards military preparations for a war with Israel, rather than to the education, welfare and redistributive projects to benefit the least well-off that Labour favoured.

Indeed, this was not the only distortion the Arab–Israeli conflict imposed upon Bevin's plans. As the officials reviewing the development schemes in 1949 observed, economic assistance to Syria, Lebanon and Jordan had necessarily taken the form of refugee aid rather than constructive development.[66] For John Troutbeck, appointed Head of the British Middle East Office in 1947, this revealed a basic weakness in Labour's strategy: it put the cart (economic development) before the horse (political stability). He therefore favoured older methods: a Western-guaranteed peace should be imposed on the region – in Troutbeck's opinion, this would be realized through the arming of Egypt to act as a counterweight to Israel – before Britain reverted to the politics of development.[67]

IV

None the less, the early post-war years saw substantial social and economic development in the Middle East, especially in Iran, Iraq and Egypt.[68] British firms won contracts in some of these projects and the Development Division of the British Middle East Office, despite its organizational weaknesses, played a small but significant part in bringing them to fruition. Indeed, as Kingston argues, the very inability of the Foreign Office to provide the necessary resources ensured that its development projects were characterized by an early recognition of the 'limits to growth'. Its projects were usually on a small scale and employed local people rather than foreign experts, and indigenous skills rather than imported technology, all techniques which later became the received wisdom of development gurus. Even its bureaucratic isolation served to liberate the developers from the political control of Whitehall, allowing them greater flexibility than they might otherwise have enjoyed.[69]

But these achievements were a product of circumstance rather than choice, and their price was the abandonment of most of the political objectives of the policy. Bevin's desire to see dynamic region-wide planning was an early victim of the decision to win the trust of governments through unobtrusive guidance tailored to the individual circumstances of each state. The work of the Middle East Office was instead from the start fragmented into cautious, slow, bilateral co-operation with individual governments. Success was greatest in those countries where British prestige was already relatively high, such as Iraq, and most of all in the small, artificial, impoverished and Anglophile Jordanian state.

In a small way, therefore, Labour's pursuit of development, far from winning the region for Britain, actually served to sharpen the divisions between those Middle Eastern governments keen to throw off British influence and those who retained their status as imperial clients. The key to success was found not in trumpeting the benefits of Anglo–Arab co-operation, as Bevin had hoped, but in the avoidance of publicity. Indeed, development schemes did best where British experts by-passed the politicians altogether and established private contact with local civil servants. Bevin's hope that development and democracy would go hand in hand also failed to materialize. The readiest acceptance of British help often came from the least-representative quarters. No matter how benevolent the autocracy of Abdallah, King of Transjordan, it was hardly congenial to a socialist administration. In 1949 in Syria, indeed, Bevin was forced to look kindly upon the Zaim military dictatorship, in the hope that it was at least no more undemocratic than the irresponsible wealthy elite it had replaced, and with the consolation that it had expressed some interest in social reform.

This was, as we have seen, in part a problem of resources. Lack of finance capital and the necessary capital goods meant that, in the phrase of the Head of the Development Division, planning for development amounted to little more than the 'training of a crew for a boat race which will never take place'.[70] Economic aid on the small scale contemplated, as one of Bevin's economic planners pointed out in a discussion of the Colombo Plan, was never likely to remake the raw material of nationalism, since it could not raise the living standards of the populace as a whole, except in small countries and over a long time-period.[71] Even with greater resources, however, it seems unlikely that Labour's policy could ever have harnessed the pressure for development in the Middle East to benefit Britain. This was partly because of the peculiar pattern of economic development in the Middle East. Resented foreign-owned enclaves in the region's oil industry were never likely to prove adequate bridgeheads from which to win local allies for development. But, above

Britain and decolonization 19

all, it was because Middle Eastern policy evolved within the tight embrace of Labour's global strategy, which precluded both the removal of British bases from the region and the open hostility to Israel demanded by Arab states. This in turn posed dilemmas for development, which Troutbeck pithily characterized as 'trying to ride two horses at the same time which were galloping in opposite directions'. Development, as he commented at the start of his posting, 'needs tranquility [*sic*], but on the one side you have the Russian menace and on the other Palestine'.[72]

These inadequacies were in large part the cause of the inability of the British to attract indigenous support for the cause of development and partnership. Their traditional clients' commitment to far-reaching reform – in many cases little more than perfunctory – was rendered irrelevant by the social and political upheavals of the war. Labour ministers faced in consequence a much less malleable nationalism, in which the anti-British theme was not incidental but central. On practically every other count, after all, Mussadeq ought to have proved an ideal ally for Labour's schemes of development. His programmes were packed with many of the same notions: land reform, industrialization and economic modernization, and many of his political supporters were young and progressive. However, his National Front coalition was cemented and underpinned less by this commitment to social reform than by anti-British and anti-monarchical sentiment.

Labour ministers often found it hard to understand this characteristic of Middle Eastern nationalism. For some, such as Bevin, it simply demonstrated opportunism and the power of vested interests, features he identified with political inexperience and the absence of proper accountability. When Egyptian Prime Minister Sidqi gave an exaggerated account of British promises over the constitutional future of the Sudan, or Iraqi premier Saleh Jabr repudiated the Treaty of Portsmouth, Bevin deplored what he termed the 'bazaar method of negotiation', so alien to the practice in trade unions, where agreements were binding and not perpetually renegotiable.[73] For Stansgate, much criticised by Bevin and other Labour ministers for fumbling the Suez negotiations of 1946, Egyptian nationalism, like its Irish counterpart, had an irrational quality that was impervious to reasoned argument.[74]

With the benefit of hindsight, it is easier to see that nationalists simply had to appeal to wide and critical audiences outside their direct control. Those who were interested in social reform were not interested in co-operation with the British, while those who were interested in co-operation with the British were not interested in social reform. At the end of their efforts, therefore, Bevin and his Labour colleagues, like a small team of foreign developers struggling to complete an over-ambitious hydroelectric dam in a hostile country, found their resources

20   *Demise of the British Empire in the Middle East*

inadequate for the task, and the great river, whose force they had hoped might drive the turbines of British influence, impossible to divert.

NOTES

I am very grateful to Dr John Darwin and the editors of this volume for helpful comments on an earlier draft.

1   Quoted in Alan Bullock, *Ernest Bevin: Foreign Secretary, 1945–1951* (Oxford: Oxford University Press, 1983) p. 155.
2   John Saville, *The Politics of Continuity: British Foreign Policy and the Labour Government 1945–46* (London: Verso, 1993) pp. 81–111.
3   Correlli Barnett, *The Lost Victory: British Dreams, British Realities 1945–1950* (London: Macmillan, 1995).
4   Wm Roger Louis, *The British Empire in the Middle East 1945–1951: Arab Nationalism, the United States and Postwar Imperialism* (Oxford: Clarendon Press, 1984); Michael J. Cohen, *Palestine and the Great Powers, 1945–48* (Princeton, NJ: Princeton University Press, 1982); Wesley K. Wark, 'Development Diplomacy: Sir John Troutbeck and the British Middle East Office, 1947–50', in John Zametica (ed.), *British Officials and British Foreign Policy* (Leicester: Pinter Publishers, 1988); Paul W. T. Kingston, *Britain and the Politics of Modernization in the Middle East 1945–1958* (Cambridge: Cambridge University Press, 1996); Robert Vitalis, *When Capitalists Collide: Business Conflict and the End of Empire in Egypt* (Berkeley, CA: University of California Press, 1995).
5   See David Goldsworthy, *Colonial Issues in British Politics, 1945–1961* (Oxford: Clarendon Press, 1971); P. S. Gupta, 'Imperialism and the Labour Government of 1945–51', in Jay Winter (ed.), *The Working Class in Modern British History: Essays in Honour of Henry Pelling* (Cambridge: Cambridge University Press, 1983); D. K. Fieldhouse, 'The Labour Governments and the Empire–Commonwealth', in Ritchie Ovendale (ed.), *The Foreign Policy of the British Labour Governments, 1945–1951* (Leicester: Pinter Publishers, 1984) pp. 83–120, at p. 89; Stephen Howe, *Anticolonialism in British Politics: The Left and the End of Empire, 1918–1964* (Oxford: Clarendon Press, 1993).
6   Stafford Cripps, 'Empire', July 1938, Cripps Papers, Box 711, Nuffield College, Oxford; 'The Commonwealth and Empire', 9 August 1943, reprinted in Stafford Cripps, *Democracy Alive* (London: Sidgwick & Jackson, 1946) pp. 120–6.
7   In a comment to Molotov in May 1946, quoted in Louis, *British Empire*, p. 281.
8   Quoted in Francis Williams, *Ernest Bevin: Portrait of a Great Englishman* (London: Hutchinson, 1952) p. 209.
9   C. R. Attlee, 'The Relations of the British Commonwealth to the Post-War International Political Organisation', June 1943, PREM 4/30/3 PRO.
10   Labour Party, *Report of Annual Conference*, May 1945, pp. 115–19.
11   Ernest Bevin, 'Middle East Policy', 25 August 1949, CP(49)183, Cab 129/36 PRO.
12   See Michael J. Cohen, *Fighting World War Three from the Middle East: Allied Contingency Plans, 1945–1954* (London: Frank Cass, 1997), and Chapter 2 in this volume.
13   John Saville, 'A Slight Case of Heresy: Clement Attlee and the Middle East, 1945–47', in *Politics of Continuity*, pp. 112–48.
14   Hugh Dalton, *High Tide and After: Memoirs 1945–60* (London: Muller, 1962) p. 105.
15   Bevin to Attlee, 9 January 1947, FO 800/476/ME/47 PRO.
16   See for example, the official views expressed in the 1945 file on Middle East planning FO 371/45252 PRO, especially the memorandum of 2 September (E6640) by Minister Resident in the Middle East and Conservative, Sir Edward Grigg (Lord Altrincham).
17   See John Darwin, *Britain, Egypt and the Middle East: Imperial Policy in the Aftermath of War 1918–1922* (London: Macmillan, 1981).
18   The claims of the following paragraph are more fully developed in my thesis: 'The Confusions of an Imperialist Inheritance: The British Labour Party and Indian Independence, 1940–1947' (Oxford DPhil, 1993).
19   War Cabinet WM(42)117, 24 August 1942, reprinted in Nicholas Mansergh *et al.*, *India: The Transfer of Power, 1942–77* (London: HMSO, 12 vols, 1970–83) Vol. II, document 621;

Britain and decolonization

'Note by Sir S. Cripps', 2 September 1942, reprinted in Mansergh, *Transfer of Power*, Vol. II, document 678; Robert Pearce (ed.), *Patrick Gordon Walker: Political Diaries 1932–1971* (London: The Historians' Press, 1991) 1 October 1942, p. 113; War Cabinet WM(43)85, 15 June 1943, reprinted in Mansergh, *Transfer of Power*, Vol. IV, document 2; Bevin to Amery, 11 June 1941, Bevin Papers, BEVN(I) 3/1; Alan Lascelles, *Diary*, 20 August 1943, Bevin Papers, BEVN 9/3, Churchill College, Cambridge.

20 On Cyprus, see Louis, *British Empire*, p. 217; on Africa, see Ronald Hyam, 'Africa and the Labour Government 1945–51', *Journal of Imperial and Commonwealth History*, 16, 3 (1988) pp. 148–72.

21 See Chapter 6 by Martin Kolinsky in this volume.

22 For details of these episodes, see Louis, *British Empire*, pp. 71–2; 86–102; 256; 632–6.

23 'Egypt and Sudan', 10 January 1948, FO 371/69192 PRO.

24 'Egypt and Sudan', ibid.; Louis, *British Empire*, pp. 226–64; F. S. Northedge, 'Britain and the Middle East', in Ovendale (ed.), *Foreign Policy*, pp. 149–80

25 Bevin, speech in House of Commons, 23 August 1945, quoted in Bullock, *Bevin*, p. 104.

26 Dixon to Sargent, 24 August 1945, FO 800/475 PRO.

27 Bevin, Record of Meeting at Foreign Office, 5 September 1945, FO 371/45252 PRO.

28 Record of Meeting at Foreign Office, 6 September 1945, FO 371/45252 PRO.

29 Louis, *British Empire*, p. 232.

30 Bevin to Campbell, 21 June 1946, FO 800/457/EG/46/32, PRO.

31 For the details of these projects, see Louis, *British Empire*, pp. 307–44; 590–603.

32 Louis, *British Empire*, pp. 54–73.

33 Bevin to Campbell, 21 June 1946, op. cit.

34 Note by H. M. Embassy, Cairo, 24 September 1945, quoted in Kingston, *Politics of Modernization*, p. 21.

35 Denis Greenhill, 'Progress Report on Recommendations of September Conference on Middle Eastern Affairs', 15 January 1946, FO 371/52318 PRO.

36 See, for example, his speech in the Commons, 23 November 1945, quoted in Kingston, *Politics of Modernization*, p. 21.

37 Conference minutes, 21 July 1949, quoted in Louis, *British Empire*, p. 606.

38 Wright to Bevin, 19 March 1949, FO 371/75064, PRO.

39 See Sargent to Campbell, 2 February 1949, FO 371/73501 PRO, for these problems of British public opinion.

40 Bevin, Record of Meeting at Foreign Office, 5 September 1945, FO 371/45252 PRO; Kingston, *Politics of Modernization*, p. 24.

41 Note by Bevin on Greenhill, 'Progress Report', op. cit.

42 Louis, *British Empire*, p. 613.

43 Record of Meeting at Foreign Office, 6 September 1945, FO 371/45252 PRO.

44 Bevin, 'Middle East Policy', CP(45)174, 17 September 1945, Cab 129/2 PRO.

45 Greenhill, 'Progress Report', op. cit.

46 Kingston. *Politics of Modernization*, p. 32.

47 Ibid., pp. 22–4.

48 Louis, *British Empire*, pp. 18, 613.

49 Bevin, Record of Meetings at Foreign Office, 5 September 1945, 10 September 1945, FO 371/45252 PRO.

50 Greenhill, 'Progress Report', op. cit.; Wark, 'Sir John Troutbeck', p. 234.

51 Killearn, Record of Meeting at Foreign Office, 5 September 1945, FO 371/45252 PRO.

52 Wright, 'Middle East Governments', 19 March 1949, FO 371/75064 PRO.

53 See Vitalis, *When Capitalists Collide* and 'The New Deal in Egypt: The Rise of Anglo–American Commercial Competition in World War II and the Fall of Neocolonialism', *Diplomatic History*, 20, 2 (Spring 1996) pp. 211–39.

54 Greenhill, 'Progress Report', op. cit.

55 Record of Meeting at Foreign Office, 6 September 1945, FO 371/45252 PRO.

56 Kingston, *Politics of Modernization*, p. 25.

57 Bevin to Campbell, 21 June 1946, op. cit.

58 Martin Wilmington, *The Middle East Supply Centre* (London: University of London Press, 1972).

59 On this point, see Israel Gershoni *et al.*, *Redefining the Egyptian Nation, 1930–1945* (Cambridge: Cambridge University Press, 1995).

60   'Anglo–Egyptian Negotiations', 6–7 June 1946, CM 57(46)1 and CM 58 (46), Cab 128/5, PRO.
61   See Chapter 12 by Avraham Sela in this volume.
62   Bevin, Record of Meeting at Foreign Office, 5 September 1945, FO 371/45252 PRO.
63   See Cohen, *Palestine and the Great Powers*. On Zionist links with Labour, see Joseph Gorny, *The British Labour Movement and Zionism 1917–1948* (London: Frank Cass, 1983).
64   Ernest Bevin, 'Middle East Policy', 25 August 1949, CP(49)183, Cab 129/36 PRO.
65   Greenhill, 'Progress Report', op. cit.
66   Louis, *British Empire*, p. 613.
67   See Wark, 'Sir John Troutbeck' for a full account of Troutbeck's views.
68   See Chapter 4 by Rodney Wilson in this volume.
69   This case is argued powerfully by Kingston, *Politics of Modernization*.
70   Bill Crawford to Wall, 14 July 1950, quoted in Kingston, *Politics of Modernization*, p. 44.
71   See the views of J. P. Stent, quoted in Louis, *British Empire*, pp. 610–11.
72   Troutbeck to Wright, 3 January 1950; Troutbeck to Wright, 31 December 1947, quoted in Kingston, *Politics of Modernization*, pp. 29, 45.
73   Bevin to Attlee, 4 August 1946, FO 800/457 PRO.
74   Stansgate to Bevin, 12 August 1946, FO 371/53309 PRO.

2

The strategic role of the Middle East after the war

MICHAEL J. COHEN

ECONOMIC AND STRATEGIC INTERESTS IN THE MIDDLE EAST

Since 1882, the hub of British interests in the Middle East had been the Suez Canal. The sprawling base installations that were built across its hinterland (38 army camps and ten airfields) made it the single largest military base in the world, until well after the Second World War. Britain's tenure of Egypt proved vital during both world wars. The Suez Canal served as a primary imperial artery, and ensured Britain's ability to bring colonial forces from India, Australia and New Zealand to the Middle East, and thence to Europe. The Canal base served as a staging area for troops and *matériel* on their way to several fronts.[1]

During the course of the Second World War, the oil resources of the Middle East had assumed unprecedented, vital military and strategic importance. The volume of oil extracted from wells in the Middle East increased by 52 per cent, a considerable proportion of which was pumped from recently developed American concessions in Saudi Arabia. Britain's revenues from her oil concessions in the region continued after the war to constitute a significant contributing factor in maintaining its balance of payments.[2]

The UK also had other substantial economic interests in the Middle East. She exported goods to the region to the value of £150 million annually, and imported considerable quantities of high-grade Egyptian cotton (see also Chapter 4 in this volume, by Rodney Wilson).

Foreign Secretary Bevin's long-term ambition was to transform the Middle East into a prosperous economic federation that, with Britain's possessions in Africa, would replace the Indian market for British goods, thereby compensating the British economy for the loss of the 'jewel in the crown'. It was Bevin's dream that the Middle East, together with the great mineral wealth (especially uranium) of the African continent, would permit Britain to retain her paramount position in the post-war

24 *Demise of the British Empire in the Middle East*

world, alongside the two new superpowers, the United States and the Soviet Union.[3]

After the Second World War, the British Chiefs of Staff (COS), in marked contrast to their predecessors in 1919, regarded the Middle East as an imperial strategic asset that was essential to guarantee Britain's continued status as a first-class military power.[4] Their position brought them into a direct clash with the new Labour prime minister, Clement Attlee.

The latter was committed less to the traditional empire than to social reform at home. In addition, Labour ministers were in general more sensitive than the military to anti-colonialist, nationalist opposition across the empire, and less willing than the latter to cling to traditional strategic footholds against the opposition of the local population. (see also Chapter 1, by Nicholas Owen).

Attlee had his own agenda, and high up on it were the resuscitation of the British economy and the establishment of the welfare state that his party had promised to the electorate during the war. Attlee clashed with his COS over global strategic priorities, and, in particular, over the need to retain Britain's traditional positions in the Mediterranean and in the Middle East. In 1945, Attlee, in some respects a British reincarnation of President Wilson (in 1919), looked forward to a peaceful world, where nations' interests would be secured and protected under the auspices of the United Nations, which body would mediate and resolve international disputes pacifically.[5]

Bevin, however, supported the COS view on retaining British bases and interests in the Middle East. Even if the Labour cabinet was willing, to a limited degree, to shed those imperial burdens that the national economy could no longer sustain, the coalition of Bevin and the COS was no more willing than the Conservatives had been to surrender Britain's Great Power status.

In 1947, after a prolonged debate within the British administration, Bevin and the COS prevailed over Attlee to retain British positions in the Middle East.[6] Nevertheless, the prime minister's central argument (ably supported by Chancellor Hugh Dalton) – that Britain no longer had the economic resources to hold and maintain large forces in the region – would ultimately prevail, and, by the early 1950s, would dictate British withdrawal from the Middle East.

None the less, in mid-February, 1947, three decisions of long-term strategic significance were taken by the British cabinet, all of which had fundamental ramifications for Britain's position in the Middle East. The cabinet decided to withdraw from India by June, 1948 (the evacuation and Indian independence were in fact brought forward to August 1947); to refer the Palestine question to the United Nations, without

Strategic role of the Middle East after the war 25

recommendations (Palestine was evacuated in May 1948); and to inform the Americans of their intention (due primarily to financial reasons) to terminate British economic and military aid to Greece and Turkey by the end of March 1947.

The decision to end aid to Greece, and to continue with very limited aid to the Turks, conveyed the same month to the Americans, prompted the issue of the Truman Doctrine the following month, underpinned by a Congressional grant of $400 million to Greece and Turkey.[7]

A NEW STRATEGIC ROLE FOR THE MIDDLE EAST

Some historians have found it difficult to comprehend why the February decisions, especially the withdrawal from India, did not bring a change in British strategic thinking on the Middle East. For example, in 1973, Philip Darby castigated British planners for failing to redefine the country's post-war imperial role, or to scale down its military commitments in the Middle East.

In 1973, Darby wrote:

> In retrospect the need for reappraisal seems so obvious that at first sight it is difficult to understand how Indian independence could pass leaving little more than a ripple on the placid surface of British political and strategic thinking.

Darby accused the COS of having confined their attentions 'to the problem of re-building an imperial strategy from what remained of the pre-war pieces'. In his opinion, the reason for their failure to address new imperial realities lay in ingrained 'patterns of thought which only slowly lost their hold on decision-making in Whitehall'.[8]

But Darby's strictures were written before the opening of the relevant British documents. A memorandum written for the cabinet by Bevin in November 1950 explains clearly the novel strategic importance assumed by the Middle East, and by the Suez Canal Base in particular, after the Second World War:

> The strategic emphasis has in fact shifted since 1936, and our primary strategic requirement is now not so much the defence of the Suez Canal itself, as the maintenance of a base in Egypt capable of rapid expansion on the outbreak of war, in order to support a major campaign in the Middle East [against the Soviet Union] and the defence of the base against air attack.[9]

Attlee's campaign to evacuate the Middle East had elicited a spate of arguments by British planners on the strategic significance of the Middle East in the new circumstances pertaining after the Second World War. In essence, the planners argued that the Allies' shortage of manpower

26 *Demise of the British Empire in the Middle East*

ruled out any thought of a land attack on the Soviet Union, at least during the early stages of a war. The air offensive, 'either by aircraft or projectile', would not only be their sole strategic weapon, but their 'only means of effective defence'. Therefore, they had to have air bases close enough to the Soviet Union to enable them to reach major strategic targets inside its territory. In this context, the Middle East was essential as a launching platform for the strategic air offensive.[10]

The COS's Joint Planning Staff (JPS) adopted and developed an argument adumbrated by Group Captain M. R. MacArthur, Deputy Director of Policy at the Air Ministry. Not only was the air offensive Britain's only strategy in the event of the Allies becoming involved in a war, they concluded that: 'the threat of attack by air or long range weapons will be our one effective military deterrent to Russian aggression'.[11] The COS stressed Britain's own vulnerability to air attack, and consequent devastation, by the new scientific weapons. They argued that the only area from which they could effectively launch an air offensive against the Soviets' vulnerable south-eastern flank was the Middle East.[12]

THE STRATEGIC AIR OFFENSIVE

American planners, basing themselves upon the experience gained during the Second World War, determined that the Soviets' industrial and petro-chemical infrastructures would be the prime targets of the Allied strategic air offensive. Given that during the early cold war period the Allies did not have an operational heavy bomber with the range to carry a full payload of ordnance from the continental United States to the Soviet Union, overseas air bases were vital.[13]

High up on the list of these potential bases were the territories under the control of the Americans' principal ally, Britain; particular interest was shown in air bases in Britain itself, and those in the Suez Base complex. In the late 1940s, construction work was begun on the Mildenhall base in Britain, and on the Abu Sueir base in Egypt. (The British had calculated that, of all the existing air bases available in the British treaty zone in Egypt, Abu Sueir would be the most economical to develop and prepare for the reception of the heavy B-29s, requiring the least expenditure in labour and money.[14]) Runways were extended, and special refuelling facilities were built, in order to accommodate the heavy B-29s, some of which (the 59th Composite Group) were specially converted to carry the atomic bomb.

American B-29s taking off from British bases would be able to attack any part of western Europe occupied by the Soviets and, in addition,

Strategic role of the Middle East after the war 27

to reach key targets such as the Ploesti oilfields in Romania, the Donbass industrial region and Moscow. None of the 140 airfields built in Britain during the Second World War could yet accommodate the B-29s, but many could be converted easily and quickly.[15]

The air bases in Britain were in many respects at a logistical *disadvantage* to those in the Middle East. Britain was expected to hold out against a Soviet offensive for between 45 and 60 days. The Cairo–Suez bases were not expected to fall to a Soviet offensive until from four to six months after D-day. In western Europe, bad weather conditions frequently inhibited flying missions; by contrast, the skies over the desert expanses of the Middle East were generally clear. And, given that the Soviets were expected to overrun most of Europe very swiftly, aircraft taking off from Britain might from an early stage of the war expect to overfly hostile, enemy-occupied territory for most of their missions; and, most important of all, the B-29s, carrying their normal payloads of 10–15,000 pounds of ordnance, were restricted to an effective maximum flying range of between 1,500 and 2,000 miles. This meant that the rich oil-producing area around Baku and the Soviet industries east of the Ural mountains would be beyond the range of B-29s based in Britain, though *within* the range of those taking off from Abu Sueir.[16]

Indeed, Egypt's primary strategic advantage over Britain lay in its closer proximity to Soviet strategic targets. A far higher percentage of those targets lay within short range of the Egyptian base, even if the percentages did even out somewhat when it came to longer-range targets.

Of the 40 most important Soviet petroleum refineries and urban areas targeted by *Makefast*, the air annexe to the American plan for a global war offensive (October 1946), their respective ranges from the Mildenhall base in England and from Cairo were calculated to be:

	1,500 miles	2,000 miles	2,500 miles
England:	5	16	30
Cairo:	12	20	32

With regard to the percentage of total Soviet petroleum-refining capacity within striking distance from bases in England and Cairo, the comparison is yet more striking:

	1,500 miles	2,000 miles	2,500 miles
England:	12%	25%	96%
Cairo:	72%	94%	99%[17]

Given the limited flying ranges of the strategic bombers available until the early and mid-1950s, the advantages of Abu Sueir over English air bases are clear.

28 *Demise of the British Empire in the Middle East*

Even when longer-range bombers became operational, during the early 1950s, the Canal Zone remained important both for the launching of medium-range bombers and as a post-strike base for landing and refuelling. An American Strategic Air Command (SAC) Emergency War plan approved by the American Joint Chiefs of Staff (JCS) on 22 October 1951 determined that medium-range bombers, starting from Britain, would fly along the edge of the Mediterranean, and deliver 52 atomic bombs on industrial targets in the Volga and Donets basins. On their return flights from their missions, these bombers were scheduled to make landings at Egyptian and Libyan air bases.[18]

In effect, British strategy for the Middle East during the early years of the cold war was reduced largely to buying as much time as possible for the American strategic air offensive from Abu Sueir to take its toll of the Soviets' war-making capacity.

BRITISH PLANS FOR THE DEFENCE OF THE MIDDLE EAST

Allied planners agreed that, in the event of a new war, the Soviets' initial strategic objective would be the conquest of western Europe. However, they also agreed that the Soviets would simultaneously have to wage a secondary campaign against the Middle East, in order to eliminate the British bases at the Suez Canal, which would otherwise pose a serious threat to their exposed left flank.

The COS believed that the Soviets would not limit themselves to air strikes, but would mount a land offensive, to ensure physical possession of the entire complex of army, air and naval bases that lay at the Allies' disposal in the Middle East, especially in Egypt.[19]

But some Foreign Office officials begged to differ, and believed that the Cs in C (Commanders in Chief) Middle East were over-anxious about the anticipated Soviet land offensive against the Middle East. One commented, somewhat facetiously:

> It seems to me rather unrealistic to assume that the Russians would launch an elaborate land attack across several deserts in order to capture the Suez Canal. They don't want the Canal for themselves but only to deny it to us. The obvious answer seems to be a few atomic bombs.[20]

Whatever the logic in that department's cynicism, it lay beyond the comprehension of Britain's military planners. The latter saw it as their duty to prepare for all contingencies, and the prospect of a Soviet Middle East land offensive, aimed at the Suez Canal, lay at the heart of their concerns.

The British plan for the defence of the Middle East, codenamed

Strategic role of the Middle East after the war   29

Sandown, was drawn up in August 1948. It envisaged that British, American and Commonwealth forces would block, and interdict Soviet land and air forces advancing on the Middle East, and bring them to a decisive battle on the coastal plain of the country then still known internationally as Palestine.

Sandown determined that the optimal position from which to defend the Middle East was the so-called *OUTER RING*. This line ran along the Taurus and Zagros mountains, which extend from Turkey to Persia, as far as Bander Abbas. This line was cut by a handful of narrow passes through which any attacking force would have to channel itself, and which would be relatively easy to defend. However, the COS determined that, for the short term, the preparation and maintenance of this line was beyond British resources. Moreover, the necessary military infrastructure, bases and logistic backing for the forces required, could not be built or supplied in the forseeable future. At best, it was hoped that these might become available ten years hence, in 1957.[21]

Owing to the paucity of allied forces available (on paper), the defensive line finally determined upon was the shortest, the so-called *Ramallah* line. This ran east from Tel Aviv through Ramallah, to Jericho, then south through the Dead Sea and along the Jordan rift valley to Aqaba. The COS favoured the *Ramallah* position, since any Soviet offensive against the Canal would be forced to traverse Palestine through 'the bottleneck formed between the Dead Sea and the Mediterranean, in the area of Ramallah'. But the key advantage of the *Ramallah* line was that it could be held by far fewer forces, with significantly less administrative backing than any other line.[22]

However, any strategy based on this line also had great disadvantages: it was perilously close to the Suez Canal; and it would mean giving up most of the Middle East oil fields in advance.[23] The planners were also aware of the political problems that the *Ramallah* line posed. Its construction would require the military collaboration of a country, Israel, the northern half of whose territory was to be thereby abandoned in advance. However, the COS were forced to conclude that, for the short term, lack of resources would compel the Allies to fall back on this strategically and politically problematic, albeit most economical and practical, defensive position.

British planners were themselves so sceptical about the prospects of *Sandown*'s success that they foresaw the possibility that the Soviets would quickly break through the *Ramallah* line, and pose a direct threat to the Egyptian base itself. If that happened, they would have to call upon the American Strategic Bomber Force to divert aircraft from their strategic targets inside the Soviet Union to Soviet tactical targets in the Middle East, in order to hold up the advance of the Red Army.[24]

Moreover, a fundamental assumption upon which *Sandown* was predicated, that of an American military contribution to this theatre, was soon shattered. At the annual (since 1947) ABC (American–British–Canadian) Planners conference held in the Pentagon in October 1949, the Americans informed their British ally that they were 'withdrawing' the American contingent hitherto earmarked for the Middle East (three-and-a-third divisions and 160 aircraft). The Americans also turned down British pleas to send at least a 'token force' to Israel. The British warned that if the Arabs received any hint that the West was going to abandon that theatre, 'then the Cold War would be as good as lost'.[25]

The British team reported back on the Washington talks to the cabinet:

> The Americans are determined not to become embroiled in a Middle East campaign which they fear will draw their forces into a 'side-show' theatre instead of allowing them to build up for the re-conquest of Europe.[26]

During the summer of 1950, international attention focused on Korea, where the first 'hot war' involving Western and Communist forces since the Second World War erupted. On 25 June 1950, North Korean forces invaded South Korea. On 8 July, in the absence of the Soviet Union, the United Nations voted to intervene on behalf of South Korea, and appointed an American officer, General Douglas MacArthur, as commander of UN forces in Korea. The Korean war also served to underline the strategic importance of the Middle East, especially the value of Allied supply lines through the Suez Canal.[27]

In June 1950, under the shadow of the developing Korean crisis, the British Defence Coordinating Committee (BDCC) Middle East (ME) reviewed *Sandown*, the Middle East theatre plan. This revision was codenamed *Celery*.

THE STRATEGIC IMPORTANCE OF ISRAEL

As part of the review, Israel's alignment with the West also received special attention. On instructions from the Foreign Office, the COS now placed more emphasis on the need to secure military and strategic rights on its territory. This was due both to Israel's abandonment of her neutrality, and its alignment with the West during the Korean War, and to the growing sense of despair of ever reaching a new base agreement with the Egyptians.[28]

The COS appreciated that Israel would be most unlikely to co-operate with the Allies on the basis of *Sandown*, a plan predicated on the abandonment in advance and probable occupation by the Soviets

Strategic role of the Middle East after the war 31

of the northern half of its territory. In that event, rather than reconcile itself to that fate, Israel was expected to seek terms with the Soviets. If that happened, the allies would have to occupy Israel by force.[29]

British concern to secure a military understanding with the Israelis or, at the very least, to guarantee and secure in advance transit rights through Israeli territory, prompted the British Government to send General Sir Brian Robertson, Commander-in-Chief British Forces, Middle East, to Israel in February 1951.[30]

However, with the American and British Chiefs of Staff preoccupied with the Far East, and the prospect of any American or Commonwealth commitment to the Middle East yet more remote, the BDCC, ME, found itself unable to agree to the COS request to move the last fortified defence line to the north of Israel, to the so-called *Lebanon–Jordan* line (running from the Mediterranean coast eastwards, from a point just north of Beirut, parallel to the main lateral road from Beirut to Damascus, thence south through Lake Tiberias and the Jordan Valley, along the 'parallel mountain ranges of the Lebanon and Anti-Lebanon running north and south on each side of the Jordan and Baalbek valleys', down to Aqaba).[31]

The *Ramallah* line remained the 'last-ditch' defence position, owing to the even more limited forces now expected to be available for the Middle East theatre. In the autumn of 1950, British planners still had no idea of how many land forces the Americans were currently willing to commit to the Middle East, nor how many American aircraft would be available. The BDCC, ME, was acutely aware of *Celery's* weaknesses, but insisted that it remained the only realistic plan in view of the limited resources at its disposal.[32]

The dangers of an Israeli refusal to co-operate were again underlined, since, by now, British planners were not confident that they would dispose of sufficient forces even to fight their way into southern Israel, if the Israeli army were ordered to resist. The JPS pointed out that the BDCC, ME, offered no solution, and no alternative course of action to this problem.

The initial phase of the war would be critical, and the British would be unable to dissipate effort and forces fighting the Israelis. The JPS warned:

> unless sufficient forces are deployed forward to deter a direct Russian advance from Iraq, we might be brought to battle at about D + 3 months on ground not of our own choosing and before our build-up had been completed.[33]

They conceded that prior studies had established the fact that the *Ramallah* line was the last possible point at which to hold up the Soviets, in order to provide sufficient depth for the defence of Egypt, and 'to prevent attack by short-range tactical aircraft'. But they protested that the Line left Israel 'wide open to Russian penetration', and again warned that 'if the Russians were on the point of entering Israel and the Allies were patently incapable of preventing them, Israel would be likely to come to an arrangement with Russia'.[34]

Therefore, the JPS reiterated, their main hope of securing the vital co-operation of Israel would be to establish their initial defence position further to the north and east, and to deploy enough forces on that line to contain the Russian threat (or at least to convince the Israelis that they could).

But, whatever the dictates of sound military doctrine, the final decision as to the Middle East defence line would depend upon which forces could be allocated initially to this theatre, how soon reinforcements could be rushed in, and upon how extensive and effective Turkish opposition (Turkey and Greece were admitted into NATO in September 1951) proved to be.[35]

In all Allied contingency plans for the Middle East, the minimum-force levels required exceeded by far those that Britain and the Commonwealth were expected to have available for the forseeable future (in September 1950 as a result of the Korean War, the British extended military conscription to two years). Everything still hinged on the American contribution, on land, sea and air. But the COS doubted whether they could count on any Commonwealth or American reinforcements within the critical first six months of the war.[36]

Thus, notwithstanding its glaring deficiencies, the *Ramallah* line was retained as the basis of Britain's Middle East defence plan. The JPS' objections may have been based upon cogent and irrefutable military logic. But, with the limited forces at their disposal, the COS were obliged to accept the risks, and to bow to the ruling of the Middle East commanders.[37]

This was tantamount to admitting that they could not in fact defend the Middle East – although at this stage, in late 1950, no one was yet willing to concede this openly.

THE DEMISE OF THE EGYPTIAN BASE

The key to Britain's strategic interests in the Middle East, in all respects, was Egypt. This was due not only to Allied plans for launching the strategic air offensive from Abu Sueir; but also to the Egyptians' insistence, since the end of the Second World War, that Britain evacuate their country and grant Egypt full independence. The British were quite creative in suggesting various plans to appease the Egyptians

Strategic role of the Middle East after the war 33

(beginning with evacuation of their forces to the Canal Zone, and ending with the plan for an Allied Middle East Command) – but all came to naught.

For the Egyptians, *British* imperialism, and *not* the Soviets represented the real enemy. Furthermore, the Egyptians regarded Israel (who had humiliated them on the battlefield in 1948) and *not* the Soviets as the more immediate military threat.

During the autumn of 1951, as yet another round of negotiations between Britain and Egypt collapsed, the country degenerated into chaos. Reinforcements had to be rushed in from Britain. Organized labour boycotted the Canal Base, British and Egyptian security forces clashed, and an indigenous guerrilla campaign harassed British forces, and sabotaged British installations. The violence in Egypt peaked on 25 January 1952, with large-scale clashes between British and Egyptian forces. The next day, the mob torched and ransacked Cairo.[38]

Quite clearly, as had been the case in Palestine, British force was unable to quash, or cope with, indigenous demands for independence. By the end of 1951, the garrison in Egypt had been reinforced from 33,500 to 64,000 troops; and 20,000 more were on their way. It was the largest concentration of British forces anywhere across the globe, and constituted a burden that Britain could no longer shoulder[39] (cf. Chapter 7 in this volume, by Charles Tripp).

Three days after the sacking of Cairo, CIGS (Chief of Imperial General Staff) Slim warned the cabinet that any further conflict with the Egyptians might require the despatch of reinforcements from Britain. However, as he also noted, they did not in fact have any additional troops to send out, since the entire strategic reserve had already been dispatched to Egypt. Slim feared that the lack of any reserve at home might encourage insurgency in other parts of the world, to which they would be unable to respond.[40]

The British garrison in Egypt, deployed in order to defend the Canal Base against a Soviet attack, had in fact become hostage to the indigenous, hostile population. As noted by Roger Allen, head of the African department at the Foreign Office:

> The truth of the matter is that we are at present keeping 80,000 men in the Canal Zone for no purpose except to maintain themselves … It is useless to maintain troops simply to be shot at.[41]

It was clear that remaining in Egypt would prove too costly, in both manpower and money.[42] But to pull out precipitately would advertise clearly to the Arabs, and to the world, British impotence. British motives were by now mixed, involving intangible, albeit vital issues such as prestige and 'loss of face'.

34 *Demise of the British Empire in the Middle East*

By the spring of 1952, the Foreign Office began to fear that the garrison in Egypt could no longer guarantee Allied strategic interests in the event of war with the Soviets, but was there primarily in order to preserve Britain's 'face' as a Great Power:

> From a long-term point of view there is much to be said for pulling as many troops as we can out of the Middle East, and so removing a major irritant to our relations with Middle East countries. On the other hand their presence there increases our prestige, and lends strength to our diplomatic arm. It boils down to whether we *really* want to keep our troops in the Middle East in order to fend off the Russians, or whether one purpose, if not the main purpose, of keeping them there is to safeguard our position in those countries.[43]

In any case, the size of the garrison now earmarked by the COS for the Middle East, a single division (of which but a single brigade was to be stationed in the Middle East) and 160 aircraft, was woefully inadequate. The Middle East commanders demanded the addition of at least an armoured force and a number of tactical bombers.[44]

THE SWITCH TO THE NORTHERN TIER STRATEGY

During the course of 1953, British planners determined on a new strategy for the Middle East, the 'Levant–Iraq', or 'Forward' strategy. The new strategy recognized the inevitability of evacuating Egypt, and planned, with the help of indigenous forces (Iraqi and Jordanian), to hold up a Soviet offensive at the northern approaches to the Middle East. The new strategy dovetailed in neatly with the Northern Tier strategy that the Americans had been pressing on their British ally for years. It would take on political expression in the Baghdad Pact, set up in 1955.

In the event of an emergency, the British garrison in the Middle East would be reinforced from a strategic reserve to be stationed in Britain. This reserve would be endowed with the ability to fly at short notice to any trouble spot across the globe. This 'mobile concept' was developed in order to cut down force levels, as required by the stringencies of budget cuts.[45]

But the new strategy was in fact but a thin veil, which barely covered Britain's military bankruptcy in the Middle East. As such, it came under scathing criticism by the Defence Coordination Committee (DCC), Middle East. With not a little sarcasm, and rancour, the DCC commented that it was its responsibility to confine itself to 'real solutions of the problem of defending this important area, and to exclude those which are only "make-believe"'.[46] If Britain could not afford 'a real solution' (whether due to political or economic reasons), but had to put forward

Strategic role of the Middle East after the war 35

'a facade', the Committee felt itself bound by good conscience to put in the following caveats:

(a) Even if we feel that we must try to deceive others, we should not deceive ourselves or the Americans.

(b) Our bluff may be called one day and British soldiers and airmen may again find themselves committed to a hopeless venture. Therefore, we should not be content with our bluff, but should strive with might and main to convert it to the real thing.

(c) The facade must not be so transparent that it fails to deceive. There is already doubt in the Arab world about our ability to defend the Middle East: hence occasional talk of neutrality. If we reach an agreement with Egypt, involving the evacuation of the Canal Zone, our ability to defend the Middle East will be the public announcement of our intentions and our answer to such questionings; the effectiveness of that answer depends upon its size ...[47]

This memorandum, written during the evolution of the new 'forward' strategy, in effect reflected the nemesis of the British imperial dream in the Middle East.

NOTES

This article is based on the author's *Fighting World War Three from the Middle East: Allied Contingency Plans, 1945–1954* (London: Frank Cass, 1997).

1   Cf. Michael J. Cohen, *Palestine and the Great Powers, 1945–1948* (Princeton, NJ: Princeton University Press, 1982) p. 34.

2   Ronald Hyam (ed.), *The Labour Government and the End of Empire, 1945–1951* (London: HMSO), series A, Vol. 2, part I, p. lviii.
      On the importance of Middle East oil from this period on, and increasing American interest in it, cf. Michael J. Cohen, *Palestine: Retreat from the Mandate, 1936–45* (London/New York: Elek/Holmes and Meier, 1978) pp. 152–4; George E. Kirk, *Survey of International Affairs, 1939–1946: The Middle East in the War* (London/New York: Oxford University Press) p. 25, note 1; Aaron David Miller, *Search for Security: Saudi Arabian Oil and American Foreign Policy, 1939–1949* (Chapel Hill, NC: University of Chapel Hill Press, 1980); and David R. Devereux, *The Formulation of British Defence Policy towards the Middle East, 1948–1956* (London: Macmillan, 1990) p. 9.

3   John Kent, 'Bevin's Imperialism and the Idea of Euro-Africa, 1945–49', in Michael Dockrill and John Young (eds.), *British Foreign Policy, 1945–56* (New York: St Martin's Press, 1989) p. 53.

4   On the Chiefs of Staffs' and War Secretary Churchill's denigration of the newly acquired territories of the Middle East, the 'New Provinces', in 1919, cf. Michael J. Cohen, *Churchill and the Jews* (London: Frank Cass, 1985) Ch. 3.

5   Cf. Michael J. Cohen, *Fighting World War Three from the Middle East: Allied Contingency Plans, 1945–1954* (London: Frank Cass, 1997) pp. 72–4.

6   On the debate on the retention of British positions in the Middle East, cf. Cohen, ibid., pp. 69–89; John Kent, 'The Egyptian Base and the Defence of the Middle East, 1945–1954', in Robert Holland (ed.), *Emergencies and Disorders in the European Empires after 1945* (London: Frank Cass, 1994); and Raymond Smith and John Zametica, 'The Cold War Warrior: Clement Attlee Reconsidered, 1945–47', *International Affairs*, 61, 2 (Spring 1985) pp. 237–52.

7   Richard N. Rosencrance, *Defence of the Realm: British Strategy in the Nuclear Epoch* (New

York/London: Columbia University Press, 1968) pp. 62–3; and Peter G. Boyle, 'The British Foreign Office and American Foreign Policy, 1947–48', *Journal of American Studies*, 16, 3 (Dec. 1982) pp. 373–89.

During 1944–47, Britain had expended $540 million on Greece, and between 1938–47, $375 million on Turkey. On British aid to Greece and Turkey, see Terry H. Anderson, *The United States, Great Britain and the Cold War, 1944–1947* (Columbia/London: University of Missouri Press, 1981) pp. 167–9.

8   Philip Darby, *British Defence Policy East of Suez, 1947–1968* (London: Oxford University Press for the RIIA, 1973) pp. 15–16.

9   Memorandum to the cabinet by the Foreign Secretary, CP (50), 283, 27 November 1950, Cab 129/43. Public Record Office (PRO).

The year 1936 was the date of the signature of the last Anglo–Egyptian Treaty, due to expire in 1956.

10   Note by Group Captain M. R. MacArthur to Director of Plans, 25 March 1946, Air 9/267, PRO.

11   Cf. Richard Aldrich and John Zametica, 'The Rise and Decline of a Strategic Concept: The Middle East, 1945–51', in Richard Aldrich (ed.), *British Intelligence, Strategy and the Cold War, 1945–51* (London/New York: Routledge) p. 244.

12   DO(46)80, *British Strategic Requirements in the Middle East*, Cab 131/3, quoted in ibid.

13   The maximum range of the B-29, carrying a full payload, was 3,200 miles, round-trip. The B-36, the propeller-driven successor to the B-29, which only came into full operation during the early 1950s, had a round-trip range of 8,000 miles. However, the B-36, which proved very vulnerable during service in the Korean War, became the subject of much criticism, and fell victim to inter-Service disputes. Cf. Cohen, *Fighting World War Three*, pp. 13–16.

14   General Hollis (Secretary, British Chiefs of Staff) to Ministry of Defence, 30 September 1948, in COS(48)138th, DEFE 4/16, PRO.

15   Elliott Vanveltner Converse, 3rd, *United States Plans for a Postwar Overseas Military Base System, 1942–1948* (unpublished PhD thesis, Princeton University, 1984) pp. 216–17.

16   Ibid., p. 217; and SAC Emergency War Pan, 1–49, 21 December 1948, quoted in T. H. Etzold and J. L. Gaddis, *Containment: Documents on American Policy and Strategy, 1945–1950* (New York: Columbia University Press, 1978) p. 359.

17   'Outline Air Plan for *Makefast*', 1 October 1946, RG 165, ABC 381 USSR (2 March 1946) section 3, NA.

18   Walter S. Poole, *The History of the Joint Chiefs of Staff*, Vol. IV, *The Joint Chiefs of Staff and National Policy, 1950–1952* (Wilmington, DE: Michael Glazier Inc., 1980) p. 170; and Peter L. Hahn, *The United States, Great Britain and Egypt, 1945–56* (Chapel Hill, NC: University of North Carolina Press, 1991) p. 95.

19   COS memorandum, DO(46)47, 2 April 1946, in Cab 131/21, PRO.

20   Minute by J. E. Cable, 7 April 1948, E4319, E4319, FO 371/68378, PRO.

21   Annex to COS(51)755, 18 December 1951, DEFE 5/35, PRO.

22   JP(49)59, 11 July 1949, DEFE 4/23, PRO.

23   Ibid.

24   JPS(48)57, August 1948, Air 8/1603, PRO.

25   Meeting between JCS and Air Marshal Tedder, 5 October 1949, CCS 337 (7-22-48) S. 1, RG 218, 1948–50, NA.

26   Annex I to JP(49)126 (Final), 3 November 1949, DEFE 4/26, PRO.

27   On the military and strategic implications of the Korean War, cf. Devereux, *Formulation of British Defence Policy*, pp. 39–40, and Hahn, *The United States*, pp. 93–4, and Chapter 9 in this volume by Hahn.

28   On Israel's policy of neutrality, and the realignment during the Korean War, cf. Uri Bialer, *Between East and West: Israel's Foreign Policy Orientation, 1948–1956* (Cambridge: Cambridge University Press, 1990).

29   JP(50)106, 1 August 1950, annex to COS(50) 135th meeting, 22 August 1950, in Air 20/8113, PRO.

30   On General Robertson's visit, cf. Cohen, *Fighting World War Three*, pp. 210–24.

31   Annex to JP(50)94 (Final), 22 September 1950, DEFE 4/36, PRO.

32   JP(50)106, op. cit., and COS to Commanders-in-Chief, Middle East, 22 September 1950, annex to JP(50)94, DEFE 6/14, and DEFE 4/36, PRO.

Strategic role of the Middle East after the war 37

33   Annex to JP(50)94, ibid.
34   Ibid.
35   JP(50)106, op. cit.
36   Ibid. In November 1950, the British still anticipated the following Commonwealth forces for the Middle East:

> *Australia*: 1–2 divisions; 1 armoured brigade; 3 fighter squadrons.
> *New Zealand*: 1 division; 1 armoured brigade.
> *South Africa*: 1 armoured division, possibly 1 further division, and 9 fighter squadrons.

Cf. annex to JP(50)167, 22 November 1950, DEFE 6/15, PRO.
37   Ibid.
38   Cf. Peter L. Hahn, 'Containment and Egyptian Nationalism: The Unsuccessful Effort to Establish the Middle East Command, 1950–53', *Diplomatic History*, 11, 1 (Winter, 1987) p. 37, and Devereux, *Formulation of British Defence Policy*, pp. 63, 137–8.
39   Cf. Kent, *The Egyptian Base*, p. 51.
40   CCs(52)8th, 28 January 1952, Cab 128/24, PRO.
41   Minute by Roger Allen, 14 February 1953, JE 1192/18, FO 371/102796, PRO.
42   Kent, *The Egyptian Base*, p. 60.
42   R. C. Mackworth-Young, minute, 9 May 1952, JE 1194/43, FO 371/96974, PRO (italics added).

Interestingly, in 1952, the British did not apparently consider the logistical problems of retaking Egypt by force, against *Egyptian* resistance. When the attempt was made in 1956, the mobile forces available proved 'altogether inadequate'; cf. Darby, *British Defence Policy*, pp. 95–6.
44   DCC(53)16, 23 February 1953, DEFE 11/58, PRO.
45   *The Radical Review: Mobility in the Middle East*, JP(53)24 (Final), 5 February 1953, DEFE 6/23, and report by *ad hoc* committee on the Radical Review, RR (*ad hoc*) (53)2, 9 February 1953, DEFE 11/87; and R. W. Ewbank, Secretary, COS Committee, to R. R. Powell, 23 February 1953, DEFE 11/87, PRO.
46   Cf. DCC(53)16, 23 February 1953, DEFE 11/58, PRO.
47   Ibid.

PART 2

ASPECTS OF ARAB NATIONALISM

3

Britain and the politics of the Arab League, 1943–50

MICHAEL THORNHILL

On 22 March 1945, Egypt, Iraq, Lebanon, Saudi Arabia, Syria, Transjordan and Yemen came together to form the Arab League. This intergovernmental organization was the practical political application of a movement towards Arab unity which had begun with the collapse of the Ottoman empire during the First World War. After 1918, Ottoman rule was replaced by British, and to a lesser extent, French control of the region. The Arab unity movement was by definition an anti-imperial venture and its final aim was the abandonment of the artificial boundaries imposed by the Great Powers. Yet the language of pan-Arabism in the European phase of Middle Eastern history was more often used as a prop by local elites for their own state-building purposes. Moreover, the arbitrary nature of the externally imposed frontiers engendered a competitive edge to this state-building process. The upshot was fierce inter-Arab rivalries, often stemming from dynastic unity schemes. The Arab countries seized the opportunity presented by the Second World War to try and loosen the imperial bindings, and an indirect challenge to Britain's position was mounted through efforts to form a regional power bloc. Rather than oppose this process, British policy-makers worked discreetly to channel it in a direction they hoped would be less harmful to their own longer-term interests. It was with this mixed – though concealed – parentage that the Arab League came into being in 1945.

PRESENT AT THE CREATION

Britain's behind-the-scenes role in shaping the Arab League was part of its approach of making tactical concessions to nationalist demands in order to preserve its position in the Middle East. Two concerns dominated British thinking in the later stages of the Second World War: the future of Palestine and the peacetime maintenance of the Suez Canal

Zone base. Both issues were produced by the drive for independence and both had the potential to destabilize Britain's wider regional interests. The strategy of British policy-makers between 1943 and the creation of the Arab League in March 1945 was to allow Egypt to play the central role in the League's foundation, the corollary of which was leadership of the Arab world. The immediate objective was to limit Palestine's influence in the proposed organization and to keep the problem of its future low on the agenda. A somewhat vaguer hope was that Egypt would steer the other League members along the road of Anglo–Arab partnership in the postwar era. However, buoyed by its new-found leadership position, Egypt used the Arab League as a vehicle for its own nationalist goals. Britain quickly lost confidence in the body, with disastrous consequences for Palestinian Arab nationalism. During the Palestine War of November 1947–January 1949, Britain adopted a pro-Transjordan policy, which placed it in direct opposition to the Arab League objective of establishing a Palestinian Arab state over the whole of mandatory Palestine. The creation of Israel and the Arab defeat was to undermine Britain's imperial position in the Middle East.

On 24 February 1943, a reply to a parliamentary question by Britain's foreign secretary, Anthony Eden, was to have a significant impact on Middle Eastern politics. The question posed by Morgan Philips Price, a pro-Arab Labour MP, concerned the delicate issue of Arab unity: would Britain, he asked, be taking any steps 'to promote greater political and economic cooperation between the Arab states of the Middle East, with a view to the ultimate creation of an Arab Federation?' Eden's response reaffirmed existing policy in that Britain would support the idea of Arab unity, but that any initiatives must come from the Arabs themselves.[1] This low-key statement was to trigger an Egyptian-led integrative process, which British officials struggled to keep in step with during the subsequent two years. To understand British thinking and policy at this time, it is useful to begin by identifying its sources.

The main tributary was the Palestinian Arab Revolt of 1936–39. The revolt's impact reverberated around the Middle East, causing an upsurge in pan-Arab and Islamic sentiment among the indigenous peoples. Arab governments responded to these domestic pressures by supporting the Palestinian Arab cause, which was pro-independence and anti-Zionist, while also promoting schemes for Arab confederation. These plans challenged the regional framework by which Britain maintained its predominant position. British officials were initially unimpressed by this talk and instead continued to emphasize their own handiwork, namely the importance of competing dynastic interests in the shaping of regional relations.[2]

This was to change, however, after Arab conferences on Palestine in

Britain and the politics of the Arab League 43

1937 and 1938. For the first time British policy-makers began to recognize the growing importance of the Arab collective will, even if serious doubts about the realism of Arab unity remained. It was decided that Britain should involve itself in future inter-Arab discussions, whether on Palestine or confederation, in order to influence their outcome. The aim as far as Palestine was concerned was to secure Arab endorsement of British policy in the mandate's affairs. In confederation discussions, the purpose was to emphasize the obstacles and minimize the prospects, although it was important for Britain not to appear to be opposed to the basic idea of unity. The brief was guidance rather than obstruction. The St James' conference in London in early 1939 was evidence of this new approach *vis-à-vis* inter-Arab politics. The official line on pan-Arabism as Britain edged towards war with Germany was to view its aims with 'sympathy' but to 'take as little initiative as possible' towards its fulfilment.[3]

While it remained easy for British officials to dismiss ideas of a one-nation super-state as an ideological fantasy, the territorial *status quo* was less secure in the face of rival dynastic unity projects. The rulers of Iraq and Transjordan, for instance, each dreamt of creating 'Fertile Crescents', the details of which varied but usually involved the absorption of Syria and Lebanon, and sometimes Palestine. The prestige to be gained from such ventures ensured the vigorous opposition of Saudi Arabia and Egypt. Nor did the Syrian, Lebanese and Palestinian populations care particularly for substituting European domination for rule by their Arab cousins. Britain opposed the dynastic unity projects because they threatened to divide the region into rival power blocs. A split in the Arab world would have compelled Britain to choose which side to support, thereby instantly losing a significant area of influence.[4]

The impact of global war was clearly a major determinant of Britain's Arab policy in 1943. Arab support or, failing that, acquiescence for the Allied war effort was perceived as vital. This requirement had determined Britain's White Paper policy of 17 May 1939, which promised a Palestinian state based on its majority Arab population within ten years. Earlier promises to the Jews were ignored. Jewish immigration was subsequently curtailed and made ultimately dependent upon Arab consent. The maintenance of Arab backing also lay behind Eden's Mansion House speech on 29 May 1941. The key passage stated that Britain would give its 'full support' to the strengthening of cultural, economic and political ties between the Arab states, provided that any scheme commanded 'general approval'.[5]

Arab support for the Allied war effort had been wavering since the collapse of France a year earlier. Britain's proclivity to maintain the regional *status quo* was in the meantime affected by Vichy French activities in Syria and Lebanon. The situation came to a head in early May 1941, when the French authorities in Syria gave assistance to Rashid Ali's pro-Axis government in Iraq. Britain's prime minister, Winston Churchill, a sympathizer with the Zionist cause, wanted to use this interference to eliminate the Vichy French in the Middle East, and in the process solve the Palestine dispute. Churchill believed that this could be achieved by implementing a proposal for the federation of the Middle East in which a Jewish state would exist in western Palestine and be an independent unit in a wider Arab caliphate. The idea had been previously broached by H. St John Philby when he was acting as an adviser to the Saudi monarchy in the late 1930s. Then, however, such federative solutions to the Palestine problem could not be made compatible with French interests in the Middle East. By May 1941, Churchill held that Vichy collaboration with Nazi Germany had removed this obstacle.[6]

Eden in the Foreign Office was more circumspect. He knew that Arab opinion opposed any form of Jewish statehood in the region, and with an Allied invasion of Syria imminent, the foreign secretary felt that Arab support had to be bolstered, not undermined. Eden's Mansion House speech thus had two purposes: to ground Churchill's federation kite, which had already been floated to some cabinet members, and to pander to Arab unity aspirations as part of a propaganda offensive on the eve of military operations in Syria. The Arab response to Eden's statement was positive but muted. Commitments made under the duress of a precarious international situation were judged in their context.[7]

It was not until the autumn of 1941 that the longer-term implications of the Mansion House policy were fully considered. This followed the establishment of a special sub-committee of the Committee of Imperial Defence in September. The timing was determined by the Anglo–Free French defeat of Vichy Syria and the questions this raised about Syria's future. The Damascus–Jerusalem linkage was underlined in the committee's terms of reference, which were to 'examine forthwith the various forms which a scheme for Arab Federation might take and to report on their advantages and disadvantages, as well as their practicability, paying special attention to the Palestine problem'.[8] Senior officials from the Foreign Office and Colonial Office were joined by representatives from the service departments, the Treasury and the India Office.[9]

The committee's deliberations centred on whether the policy of supporting Arab unity initiatives should be taken one step further and whether Britain should actually lead the process. The views of the Foreign and Colonial Offices finally prevailed. Influenced by representatives in the region, the thinking was that political federation was still an unrealistic proposition and that greater economic co-operation

Britain and the politics of the Arab League   45

was the only possibility. The Middle East Supply Centre, established in April 1941 to regulate civilian supply needs, was held as the beacon in this respect. Britain's ambassador in Egypt, Sir Miles Lampson (Lord Killearn, January 1943), best encapsulated the preferred line when he wrote that Britain should confine itself to 'vague expressions' of support for Arab unity.[10]

This, then, was the broad thrust of British thinking on Arab unity when Eden repeated his Mansion House pledge in the House of Commons in February 1943. The reason the second statement served as a catalyst for the concerted negotiations which led to the signing of the Arab League in March 1945 was Britain's victory at El Alamein in November 1942. With the German threat to the region diminishing, the Arab states were obliged to square their own national aspirations with the continuation of British imperium.

The pace of the integrative process was determined by the relationship between inter-Arab rivalries and a power struggle in Egypt. Regional manoeuvring began as soon as the implications of the German defeat in the Western Desert became apparent. The Iraqi prime minister, Nuri al-Said, set the ball rolling when he outlined his new Fertile Crescent thinking to the British ambassador in January 1943. Syria, Lebanon and Palestine would be joined with Transjordan, and an Arab league would be created between this new state, Iraq, and the other Arab countries. Ever the wily politician, Nuri coupled this initiative with a declaration of war against the Axis powers.[11] Iraq's premier followed this up with a letter to Egypt's Wafd prime minister, Mustafa al-Nahas, on 17 March suggesting an inter-Arab conference. The status of the meeting – i.e. governmental or unofficial – was left open.[12] The struggle for Arab leadership between Egypt and Iraq had therefore started even before Eden's statement on 24 February.

Al-Nahas' immediate preoccupation, however, was with his domestic position. King Faruq deeply resented having the Wafd ministry imposed upon him by British tanks in February 1942, and his abiding aim was to get rid of al-Nahas as soon as he could. Faruq also had regional ambitions of his own and dreamed of becoming the Caliph of all Muslims. Al-Nahas was concerned that Nuri's lack of precision over the nature of the Arab conference would enable Faruq to play a central role in the proceedings. These fears increased after Eden's statement on 24 February prompted the leading Egyptian pan-Arabist journalist and former minister Abdul Rahman Azzam to write a newspaper article calling for a 'free Arab conference'.[13] The domestic threat of the Palace and the external challenge of Nuri prompted al-Nahas to make a highly significant announcement in the Egyptian parliament. On 30 March, the Wafd government stated that it intended to begin bilateral negotiations with Arab governments on the subject of future Arab political co-operation. When this process was completed, Egypt would sponsor an official Arab conference.[14]

The 30 March initiative by al-Nahas began an Egyptian move for leadership of the Arab world. The Wafd government's reliance on British backing to remain in office during 1943–44 could suggest that Britain was underwriting the leadership bid. However, two qualifying points should be made. Firstly, Egypt's interest in regional leadership derived from far deeper well-springs than al-Nahas' concerns of early 1943. Egyptian pan-Arabism emerged as a force to be reckoned with during the Palestine Revolt. But even then domestic factors were important. Wafdist interests in pan-Arabism were partly a ploy to offset the influence of Faruq's thinking on the Caliphate.[15] Another domestic motivation was the need to try and limit the growth of extra-parliamentary pressure groups like the Muslim Brotherhood. The trend from the late 1930s was for nationalist and Islamic opinion to be canalized outside the parliamentary framework. The creeping effect was to weaken the appeal and stability of the established governmental structures.[16]

Short-term political advantage was therefore responsible for the timing of al-Nahas' initiative, but the roots of Egyptian interest in regional leadership were clearly traceable to the 1930s. The second point to be made about al-Nahas' leadership bid being backed by Britain related to geopolitical realities on the ground. Egypt's pre-eminent position in the Arab world was in many ways conferred by its size and geographical centrality, its large and homogeneous population, and the relatively large measure of independence it had already acquired. In this respect, Britain's policy of backing the al-Nahas–Egyptian leadership drive was akin to swimming with the tide.

The Arab states reacted to the al-Nahas initiative in a number of ways. For Syria and Lebanon, the two countries most often threatened territorially by Hashemite unity schemes, Egyptian leadership was welcomed enthusiastically. By the same token, Transjordan and Iraq felt not a little bitter as their Fertile Crescent dreams faded. Nuri was further piqued by al-Nahas' first stealing and then trumping his Arab conference card. Saudi Arabia was the state most wedded to the *status quo* and was wary of any moves which challenged it. Consequently, Ibn Saud's reluctant participation in the unity process was the result of anti-Hashemite sentiments deriving from rivalries over dynastic prestige, coupled with an anxiety to press for a looser form of confederation.[17]

In short, the unity movement under the Egyptian bloc was primarily a containment strategy of Hashemite dynastic ambitions. Although the existing political framework was clearly the preference for British policy-makers, the Egyptian-led process offered the best prospect for guiding the proceedings in a favourable direction. Indeed, the sheer physical

Britain and the politics of the Arab League 47

presence of Britain's military build-up in Egypt during the war, together with the embassy's concerted involvement in Egyptian domestic affairs because of the *état de siège* and the need to keep the Wafd in power, encouraged British officials to think that they could influence al-Nahas' hand in the inter-Arab negotiations.[18]

When Britain's senior military and political authorities in the region gathered in Cairo in May 1943 for a meeting of the Middle East War Council, the usual concerns with political unity were expressed. The recommendation which followed was to offer the Arab states encouragement only in the cultural and economic spheres.[19] A few weeks later, on 19 July, the War Cabinet reached the same conclusions. Caution was the watchword because of Palestine and the future of the French position in the Levant. Nevertheless, the basic approach of avoiding the appearance of blocking the unity movement remained in place, as did the declaratory policy of support for it. As a consequence, British diplomatic efforts were targeted at discouraging, albeit in an indirect way, the idea of a general Arab conference, where the subjects of Palestine and Syria were bound to be raised.[20]

By the spring of 1944, the bilateral process was reaching its final stages and could not be drawn out any longer. The prospect of a general Arab conference loomed large. On 5 June, Killearn broke the cover of informal representations and urged one of al-Nahas' chief aides to allow the conference idea to 'peter out'. The message went on to remind al-Nahas that Nuri's resignation as Iraq's prime minister in May had removed the personal challenge to his leadership of the Arab world.[21]

Once again, al-Nahas' more immediate concerns related to his domestic position. Corruption allegations levelled at his government by a former minister had damaged the Wafd's already faltering position. It appeared as though British support and the separate Arab unity negotiations were the only obstacles to the Palace's dismissing the Wafd and appointing a new government. Yet, with the 5 June *démarche*, Killearn was making an implicit linkage between the continuation of British support and an end to the unity discussions if a general Arab conference was planned. Herein lay the dilemma for al-Nahas. Reliance alone on British backing could destroy the Wafd as a political force in Egypt. With this in mind, the Egyptian premier decided to ignore the *démarche* and instead sought to rebuilt his domestic standing by pursuing an increasingly independent line *vis-à-vis* Britain. The main prop of this entailed accelerating the Arab unity discussions. Al-Nahas' next move therefore was to invite the main Arab governments to form a preparatory committee as a prelude to a general conference. The question of Palestinian representation was explicitly raised.[22]

The Cairo embassy was informed of al-Nahas' intentions but by the time Killearn had received instructions from London, the invitations had been dispatched to the Arab heads of state. Killearn was embarrassed at being out-manoeuvred and, like the Foreign Office, incensed at the names suggested for the Palestinian delegation: two of the leaders mentioned were internees in British camps.[23] In order to mend fences with Britain, al-Nahas subsequently did his utmost to reassure Killearn that discussions on the Palestine question would be conducted in a sober manner. To this end, the moderate Palestinian leader, Musa al-Alami, was chosen to head Palestine's delegation. These reassurances on Palestine went some way to soothing Britain's fears as regards the calling of an Arab conference while the war was still on. British officials also took heart from the Saudi monarch's anger at not being given prior notice, let alone consulted, about the conference's timing. Indeed, it was perhaps only because Britain advised Ibn Saud to accept the invitation if the balance of other Arab states did likewise that Saudi Arabia eventually agreed to attend the conference.[24]

Between 25 September and 6 October 1944, the leaders of the Arab world gathered in Alexandria, Egypt, to discuss the momentous question of Arab unity. While Britain was unable to halt this conference (without, that is, losing face on its claims to support the unity idea), its influence on proceedings was nevertheless significant. Most importantly, al-Nahas continued to assuage Britain on Palestinian issues. The weakening of the Saudi–Egyptian axis, because of continuing tensions over the invitation *faux pas*, also had its diplomatic advantages. That said, the anti-Hashemite bloc was still able to keep the inherently destabilizing Fertile Crescent schemes off the agenda. The ingredients were thus present for a loose confederation of Arab states being proposed, something Britain's imperial interests could live with. At the end of the two-week conference, a protocol was signed outlining the principles for the establishment of a league of independent Arab states. The purpose was to protect state sovereignty and increase co-ordination of political policy. The phrase 'Arab unity' was notably absent from the protocol's wording.[25]

The day after the signing of the Alexandria Protocol King Faruq dismissed the Wafd government. Britain's policy of maintaining al-Nahas in power had been quietly abandoned. Al-Nahas' conference invitation *fait accompli* of June 1944 was certainly a major factor in confirming this decision. Yet it was his desire to appease Britain after his errant behaviour which made him such a good conduit for Cairo embassy guidance on Palestinian topics at the Alexandria Conference. Their needs having been served, Britain's inclination to prop up al-Nahas' Wafd ministry finally melted away. Faruq must have sensed this drift – evidenced by Killearn's absence on holiday in South Africa – and

Britain and the politics of the Arab League 49

awaited his moment. This came with the ending of the inter-Arab conference. An earlier dismissal might have led to a charge of the Palace's being unsympathetic to the pan-Arab cause.[26] Continuation of Egypt's regional policy was passed to the new coalition government headed by Ahmad Maher and, after his assassination in February 1945, to Muhammad al-Nuqrashi. The pan-Arabist campaigner, Azzam, was brought in as minister for Arab affairs. As such, he was responsible for turning the principles of Alexandria into a working organization.

Britain's influence over the final stages of the negotiations remained extensive for two crucial reasons: Syria and Palestine. Firstly, the Arabs feared the re-establishment of French interests in Syria, and Britain was in a strong position to block this. Secondly, the Arab states demanded the full implementation of the Palestine White Paper policy of 1939. Again, Britain appeared to hold the key. In a telegram to Killearn (repeated to other Middle Eastern missions) dated 4 January 1945, Eden underlined the official policy of support for the post-Alexandria league negotiations, albeit out of the customary desire of not wanting to be seen to obstruct the unity process. The dispatch went on to note that Britain would oppose the French use of force to retrieve its position in the Levant.[27]

To the last, concern over Palestine dominated British policy. In early March 1945, the political sub-committee established at Alexandria to work out the details of the league framework over-stepped what Britain thought permissible. The problem was a text that recognized the right of the Palestinian Arabs to participate in the proposed organization on an equal standing with the founding members. Al-Nahas certainly had not gone so far at Alexandria, and Britain placed the opprobrium for this 'fanaticism' at Azzam's door.[28] The British view was that observer status was the best Palestine could expect because it was still under mandatory rule. Strong representations were made to the Arab drafting delegates, resulting in the clause's being dropped.[29] Syria, Lebanon and Transjordan – the other mandates in the region – were spared this reasoning. The upshot was that Palestine was relegated to an annex of the pact. This was a pointed downgrading, even from the Alexandria proceedings. The Palestinian moderate, Musa al-Alami, was in no doubt about the implications: Palestine had been deliberately marginalized and the Arab League structure was a glorified debating society.[30]

British policy-makers could be satisfied with the outcome of the unity negotiations prompted by Eden's Commons statement in February 1943. To be sure, Britain was out-paced at times during the process, but, come the finishing line, it was exactly where it wanted to be. Most crucially, the intimate relationship between the pan-Arab movement and Palestine, which had developed in the late 1930s, had been

50   *Demise of the British Empire in the Middle East*

weakened. Furthermore, the Arab League Pact, like the Alexandria Protocol, made no mention of 'Arab unity'. One British official noted smugly that the powers of the new body were somewhat less binding on the member states than the rules of the Royal Automobile Club.[31] Another London-based diplomat took the view that *'Divide et impera* may be a risky motto for us in the future'; he suggested that there would be 'real advantages' in 'promoting solidarity' among the Arab states and in encouraging them to look to Britain for leadership and help, as there was 'a strong tendency for them to do'.[32] Killearn, from the vantage of the Cairo embassy, was more cautious in his estimate. Officially, he noted that the Arab League was an Egyptian triumph over Hashemite unity schemes and its formation inaugurated an era of Egyptian leadership in inter-Arab politics. To his diary, however, he confided that he was 'still afraid that the zealots of pan-Arabism were going to force the unfortunate child [the Arab League] to run before it had even begun to walk'.[33]

FORMATIVE YEARS

Britain's harmonious relations with the Arab League ended soon after British forces had compelled the French to stop their bombardment of Damascus and other Syrian towns in late May 1945. With the French threat over, the League began to pursue a more independent line. Neither Egypt nor the Egyptian-dominated Arab League framework were willing to act as Britain's partners in the Arab world. Under Azzam's leadership, the Arab League developed into a tool for ending British control, with Egypt the priority and the rest of the region to follow. This was not the bellwether role Britain had envisaged. The irony of having backed Egypt's pre-eminent position was not lost on British officials, who were soon likening the organization to Frankenstein's monster. Moreover, the political pay-off on Palestine proved to be short-lived. International pressures in the wake of the Holocaust meant that the problem did not stay low on the agenda for long. By 1947, the future of the mandate dominated League Council proceedings, even to the detriment of Azzam's Egypt-first approach, and the centrality of the dispute was made permanent with the creation of Israel in 1948. The Palestinian issue in one form or another thus came to dominate Britain's relations with the Arab League after 1945.

    As secretary-general until 1952, Azzam incurred much of the blame from British policy-makers for the political direction of the fledgling organization. In 1939, he had been against an Egyptian declaration of war and, as a close confidant of the troublesome Ali Maher, was lucky

Britain and the politics of the Arab League   51

to have avoided internment. During the final drafting stages of the Arab League Pact, he annoyed Killearn by his championing of representation for the non-independent Arab countries of north Africa. There was also, of course, his text for equal Palestinian representation in the League. The ambassador informed Eden on 9 March that he was 'frankly apprehensive of his [Azzam's] lack of responsibility and his amateur methods'.[34] However, Azzam's assumption of the secretary-general post was guaranteed by the success of his mission to Ibn Saud in January 1945, in smoothing the feathers al-Nahas had ruffled in his haste to call an Arab conference in 1944.[35]

Azzam interpreted the pan-Arab charter of the Arab League as a mandate for securing the complete independence of the Middle East. He believed that this could be achieved by first securing Egyptian nationalist goals. Besides engendering predictable friction with Britain, this Egypt-first strategy also annoyed the Palestinian 'observers' when the League Council met in Cairo in November 1945. The Palestinians argued that their own national cause was more urgent and they left the meeting with their fears of marginalization confirmed.[36] At the start of the Anglo–Egyptian treaty negotiations in 1946, Azzam announced – without much pretence of consulting any other delegates – that the Arab League gave its full support to Egypt's demands for the unconditional withdrawal of British military forces and for union with Sudan.[37]

An important element in the 1946 Egyptian negotiations was Britain's attempts to establish a Middle Eastern defence system to ease its reliance on the Canal Zone installations. Despite this regional aspect, Britain refused to use the Arab League as a forum for negotiations and insisted that they remained on a strictly bilateral basis.[38] The idea of Azzam in a mediating role was simply not practicable. Nevertheless, Britain did use Arab friends like Nuri to try and pressure Egypt through the League into accepting Britain's modified military requirements. Nuri took an instant dislike to Azzam and believed that he had hijacked the Arab League for Egyptian interests.[39]

The main feature of the 1946 negotiations was the British offer to withdraw from the Canal Zone base by 1949. This concession was made because Palestine was viewed (by the military at least) as an alternative main base in the Middle East. The offer to redeploy from Egypt was a highly significant development and the influence of the Arab League should not be understated. International weight was being added to the Egyptian case through Azzam's leadership of the Arab bloc. While the secretary-general's use – or manipulation – of 'Arab identity' for Egyptian ends certainly had its critics in the Middle East, delegates in the Cairo head offices of the Arab League could see at first hand the strength of Egyptian nationalist agitation, especially during the

52   *Demise of the British Empire in the Middle East*

demonstrations of January–February 1946. The on-looking Saudi representative was especially worried that a revolution was imminent, a fear no doubt repeated among the other narrowly based elites of the region.[40]

When Britain's foreign secretary, Ernest Bevin, met Azzam in September 1946, he came away with his own anxious analysis of the connection between the Egyptian situation and mass movements throughout the Middle East. The link, as ever, was Palestine. The import, as Roger Louis writes, was that 'the Arab states feared Zionist expansion to the extent that they would support the Egyptians against the British in return for assurance of a united Arab front under Egyptian leadership in Palestine'. The upshot was that 'the Egyptians held the hand of an anti-British whip, in part because of Azzam's grip over the Arab League'.[41]

This situation prompted Foreign Office officials during the summer of 1947 to contemplate toppling Azzam from his position as secretary-general, despite the Bevin-imposed principle that Britain should avoid intervention in the internal affairs of the Arab states.[42] The immediate background was the Egyptian decision to take the Canal Zone dispute to the Security Council of the United Nations. The main proponent for ousting Azzam was the head of the Foreign Office's Egyptian department, Daniel Lascelles. Referring to the Arab League, he minuted on 5 May: 'Can we do anything about this Frankenstein of ours beyond trying to get rid of Azzam or put him in his place?' 'If the upshot were the disruption of the League, how much would we care?' He concluded by observing: '*Divide et impera* is still a good maxim, though much blown upon of late.'[43] On the other side, Peter Garran of the Eastern department (under which Palestine was subsumed) was reluctant to write off the Arab League merely because of Azzam. In his opinion, the organization served as 'a convenient safety-valve for Arab nationalist sentiment' and it was better to have this than other 'outlets' like the Muslim Brotherhood. It was this view that prevailed and British policy became one of checking Azzam's ambitions and extravagances rather than drastic measures.[44]

After the Egyptian Security Council action in July 1947, the Arab League's Egypt-first policy was pushed aside by the worsening crisis over Palestine's future. The establishment of the Anglo–American Committee in November 1945 had been interpreted by the Arabs as a direct challenge to the White Paper policy of 1939. It was at this point that Musa al-Alami and other Palestinian leaders lost their patience with Azzam's Egyptian preoccupations in the Arab League. A Council resolution of December 1945 calling for the boycott of Jewish goods was perceived as a step in the right direction, but little attention was given

Britain and the politics of the Arab League   53

to the means of implementation until the next summer.[45] Even then, the actions taken at the Inshas summit in Egypt in May 1946 (the first ever held between Arab heads of state) and another in Bludan, Syria, the following month, were a response primarily to domestic pressures in Arab countries on the Palestine issue.[46]

The Bludan meeting nevertheless stands out as the moment when custody of the Palestinian Arab cause was formally taken over by the Arab League.[47] This trusteeship was to have a decisive impact on subsequent events. Significantly, the custodial role was grafted on to an organization that still bore the imprint of British influence at its inception – no voting rights and observer status only for the Palestinian Arabs. Britain's position on this issue was determined largely by its attitude towards Haj Amin al-Hussaini, the Grand Mufti of Jerusalem. After leading the 1936–39 revolt, Haj Amin had thrown his lot with the Nazis during the Second World War. Moreover, his support for the Rashid Ali forces in Iraq in 1941 guaranteed the lasting hostility of the Hashemites. But even if the Mufti had few friends in the Arab League, he remained the standard-bearer of Palestinian national hopes.[48]

Meanwhile, Britain's commitment to the 1939 White Paper policy was being eroded by international pressures, not least from the United States. Sensing this drift, the Arab League countries protested vigorously against the idea of partition during an emergency conference in London at the start of October 1946. In their view, the creation of a Jewish state in any part of Palestine would be tantamount to establishing a settler colony and an infringement of the right to self-determination for the Arab majority. The conference was barely over when President Truman made his 'Yom Kippur' speech of 4 October, in which he appeared to endorse partition. The subsequent exacerbation of tensions in Palestine coincided with the breakdown of the Anglo–Egyptian negotiations. Britain's military chiefs responded by sending troop reinforcements from Egypt to Palestine, a clear indication that the Palestine main base idea was still alive.[49] For his part, Bevin was preoccupied in late 1946 with preserving what was left of Arab goodwill towards Britain. He was beginning to think that the best way of doing this was to hand over the Palestine problem to the United Nations. The ultimate aim was to maintain British imperial interests in post-mandatory Palestine. As for Egypt, the intention was to stand firm on existing treaty rights.[50]

During 1947, three momentous events *vis-à-vis* Palestine tested the collective will of the Arab League, one by Britain followed by two UN decisions. On all three occasions, the collective stance was fractured. The first was Britain's decision to refer the Palestinian issue to the United Nations, announced on 18 February. The Arab League reacted by calling a Council session in Cairo between 17 and 19 March. At this meeting,

54   *Demise of the British Empire in the Middle East*

the Transjordanian delegate made known his government's intention 'to safeguard its right to take an independent course of action'.[51]

The next test came in September, when the United Nations Special Committee on Palestine (UNSCOP) published its minority and majority reports and presented them to the General Assembly. The majority report favoured partition, with an Arab state, a Jewish state and a separate status for Jerusalem. The minority report was for a federal state with Jewish and Arab components, and Jerusalem as its capital. Six of the seven delegates on the Arab League's Committee on Palestine declared their fundamental opposition to the partition plan as a violation of the UN charter and the democratic rights of the Palestinian people. The seventh member, Transjordan, abstained.[52]

The third and greatest test for the Arab League came after the General Assembly's vote for partition on 29 November. Britain's 26 September decision to quit Palestine on 15 May 1948 meant that this established a five-and-a-half month timetable in which to prepare the ground for an independent Palestinian Arab state. As the Arab League prevaricated during the subsequent weeks, Britain came to adopt a pro-Transjordan approach regarding Palestine's future. This strengthened Abdallah's resolve to break from Arab League policy and pursue a separate partition solution.

THE PALESTINE WAR

The Palestine War had two distinct phases: the civil war between November 1947 and 14 May 1948, and the Arab–Israeli war from 15 May 1948 until January 1949. Britain was directly involved in the former because of its responsibility to maintain law and order during the final months of the mandate. Its involvement in the second phase – the inter-state conflict – was indirect. The precise nature of Britain's role through-out the Palestine War is the subject of heated historical controversy, particularly among Israeli scholars.[53] The debate centres on the role of Transjordan and whether an agreement was reached between Abdallah and the Jewish Agency Executive following meetings with Golda Myerson (Meir) in November 1947 and May 1948. One of the main disputed points concerns Bevin's response to Abdallah's intention to enlarge Transjordan's borders. Whatever its substance, the Transjordan–Britain connection must reside at the heart of any assessment of British policy towards the Arab League during the Palestine War. The following analysis argues that Britain and Transjordan did reach a tacit under-standing in February 1948.[54] This was then developed in a piecemeal and pragmatic manner, which was to have detrimental effects on the

Britain and the politics of the Arab League

Arab League's military aims and its attempts to establish an independent Palestinian Arab government.

A portent of the Arab League's lack of unity during the Palestine War evidenced itself at the Council meeting in Sofar, Lebanon, between 16 and 19 September 1947. The League deliberated on whether to implement earlier secret resolutions passed at Bludan in 1946, specifically on the use of an oil embargo. This was the Arab bloc's strongest lever against the increasingly oil-hungry Western powers. Iraq was a strong advocate of the oil sanction, but mainly as a means of embarrassing the reluctant Saudis, who had more to lose.[55] This petty manoeuvring was indicative of inter-Arab tensions within the League framework.

The next Council meeting was in October at Aleyh in Lebanon. The military situation dominated the proceedings because of the circulation of a report by a specially established technical committee. It made gloomy reading for the delegates, detailing the advanced state of Zionist administrative and institutional capabilities, together with an alarming but accurate assessment of Jewish military superiority. The strong recommendation was for urgent remedial action, especially in the military sphere.[56] Although Egypt made an extremely able leader of the Arab states in terms of rhetoric and posturing, it was to prove less capable of instigating concrete actions. In this instance, the Egyptian government responded to the technical report's recommendations by down-playing its ability to contribute forces because of internal issues connected with the British occupation.[57] By contrast, when Syria declared its willingness to make substantive troop deployments, its motives were viewed suspiciously by the other Arab states.[58] Such was the spirit in which the Arab League prepared for war.

The failure at Aleyh to address systematically the League's military shortcomings meant that this topic also dominated the next Council session in Cairo in December. The Arab states had the added impetus of internal pressures from agitated public reactions to Palestinian defeats during the first weeks of the civil war. It was at this meeting that a formal political commitment was made to support the Palestinian Arabs in defence of all Palestine. On a practical level, the Arab League promised 10,000 rifles, a 3,000-strong volunteer force, and financial assistance.[59] The effect of this was to sideline the Palestinian Arab war efforts and push the Arab League's contribution to the fore. As a consequence, Palestinian political marginalization came to be coupled with military marginalization.

The more determined resolve at the Cairo meeting was shrouded in a thicker veil of secrecy over its proceedings. Even Nuri was reticent to tell the British what measures were being undertaken. Britain's ambassador in Iraq concluded that this probably meant that the Arab

League 'had done little more than wrangle'.[60] This observation was symptomatic of British attitudes towards the organization, not least in the area of military decision-making. Yet, despite the secrecy, Britain, as the arms supplier to the region, remained in an excellent position to assess the fighting worth of the Arab armed forces. Britain believed that the Arab armies – with one exception – were poorly organized and badly equipped, and taken together compared unfavourably with the Jewish forces. Transjordan's British-led, trained and subsidized Arab Legion was the exception.[61]

This was the military situation when Bevin and the Transjordanian prime minister met on 7 February 1948. The meeting was a turning point in British policy towards the Middle East, in that Bevin chose to co-operate with Abdallah to secure the expansion of Transjordan over the areas allotted by the UN to Arab Palestine.[62] A corollary of this policy was the need to obstruct the creation of a Mufti-led Palestinian state. Britain was nevertheless anxious for Abdallah to abstain from using the Arab Legion for aggressive purposes. These were defined as military actions in territories allotted to the Jews by the UN. British officials hinted to Abdallah that the financial subsidy given to Transjordan's Arab Legion, together with the British officers who served in it, would be withdrawn if it occupied or was used against Jewish areas.[63] Abdallah duly assured Britain on 13 February that his goal was to occupy only the Arab-designated areas of Palestine. Any public pronouncements to the contrary were intended solely to forestall accusations that he was implementing partition. The publicity aspect touched a British concern over the possible alienation of Transjordan in the Arab League. Abdallah was therefore advised to secure Iraqi support before making a start on his plans.[64]

A succession of Palestinian military defeats in the final six weeks of the mandate compelled the Arab League to abandon its policy of using volunteer forces. Apart from sidelining Palestinian units, the volunteers had made little impact on the war effort and were ill matched against the well-organized Jewish forces. In addition, the effects of incidents like the Deir Yasin massacre on 9 April exerted domestic political pressures on Arab governments for greater involvement in the war. Egypt had previously stressed the need for its army to stay at home for policing duties; but mounting domestic pressures meant that elements of the Egyptian army had to be deployed in Palestine precisely to prevent disturbances in Egypt. Other Arab states had similar national agendas.[65] Consequently, on 16 April, after a week of discussions in Cairo, the Arab League finally committed itself to sending regular troops to Palestine.[66] The question of leadership for these forces was not decided until a few hours before the end of the mandate.

Britain and the politics of the Arab League   57

In the second week of May, the secretary-general of the Arab League travelled to Amman to see Abdallah and Sir John Glubb, the senior British officer with the Arab League. Azzam's mission was to offer titular control of the Arab League forces to Abdallah and the commander-in-chief position to Glubb. The motives for this action remain a source of controversy. It may have been that Azzam wanted the command of the League forces to go to the most experienced officer in the strongest of the Arab armies. He may also have been trying to tie down Transjordan politically to Arab League war aims. In this respect, doubts and rumours about Abdallah's commitment to the collective Arab policy of opposition to partition had long been a feature of political gossip. For instance, an Egyptian newspaper article in 1947 had reported Ibn Saud as saying that Abdallah was 'just a minor Ottoman official' who had managed 'to get himself crowned king', and that he was 'a secret ally of the Zionists'.[67] Suspicions about Transjordan's contacts with the Jewish Agency gained in currency in early 1948. British actions were also under a cloud of suspicion, not least after the swift military withdrawal from Haifa on 21 April paved the way for its fall to Jewish forces on 22–23 April.[68]

Given the extent of mutual distrust, it is probable that Azzam had ulterior motives for offering the command of the Arab League forces to Abdallah and Glubb. Moreover, Azzam was well aware that the Arab armies were woefully unco-ordinated and poorly prepared for war. The very fact that the senior command positions were not filled until two days before the end of the mandate was further testament to that. Glubb's own feeling was that Azzam, in making the offers, was looking for future scapegoats.[69] There were few better candidates than an unreliable ally (Abdallah) and a living totem of British imperialism (Glubb). While Abdallah accepted Azzam's offer, Glubb declined – so explicit a British connection to the Arab armies would have been a major blow to imperial prestige in the event of the anticipated military defeat. The Arab League forces therefore came under the leadership of Abdallah.[70] This placed him in an ideal position to shape the Arab bloc's invasion strategies to further his own goals for a greater Transjordan. Britain's tacit support for Abdallah's war aims guided its policy throughout the Arab–Israeli phase of the Palestine War.[71]

The Arab League's administrative arrangements for post-mandatory Palestine were also hindered by inter-Arab differences. The Mufti was largely responsible for the confusion. His mere presence at Council meetings in late 1947 acted as a brake on preparations for Palestinian statehood. The Iraqi delegate at Aleyh in October refused even to meet with him, let alone support his demands for a 'government-in-exile', because of memories of 1941.[72] The Mufti's demands served to obfuscate the League's trusteeship of the Palestinian cause when the civil war

58   *Demise of the British Empire in the Middle East*

began. The member states were well aware of the Jewish Agency's administrative and organizational lead because of the aforementioned technical report findings in October. Nevertheless, at Cairo in December, the League Council managed only to agree on increasing military assistance. As the end of the mandate approached, the problem of establishing a Palestinian government-in-waiting became more acute. Continued wrangling in February 1948 led to a decision-to-defer-a-decision until Palestine had been conquered.[73] February, of course, was the month of the reorientation in Britain's Middle Eastern policy. An important influence on this shift was the Arab League's inability to establish blueprint administrative structures for after 15 May 1948. By contrast, the Transjordan option appeared to offer the best prospect of stability and security once the British mandate had ended.

The Arab League's negligence in failing to prepare administratively for the end of the mandate stood in stark contrast to the Zionist efforts. It was not until 8 July that the League Council relented in its anti-Mufti stance and accepted a temporary civil administration under his direction.[74] Not surprisingly, Abdallah saw this institution as a direct threat to his own ambitions and wanted to end its existence as soon as he could. A major split between Transjordan and the Arab League therefore occurred when the League Council turned the Mufti's temporary administration into a permanent body through the proclamation of the 'All-Palestine Government' on 22 September.[75] The Arab delegates were motivated by three main aims: the familiar need to appease domestic pressures; Arab claims to sovereignty over the whole of Palestine also needed to be preserved; but, most important, the All-Palestine Government was a means of blocking Abdallah's thinly veiled annexationist plans.[76]

The Mufti realized that the inter-Arab rivalries responsible for establishing the All-Palestine Government could also destroy it. Therefore, to give the government a lasting legitimacy, he announced founding elections for 1 October. Abdallah responded by convening a congress of Palestinian notables in Amman on 30 September.[77] In the battle of rival governments which followed, Britain worked assiduously to prevent international recognition for the Arab League-sponsored Palestinian government. As before, a strong desire to prevent the creation of a Mufti-led Palestine went hand in hand with support for Abdallah's 'Greater Jordan' policy. British officials also attempted to win Iraq's support for an enlarged Transjordan in the wider interests of the Hashemite houses, but little progress was made because the Iraqi Regent feared the likely public reaction to partition.[78] A more telling blow to the All-Palestine Government was dealt in mid-October when Glubb's Arab Legion forces dismantled the Mufti's Holy War Army because of attacks on UN observers.[79]

Britain and the politics of the Arab League 59

The timing could not have been worse. On 15 October, the second truce was broken by an Israeli attack on Egyptian positions in the south of Palestine. Egypt's army was pushed into a rapid retreat, prompting the Gaza-based All-Palestine Government to flee to neighbouring Arab states. With its foothold on Palestinian soil abandoned, the Mufti government lost much of its prestige and authority, leaving the Palestinian Arabs little choice but to look to Abdallah for protection.[80] Abdallah obliged by holding a second meeting of Palestinian notables. It was at the Jericho conference of 1 December 1948 that a motion was passed calling for the unification of Palestine and Transjordan into one kingdom. This resolution was condemned by the other Arab states as being contrary to the Arab League's pre-invasion commitment to enter Palestine for rescue purposes only.[81] Consequently, throughout 1949, the Arab League sought to prevent Abdallah, who was seen as a 'land-grabber', from formally annexing the Palestinian territory under his control.[82] The other major concern was that a separate peace treaty would be signed between Jordan (the 'Trans' prefix was dropped in 1949) and Israel under the cover of the armistice negotiations. Meanwhile, Britain urged caution on Abdallah and encouraged him to try and improve his relations with the other Arab states.[83]

The annexation issue finally came to a head in the spring of 1950. The crisis began in March when the All-Palestine Government, which was leading a nominal existence in Cairo, complained that it was being denied representation in Arab League Council meetings. A resolution was duly passed inviting the exiled government to send a representative to future sessions.[84] Abdallah was concerned that increased visibility for the Mufti government would further undermine Jordan's post-Jericho claims that it represented Palestinian interests in the Arab League.[85] Shortly afterwards, Jordan's own position in the League was questioned following reports of secret peace negotiations with Israel. In a thinly veiled warning to Abdallah, an Egyptian-drafted resolution dated 1 April stipulated that any Arab state recognizing or making peace with Israel would be expelled from the Arab League.[86] Abdallah's next gambit for securing his gains from the 1948 war was to hold a general election on 11 April. The purpose was to facilitate Palestinian representation from the occupied West Bank in Jordan's parliament. With this achieved, Amman announced on 24 April that it was uniting the two banks of the river Jordan. Formal British recognition came three days later.[87]

This disappearance of Arab Palestine in this way had serious implications for all the Arab regimes, which were already in jeopardy after the 1948 defeats.[88] Meeting on 15 May, the Arab League rejected the annexation as a unilateral act in defiance of previous Council resolutions.[89] Egypt, Lebanon, Saudi Arabia and Syria also wanted to expel

60

Jordan from the League framework. However, the Iraqi and Yemeni delegates needed to consult their respective governments and so a decision was delayed until June. The breathing space permitted mediation efforts by Iraq and (following a change of mind) Lebanon aimed at keeping Jordan in the Arab League. These negotiations paved the way for a compromise solution at the next Council session on 12 June. This was based upon Jordan's holding on to the West Bank until a final settlement of the Palestine question was reached. For its part, Jordan promised to accept the unanimous decision of the other member states when this time came.[90] Not for the first time, the Arab states had accorded a higher priority to maintaining the integrity of the bloc of 'seven' than to protecting the Palestinian national cause.

Between 1943 and 1945, Britain quietly backed Egypt's leadership of an Arab unity process, which became, in effect, a Hashemite containment strategy. This pleased British officials because Iraqi and Transjordanian Fertile Crescent schemes had been the most destabilizing external influences on the situation in Palestine. Three years later – and after the embittering experience of seeing the Arab League turn into a vehicle for uncompromising Egyptian nationalism – Britain conducted a *volte face* in its Middle Eastern policy. Abdallah was given a green light to seize the UN-designated Arab parts of Palestine. Again, British officials played a behind-the-scenes role. The creation of a 'Greater Jordan' at the expense of a Mufti-led Palestinian state was a bid to preserve Britain's influence after the mandate had ended. Throughout these years, the Arab League proved to be an unsuitable guardian for the Palestinian Arab national cause. In fact, the ambitions and rivalries of the seven member states played a crucial part in frustrating the emergence of a Palestinian Arab state. But just as Britain's imperial position in the Middle East was undermined by the emergent Arab–Israeli conflict, so too was the stability of the king–pasha order.

NOTES

1   Parliamentary Debates, House of Commons, Vol. 387, 5 series, c. 139.
2   Yehoshua Porath, *In Search of Arab Unity 1930–1945* (London: Frank Cass, 1986) p. 234.
3   Minute by Seymour, 20 January 1939, FO 371/23245 E1274/29/31.
4   See Porath, *Arab Unity*, Ch. 4, pp. 197–256.
5   Michael J. Cohen, 'A Note on the Mansion House Speech, May 1941', in *Asian and African Studies* 11, 3 (1977) p. 375.
6   Porath, *Arab Unity*, pp. 91–3.
7   Ibid., pp. 247–9.
8   Cab 95/1 Middle East (Official) Committee Report on Arab Federation, 9 January 1942.
9   Ibid.
10 Lampson (Cairo) to Foreign Office, 14 October 1941, FO 371 27045 E6636/53/65.
11 Israel Gershoni and James P. Jankowski, *Redefining the Egyptian Nation, 1930–1945* (Cambridge: Cambridge University Press, 1995) p. 197.

Britain and the politics of the Arab League

12 Copy of Nuri to al-Nahas, 17 March 1943, FO 371/34956 E2027/506/65.
13 Gershoni and Jankowski, *Redefining the Egyptian Nation*, p. 198.
14 Lampson (Cairo) to Foreign Office, 1 April 1943, FO 371/34957 E2096/506/65.
15 See Ralph M. Coury's two-part article 'Who "Invented" Egyptian Nationalism?', *International Journal of Middle Eastern Studies* 14 (1982) pp. 249–81 and 459–79.
16 M. E. Yapp, *The Near East since the First World War* (London: Longman, 1991) pp. 63–5.
17 For the origins of the Hashemite–Saudi tensions see Nadav Safran, *Saudi Arabia: The Ceaseless Quest for Security* (Ithaca, NY: Cornell University Press, 1988) Ch. 2, pp. 28–56; also pp. 62–3.
18 For Britain's involvement in Egypt's internal politics during the war, see Chapter 6 by Martin Kolinsky.
19 Porath, *Arab Unity*, p. 291.
20 Ibid., pp. 293–5.
21 Killearn (Cairo) to Foreign Office, 5 June 1944, FO 371/39988 E3374/41/65.
22 Killearn (Cairo) to Foreign Office, 23 June 1944, FO 371/39988 E3686/41/65.
23 Ahmad M. Gomaa, *The Foundation of the League of Arab States* (London: Longman, 1977) p. 202.
24 Ibid., p. 206.
25 Porath, *Arab Unity*, pp. 282–3.
26 Killearn went on leave from 12 September until his recall following Lord Moyne's assassination on 6 November. He arrived back in Cairo on 12 November. His diary entry for the 14th notes a conversation with al-Nahas' chief aide, in which he reports himself as saying that 'it was no bad thing that the [Wafd] government had gone. They had had a long innings and it would do them no harm to be out of office for a while.' Assessing the previous year on 1 January 1945, Killearn observed that 'it was certainly for the good' that the Wafd's dismissal happened while he was in South Africa. See Killearn Diaries, 14 November 1944 and 1 January 1945, Middle East Centre Archive, St Antony's College, Oxford.
27 Eden to Killearn (Cairo), 4 January 1945, FO 371/40307 E7878/23/89.
28 Killearn wrote in his diary on 3 March that Azzam's 'zeal in the Arab cause had so often outrun his discretion during the present Arab conference'. Killearn Diaries, Middle East Centre Archive, St Antony's College, Oxford.
29 Gomaa, *League of Arab States*, pp. 258–61.
30 Killearn (Cairo) to Eden, 23 March 1945, FO 371/45237; Killearn (Cairo) to Foreign Office Weekly appreciation, 29 March–4 April, FO 371/45930.
31 'Embassy Note on the Present State of the Arab Unity Conversations', 11 March 1945, FO 141/1010 32/77/45.
32 Minute by Hankey, 30 March 1945, FO 371/45237 E2091.
33 Killearn (Cairo) to Eden, 23 March 1945, FO 371/45237 E2091/3/65; and Killearn Diaries, 22 March 1945, Middle East Centre Archive, St Antony's College, Oxford.
34 Killearn (Cairo) to Eden, 9 March 1945, FO 371/45237 E2091.
35 Porath, *Arab Unity*, pp. 288–9.
36 Walid Khalidi, 'The Arab Perspective', in Wm Roger Louis and Robert W. Stookey (eds.) *The End of the Palestine Mandate* (London: I. B. Tauris, 1986) p. 109.
37 H. Rahman, *A British Defence Problem in the Middle East: The Failure of the 1946 Negotiations* (Reading: Ithaca, 1994) pp. 63–4.
38 Bowker (Cairo) to Foreign Office, 12 March 1946, FO 371/53288.
39 Minute by Clayton (British Middle East Office, Cairo), 28 May 1946, FO 371/52313. The British Middle East Office was responsible for liaising with the Arab League, although no formal relationship existed. See Sir Thomas Rapp, *Memoirs* (unpublished), p. 373. A copy is held in the Middle East Centre Archive, St Antony's College, Oxford.
40 Hoda Gamal Abdel al-Nasir, *Britain and the Egyptian Nationalist Movement 1936–1952* (Reading: Ithaca, 1994) p. 157.
41 Wm Roger Louis, *The British Empire in the Middle East 1945–1951* (Oxford: Clarendon Press, 1984) p. 136.
42 Ibid., p. 3.
43 Minute by Lascelles, 5 May 1947, FO 371/61524 E4697.
44 Minute by Garran, 2 May 1947, FO 371/61524; for a detailed account of this internal Foreign Office debate see Louis, *The British Empire in the Middle East*, pp. 138–46.

62   *Demise of the British Empire in the Middle East*

45   Hussein A. Hassouna, *The League of Arab States and Regional Disputes* (New York: Oceana Publications, Dobbs Ferry, 1975) p. 269.

46   Leila S. Kadi, *Arab Summit Conferences and the Palestine Problem 1936–1950* (Beirut: Palestine Liberation Organization Research Centre, 1966) pp. 27–9.

47   Khalidi, 'The Arab Perspective', p. 111.

48   The best account on Haj Amin is Zvi Elpeleg, *The Grand Mufti: Haj Amin Al-Hussaini* (London: Frank Cass, 1993).

49   Ritchie Ovendale, 'The Palestine Policy of the British Labour Government', *International Affairs*, 55, 3 (1979) p. 430.

50   Alan Bullock, *Ernest Bevin Foreign Secretary 1945–1951* (Oxford: Oxford University Press, 1985) pp. 332–6.

51   Kadi, *Arab Summit Conferences*, p. 53.

52   Ibid., p. 51.

53   See Avi Shlaim, 'The Debate about 1948', *International Journal of Middle Eastern History*, 27 (1995) pp. 287–304.

54   Three previously retained Amman embassy files for 1947, 1948 and 1949 were released in August 1995 and shed interesting new light on the conduct of Britain's policy during these years. See FO 816/111, 115 and 116. The files are all entitled 'Partition of Palestine'.

55   Kadi, *Arab Summit Conferences*, p. 53.

56   Khalidi, 'The Arab Perspective', p. 118.

57   Ibid., pp. 118–19.

58   Ilan Pappé, *The Making of the Arab–Israeli Conflict, 1947–1951* (London: I. B. Tauris, 1992) p. 103.

59   Khalidi 'The Arab Perspective', p. 123; also Haim Levenberg, *The Military Preparations of the Arab Community in Palestine 1945–1948* (London: Frank Cass, 1992) pp. 180, 189, 200. Levenberg points out that neither the full quota of volunteers nor financial assistance ever reached Palestine.

60   Baghdad to Kirkbride (Amman), 30 December 1947, FO 816/111 tel. 94.

61   Ilan Pappé, *Britain and the Arab–Israeli Conflict, 1948–51* (London: Macmillan, 1988) pp. 23–5.

62   Avi Shlaim, *Collusion Across the Jordan* (Oxford: Oxford University Press, 1988) pp. 138–9. It should be noted that the Transjordan option had in a different form been the basis of the Peel Royal Commission's Report of 1937.

63   Kirkbride (Amman) to Foreign Office, 13 February 1948, FO 816/116 tel. 90.

64   Ibid.

65   On the Palestinian military defeats in the final weeks of the mandate see Yoav Gelber, *Jewish–Transjordanian Relations 1921–48* (London: Frank Cass, 1997) pp. 266–7; also Levenberg, *Military Preparations of the Arab Community*, pp. 208–10. Pappé details the various national agendas of the Arab states in *The Making of the Arab–Israeli Conflict*, p. 127.

66   Kadi, *Arab Summit Conferences*, p. 57.

67   Reported in George Kirk, 'Cross Currents within the Arab League', *The World Today* (January 1948) p. 21.

68   Khalidi, 'The Arab Perspective', p. 129.

69   John Bagot Glubb, *A Soldier with the Arabs* (London: Hodder & Stoughton, 1957) pp. 84–5.

70   Ibid.

71   Pappé, *Making of the Arab–Israeli Conflict*, p. 127.

72   Khalidi, 'The Arab Perspective', p. 119.

73   For the background on the Mufti's attempts to persuade the Arab League to establish a government-in-waiting, see Avi Shlaim, 'The Rise and Fall of the All-Palestine Government in Gaza', *Journal of Palestine Studies*, 20, 1, 77 (1990) pp. 37–8; also Elpeleg, *The Grand Mufti*, pp. 85–92.

74   Shlaim, 'All-Palestine Government', p. 39.

75   Hassouna, *League of Arab States*, p. 266.

76   Itamar Rabinovich, 'Egypt and the Palestine Question Before and After the Revolution', in Shimon Shamir (ed.), *Egypt from Monarchy to Republic* (Boulder, CO: Westview Press, 1995) p. 327; also Elpeleg, *The Grand Mufti*, pp. 105–7.

77   Shlaim, 'All-Palestine Government', p. 44.

78   Ibid., pp. 46–7; and Elpeleg, *The Grand Mufti*, pp. 105–7.

Britain and the politics of the Arab League

79   Glubb, *A Soldier with the Arabs*, p. 192.
80   Shlaim, 'All-Palestine Government', p. 48.
81   Hassouna, *League of Arab States*, pp. 33–4.
82   Troutbeck (British Middle East Office, Cairo) to Wright, 3 March 1949, FO 371/75064.
83   Mary C. Wilson, *King Abdullah, Britain and the Making of Jordan* (Cambridge: Cambridge University Press, 1987) p. 184.
84   Hassouna, *League of Arab States*, pp. 266–7.
85   Ibid., p. 256.
86   Pappé, *Making of the Arab–Israeli Conflict*, p. 261.
87   Wilson, *King Abdullah*, p. 197.
88   Ibid.
89   Hassouna, *League of Arab States*, pp. 33, 39.
90   Ibid., pp. 39–40.

4

Economic aspects of Arab nationalism

RODNEY WILSON

Determining causation between economic and political factors is always difficult, but careful appraisal of the historical facts and economic circumstances can provide valuable insights. The major premise of this chapter is that it was Britain's severely weakened domestic economic circumstances in the immediate post-war period that was responsible for its withdrawal from the Arab world.

After a review of Britain's economic interests in the Arab world, consideration is given to the economic aspects of Arab nationalism, focusing in particular on Egypt, which was at the centre of the movement. The ideology of Britain's immediate post-war Labour government resulted in a growing desire to move from an economic relationship based, at least on some interpretations, on imperialist exploitation, to a partnership, where Arab economic development could be linked to Britain's own interests. It is clear not much progress was made with this policy shift, as there was arguably more rhetoric than substance, but the Sudanese development experience is examined to throw some light on this issue. Finally, the question of Britain's role in the region's oil production is examined, particularly its involvement in Iraq and Kuwait.

BRITAIN'S ECONOMIC INTERESTS

Elizabeth Monroe, who worked for the Ministry of Information during the war, had some pertinent observations on Britain's interests in the Middle East in the 1940s. She asked: 'What constitute interests? Are they purely material – supplies, markets, airlines, pipelines – or are they also psychological, entailing prestige and moral ties such as alliances?'[1]

While recognizing the importance of the 'psychological' factor, I will consider here only the 'material' aspects. It is important to evaluate the extent to which the Arab world represented an asset or a liability to Britain. The evidence from the 1943–55 period seems to point to the latter, at least in strictly economic cost–benefit terms, despite the

Economic aspects of Arab nationalism 65

continuing importance of the Suez Canal and the growing significance of the region for oil production. In the late 1940s it was Iran rather than the Arab countries that was of most significance for Britain's oil interest, hence there appeared to be less economic purpose to be served by maintaining a British presence in the Arab states on the scale that was necessary during the Second World War.

It can, of course, be argued that the British involvement in the Middle East was not simply to serve its own, narrowly defined, national economic interests, and there were wider strategic issues. Its original involvement had been to serve the needs of its broader empire in Asia and Africa, and to counter the threat from other European powers, especially Germany and Italy, in the period up to 1943. After the Second World War, and especially following the withdrawal from India in 1947, the prime, and novel, strategic importance of Egypt lay in the Suez Canal Base, rather than in the Canal itself, which was now to serve as the launching pad for the allied strategic air offensive against the Soviet bloc, in the event of a Third World War (see Chapter 2, this volume).

The British government became very upset about competition from the United States, partly because of tensions that had arisen in the Middle East Supply Centre, which had been created to make the region more self-sufficient during the Second World War.[2] Britain wanted to perpetuate its imperial preferences, but the United States favoured an 'open-door' policy and non-discriminatory trade.[3] Nevertheless, there was a degree of co-operation over oil, despite some British resentment over United States involvement in Saudi Arabian oil. Britain's economic interests were in any case well served through the Anglo–Iranian Oil Company, and British and American oil companies shared in the ownership of a number of oil companies in the Arab world, including the Iraq Petroleum Company.

Britain's trade with the Middle East during the 1943–55 period was much more significant than that between the United States and the region. The Middle East accounted for over eight per cent of United Kingdom exports in 1946, and almost five per cent of its imports.[4] Of this the Arab countries accounted for most of the share, Iran being the other major partner, much of its trade being associated with the activities of the Anglo–Iranian Oil Company. Britain maintained a trade surplus with its leading Arab trading partners as Table 4.1 shows, although with increasing dependence on Gulf oil in the 1950s, the overall balance moved into deficit.

It was important for Britain to maintain a trade surplus in the early post-war years, as it had incurred enormous debts as a result of its wartime expenditure. In 1939, United Kingdom external debt amounted to £476 million, but by 1945 this had risen to £3,355 million, largely as a

TABLE 4.1
Britain's trade with the Arab world (£ million)

		1938	1946	1947	1948	1949	1950	1951	1952	1953	1954	1955
Aden	X	0.5	2.2	2.0	2.5	2.8	3.5	4.6	11.9	19.6	14.3	7.3
	I	0.1	1.5	0.6	0.9	0.9	1.0	2.3	1.3	1.3	2.4	4.8
	V	+0.4	+0.7	+1.4	+1.6	+1.9	+2.5	+2.3	+10.6	+18.3	+11.9	+2.5
Egypt	X	8.9	23.7	22.2	34.6	36.5	43.0	39.0	33.0	21.4	21.5	29.1
	I	11.6	15.3	14.8	47.6	29.0	40.2	47.4	12.9	15.3	16.7	9.7
	V	−2.7	+8.4	+7.4	−13.0	+7.5	+2.8	−8.4	+20.1	+6.1	+4.8	+19.4
Iraq	X	2.5	10.7	14.5	17.6	14.4	14.6	15.9	22.4	29.4	23.6	26.7
	I	2.7	2.0	3.3	7.2	6.6	8.7	13.8	51.9	64.5	44.5	32.6
	V	−0.2	+8.7	+11.2	+10.4	+7.8	+5.9	+2.1	−29.5	−35.1	−20.9	−5.9
Kuwait‡	X	0	0	3.3	8.6	8.3	7.0	7.5	10.1	16.5	10.2	8.1
	I	0	0	3.1	6.2	17.8	34.8	79.3	136.0	129.5	134.5	125.4
	V	0	0	+0.2	+2.4	−9.5	−27.8	−71.8	−125.9	−113.0	−124.3	−117.3
Palestine/Israel†	X	1.6	17.1	17.6	10.2	6.6	8.7	11.7	9.1	9.0	7.0	9.9
	I	3.1	5.7	13.0	12.9	5.6	5.2	5.9	5.9	6.3	9.1	7.7
	V	−1.5	+11.4	+4.6	−2.7	+1.0	+3.5	+5.8	+3.2	+2.7	−2.1	+2.2
Saudi Arabia	X	0.1	0.5	0.8	1.6	3.5	2.9	3.3	7.4	6.0	5.7	7.9
	I	0	0	1.5	5.3	6.8	8.2	30.2	35.6	2.2	1.8	3.2
	V	+0.1	+0.5	−0.7	−3.7	−3.3	−5.3	−26.9	−28.2	+3.8	+3.9	+4.7

Source: Frank Brenchley, *Britain and the Middle East: An Economic History, 1945–87* (London: Lester Crook Publishing, 1989, Table 2) pp. 40–3 and Table 3, pp. 113–15. Brenchley compiled the data from the *Accounts Relating to Trade and Navigation of the United Kingdom*.

Notes: X = exports; I = imports; V = visible trade balance.
† Refers to Palestine, including Transjordan, before 1947 and Israel from 1948.
‡ Refers to Kuwait, Bahrain and the Trucial States.

Economic aspects of Arab nationalism   67

consequence of military expenditure in the Middle East and Far East, including infrastructure spending on airfields, railways, roads and harbours, and payments to local labour and suppliers.[5] This debt was still accumulating after the war, with the maintenance of British troops in Egypt and Palestine. In 1946, Britain's overseas military expenditure still amounted to £216 million, of which £61 million was spent in the Middle East.[6] There were strong pressures on the British Labour government of 1945–51 to reduce this expenditure, not least from the Conservative opposition, with even Churchill, the great statesman of the empire, attacking the government of Attlee for throwing away between £30 million and £40 million of hard-earned money in Palestine.[7]

Although much of Britain's debt was to the United States, a sum estimated at £588 million was to Middle Eastern governments,[8] over one-sixth of the total. Much of this debt was to the government of Egypt, the base for Britain's Middle Eastern and Balkan campaigns during the war. Egypt, like the Sudan, Palestine and Transjordan, was part of the Sterling Area. This meant it had accumulated financial reserves that were effectively tied to the purchase of British goods and services, but which could not be used to finance imports from other sources such as the United States. Egypt was the major holder of these balances, as its sterling holdings rose from £190 million in 1943 to £390 million in 1945, and subsequently peaked at £470 million in 1947.[9] The other significant holders of sterling assets were the governments of Palestine (£120 million) and Iraq (£70 million), with Aden, Transjordan and the Sudan holding around £10 million each in 1945.[10]

Not surprisingly, the Arab governments, especially the government of Egypt, were unhappy with these arrangements. There were negotiations in 1945 which resulted in an Anglo–Egyptian Financial and Commercial Agreement. This permitted Egypt to spend up to £10 million outside the Sterling Area, of which the maximum for visible imports was £7.5 million, £1.5 million for invisibles and £1 million for contingencies such as import price rises resulting from any fall in the value of sterling or a rise in dollar prices. Under a further interim agreement, in January 1946, the Egyptians were allowed to spend a further £4 million for the period to April. Subsequently, for the year starting in April 1946, a ceiling of £12 million was set for hard-currency, non-sterling purchases.[11]

THE ARAB NATIONALIST RESPONSE

Needless to say, the Egyptian government felt obliged to resist these constraints on its trading policy and its lack of financial independence. It was seen as another manifestation of British imperialism, which was so much resented by those involved in politics in Egypt. Given the strong nationalist feelings, and resentment at Britain's meddling in Egyptian internal affairs, its continuing military occupation of the Canal Zone, and its policies in the Sudan and Palestine, no Egyptian government could be seen as being too compromising to Britain. The weakness of the coalition governments in Egypt meant that even those who thought they might get some benefit from British support could not openly speak out. The political climate was such that London's support for the Wafd party leader Mustafa al-Nahas, who was accused of corruption after he relinquished power in 1944, proved counterproductive, and al-Nahas, seeing this, took an anti-British stance.[12]

Egypt pressed to leave the Sterling Area, which the United Kingdom formally agreed to in June 1947. The departure was made conditional on Egypt transferring an estimated £400 million of sterling holdings to a blocked account, with £30 million to be made available for purchases from hard-currency countries in 1947.[13] Further allowances were made for the release of funds in 1948, 1949 and 1950, but even in March 1951 Egypt still had blocked sterling funds worth £230 million. Under an agreement later that year a further £150 million was to be released over a 10- to 13-year period, hardly a satisfactory situation for a country supposedly given monetary and commercial independence from Britain.[14] The reality was that, despite the appearance of Egypt's leaving the Sterling Area, Britain was still in a strong position to dictate reserve policy, given that it was the United Kingdom's currency that was involved.

As Raymond Mikesell, a well-known American monetary economist of that period, noted: 'Egypt's departure [from the Sterling Area] appears to have been motivated by a desire for an outward expression of independence from Britain and not to have been based on a careful calculation of the economic consequences.'[15]

The extent to which economic discontent underlied Arab nationalism must be open to doubt. The Arab countries were extremely poor, with widespread malnourishment, bad housing, a lack of adequate sanitation and much disease. The amelioration of these problems did not appear to be a high priority for the pre-revolutionary governments in Egypt or Iraq, however, during the 1940s and early 1950s. Arab economists themselves saw this poverty as a condition that had existed for centuries, and that they believed was likely to continue to prevail, as it reflected the meagre resources of the region, apart from oil.[16] Social structures also served to hinder economic development, notably the feudal land-tenure systems, which often resulted in large absentee landlords controlling much of the countryside, while the majority of their tenants lived in absolute poverty and were burdened by debt.[17] Such agricultural systems resulted in under-investment and inefficient

Economic aspects of Arab nationalism 69

production, but the governments in Cairo before 1952 and Baghdad before 1958 were reluctant to undertake land reforms, as the landlords were a major force in nationalist politics. Selma Botman has calculated that of the 50 cabinets formed in Egypt from the time of Husayn Rushdi in 1914 to Ali Maher in 1952, 58 per cent of the ministers were themselves large landlords.[18]

There was also the vexed issue of the relationship between Arab nationalists and Islamic political movements, which had implications for economic development. Controversially, there were some economists, notably Alfred Bonné, Professor of Economics and Director of the Economic Research Institute at the Hebrew University in Jerusalem, who blamed Arab backwardness on Islamic economic ethics.[19] Perhaps the most revealing passage is where he asserts: 'In comparison to the social ethics of Calvinism and Protestantism and similarly also of late Judaism, with the high demands they made at all times on the conduct of their followers, Islam was a non-committal, indulgent, easy-going form of religion.'[20]

Furthermore, Bonné draws attention to: 'the contrast between the significance of the time factor in Islam and its role at the beginning of modern development in the West ... On no account must there be any acceleration of the natural slow course of events. "Hurry is the Devil's work" is a classical saying commonly quoted by Muslim moralists.'[21]

Empirical evidence of a rather casual kind is cited by Bonné to support his case: 'The practice of Muslim life itself supplies ample material in support of our theses. The lack of initiative, the absence of creative ideas among many native merchants and entrepreneurs is a phenomenon soon apparent to all who have lived for any length of time in Oriental countries.'[22]

I would suggest that the Islamic responses to modernization were more complex, some following the modernizing thinking of al-Afghani, while others followed the more conservative line of the Muslim Brotherhood, which shunned capitalism, and abhorred the secularist attitudes and lifestyles of those who were influenced by British ideas. Arab nationalists who could be categorized in this way were regarded as hypocrites even if they rejected British imperialism. The Muslim Brotherhood was especially active in Egypt during the 1945–48 period, sabotaging meetings of the Wafdists and leftists, who were regarded as too secularist.[23] In these circumstances successive Egyptian governments had to be extremely sensitive in handling issues which might antagonize Islamists, even those who held moderate views. This represented a real constraint on any radical thinking in the conduct of domestic economic policy, and encouraged governments to adopt a conservative line while venting their frustrations on the British, opposition to whom was a unifying factor.

70   *Demise of the British Empire in the Middle East*

Peter Franck, one of the earliest American economic-development specialists, provided a wide-ranging assessment of the economic implications of nationalism in the Middle East in 1952 for the Near East Studies Programme of the University of Michigan.[24] Economic nationalism was an alien concept for the Arabs and Turks, he believed, but in the nineteenth century European nationalism had a profound influence on the Middle East, not only in reshaping the economies of the region, but also in influencing popular attitudes towards the role of nation-states. As Franck asserts, from the perspective of the politically concerned in the Middle East: 'The power of those [European] nations was to them [Arabs and Turks] a reflection of the superiority of the combination of a cultural and political heritage, of political centralisation with economic viability, over the decentralised political entities which were the Arab or Ottoman empires.'[25]

It was the power and success of Britain in particular from which lessons were drawn, and, even though its power was clearly reduced by the mid-1940s, it was still in a position to secure victory over its European rivals. This arguably increased its esteem among the Arab political classes, even if it did not bring admiration. Arab nationalists had no preferences between the European powers, resenting them all, and the waning support for Germany in 1942 and 1943 merely reflected the perception that there was no point in siding with losers. Indeed, the Wafd in Egypt, who had been highly critical of the British in opposition, saw much to be gained by collaborating with the British occupying forces when in government during the war.[26] By contrast, in Iraq, the army seized the opportunity of a weakened British position in 1941 to take over power, installing a pro-Axis prime minister, Rashid Ali al-Gaylani.[27]

Two major policies were urged by Arab nationalists in the economic sphere: first, tariffs, and, second, other protective measures so that local business would not have to compete with British firms in their own markets. The latter sought controls over foreign ownership of local assets and foreign direct investment more generally. The problem with both of these policies in the Middle East in the 1940s and early 1950s, according to Franck, was that when implemented they resulted in unscrupulous behaviour by local business groups.[28] The Pashas supported economic xenophobia for their own ends, not only to deflect domestic criticism,[29] but to create commercial opportunities for themselves and their local business associates. They were unconcerned about the conditions of the poor, or issues of fair prices for consumers.

Franck cites the case of Egyptian cotton textiles as a good example of this abuse of tariffs.[30] After 1930, the ban on raw-cotton imports and the high tariffs on imported cotton goods encouraged a tenfold increase in local textile production in the period up to the Second World War.

Economic aspects of Arab nationalism 71

However, the industry was so inefficient and the output so expensive that the masses of *fellahin* could not afford the cloth, even though subsidies had to be paid to the local textile owners to keep them competitive. Meanwhile, Britain switched to purchasing Sudanese raw cotton, leaving Egyptian cotton producers with substantial unsold stocks.

There were, nevertheless, cases where local production was justified, but where Britain took a negative stance in response to lobbying from its own producers. In the late 1940s, Egypt wanted to establish a fertilizer industry, as each year around $30 million was spent on imported fertilizers, mostly from the United Kingdom. Britain's Imperial Chemicals Industry (ICI) opposed any Egyptian venture, even though there were abundant local raw chemicals.[31] Not only did ICI fear losing the Egyptian market, but it saw production there as a potential threat to its sales to India. British banks refused to finance the venture, even though the Egyptian government was prepared to offer some of its sterling holdings as collateral. In the end the United States Export–Import Bank financed the venture, much to Britain's annoyance.

BRITAIN'S ROLE IN ARAB ECONOMIC DEVELOPMENT

Such examples of Britain's deliberately inhibiting Arab development were the exception by the late 1940s. It can be argued that, as already indicated, Ernest Bevin's approach was ideologically different from that of previous governments, but his intention to retain British dominance was unambiguous. 'Altruism' and 'economic justice' were phrases that were little more than gloss, and the Egyptians were not in the least taken in. Again, it is instructive to read Vitalis on how certain Egyptian–American business links undermined the British economic and political position. The Labour government of 1945–51 took a different ideological stance from its predecessors, and did not want to be accused of perpetuating colonialist exploitation and economic imperialism. Bevin, who was British foreign secretary until almost the end of the period of the Labour government, supposedly sought the transformation of imperial relations into more of a partnership of equals. Practice did not match ideology, however, as Bevin still believed that Britain had a special, perhaps even a paternalistic, role, given its vast experience of empire. Unlike Attlee, Bevin thought that Britain had a continuing major part to play in the Middle East, including the development of the region's oil resources.[32] In practice, this was really a continuance of the old dominance, although oil was to be exploited in order to help the British Empire as a whole, and the countries of the region, rather than to benefit narrow capitalist interests.[33]

72   *Demise of the British Empire in the Middle East*

Although economic development as a sub-discipline of economics was in its infancy, and the concept of underdevelopment was only just emerging, Bevin had an optimistic view on the possibility of economic progress which would benefit the common man. The view that progressive change was impossible in a region such as the Arab world was rejected. Despite Britain's very limited resources in the aftermath of the Second World War, economic development of the empire and the countries of the Middle East was given a much higher priority than hitherto. With independence for India, Bevin turned his attention to Africa, a region he believed to be of enormous economic potential and value to the empire, where Britain, with its experienced colonial officers, had an important role to fulfil.[34] The Middle East was valued not only for its own resources, notably oil, but as a gateway to Africa, with Egypt and the Sudan being the focus of particular attention.

The greater priority given to Middle Eastern economic development by the British Labour government reflected its own ideology and convictions rather than any pressures from the region itself. Indeed, the governments of Egypt, Iraq and other Middle Eastern countries within the British domain were mainly concerned with maintaining their own power, and saw development as a potentially destabilizing factor rather than as an opportunity. The government of al-Nahas Pasha in Egypt represented the feudal landlords who dominated the Wafd Party, not the landless labourers, nor the urban poor, nor even the urban middle classes who supported reform. Nevertheless, there were forces for change, and Egypt in particular had an extremely active labour movement, which no government could ignore,[35] but the extent to which this movement was concerned with wider economic development issues or simply the narrower concerns of its own members must be open to debate.

Although Palestine absorbed most of the political energy of the British Labour government in the Middle East during the period after the war, the Sudan was the major focus of the development effort. The Sudan was arguably a great source of hope, unlike Britain's other involvements in the Arab world, which were often viewed with despair. Sudan had its discontented educated minority, the Graduates Congress, and rivalry between the followers of the Mahdi's posthumous son, Sayed Abdulrahman, and the anti-Mahdist, Khatmiyya, led by Sayed al-Mirghani.[36] Nevertheless, the country was well administered and largely content, Sir Hubert Huddleston being an especially enlightened British Governor General during the 1940–46 period. Sir James Robertson, who had been with the Sudanese Political Service since 1922, and was head of the civil service in Khartoum between 1945 and 1953, had a great interest in agricultural development issues and the Gezira scheme in particular.[37]

Economic aspects of Arab nationalism 73

The area between the White and Blue Nile to the south of Khartoum had been developed for cotton cultivation by the British, the major work being the construction in the late 1920s of a large dam at Sennar and irrigation channels to provide water to an area of over 300,000 feddans.[38] Much effort had been expended on the Gezira scheme, and the British administrators in the Sudan were extremely proud of the results of their efforts. There were marketing and pricing difficulties with the cotton itself, and serious problems of indebtedness among some of the tenants on the scheme,[39] but, in terms of irrigation extension and agricultural production, the scheme was seen as a great success.

Much was done to combat the social problems that had resulted in the indebtedness, and to put the scheme on a sound financial footing. Sir James Robertson saw Gezira as: 'not just a machine for the production of cotton and money: it might be the scene of a real experiment in mass education, in social improvements, in co-operative enterprises, in democratic control of local administration, as well as an agricultural scheme of great importance to the Sudan'.[40] With the British Labour government's interest in economic and social development, Robertson expressed the view in a 1947 memorandum that: 'we have a magnificent chance of making something unique out of Gezira if we can capture the imagination of the British and Sudanese'.[41] In fact, it was not so much a matter of additional external funding, as there was little prospect of that, given Britain's financial position, but rather of administrative and organizational change, and investment in social provision such as better housing and water supplies, better diet and healthcare, and improved education.

Interestingly, much of this organizational change was to survive after Sudanese independence in 1956, although the long-term sustainability of the social development in such an underdeveloped country was more open to question. What was not maintained was the physical infra-structure, which was to deteriorate throughout the Sudan, with meagre and inefficient investment, as political corruption and civil strife took their toll.

THE BRITISH AND ARAB OIL

Much of Britain's interest in Middle East oil was focused on Iran during the 1943–55 period, especially given its interest in the Anglo–Iranian Oil Company, whose Iranian assets were nationalized by Mosaddeq in 1951.[42] Iraq, however, also had significant supplies of oil, and Kuwait and the other Gulf Arab states protected by Britain were also obvious alternative sources of oil. Britain's interests in the Gulf dated from the

74   *Demise of the British Empire in the Middle East*

East India Company's agency in Basra in 1723,[43] the start of a long historical involvement, which was always as much about 'economic insurance' as political strategy. There was, on the one hand, the desire to maintain a British presence and exclude both other European powers and, by the 1930s, the United States, with its growing interests in Saudi Arabia. On the other hand, there was the security of having a diverse portfolio of actual or potential oil supply, so that if difficulties arose in one location, either operational or political, the supply from another source could fill any gap.

Oil was first discovered in Iraq in 1927. From the start it was the Iraq Petroleum Company that was involved, a British-registered company with a British chairman, which obtained a 75-year concession to exploit most of the country's resources.[44] British oil companies still had a substantial stake in the Iraq Petroleum Company in 1945, with the Anglo–Iranian Petroleum Company (later British Petroleum, BP) owning 23.75 per cent and Shell (Anglo–Dutch) owning a further 23.75 per cent, with American and French companies owning the remainder.[45] After the Second World War, in order to increase Iraq's export capacity, the Iraq Petroleum Company began the construction of a 16-inch pipeline between Kirkuk and Haifa parallel to an existing 12-inch pipeline that carried oil to the Mediterranean. The Iraqis would have liked an even larger pipeline, but 16 inches was the maximum size of pipeline that could be manufactured in Britain, and the British government was unwilling to supply hard currency for the purchase of pipes from a United States company.[46]

Britain's withdrawal from Palestine was to prove a major setback for the Iraqi economy, owing to the disruption of oil exports. Just as work on the 16-inch pipeline was nearing completion in 1948 the war in Palestine erupted, with Iraq joining the Arab forces fighting the new state of Israel, which had been created on the 14 May. Iraq ordered the closure of the 12-inch pipeline to prevent the oil from falling into Jewish hands, the revenue from this oil being worth £1 million a year. Furthermore, with the failure to complete the 16-inch pipeline, a further £2 million of potential revenue was lost.[47] The Iraqi government's financial problems were compounded by a an invasion of locusts and a severe drought in 1947 and 1948, which cut the wheat harvest by almost 40 per cent. Domestic price rises forced the Baghdad government to pay more for wheat purchased for the urban poor, and increased imported wheat purchases. As the urban poor were politically militant, and the governments of al-Sadr and al-Pachachi were weak, they had little choice but to continue this policy of food subsidy, even though they had not the resources to sustain it.

With an increasing budget deficit, the government asked Britain for

Economic aspects of Arab nationalism 75

a loan of £2 million in 1948. Although all this amounted to was, in effect, a request for the release of Iraq's blocked sterling balances, Britain refused partly because of its own financial difficulties, but also because of Iraqi repudiation of the Treaty of Portsmouth governing the British military bases in Iraq. The Iraqi government was having difficulty in collecting taxes, and could not borrow internally, as affluent Muslims and Christians lacked confidence in the government's ability to honour its commitments, and affluent Jews abhorred its policies towards both them and Palestine. The Iraq Petroleum Company was also reluctant to make funds available, as they were unhappy about the closure of the Haifa pipeline, although in the end they agreed to bring forward a £1 million royalty payment from 1950 to 1949.[48] Britain finally agreed in 1949 to make some money available, which was tied to the purchase of British railway equipment that had already been ordered, as the cancellation of the order would have created major problems for the company involved.

In the end, Iraq's financial position was rectified, thanks to a loan of $12.8 million from the World Bank in July 1950[49] and rapidly rising oil revenues during the early 1950s.[50] The government of Nuri Pasha was much more pragmatic than the government of Iran in reaching a settlement in the economic interests of both Iraq and Britain.[51] The World Bank mission to Iraq in 1951 was able to report on the plans for rapid rises in output from 6 million tons in 1950 to 30 million tons in 1955.[52] Oil revenue subsequently rose more than fivefold over the 1950–55 period,[53] with much of it assigned to the Development Board charged with overseeing infrastructure improvement and agricultural and industrial development.[54] By then the Americans and the World Bank were playing a major part in Iraq's development, somewhat eclipsing the role of Britain.

As the Anglo–Iranian Oil Company owned 50 per cent of the Kuwait Oil Company,[55] the emirate was an obvious location from which to expand production, both as a precaution against potential problems in Iran itself, and as a consequence of the realization of Britain's worst fears with the nationalization by Mosaddeq. Oil production in Kuwait was increased from 5.9 million barrels in 1945 to 125.7 million barrels in 1950, and subsequently to 402.7 million barrels by 1955.[56] As a consequence, Kuwaiti government oil revenue was to rise from a mere $760,000 in 1946 to $16 million by 1950, and $281 million by 1955. Kuwait was transformed from a small backwater at the head of the Gulf into a major centre for oil production, to the satisfaction of both the British and the emir. Although there had been some stirrings for reforms in government in Kuwait dating from 1938 in response to maladministration by the ageing ruler, Ahmad bin Jabars, the ruler was to hold on until the mid-

76 *Demise of the British Empire in the Middle East*

1950s when the less conservative Sheikh, Abdallah as-Salem, took over.[57] Some of the more internationally aware Kuwaitis resented British policy in Palestine, but the currents of Arab nationalism did not take hold in Kuwait, and there was no general disquiet with British foreign policy or the role of the British political agent.

CONCLUSION

The central thesis of this chapter is that Britain's weak economic position at home in the post-war period dictated much of its policy towards the Arab world, and that Arab nationalism, with the possible exception of Egypt, had a more limited impact. Certainly, Britain's oil interests in the Arab world were not curtailed by nationalist pressures, although the situation was very different in Iran. The Anglo-Iranian oil company was able to develop its interests in Kuwait, and in Iraq, despite the deep hostility to British policy in Palestine and the closure of the pipeline to Haifa. Furthermore, it is clear that it was Iraq and not Britain that suffered from this action.

Britain did not have the resources to take economic development schemes, such as that in the Gezira region of the Sudan, much further, in spite of the advocacy by supporters of the Labour government of such schemes. Ultimately, it was international bodies such as the World Bank and the United States that were to have more impact on Arab economic development, but there are no indications that Arab nationalism deterred Britain. Indeed, the nationalists had a common cause with those in the Labour Party who wanted to replace economic relationships that they regarded as imperialistic with those based on partnership. There was little evidence, however, that Arab nationalists took advantage of this, as their agenda was primarily concerned with Arab rights, and economics was not seen as a priority. Not surprisingly, Arab governments were absorbed by their own domestic issues and had little understanding of, or interest in, British politics and Labour Party ideology.

Egypt was a good example of this Arab concern for politics rather than economics. It had arguably the strongest Arab nationalist movement, which was to undermine Britain's strategic interests, especially in Suez. However, Egypt's governments acquiesced in the major economic policy that really mattered in the post-Second World War period, the blockage of the sterling balances, which severely limited economic sovereignty. Although Egypt formally left the Sterling Area, it could still not utilize most of its balances. Arab nationalists were more concerned with broad political issues, with form rather than substance.

Economic aspects of Arab nationalism 77

The blocked sterling balances were seen as a mere technical matter, and there was little appreciation of their economic significance.

NOTES

1 Elizabeth Monroe, 'British Interests in the Middle East', *Middle East Journal*, 2, 2 (1948) pp. 129–46. Quotation on p. 131.
2 Martin W. Wilmington, *The Middle East Supply Centre* (London: University of London Press, 1971) pp. 64–83.
3 Robert Vitalis, 'The "New Deal" in Egypt: The Rise of Anglo–American Commercial Competition in World War II and the Fall of Neocolonialism', *Diplomatic History*, 20, 2 (Spring 1996) pp. 211–39. Also Robert Vitalis, *When Capitalists Collide: Business Conflicts and the End of Empire in Egypt* (Berkeley: University of California Press, 1995). For details of British efforts to control United States involvement in Egypt see pp. 130–1. For a discussion of development implications see Wesley K. Wark, 'Development diplomacy: John Troutbeck and the British Middle East Office, 1947–50', in J. Zametica (ed.), *British Officials and British Foreign Policy, 1945–50* (Leicester: Leicester University Press, 1990) pp. 228–49; also John Kent, 'Bevin's Imperialism and the Idea of Euro-Africa, 1945–49', in Michael Dockrill and John Young (eds.), *British Foreign Policy, 1945–56* (London: Macmillan, 1989) pp. 47–76.
4 Frank Brenchley, *Britain and the Middle East: An Economic History, 1945–87* (London: Lester Crook Publishing, 1989, Table 2) pp. 40–3.
5 Daniel Silverfarb, *The Twilight of British Ascendancy in the Middle East* (London: Macmillan, 1994) p. 74.
6 Ibid., p. 75.
7 Michael J. Cohen, *Palestine and the Great Powers, 1945–1948* (Princeton, NJ: Princeton University Press, 1982) p. 246.
8 Monroe, 'British Interests in the Middle East', p. 134.
9 Brenchley, *Britain and the Middle East*, p. 17.
10 Ibid., p. 16.
11 Ibid., p. 23.
12 Hoda Gamal Abdel al-Nasir, *Britain and the Egyptian Nationalist Movement, 1936–1952* (Reading: Ithaca Press, 1994) pp. 115–16.
13 Brenchley, *Britain and the Middle East*, p. 24.
14 Ibid., pp. 26–7.
15 Raymond Mikesell, 'Sterling Area Currencies of the Middle East', *Middle East Journal*, 2, 2 (1948) pp. 160–74. Quotation from p. 174.
16 Sa'id B. Himadeh, 'Economic Factors Underlying Social Problems in the Arab Middle East', *Middle East Journal*, 5, 3 (1951) pp. 269–83.
17 Doreen Warriner, *Land and Poverty in the Middle East* (Oxford: Oxford University Press, 1948) pp. 12–13.
18 Selma Botman, *Egypt from Independence to Revolution: 1919–1952* (Syracuse, NY: Syracuse University Press, 1991) p. 79.
19 Alfred Bonné, *State and Economics in the Middle East*, (London: Routledge & Kegan Paul, 1948, 1st edn; 2nd edn 1955). The economic ethics of Muslim society are discussed on pp. 352–61 of the 2nd edition.
20 Ibid., p. 356.
21 Ibid., p. 360.
22 Ibid.
23 Botman, *Egypt from Independence to Revolution*, p. 122.
24 Peter G. Franck, 'Economic Nationalism in the Middle East', *Middle East Journal*, 6, 4 (1952) pp. 429–54.
25 Ibid., p. 430.
26 Abdel al-Nasir, *Britain and the Egyptian Nationalist Movement*, pp. 78–90.
27 Silverfarb, *Twilight of British Ascendancy in the Middle East*, pp. 1–2.
28 Franck, 'Economic Nationalism in the Middle East', p. 436.
29 Ibid., p. 431.

78 — Demise of the British Empire in the Middle East

30 Ibid., pp. 437–8.
31 Ibid., p. 433.
32 William Roger Louis, *The British Empire in the Middle East, 1945–1951* (Oxford: Oxford University Press, 1994) p. 6.
33 For an analysis of these issues see Paul W. T. Kingston, *Britain and the Politics of Modernisation in the Middle East* (Cambridge University Press, Middle Eastern Studies Series, no. 4, 1996).
34 Louis, *British Empire in the Middle East*, p. 16.
35 William J. Handley, 'The Labour Movement in Egypt', *Middle East Journal*, 3, 3 (1949) pp. 277–92.
36 Glen Balfour-Paul, *The End of Empire in the Middle East: Britain's Relinquishment of Power in her Last Three Arab Dependencies* (Cambridge: Cambridge University Press, 1991) p. 21.
37 Arthur Gaitskell, *Gezira: A Story of Development in the Sudan* (London: Faber & Faber, 1959) p. 246. The official papers of Sir James Robertson are housed in the Durham University's Sudan archive. Details of his papers are available on the World Wide Web: [http://www.dur.ac.uk.Library/asc/Sudan/Sudan.html#JWR].
38 Gaitskell, *Gezira*, p. 99. A 'feddan' is approximately an acre.
39 For a discussion of some of the indebtedness problems and the tenancy arrangements see Tony Barnett, *The Gezira Scheme: An Illusion of Development* (London: Frank Cass, 1977) pp. 73–100.
40 Gaitskell, *Gezira*, p. 246.
41 Ibid.
42 Rodney Wilson, *The Economies of the Middle East* (London: Macmillan, 1979) p. 4.
43 Balfour-Paul, *End of Empire in the Middle East*, p. 96.
44 Brenchley, *Britain and the Middle East*, pp. 104–5.
45 Ibid., p. 19.
46 Silverfarb, *Twilight of British Ascendancy in the Middle East*, p. 217.
47 Ibid., p. 189.
48 Ibid., p. 198.
49 Ibid., p. 201.
50 Daniel Silverfrab, 'The Revision of Iraq's Oil Concession, 1949–52', *Middle Eastern Studies*, 32, 1 (1996) pp. 69–95.
51 Ibid., p. 90.
52 International Bank for Reconstruction and Development, *The Economic Development of Iraq* (Baltimore, MD: Johns Hopkins University Press, 1952) pp. 34–5.
53 Ferhang Jalal, *The Role of Government in the Industrialisation of Iraq, 1950–1965* (London: Frank Cass, 1972) p. 11.
54 Ibid., pp. 14–31. See also Kathleen M. Langley, *The Industrialization of Iraq* (Cambridge, MA: Harvard University Press, 1962) p. 86.
55 M. W. Khouja and P. G. Saddler, *The Economy of Kuwait* (London: Macmillan, 1979) pp. 77–80.
56 Ibid., p. 26.
57 Balfour-Paul, *End of Empire in the Middle East*, p. 113.

5

A new Middle East?
The crystallization of the Arab state system after the Second World War

BRUCE MADDY-WEITZMAN

The imminent end of the Second World War seemed to herald great change in the Arab Middle East. A generation of British and French domination was coming to a close, ignominiously, in France's case. An Arab 'proto-system' of sorts had already emerged during the inter-war years. In March 1945, the ruling Arab elites of the incipient system's 'core' – Egypt, Iraq, Syria, Lebanon and Transjordan – joined together with Saudi Arabia and Yemen to establish the League of Arab States, a framework designed to advance their declared common goal of intensified co-operation, particularly in the face of external challenges, and to regulate relations properly between them. To be sure, the new arrangement was a far cry from the unity ideal championed by opposition pan-Arab elements within their societies. Nonetheless, the League's creation was a milestone in the history of modern Arab politics, establishing both an organizational framework through which Arab states could formulate and co-ordinate common policies, and normative standards of conduct by which regimes could be measured. Taken together with the concurrent, irreparable decline in British and French capabilities in the region, one may speak of 1945 as marking a historical watershed, inaugurating a fully fledged Arab state system.

At the same time, the Arab League framework, constituting a compromise formula between the advocates of closer, more integral ties and the proponents of a regional *status quo* and the protection of individual sovereignties, provided only the barest of guidelines for Arab policy-makers as they entered the new era. The issues facing them were fundamental: what was the preferred formula for advancing agreed-on all-Arab interests – co-operation among the existing sovereign states, implementing partial unification schemes among neighboring entities, or adopting a more comprehensive approach that would fundamentally alter the region's post-Second World War territorial boundaries? How

80 *Demise of the British Empire in the Middle East*

did Arab leaders guard and enhance their own particular interests both domestically and within the wider Arab setting? More generally, what was the relationship between the vision of Arab nationalism and the reality of Arab particularism?

On the concrete level, how did the Arab states cope with the challenge posed by the Zionist movement in Palestine? How did ruling elites manage their relations with Britain, whose influence in the Middle East, while having waned, remained pre-eminent among the Great Powers? And how did they manage their own internecine rivalries?

The answers to these questions, as they would evolve on the plain of history over the following decade, the 'dynastic phase' of inter-Arab relations, resulted in a more definitive crystallization of the Arab state system. The system was state-centric, marked by high levels of both conflict and co-operation, and with a particular *modus operandi* based on loosely structured, shifting coalitions, while an overall equilibrium was maintained through checks and balances. At the same time, 'Arabism' was confirmed as an unchallenged normative value in both domestic and regional politics. As such it helped to prepare the way for Gamal Abd al-Nasir's challenge to the existing Arab order beginning in 1955.[1] Nonetheless, the consolidation of the Arab state system during the preceding decade significantly inhibited the subsequent efforts of radical Arab nationalists to implement their vision of revolutionary transformation of Arab societies and the Arab regional order.[2]

The dynamic, complex interactions between domestic, regional and international factors that produced this outcome are the subject of this chapter. Three overlapping issue areas are treated: the future of Syria, the question of Palestine, and Arab–British relations.

THE FUTURE OF SYRIA

Syria's place in the Arab firmament was a subject of almost continuous dispute during the system's formative years between what can be termed the 'Hashemite' and 'anti-Hashemite' camps.[3] The former consisted of Iraq and Transjordan, the latter of Egypt, Saudi Arabia and Lebanon, and nearly always the Syrian regime itself. Patrick Seale dramatized the dispute as the 'struggle for Syria', placing it at the center of Middle East regional dynamics.[4] Even if Seale's geopolitical-centered analysis does not always stand up to rigorous examination, it still has much merit.

At stake between the two loose coalitions was the determination of a considerable portion of the regional balance of power. The Hashemite grouping was, in essence, unhappy with the regional *status quo* and

A new Middle East? 81

sought to alter it, albeit in an unco-ordinated fashion, to their respective advantages. The first post-war effort was by Transjordan's King Abdallah in 1946–47. The second, more serious, one was spearheaded by Iraq in 1949. Their actions drew sharp responses from the other Arab states, which consolidated into an Egyptian-led bloc.

From the moment that France evicted Faysal from Damascus in 1920 and abolished his short-lived Syrian kingdom, his brother Abdallah had cast his eyes on Syria as an appropriate place to fulfill his own, and his family's ambitions for Arab leadership. These ambitions had originated in the Hashemite-led 'Great Arab Revolt' against the Ottomans in the First World War. By the 1940s, Syria had become somewhat of an obsession for this senior surviving member of the Hashemite house, now ensconced in a small desert kingdom between his ancestral home in the Hijaz and the 'prize' that Damascus and the 'Fertile Crescent' embodied. But his entreaties to Britain in 1939–40 to fulfill what he viewed as Winston Churchill's 1920 promise to restore Hashemite rule in Syria were brushed aside.[5] Similarly, his efforts to promote a Greater Syrian federation under his own leadership during the 1943–44 discussions, which led to the establishment of the Arab League, produced no results.[6] Nonetheless, he remained seized by the matter.

Abdallah launched a new bid during 1946–47. One aspect of his efforts was the tendering of financial support for various opposition elements within Syria.[7] Another, more vocal and thus more irritating to his rivals, was his tendency to issue grandiose pronouncements on the issue. His 11 November 1946 speech on the need for Syrian–Transjordanian unity generated swift Syrian and Lebanese condemnations. The Arab League Council took up the matter as well, despite Abdallah's vigorous opposition to League involvement.[8] Throughout the following year, Abdallah continued to promote his scheme, highlighted by an 11 August 1947 proclamation inviting 'the regional Syrian governments' to convene jointly a constitutional assembly to lay down a constitution for Greater Syria, on either a union or a federative basis. Syrian President Shukri al-Quwwatli responded in kind, rejecting Abdallah's 'false federation' and emphasizing that if any of the Arab states was historically illegitimate, it was Abdallah's 'princely throne' that had been 'detached from the [Syrian] motherland'.[9]

Abdallah was either unwilling or unable to take real risks on behalf of his dream, and his challenge to the republican *status quo* in Syria faded in importance during the remaining four years of his life. Nonetheless, Transjordan's effort and Syria's responses during 1946–47 highlighted three important features of inter-Arab politics during these years: (1) the intermeshing of ideological and pragmatic political considerations; (2) the intense personal rivalries between Arab leaders; and (3) the

82 *Demise of the British Empire in the Middle East*

importance of what Stephen Walt calls the 'balance of threat' mode of politics, demonstrated in this case by Quwwatli's hasty mobilization of Egypt and Saudi Arabia to counter Abdallah's designs.[10]

For its part, Iraq had no interest in Abdallah's designs on Syria, and on occasion even served as a mediator between Jordan and the anti-Hashemite camp.[11] Rather, the Iraqi leadership, particularly Nuri al-Sa'id, the strongman of Iraq for nearly four decades, and Crown Prince and Regent Abd al-Illah had their own (sometimes conflicting) designs on Syria. Nuri's conceptual framework was first laid out in his 1943 'Fertile Crescent' project, which envisioned a Greater Syrian entity linked together with Iraq in an 'Arab League' (without Egypt or the Arabian Peninsula).[12] Notwithstanding the Egypt-centered League that emerged, Nuri never abandoned his geopolitical focus on the Fertile Crescent. In 1946, he sought a bilateral pact with Syria to complement a recently concluded accord with Turkey.[13] Concurrently, he rebuffed Abdallah's efforts to forge closer ties, forcing him to settle eventually for a watered-down treaty of 'Brotherhood and Alliance'.[14]

The peak of Iraqi efforts in Syria came in 1949, a year of unprecedented internal instability there. The successive military coups of 30 March and 14 August offered Iraq an unprecedented opportunity to alter the regional balance of power in its favor. However, countervailing regional and internal Syrian factors, as well as a lack of Iraqi resolve, blocked the realization of the ambitions of Nuri and the Regent.

The overthrow of Quwwatli's government by the Army Chief of Staff, General Husni al-Za'im, on 30 March caught the whole region by surprise. Both the Regent and Nuri were apprehensive about the implications of the coup, fearing that it might have a contagious effect on the Iraqi army, which was concurrently withdrawing from Palestine following its less-than-glorious campaign there. At the same time, they recognized that the coup provided them with new opportunities. Za'im himself also displayed interest in strengthening Syrian–Iraqi ties in order to bolster his position in the forthcoming armistice negotiations with Israel and to legitimize his takeover in the eyes of the international community. However, after three hectic weeks of meetings and contacts, including a stormy *tête-à-tête* between Nuri and Za'im in Damascus,[15] Za'im restored Syria's place within the Egyptian-led anti-Hashemite camp. Nuri's innate caution had deterred him from bold intervention, while his hopes that Syria's civilian politicians would take the lead toward an Iraqi–Syrian merger were disappointed.

Iraqi–Syrian relations during the following months were mostly sour, and Iraq pursued contacts with dissident factions within the Syrian officer corps. However, Nuri was unwilling to adopt their plans for a coup wholeheartedly: consequently, Za'im's overthrow by Colonel

A new Middle East? 83

Sami al-Hinnawi on 14 August again caught the Iraqis by surprise. This time, the opportunity for merger or federation seemed more propitious, and two months of discussions ensued. But again, Nuri was cautious, depending on pro-Iraqi civilian and military figures in Syria to neutralize the anti-merger forces. By mid-October, enough progress had been made to begin drawing fire from the anti-Hashemite countries, who used the Arab League to adopt an all-Arab collective security package as an alternative to Syria's exclusive dependence on Iraq. The Iraqis had again been outmaneuvered on the inter-Arab stage.

Their last chance came with the Syrian elections for a Constituent Assembly in mid-November. However, their efforts to promote pro-unionist forces did not bear sufficient fruit. The latter managed only to galvanize anti-union sentiment in the army, leading to Hinnawi's arrest on the night of 18–19 December by Colonel Adib Shishakli. The Syrian army became the ultimate arbiter of Syrian political life, a pattern which would repeat itself in other Arab states in the coming year.

Politically, the inter-Arab system of checks and balances had triumphed over Iraqi Hashemite revisionist aspirations: Syria was kept within the Egyptian–Saudi fold, the 'co-operation' mode of inter-Arab relations, as opposed to the 'federation' or 'unity' mode remained dominant; and overall systemic equilibrium was maintained. Iraq (and Jordan, until Abdallah's death in 1951) engaged in periodic intrigue in Syrian affairs during the following years. The Iraqis continued their support of opposition military elements and tendered various federation plans. But the regional *status quo* remained unchanged.

THE QUESTION OF PALESTINE

From the mid-1930s, the fate of Palestine had become a litmus test for fidelity to rising Arab nationalist values among both Arab regimes and their increasingly politicized publics.[16] The inclusion in the Arab League Charter of a special annex on Palestine provided tangible evidence of the centrality the issue held for its members. Indeed, the overwhelming majority of Arab League meetings during the following decades would be devoted to the subject.

The rush of events in Palestine after 1945 posed the first real test of the fundamental tenets of all-Arab solidarity and collective will, enshrined in the Arab League Charter. The Arab countries tried to rebuff the challenge posed by the Zionist movement and sought to preserve what they viewed as a central part of the Arab patrimony. But, as it turned out, the picture of Arab unity of ranks and purpose, embodied by the all-Arab war coalition that attacked Israel on the morrow of the

84 *Demise of the British Empire in the Middle East*

British withdrawal from Palestine on 14 May 1948, proved to be a thin facade. Competing interests, acute suspicion toward fellow Arab states and a lack of resolve dominated Arab state behavior during the 1948 war. Consequently, they failed to achieve their declared goal of preventing the establishment of a Jewish state in Palestine, with their armies suffering an ignominious defeat on the battlefield (see Chapter 12 by Avraham Sela in this volume).[17]

The exception to this sorry state of affairs was Transjordan. Alone among the Arab states, it demonstrated a clear sense of purpose, growing out of Abdallah's interest in expanding his kingdom and blocking the challenge posed by radical Palestinian nationalism. The linkage to his Syrian ambitions was only minimal. To be sure, Abdallah occasionally speculated about Palestine being a stepping stone to Syria, but the rush of events in Palestine and the opportunities available for him there made Palestine a vital arena for action in and of itself. Moreover, in contrast to his ambitions regarding Syria, Abdallah possessed the means to implement his program in Palestine: a strong, albeit small fighting force, the Arab Legion, plus the required geographical proximity to Palestine's heartland. Two other elements were no less crucial to his success: a pragmatic, and realistic, view of the capabilities of the Zionist movement; and the quiet support of Britain.[18]

Arab suspicions regarding Abdallah's intentions in Palestine, his own mere lip service to the collective Arab line that their intervention in Palestine was merely of a temporary nature, and his ability to maneuver adroitly between collective Arab requirements and his own particular interests, are well known. Less well understood is one important aspect of this maneuvering: the fashioning of a temporary Jordanian–Egyptian axis during the crucial days just prior to the British withdrawal and Arab attack, which lasted throughout the first round of Arab–Israeli fighting between 15 May and 11 June. This alignment, between the main Arab aspirant in Palestine (Transjordan) and the Arab country capable of posing the biggest obstacle to these ambitions (Egypt), enabled Abdallah to establish a presence in the West Bank and Jerusalem, which he would never relinquish, while demonstrating Egypt's own contradictory policy of half-measures regarding the Palestine question.[19]

Paradoxically, this tacit, temporary but crucial alliance came on the heels of Egypt's King Faruq's 12 April 1948 declaration that any Arab action in Palestine must be regarded as temporary, following which 'Palestine must be handed over to its own people'. Abdallah subscribed publicly to the notion, and then moved to legitimize his army's future activities by placing them within the framework of an all-Arab military action. One month later, on the eve of the invasion, Abdallah

A new Middle East?   85

successfully changed the invasion plans to his benefit and was named overall commander in chief. Both actions were done with the approval of Egypt, which dispatched staff officers to Amman to help co-ordinate their upcoming actions. The changes in the plans made military sense for both sides, as each would provide support for the other's flank, with the Egyptians even providing volunteer units to shore up the Arab Legion's position in the Hebron–Bethlehem area, right up to the outskirts of Jerusalem (these units would later be the cause of much friction between Jordan and Egypt).[20]

Egyptian and Jordanian interests diverged following the first ceasefire. Abdallah, however, had exploited his hand to the fullest, and was now, territorially speaking, in the driver's seat. The Egyptians, for their part, had recognized that the Arab cause would be utterly hopeless without Abdallah, and thus acquiesced in his change of military plans. Moreover, their subsequent promotion of a Palestinian alternative to Abdallah was done in a restrained fashion, more for the purpose of demonstrating Egyptian fidelity to the cause of Arab Palestine than to block Abdallah's territorial aggrandizement.

The successful negotiation of separate armistice agreements between Israel and its Arab neighbors during 1949 was for the Arab states, in a sense, a triumph of *raison d'état* over the doctrine of pan-Arabism. At the same time, the limitations on Arab states' individual freedom of action in the Arab–Israeli sphere was highlighted on two fronts: the Palestine Conciliation Commission collective negotiating framework, and Jordan's efforts to achieve a separate, non-aggression treaty with Israel. Jordanian–Israeli secret diplomacy during the winter of 1949–50 produced a draft non-aggression agreement, but thanks to Egyptian and domestic constraints, Abdallah was incapable of seeing it through. Instead, on 1 April 1950, the Arab League laid down a basic 'rule of the game', which would guide Arab behavior toward Israel for almost three decades: Arab states were henceforth forbidden from negotiating or concluding 'a separate peace or any political, military or economic agreement with Israel'. Two weeks later, the Arab League Council spelled out the consequences for possible violators: expulsion from the League, political and economic sanctions, the severance of all relations and the closing of common frontiers.[21]

Abdallah had not given up hope of pursuing an agreement with Israel, but the die had been cast as far as the Jordanian political elite had been concerned. More important for them was the need to consolidate Jordanian control in the West Bank and neutralize Egyptian threats to expel Jordan from the League for this as well. As it happened, Jordan managed to parry the Egyptian moves and rebuff the League's efforts to place Jordanian rule under a temporary, trusteeship framework.[22] The

86 *Demise of the British Empire in the Middle East*

de facto legitimacy of its authority over the rump of Arab Palestine was not called into question for a decade, and was seriously reopened only after the June 1967 War. In addition, the consolidation of the Jordanian entity continued apace during the crucial years of uncertainty between the time of Abdallah's assassination in 1951 and the young King Husayn's full assertion of authority in 1956.[23]

As for the other Arab regimes involved in the 1948 war, the failure in Palestine would cost many of them dearly, catalyzing political opposition among alternative elites and newly mobilized sectors of the population alike, and contributing to their ultimate downfall. On the ideological level, the *nakba* (catastrophe) of 1948 contributed to the emergence of a more strident, militant brand of Arab nationalism, which dominated Arab political life for a generation.

ARAB–BRITISH RELATIONS

Contrary to long-held belief, Britain was not the driving force behind the creation of the Arab League in 1945.[24] Rather, it was compelled to follow Egypt's lead in supporting the creation of a loose co-operative framework, at the expense of the more compact, Hashemite-inspired unity schemes. Nonetheless, Britain did play a role in its formation, encouraging the various, often competing, clients to damp down their differences on behalf of the common good. It was Britain's hope that this 'common good' would be commensurate with British interests, inaugurating a new era of Arab–British partnership. To that end, in May 1945, Britain imposed on France an unconditional withdrawal of its forces from Syria and Lebanon. However, the Arab League proved to be a disappointment to the British, serving as a forum to promote more strident Arab nationalist interests, usually under Egypt's guiding hand.[25] Nonetheless, periodic discussions among British (and American) policy-makers regarding the desirability of the League's continuation or termination always reached the conclusion that a break-up of the League would be even more destabilizing to inter-Arab relations and thus to British and Western interests.[26]

Part of Britain's efforts to fashion a post-war order that would continue to serve its interests focused on the renegotiation of existing bilateral treaties with Egypt and Iraq. These efforts turned out to be both unsuccessful and traumatic. The 1946 Bevin–Sidqi draft agreement, which was to have replaced the 1936 Anglo–Egyptian Treaty, never came to fruition, leaving Anglo–Egyptian relations fraught with ill will and tensions. The January 1948 Portsmouth Agreement with Iraq, designed to replace the 1930 Anglo–Iraqi Treaty, was renounced within days by

A new Middle East?   87

the Iraqi Regent following large-scale rioting, which threatened the stability of the regime.[27] (For details on Egypt and Iraq, see Chapters 9 and 10, by Peter Hahn and Michael Eppel respectively, in this volume.) Only with Transjordan did matters proceed smoothly, with cosmetic changes being made in 1948 to a 1946 bilateral treaty.

Britain's efforts to advance its interests and strengthen its numerous allies in the region were also complicated enormously by inter-Arab differences and rivalries. Abdallah's machinations regarding Syria repeatedly raised the ire of his Arab rivals against Britain, which, they assumed, could easily have restrained Abdallah should it so desire. In fact, however, Britain was caught in the middle, and thus adopted a posture of strict neutrality regarding all Arab unity schemes, on the condition that they were being advanced peacefully.

Britain's representatives in Amman did try periodically to moderate Abdallah's utterances, albeit with extreme caution so as to 'not drive him to some act of folly on the spur of a moment of irritation'.[28] Similarly, Britain repeatedly cautioned the Iraqis against any thoughts of military intervention in Syria during the unstable times of 1949. It also avoided giving definitive clarifications and encouragement to Iraqi and Syrian leaders during their federation discussions in the fall of 1949. That would have enabled Syrian Foreign Minister Nazim al-Qudsi to counter domestic criticism that the federation would bring Syria under the thumb of British domination, through the application of the existing Anglo–Iraqi treaty to Syria.[29] An additional geopolitical factor in British calculations was Israel's likely behavior in the event of a Syrian–Iraqi union, or the breakdown of order in Syria. Along with the USA, Britain feared possible Israeli intervention in Syria to block a Syrian–Iraqi union. At the same time, Britain and Jordan were concerned that chaos in Syria would lead to an Israeli move against Jordanian forces in the Jordanian-held areas of the former mandated Palestine.

Inevitably, the Palestine question placed Britain, as the responsible mandate power, in an enormously difficult position *vis-à-vis* its Arab allies. As arbiter of an unstable, and ultimately untenable situation, Britain was keen on avoiding responsibility for any outcome which the Arab world might deem unfavorable. Inter-Arab divisions over Palestine further complicated its possible policy choices.

In early December 1947, on the morrow of the UN General Assembly partition vote, Arab leaders meeting in Cairo appealed to Britain to extend the mandate. Notwithstanding the negative reply, they still believed for a time that Britain would not in the end withdraw, if only because Palestine was viewed by them as the most likely alternative site for a British base once Britain withdrew its forces from Egypt. Their evaluation of Britain's strategic needs was not totally groundless, as a

September 1947 report by Britain's general staff had said as much.[30] However, Arab leaders failed to calculate the costs Britain would incur by remaining in Palestine, and their optimism proved not only premature but also damaging, since it contributed to the slowness of their own response to the developing situation.

Abdallah's ambitions in Palestine were viewed guardedly at first among British policy-makers. Many were especially concerned that his more pragmatic policies towards the Zionists and his territorial aspirations would lead to Transjordan's isolation from the other Arab states and consequently destabilize his position. They also feared UN sanctions against him were he to dispatch his forces into areas assigned to the Jewish state. On the other hand, Transjordan's explicit plans to occupy the Arab areas of Palestine adjacent to Transjordan, laid down by Prime Minister Tawfiq Abul Huda to Foreign Secretary Ernest Bevin on 4 February 1948, dovetailed with Britain's preference to wash its hands of the problem. Bevin thus tendered his silent approval to Abul Huda's plan.[31]

Some British officials were also enamored with the idea of detaching the Negev from the as yet unborn Jewish state, in order to assure territorial contiguity between Egypt, Transjordan and Iraq, for the sake of Britain's military interests[32] (on British military interests in the Negev, see Chapter 2 by M. J. Cohen in this volume). The idea resurfaced in the recommendations of the UN mediator Bernadotte in September 1948, and in periodic British efforts to coax Cairo and Amman toward a common position that would dovetail with British strategic interests.[33] However, the matter was never given high priority among British policy-makers, and the reluctance of Egypt and Jordan to co-ordinate their own policies was a source of constant frustration to Britain. More generally, the Bernadotte Plan seemed to offer an opportunity for Britain to strengthen its interests. However, the plan could be imposed over Israeli and Arab objections only with the co-operation of the USA. When the latter prevaricated, the plan was doomed, and Britain's ability to shape regional events continued to decline.[34]

Overall, Britain's refusal to support the UN plan for the partition of Palestine, its studied neutrality during the war, and its quiet support for Abdallah left it room to repair and maintain its relationships with ruling Arab elites. None the less, blame for the defeat of the Arabs in Palestine and the emergence of Israel could easily be traced to Britain's door: after all, it was Britain that had committed what in Arab eyes was the original sin, the issuing of the Balfour Declaration. For the rising generation of an increasingly politicized Arab public, Britain shouldered much of the blame for the events in Palestine, as it did for so many of the other perceived evils in the region. Britain's intimacy with Arab ruling elites did not provide a sufficient counter to this view, and in fact reinforced it.

A new Middle East?
89

Whereas Britain was entangled in Palestine over a 'core' Arab concern, its strategic planning was bedeviled by its unresolved dispute with Egypt over the future of the British base in Suez and of the Sudan. Much to Britain's disappointment, the other Arab states, while privately exhibiting little sympathy for the Egyptian position, publicly toed the all-Arab line in support of Egypt's position.[35]

British–Egyptian negotiations, Western powers' defense proposals (the Middle East Command and the Middle East Defense Organization) and inter-Arab contacts on finalizing their 1949 Joint Defense Pact became closely intertwined between 1950–52. Nuri al-Sa'id of Iraq was active in pushing for closer Arab–Western ties, and at times sought to mediate between Egypt and Britain. However, it was Egypt's position that continued to be decisive on both Arab–Western and inter-Arab matters. Egypt's rejection of Western defense proposals designed to supersede the Anglo–Egyptian impasse, and its ability to mobilize Arab support behind its demands for unconditional British withdrawal continued to confound British policy-makers. In turn, Britain continued to recognize the primacy of Egypt's strategic value versus Iraq's secondary status, much to Nuri al-Sa'id's chagrin.[36]

The overthrow of Faruq and the consolidation of power by the Free Officers Movement in Egypt, in July 1952, changed the focus of both Britain and Egypt and led to a resumption of negotiations. Agreements on the Sudan and on British withdrawal from Suez were concluded during 1953 and 1954. Inexorably, the USA was supplanting Britain as the Western power primarily responsible for the defense of the area, and would become increasingly entangled in the intricacies of inter-Arab affairs as well. Concurrently, Britain and (unofficially) the USA scaled down their defense plans into a 'Northern Tier' policy, given public expression in the Baghdad Pact. In doing so, they ignored the likely destabilizing effect this would have on inter-Arab affairs. Throughout the previous decade, Britain's old ally Nuri al-Sa'id had reluctantly acquiesced to the Egyptian-centered Arab League framework. Consequently, his embrace of a non-Arab centered regional defense framework marked a bold departure from past policies. This inaugurated a new, and more volatile, era in inter-Arab relations.[37]

CONCLUSION

Ruling Arab elites had entered the post-Second World War era with varying agendas: the Egyptians were determined to assume the position of *primus inter pares* among the Arab states while simultaneously freeing themselves from the remaining British shackles; the Iraqis still nurtured dreams of playing Prussia to the Arabs of the Fertile Crescent; in Transjordan, Abdallah was at times obsessed with Greater Syria but

90 *Demise of the British Empire in the Middle East*

sharply focused on Palestine; the Syrians needed support to rebuff Hashemite designs; Saudi Arabia's Abd al-Aziz saw Hashemite conspiracies at every turn; and the Lebanese were wary of everyone. Consequently, the chance that Arab elites would develop a sustained co-operative mode of relations among themselves and with Britain, and begin to reverse what Arab nationalists condemned as the 'Balkanization' of the Arab world after the First World War, was remote.

What crystallized, instead, was a state-centric system adhering to a common ideology of fidelity to Arabism, marked by sharp swings between co-operation and conflict, and the fashioning of loosely structured and shifting coalitions. The issues of the day – the future of Syria, the question of Palestine (and Israel), and the future relations with Britain – produced innumerable bouts of inter-Arab tension. However, irreversible schisms were avoided, sometimes by design, sometimes by an almost mechanical process of systemic checks and balances.

At the same time, the status of the Arab League, whose founding had engendered considerable hope among the Arab political public, was irreparably eroded, becoming instead a symbol of impotence. Its fading into irrelevance helped prepare the ground for the emergence of a more militant, mass-based, radical pan-Arab ideology, beginning in the mid-1950s. However, the intricate system of inter-Arab checks and balances which had emerged during the first decade after the Second World War, coupled with the failure of Arab states even to begin to develop interlocking economic interests, contributed heavily to inhibiting the implementation of the radical pan-Arabist revisionist vision in the years ahead.

For Britain, the ultimate inhibition of radical pan-Arabism was of scant comfort. The decline in its ability to shape Middle Eastern events reverberated throughout the first post-war decade, particularly over the Palestine question, as well as with regard to its efforts to consolidate regional defense arrangements and bilateral security links with Egypt and Iraq. Thus, the Suez debacle and the violent death of the pro-British Hashemite regime in Iraq in 1958 were, in a sense, only the last nails in the coffin of British influence in the region, after two generations of pre-eminence. The terminal decline of Britain's position was intimately linked with the emergence in 1945 and subsequent evolution of a contentious and quarrelsome Arab state system.

NOTES

1   Michael N. Barnett, *Dialogues in Arab Politics: Negotiations in Regional Order* (New York: Columbia University Press, 1998).
2   For a fuller treatment of these developments, see Bruce Maddy-Weitzman, *The Crystallization of the Arab State System, 1945–1954* (Syracuse, NY: Syracuse University Press, 1993).

A new Middle East? 91

3   For a series of scholarly studies on various aspects of the Hashemite monarchies, see Asher Susser and Aryeh Shmuelevitz (eds.), *The Hashemites in the Modern Arab World* (London: Frank Cass, 1995).

4   Patrick Seale, *The Struggle for Syria* (London: Oxford University Press, 1965).

5   Maddy-Weitzman, *Crystallization*, p. 11.

6   Yehoshua Porath, 'Abdallah's Greater Syria Programme', *Middle Eastern Studies*, 20, 2 (1984) pp. 172–89.

7   United Kingdom, Public Record Office, Foreign Office (FO) 371, 61492/E2529, Vaughan-Russell, memorandum, Aleppo, 27 February 1947; FO 371, 61497/E9137, 'The Greater Syria Movement', 10 January 1948.

8   Maddy-Weitzman, *Crystallization*, pp. 38–9.

9   US Department of State, National Archives, RG59/890D.00, enclosure, Patterson (Cairo) to Secretary of State, # 2838, 21 August 1947; and enclosure, Childs (Jidda) to Secretary of State, # 351, 26 August 1947; RG59/890D.001, enclosure, Hinton (Damascus) to Department of State, # 775, 22 September 1947; Mary Wilson, *King Abdullah: Britain and the Making of Jordan* (Cambridge: Cambridge University Press, 1987) pp. 158–9.

10 Stephen M. Walt, *The Formation of Alliances* (Ithaca, NY: Cornell University Press, 1987) Maddy-Weitzman, *Crystallization*, p. 43.

11 Maddy-Weitzman, *Crystallization*, p. 44.

12 Porath, 'Nuri al-Sa'id's Arab Unity Programme', *Middle Eastern Studies*, 20, 4 (1984) pp. 76–98.

13 For the minutes of Nuri's meeting with the Syrian prime minister on this subject, see RG59/790D.90G, Schoenrich (Baghdad) to Secretary of State, # 1467 and enclosure, 22 October 1946.

14 For the text of the treaty, see Muhammad Khalil (ed.), *The Arab States and the Arab League*, Vol. 2 (Beirut: Khayats, 1962) pp. 226–8.

15 Maddy-Weitzman, *Crystallization*, pp. 109–10.

16 Michael Eppel, *The Palestine Conflict in The History of Modern Iraq: The Dynamics of Involvement, 1928–1948* (London: Frank Cass, 1994) pp. 30–79; Barry Rubin, *The Arab States and the Palestine Conflict* (Syracuse, NY: Syracuse University Press, 1981) pp. 53–65.

17 Maddy-Weitzman, *Crystallization*, pp 55–90; Avi Shlaim, *Collusion Across the Jordan* (Oxford: Oxford University Press, 1987) pp. 122–338; *Behind the Curtain: [Report of the] Iraqi Parliamentary Committee [of Inquiry] on the War in Israel [Palestine Problem]* (Hebrew translation by Shmuel Segev of Arabic original; Tel Aviv: Ma'arakhot, 1954); J. C. Hurewitz, *The Struggle for Palestine* (New York: Schocken Books, 1976); Dan Kurzman, *Genesis 1948: The First Arab–Israeli War* (London: Vallentine Mitchell, 1972); William Roger Louis and Robert W. Stookey (eds.), *The End of the Palestine Mandate* (London: I. B. Tauris, 1986).

18 For a detailed, and controversial examination of the Abdallah–Zionist–British relationship, see Shlaim, *Collusion Across the Jordan*.

19 Earlier writings on inter-Arab manueverings during this crucial period immediately preceding the end of the mandate include Jon and David Kimche, *Both Sides of the Hill* (London: Secker & Warburg, 1960); Yaacov Shimoni, 'The Arabs [Heading] Towards the Arab–Israel War, 1945–1948', (in Hebrew), *The New East [Hamizrah Hehadash]* 12, 3 (1962) pp. 189–211; Thomas Mayer, 'Egypt's 1948 Invasion of Palestine', *Middle Eastern Studies*, 22, 1 (1986) pp. 20–36.

20 Maddy-Weitzman, *Crystallization*, pp. 64–9.

21 Ibid., p. 131–6.

22 Ibid., pp. 137–41.

23 Robert Satloff, *From Abdullah to Hussein* (New York: Oxford University Press, 1994); Maddy-Weitzman, 'Jordan and Iraq: Efforts at Intra-Hashimite Unity', *Middle Eastern Studies*, 26, 1 (1990), pp. 65–75.

24 A contemporary version is contained in US Office of Strategic Services, Research and Analysis No. 1754, 'Notes and Comments on Arab Federation and Arab Unity, Covering August to December 1943'. Asher Goren's *The Arab League* (in Hebrew; Tel Aviv: 'Eynot, 1954), gave primary weight to the external factors. Elie Kedourie's seminal article, 'Pan-Arabism and British Policy', in his *The Chatham House Version and Other Middle Eastern Studies* (London: Weidenfeld & Nicolson, 1970) pp. 213–35, was often misunderstood as ruling out the input from local factors. Michael J. Cohen, *Palestine: Retreat From Mandate*

92 *Demise of the British Empire in the Middle East*

(New York: Holmes and Meier, 1978) pp. 144–50, pointed to Britain's reluctance to encourage Arab politicians to go forward, out of fears regarding the Palestine question. Book-length scholarly studies emphasizing the primacy of Arab factors in the League's creation are Yehoshua Porath's *In Search of Arab Unity, 1930–1945* (London: Frank Cass, 1986), and, earlier, Ahmad Gomaa, *Foundation of the League of Arab States* (London: Longman, 1977). For a discussion of the 'old paradigm', which led both British and Arab officials to overemphasize Britain's primary role in the League's formation, see Israel Gershoni, 'The Arab League as an Arab Enterprise', *Jerusalem Quarterly*, 40 (1986) pp. 88–101.

25 Wm Roger Louis, *The British Empire in the Middle East, 1945–1951*, (Oxford: Clarendon Press, 1985) pp. 128–47.

26 For example, *Foreign Relations of the United States*, Vol. 5, 1947 (Washington, DC, Government Printing Office, 1971), 'Statement by the United States and the United Kingdom Groups', 'Problem: The Arab League' (undated, 1947) pp. 606–7.

27 Louis, *British Empire in the Middle East*, pp. 226–64; 307–44.

28 FO 371, 61497/E8901, Pirie-Gordon (Amman) to Garran (London), 18 September 1947.

29 Maddy-Weitzman, *Crystallization*, p. 119.

30 Wahid al-Dali, *The Secrets of the Arab League and 'Abd al-Rahman al-'Azzam* (Arabic) (Cairo: Ruz al-Yusuf, 1982) p. 232; Al-'Azzam, 'Abd al-Rahman, 'Memoirs of the Secretary-General of the League of Arab States 'Azzam Pasha', (Arabic); *al-Usbu' al-'Arabi*, 7 February 1972; Gabriel Cohen, 'British Policy on the Eve of the War of Independence', in Yehuda Wallach (ed.), *We Were Like Dreamers* (Hebrew) (Ramat Gan, Israel: Massada, 1985) pp. 121–8, 171–2.

31 FO 371, 68366/E1916, 'Conversation with the Transjordan Prime Minister', Bevin (London) to Kirkbride (Amman), # 19, 9 February 1948; Shlaim, pp. 132–40; Ilan Pappé, *Britain and the Arab–Israeli Conflict, 1948–1951* (New York: St Martin's Press, 1988) pp. 1–16; Michael J. Cohen, *Palestine and the Great Powers, 1945–1948* (Princeton, NJ: Princeton University Press, 1982) pp. 325–31. For a contrary view, see Efraim Karsh, *Fabricating Israeli History* (London: Frank Cass, 1997) pp. 109–42.

32 FO 371, 68367/E2163 and E2696, Foreign Office 'Minute', 13 February 1948.

33 Maddy-Weitzman, *Crystallization*, pp. 78–9, 86–7, 90, 130.

34 Sune O. Persson, *Mediation and Assassination: Count Bernadotte's Mission to Palestine in 1948* (London: Ithaca Press, 1979); Amitzur Ilan, *Bernadotte in Palestine, 1948* (Basingstoke: Macmillan, 1989).

35 Peter Hahn, *The United States, Great Britain and Egypt, 1945–1956* (Chapel Hill, NC: University of North Carolina Press, 1991).

36 Ibid, pp. 143–55.

37 Elie Podeh, *The Quest For Hegemony in the Arab World: The Struggle over the Baghdad Pact* (Leiden: E. J. Brill, 1995).

PART 3

EGYPT IN CONFLICT
WITH BRITAIN

6

Lampson and the wartime control of Egypt

MARTIN KOLINSKY

During the Second World War, Egypt was at the centre of Britain's military efforts in the Middle East and Mediterranean theatres. The headquarters of the army and air forces were in Cairo, and the headquarters of the Mediterranean Fleet were at Alexandria. Egypt was turned into a vast military complex, with extensive bases in the Delta and the Suez Canal area, and with networks of ammunition dumps, stores, workshops and hospitals.

A prime concern of the British authorities was for the internal security and political tranquillity of this crucial base, with its direct links to India and the Far East. Highly suspicious of the intentions of some of the leading Egyptians, the British monitored domestic political affairs closely, and were prepared to intervene directly when they thought it necessary to do so. The most notable and notorious intervention occurred in February 1942, when King Faruq was threatened with dethronement if he did not appoint a prime minister of Britain's choosing.

This was a major turning point in Anglo–Egyptian relations, provoking a sense of humiliation and frustration, which had profound political repercussions. It could be argued that all that mattered at a time of acute danger was to ensure that the Egyptian Government was fully supportive of Britain's war effort. This was the position of the British ambassador in Cairo, Sir Miles Lampson,[1] of the foreign secretary, Anthony Eden, and of the war cabinet. Yet some senior British military officers[2] doubted the wisdom of forcing the change. The interpretation presented in this chapter vindicates their misgivings. I shall argue that the intervention would have been unnecessary in February 1942 had Lampson taken appropriate measures earlier; and that Lampson's mistaken political evaluations contributed significantly to the crisis. Had he been more detached, and not motivated by a desire to settle his personal account with the young King Faruq, the situation might have been resolved in a much less spectacular manner.

But once Faruq was threatened by force publicly there was no going

96   *Demise of the British Empire in the Middle East*

back. Neither Lampson nor Eden took account of the consequences, which were to weaken the Wafd party by making them appear subservient to the foreign power. The humiliated monarch attracted widespread sympathy and was in due course able to regain a strong position. Consequently, the British began to lose control, being tied to a diminishing asset, the Wafd party. Responsibility for these major errors of policy lay as much with Eden as with Lampson, since the former gave his man on the spot full support.

This gives rise to a further issue: was Eden at fault for keeping the ambassador in Egypt too long? Lampson had taken up his post in Cairo in 1934 and had become deeply involved in domestic politics. Perhaps too deeply, in that he moved beyond being an arbiter to a participant with personal emotional involvement. His partnership was ultimately detrimental to the long-term British objective of retaining influence in Egypt.

The questions to be explored in this chapter are: Why did the February 1942 crisis occur? Could it have been avoided? What were the consequences for Anglo–Egyptian relations? Discussions of these issues requires a brief review of developments prior to the beginning of the Second World War.

A key element in the situation was that Fuad (sultan 1917–23, king 1923–36), with the support of the old Turkish ruling stratum, was not content to be merely a constitutional monarch. His aim was to expand his prerogatives beyond such limitations and to subordinate parliament when he could not dispense with it altogether. He was successful in the main, and on three occasions removed the Wafd party from power. The British did not interfere, which attracted the criticism that they were interested in upholding a corrupt autocracy.

Faruq, who reigned from 1937–52, tried to emulate his father in manipulating elections and in outmanoeuvring Lampson. By acting with apparently scatter-brained insouciance and lack of discipline, the young king disconcerted the powerful British ambassador. Lampson's desire to get to grips with 'the boy' was often frustrated, even during the war years. Faruq was far more influenced by Ali Maher, who was prime minister on several occasions,[3] and by his tutor, Ahmad Hassanein – both of whom served as Chief of the Royal Cabinet – and by lesser members of the court, some of whom were Italian nationals.[4]

Parliament was dominated by politicians of the pasha class, landowners and notables who formed in-bred cliques, seeking positions of influence from which to dispense patronage to their followers. As such, expediency and inevitably corruption were the springs of political motivation, rather than ideological or moral principles.[5] The nationalistic

Lampson and the wartime control of Egypt

Wafd party conformed to this model,[6] yet was different in significant respects. Its emphatic commitment to nationalism and its organizational capabilities endowed it with a much broader mass appeal than the others. It was dominant in the cities and in many rural areas, with support from schoolteachers and village headmen. It was a party of government, which was often denied its role in government, and therefore was not loathe to resort to violent agitation and demonstrations, and to organize the paramilitary Blue Shirts during the 1930s.[7] Moreover, the Wafd as a mass party consisted of different wings, which represented diverse social groups. Hence the internal struggles within the Wafd were something more than the competition of cliques: they can be seen as a struggle for dominance between rural landowners and the urban middle-class *effendis*. The former eventually won, personified by the transition of al-Nahas himself from leader of the urban middle-class elements to supporter of the conservative rural landowners.[8]

LAMPSON'S ABANDONMENT OF THE WAFD

King Fuad died in 28 April 1936. Shortly afterwards elections were held and the Wafd came to power for the fourth time. Prime Minister Mustafa al-Nahas negotiated the Anglo–Egyptian treaty, which was signed in August. It was a 20-year military alliance, which was to become a focal point of tension between the two countries, as is discussed in the following chapters. Of more immediate significance was the bitter internal dispute within the Wafd government, which led to the expulsion of Ahmad Maher and Mahmud al-Nuqrashi (both future prime ministers) in the autumn of 1937. They formed a new entity, the Saadist party, which represented emergent industrial interests.

Faruq was eager to take advantage of the split that had weakened the Wafd. The king, who came of age to ascend to the throne in July 1937, wanted his own men in charge. He reappointed Ali Maher as Chief of the Royal Cabinet, a move which al-Nahas opposed because he realized that it would create trouble for him. The palace sought vigorously to assert its control over the budget and to increase its support within the key institutions of the senate, the army, and the Al-Azhar religious university. Faruq was an attractive figure to many Egyptians, being young, handsome and full of promise. His popularity grew at the expense of the Wafdist government, and at the end of December 1937 Faruq judged that al-Nahas was sufficiently weakened to dismiss him.

Lampson tried to prevent the king from acting in such an arbitrary way, and warned against dismissing the head of an elected government. But it was to no avail. Worse was to follow. The elections of April 1938 were rigged to reduce severely Wafd representation. By allowing the palace to get away with these actions, the British ambassador was storing up difficulties for the future. Lampson was aware of the damage that was done to the cause of democracy in Egypt, but neither he nor the Foreign Office were willing to take action. The probable explanation is that they saw no immediate threat to fundamental British interests in Egypt, and they were reassured that the man who replaced al-Nahas, the Oxford-educated Muhammad Mahmud, a former Liberal Constitutional prime minister, was well disposed towards them. Heedless of the long-term consequences, they did nothing to protect the institution of parliament and responded opportunistically. The fact that Mahmud was a weak leader, without popular support, who depended on the embassy for guidance and encouragement, was advantageous to them.

The combination of inertia, opportunism and lack of foresight meant that Lampson had abandoned the Wafd to the arbitrary actions of the palace. The ambassador subsequently made no effort to rectify the situation. He was more concerned about his inability to influence the young king.[9] For his part, al-Nahas reacted with bitterness against the British, with whom he had negotiated the historic treaty. The new *modus vivendi* that the treaty represented was thrown into doubt. He and William Makram Ebeid, the prominent Wafdist politician who served as minister of finance in 1936, led an agitated extra-parliamentary campaign. They criticized the British for seeking to reimpose control over Egypt by supporting a weak government in office. This had the effect of keeping up the pressure on Mahmud, and of reinforcing their own position in the country.

The situation continued unchanged after Mahmud was forced to resign because of ill-health on 12 August 1939. The resignation might have provided Lampson with an opportunity to press for the restoration of the Wafd to government, but he did not do so. Instead he left the initiative to Faruq, who appointed his adviser Ali Maher as prime minister. It was a political error of the first magnitude on the eve of the Second World War. Instead of ensuring that a popular, pro-British government was installed at this crucial point, Lampson acquiesced in the continuation of unrepresentative government. The consequence was that the movement for neutrality remained unchecked and allowed to grow.

EGYPTIAN NEUTRALITY

The movement for neutrality, which Lampson suspected was covertly supported by the king, was sufficiently strong to prevent Egypt from issuing a declaration of war on Germany in September 1939. A significant

Lampson and the wartime control of Egypt   99

pointer to post-1945 developments was that some of Ali Maher's cabinet, led by Abdel Rahman Azzam (who in 1945 became secretary general of the Arab League), were holding out for a promise that at the end of the war Britain would negotiate a revision of the Anglo–Egyptian treaty.[10]

Lampson rejected the notion of treaty revision outright; the upshot was that, although Egypt co-operated fully with British requirements, the government did not declare war. Diplomatic relations with Germany were severed. Censorship was imposed under a regime of martial law known as the *état de siège*. An embargo was imposed on trade with Germany, and neutral ships in Egyptian waters were searched. A strict economic regime was established, and the prices of foodstuffs and essential commodities were controlled.[11] In those circumstances, the British government decided not to press the Egyptians further on the issue of the declaration of war.[12]

But suspicions had been aroused, fed by intelligence reports that Ali Maher was maintaining secret contact with both the Italian and the German governments. Moreover, his dismissal of a number of pro-British officials from his administration added to Lampson's doubts about his trustworthiness.

Matters came to a head in June 1940 with the collapse of France, the expulsion of British troops from the European continent, and the Italian declaration of war. The movement of opinion towards Egyptian neutrality gained strength. Faruq and Ali Maher were anxious to reinsure with the Italians, at the very least by not offending them. The Maher government wanted to proclaim Cairo as an 'open city', which would have necessitated the removal of British troops and anti-aircraft defences, to prevent it from being bombed. Lampson, with the strong approval of the Foreign Office and the military chiefs in Egypt, prevented him from doing so.

On 12 June, two days after the Italian declaration of war, Ali Maher broke off diplomatic relations with Italy; but his statement in the Egyptian parliament indicated that the government would not declare war if Italy did not attack Egypt. The British Embassy was alarmed by this, and their anxiety was increased by the slowness of the Egyptian government in expelling Italian diplomats, and in interning suspected Fascists. Lampson was convinced that the prime minister was endeavouring to maintain good relations with the Italians and was working against British interests, a conviction strengthened by reports that the Egyptian minister in Rome was advocating Egyptian neutrality.

Afraid that the prime minister's attitude would spread defeatism and undermine Britain's position just as military action was about to begin, Lampson intervened forcibly. He told Faruq on 17 June that he had to dismiss Ali Maher.[13] Lampson also insisted that Maher should not be allowed to return to a position of influence in the palace. Failure to comply, he warned, would bring Faruq into confrontation with General Wavell, the Commander-in-Chief, Middle East, a thinly veiled reminder of the dethroning of the Khedive Abbas Hilmi in 1914.[14]

Al-Nahas wanted elections to be held, but Lampson did not agree, using the war as an excuse. This was another mistake, of the same order as before, because the Wafd then decided to stay out of government. They were certain that they would win an overwhelming majority and saw no reason to be compelled to rule through a coalition for Lampson's convenience. Thus another opportunity was missed to legitimize the accession to power of a friendly government, which would have been based on mass support. Instead, Faruq was again handed the initiative and he chose as prime minister Hassan Sabry, who lacked political standing though his views were pro-British. His cabinet consisted of Saadists, Liberals and Independents.

The feeble political standing of the cabinet allowed the Palace to retain considerable influence over policy.[15] Thus the actions of the embassy continued to support the palace to the detriment of parliament, though Lampson was convinced that the Wafd were much more reliable from a British point of view than Faruq.

On the issue of neutrality, the new government followed the same policy as Ali Maher had done. In June, the war cabinet gave Lampson discretion not to insist on an Egyptian declaration of war, provided that they co-operated on internal security matters, did not hinder British military actions and broke off diplomatic and trading relations with Italy. The Egyptians were reluctant to declare war, even when the Italians penetrated over 70 miles into the Western Desert, because they were fearful of exposing their cities to bombing. But by then, the British military commanders in the Middle East no longer thought an Egyptian declaration of war to be necessary, as long as the Egyptian prime minister co-operated fully with the British war effort.[16]

The pro-British elements in Egyptian political circles were strengthened by the outcome of the Battle of Britain, and by Lampson's success in persuading the Treasury to help financially with credits for arms and to purchase the cotton crop. In addition, the loss of export trade was compensated by the expenditure of the imperial forces on local Egyptian goods and services.

Nevertheless, the positive effects were offset by the consequences of an internal political crisis between the prime minister and his Saadist colleagues. Some of the acrimony was personal, but more important was the question of Egypt's position, as war threatened the western frontier. Unlike his brother Ali, the Saadist leader Ahmed Maher was

Lampson and the wartime control of Egypt 101

strongly pro-British, and responded to the Italian invasion of Egypt by campaigning for active Egyptian participation alongside Britain in the defence of the country. But the prime minister refused to go beyond the cautious inaction of his predecessor, and wished to postpone defining the red line that would necessitate Egyptian participation in a war confined so far to distant areas of desert. He forced the Saadist ministers to resign. Lampson confined himself to verbal protests to Hassan Sabry, and made no attempt to have them brought back into the government. The result was to demoralize the Saadists and with them the pro-British elements.

On 15 November the new parliamentary session began. It was marked by a dramatic incident: Hassan Sabry collapsed and died while reading the king's speech. A few days later, Husayn Sirry became the new prime minister, and affirmed the continuity of Egyptian policy, in particular, that of refraining from declaring war on the Italians. The new government was composed of Liberals and Independents. It faced a twofold opposition. The Wafd remained outside government, and were critical of the embassy for again supporting an unrepresentative minority government, which enabled the palace to retain much power. The Saadists disdained the minor cabinet posts offered them. They again campaigned for more active participation in the war in order to strengthen Egyptian claims at the peace settlement. At the end of December 1940, while Wavell's forces were routing the Italians in the Western Desert, parliament debated the question raised by the Saadists. The result was a government victory (122 votes to 68) on a vote of confidence. The Wafd, still hostile to Ahmad Maher and the Saadists for splitting away in 1937, voted for the government.[17]

THE THREAT OF ROMMEL

The build-up of the German air force in Sicily and the Dodecanese islands during January 1941 seriously affected the strategic situation in the Mediterranean. Heavy bombing of the port of Benghazi from mid-February forced the British to revert to Tobruk, some 200 miles to the east, as their supply base. The British commitment to Greece weakened their position in Libya, and Rommel's first offensive at the end of March came much sooner than Wavell had expected. Six days later, the Germans invaded Yugoslavia and Greece.

The rapid advance of the Axis forces under Rommel alarmed the Egyptian public and even overshadowed the *coup d'état* in Iraq on 1 April by the pro-Axis Rashid Ali. With the important exception of the Wafd, the political parties supported the government's policy, which the prime minister explained in a secret session of parliament on 14 April. The policy was to co-operate with Britain, uphold public morale, and employ the Egyptian Army mainly on internal security duties, especially protection of the vital infrastructure of communications, such as bridges and public utilities.[18]

The Wafd was highly critical of the British for maintaining an undemocratic government during such a crisis. But, from Lampson's point of view, the prime minister was doing a good job of deflating Ali Maher and counter-acting defeatist and anti-British tendencies.[19] The danger of spying and sabotage had increased greatly, and the para-military formations led by Abdul Rahman Azzam and Taher Pasha were under suspicion. Ali Maher had turned to Islamic organizations as a means of preserving his influence, but Husayn Sirry had weakened them by exiling Hassan al-Banna, the head of the Muslim Brotherhood, and was planning to imprison Ahmed Husayn, the head of the National Islamic Party, formerly 'Young Egypt'. Moreover, Husayn Sirry gave Ali Maher the alternative of accepting the position of Egyptian minister in Washington or of being confined to his country house.[20]

Husayn Sirry attempted to secure the agreement of the party leaders for a government of national unity, but al-Nahas was not interested: he wanted parliament dissolved and new elections held. However, the other parties did not agree, and negotiations broke down. The upshot was that at the end of July 1941, Sirry reconstituted his cabinet. It included five each of Liberals, Independents and Saadists. Neither Ahmed Maher nor al-Nuqrashi were among the latter because they refused to take minor positions. For its part, the Wafd was incensed and loudly exploited the unpopularity of the new cotton agreement with Britain, which disposed of only half the crop. Al-Nahas severely criticized the British for undermining the economy and independence of Egypt and claimed that they were violating the treaty he had negotiated with them. After his first speech, he was received by the king, which made it appear that Faruq was encouraging his attacks on the British. For Lampson, it was a novel and unwelcome development: the new royal–Wafd rapprochement weakened the prime minister. The latter, having lost the king's favour, was exposed as ruling only through British support. Many senators and deputies followed the trend, shifting their allegiances away from the prime minister, and others, mainly Saadists and some Liberals, supported the weakened government without enthusiasm.[21]

Lampson's previous political miscalculations and opportunism had created an impasse. By the autumn, Lampson felt that there was only one solution: he wanted to bring the Wafd into the government, but could not find a way to do so. He knew from past discussions that the

Lampson and the wartime control of Egypt

British military would be opposed to using force to make Faruq accept al-Nahas as long as there was no obvious internal threat to the stability of the Egyptian base. His best hope was to try to establish a national coalition in which the Wafd would play a leading role,[22] but that was not what al-Nahas wanted. The latter was convinced that elections would give him a clear majority, and he saw no reason to accept less.

THE ULTIMATUM TO FARUQ

The Japanese attack on American and British positions in the Far East in December 1941 had serious economic repercussions in Egypt. The restriction on imports aggravated the shortages of cereals and other supplies and gave further impetus to inflation, resulting in strikes and agitation. Lampson was critical of the prime minister for his lack of control, and for his failure to explain to a fearful public that it would be impracticable to declare Cairo an 'open city' to shield it from bombing. The ambassador increasingly felt the strain of 'backing a minority though entirely friendly government, against a hostile majority'.[23] His involvement in the situation, and desire to reconstruct it to his personal satisfaction, which included ousting the king, lay behind the sudden development of a crisis.

On 6 January 1942, the Egyptian government, at the request of the British, broke off diplomatic relations with Vichy France because it was assisting the Axis armies through Tunisia. This act did not attract much attention in the Egyptian press, and its connection with the sudden resignation of the prime minister on 2 February was not immediately perceived. Faruq had objected to the rupture of relations with Vichy, especially as he had not been consulted, and he forced the resignation of the Foreign Minister Salib Sami. This provoked Sirry Pasha, who was not willing to tolerate such blatant interference from the king, to resign in protest. In turn, the British authorities were angered because they had initiated the severing of relations with Vichy.[24] Lampson suspected that Faruq had acted upon the advice of Ali Maher, and was determined to end the latter's influence.[25] Moreover, Lampson, fed up with the antics of the king, was eager to remove him.

Eden gave his full support to bringing the Wafd to power. He recommended that al-Nahas be sounded regarding the elimination of 'insidious influences in the palace' and the fulfilling of Egypt's obligations under the treaty. He wanted Lampson 'to make it plain to al-Nahas Pasha that we do not intend to allow any question of treaty revision to be raised so long as the war lasts'. Eden then stated, with supreme cynicism and arrogance:

104   *Demise of the British Empire in the Middle East*

> Should Nahas Pasha offer satisfactory assurances ... (and I should value such assurances, not because I necessarily expect him to keep them, but because if he does not, they will afford us strong grounds for turning him out) ... you will feel at liberty to encourage the king to follow Husayn Sirry's advice and form a Wafdist Government.

But if the king wanted to nominate his own prime minister, Eden continued, 'you should acquiesce in his doing so' (apart from Ali Maher), while at the same time warning him that 'we in London are wondering whether the only way to get rid of a cycle of which we are heartily tired would not be by reducing the governing factors from 3 to 2'.[26] The threat to Faruq was undisguised; but Eden had not considered the longer-term consequences.

Thus armed, Lampson sent the king an ultimatum on Wednesday 4 February. The issue was dramatized to the full when the Abdin Palace was surrounded by British troops and tanks. Lampson, General R. G. Stone, Commander of British Troops in Egypt, and armed officers, arrived at 9 p.m., four hours after the expiry of the ultimatum.[27] Within an hour, Faruq appointed al-Nahas as prime minister. The humiliation of the king was felt widely in Egypt, particularly among Army officers,[28] as an affront to national dignity.

The consequences of the humiliation far outweighed the gains. Britain's position in the country had not been threatened seriously by internal political movements and conspiracies, and far less obtrusive measures could have been taken to resolve the problem. Lampson could have supported the prime minister by insisting on the reinstatement of the foreign minister, a measure that would have checked the palace without precipitating a major crisis. Alternatively, he could have pressed for new elections, which would have had the effect of bringing the Wafd to power in a legitimate manner. But Lampson wanted to settle his personal vendetta with the king. As a consequence the Wafd were imposed on the palace, and were thereafter visibly dependent on the British. It was deeply damaging, though not fatal, to a party which had spearheaded the Egyptian independence movement.

Notwithstanding the need for a new personality and a fresh, less emotional approach, Lampson was kept on. He retained the confidence of Eden, not simply because he was zealous in his flattery of the rather vain foreign secretary. More fundamentally, they saw eye to eye on the handling of political matters. Lampson was rewarded by being raised to the peerage in 1943 for services, which in effect had undermined British influence in the country after the February coup.

Elections were held in March, and were boycotted by the Saadist and Liberal parties. Although the Wafd won an overwhelming majority with over 85 per cent in the Chamber of Deputies, and over 50 percent in the

Senate, Lampson was concerned about the negative reactions of the Saadists and Liberals to the new government. They had been highly supportive of the British alliance, and were now faced with the unpleasant fact that their loyalty had been rewarded by British intervention in favour of their political rivals. He feared they might turn against the treaty.[29]

The Muslim Brotherhood responded in a more extreme and hostile manner, but al-Nahas struck back at them by ordering their leader Hassan al-Banna to withdraw from the elections and by arresting their ally Ali Maher in April. Some months later, after some of their leaders had made pro-German speeches, al-Nahas banned their public meetings.[30]

The reactions in the Egyptian Army were potentially more serious, as they might have had an effect on the British war effort, given their services in connection with aerial defence and protection of the lines of communication. The Egyptian army resented the pressure employed against the king in bringing the Wafd to power. There were some thoughts among the junior officers of taking action against the British, but these were discouraged by their superiors.[31] General Wilson, who had commanded British troops in Egypt until February 1941, and served subsequently in Greece, Palestine, Syria, Iraq and Iran, credited its Chief of Staff, Atallah Pasha, with preventing any serious incidents. Wilson, with considerable justification, blamed the British ambassador for creating the tense situation. The general endorsed the view of Hassanein, the head of the Royal Cabinet, that it had not been necessary to force the issue with the king. Wilson insinuated that Lampson's ham-fisted approach was due to personal shortcomings rather than to any inherent political necessity.[32]

A year later the situation had improved considerably, according to a review by General Stone, who before becoming GOC (General Officer Commanding) British Troops in Egypt had been head of the military mission. He regarded the Egyptian army as fully co-operative. But he warned that 'if we took any form of military action against the king, the Egyptian army, even though unable successfully to oppose our action, would almost certainly cease to co-operate with us'.[33] The danger was not of an overt rebellion, but of a sullen refusal to service British wartime needs. Moreover, the discontent would probably have been much more serious and widespread than that manifest in abortive attempts by young officers like Anwar Sadat to contact the Axis.[34]

POLITICAL DISARRAY

The Wafd government fulfilled the immediate British requirements for wartime co-operation, suppressing defeatist propaganda and imprisoning those suspected of Axis sympathies. But the embassy became

106 *Demise of the British Empire in the Middle East*

increasingly anxious about the government's underlying instability because of the development of serious conflicts. As early as April 1942 the rift between al-Nahas and Makram Ebeid, the minister of finance, was becoming irreparable. It was provoked by the latter's resistance to promotions for favoured Wafdist bureaucrats as well as his reluctance to grant special import licences which al-Nahas' wife, the daughter of a landowner, wanted for her relatives.[35] The split affected the Wafd Party at the highest level, because Makram was also the party's secretary general and commanded the allegiance of many of his fellow Copts. The conflict made it easier for the palace to undermine the Wafd in preparation for eliminating them from the government.[36]

Makram, who was increasingly wooed by the king, was left out of the government when al-Nahas recast it in May. The popularity of the Wafd government eroded over the summer, owing to persistent charges of corruption and nepotism. In addition, government officials and police were disgruntled; and potentially more dangerous was the anti-government attitude spreading in the army, which was upset by appointments and transfers designed to reduce the influence of the palace. Faruq was still regarded sympathetically throughout the army as a symbol of the national humiliation imposed by the British. Embassy officials were aware that it was only the British commitment to al-Nahas that pre-vented the king from sacking him.[37]

Matters became far worse when Makram, who was also expelled from the party in July 1942, formed his own group, the Independent Wafdists. He co-operated with other opposition leaders and with the palace. He severely damaged the government in the spring of 1943 when he published a sensational document, called the *Black Book*, which gave a detailed account of the alleged corruption and misdeeds of al-Nahas, his wife, her relations and other Wafd politicians. Al-Nahas' response was to accuse the palace of having promoted this book to discredit and get rid of him.

The Foreign Office was worried, and instructed Lampson to play a more active role in defending al-Nahas, in particular, to prevent Faruq from seizing the opportunity to dismiss him. The calculation was that 'if we let Nahas Pasha go (and the prospect is one of minority government with no solid foundation) the Wafd is almost bound to return to power once more and if they were convinced that we had let them down after their record last summer we should find collaboration with them difficult indeed'.[38]

However, the British service chiefs took a different view of the situation. Because of pending military operations, they were unwilling to resort to force if Faruq decided to dismiss the Wafd. Moreover, they thought that it would be more dangerous from a security point of view to have the palace and the army hostile than it would be to incur the animosity of the Wafd. Both the minister of state, Richard Casey, and his deputy, Lord Moyne, agreed, but Lampson did not. The latter argued in the Middle East War Council that the Wafd in opposition would be most troublesome because of its mass support, and in its feeling of betrayal would beat a frenzied chauvinistic and anti-British drum. Casey referred the issue to London, and to Lampson's delight the prime minister supported his position.[39]

However, the problem diminished in importance in May because of Allied success in Tunisia, and the elimination of the Axis from north Africa. Moreover, al-Nahas successfully defended himself against the accusations of corruption and nepotism, and won a decisive vote of confidence in parliament. This made it hard for the king to act against him directly.[40]

DISMISSAL OF THE WAFD

Lampson had no grounds for complaint about the government in terms of its co-operation on war measures. But its decline in popularity created two major problems for the British. One was that they were publicly obligated to the Wafd because their force had been used to bring it to power; there was no one else to whom the embassy could turn. Moreover, Lampson took a certain pride in being loyal and could not in good conscience simply let the government fall – though it did come to that at a later stage.

The second problem was that al-Nahas sought to overcome his government's loss of domestic support by vigorous nationalism in foreign policy. A key feature of this was the promotion of cultural relations with other Arab countries. Egypt's claim to leadership in that domain was strengthened by his attempts to interfere in the affairs of Syria, Lebanon and Palestine. This aroused Lampson's concern, as did the likelihood that al-Nahas would insist on Egypt's claims to a role in future peace negotiations.[41] It was a surefire way to rally political support in Egypt, as no matter what the differences between the parties, they all agreed on the need to achieve independence in the post-war period and to secure their longstanding claims to 'the unity of the Nile Valley' (i. e. to control the Sudan) and to influence in the region. These goals could be attained only at the expense of the British, whose withdrawal from the country was fervently desired. As the war receded from the Egyptian frontier, Egyptian nationalist feeling began to rise, with an increasingly sharp

108   *Demise of the British Empire in the Middle East*

anti-foreign, especially anti-British, tone. It was to culminate in strikes and rioting in February 1946, as is discussed in the following chapters.

Meanwhile, the opposition parties were anxious to take advantage of the government's weakness, and were able to overcome their internal differences to establish a 'National Front'. In February 1944, a second edition of Makram's indictment of the al-Nahas government, *The Black Book*, was published. The National Front followed this up in May with a list of repressive acts that the government had taken, accusing it of abusing the provisions of martial law for its own political purposes.[42] On 12 April, Faruq, confident of the loyalty of the Egyptian army, informed Lampson that he wanted to replace the Wafd government with one of his own. It was to be headed by Hassanein, whom Lampson had begun to distrust after having previously accepted his appointment as Chief of the Royal Cabinet.

Neither Lampson nor the War Cabinet in London wanted a change of government. They realized that its successor would be highly dependent upon Faruq, whom Lampson ached to depose and whom Churchill characterized as 'an Oriental despot who on every occasion has proved himself a poor friend of England'.[43] Lampson was authorized by Churchill to use force, if necessary, to prevent Faruq from dismissing al-Nahas, despite the reluctance of the military authorities, who were preoccupied with Greece.[44]

But the position of the Wafd in the country had weakened to such an extent that Lampson was becoming resigned to its demise. He was increasingly aware of the disadvantages of prolonging the association with what was widely perceived as a corrupt, autocratic government.

On 8 October 1944, while Lampson was on a visit to South Africa, Faruq seized the opportunity to get rid of al-Nahas and dismissed the Wafd.[45] The king then appointed the Saadist leader Ahmed Maher as prime minister. It was difficult for Lampson to object to Ahmed Maher because he was a long-standing advocate of full alliance with Britain in the war. In any case, the writing had been on the wall for some time, and Lampson was relieved that the sacking had occurred during his absence.[46] No vital British interests were at stake, and Lampson did not seem worried that Faruq might have outwitted him. For his part, Faruq knew the limits of his power and did not attempt to push matters with Lampson further. The choice of Ahmed Maher was opportune and astute.

The elections held in January 1945 were boycotted by the Wafd. Ahmed Maher's government took measures to meet the economic distress of inflation and food shortages, and released all political prisoners. On 24 February, parliament approved the prime minister's proposal to

Lampson and the wartime control of Egypt

declare war on Germany. Although coming very late in the war, the intention was to secure a seat at the United Nations in order to fulfil Egypt's post-war aims.[47] On leaving parliament, Maher was shot dead by a terrorist.

The political degeneration which had been such a long-standing feature of the Egyptian scene worsened. December 1937 had been a low point with Faruq's abrupt dismissal of the Wafd government, and the naked exercise of British power in February 1942 had provoked a widespread sense of humiliation. The Wafd, hoisted to power by Lampson, was consequently undermined and the parliamentary process was brought into disrepute. It was a turning-point, after which the British authorities began to lose control.

Although rewarded with a peerage, Lampson had in fact failed. His action in February 1942 was unnecessarily overdone because all he had to do to curtail Faruq and support the prime minister was to insist on the restoration of the foreign minister. Previously, he had reacted passively to Faruq's arbitrary actions. He knew Faruq was out of bounds in December 1937 when he dismissed the popularly elected Wafd government, and when Faruq grossly manipulated the 1938 elections to keep out the Wafd. For the next four years, he and the British government were content to have unrepresentative governments, entirely dependent on embassy support. The effect of this short-sighted opportunism was to damage parliament, and to let the king persist in acting beyond constitutional limits. The 1942 action was supposed to have been a 'correction', but it made matters far worse because the army and the country were humiliated. The Wafd party was damaged because it was then seen to depend on Lampson.

The end of the war was heralded by political assassination. Lampson was still in charge of the embassy, and the British military presence gripped Egypt. The British wartime aim of stability in Egypt had been attained, but at a high political cost. British support, as al-Nahas saw clearly, was an important asset in the deadly political game. But it was not enough to offset the palace; and it was not constant, being guided by imperial interests, not those of Egyptian democracy. There was less and less to show for the decades of British influence and manipulation. Ernest Bevin, foreign minister in the new Labour government, professed an ideology of 'development' and 'partnership',[48] which attempted to breathe new life into the nearly defunct relationship; but it had no meaning for the Egyptians. By the end of the war, they wanted merely to be rid of Britain's self-interested presence, which had produced little for Egypt beside the wreckage of political vendettas.

110   *Demise of the British Empire in the Middle East*

NOTES

I wish to thank Dr Michael Thornhill for his research assistance.

1   Sir Miles Lampson became the first Lord Killearn in 1943; but for the sake of simplicity he will be referred to as Lampson throughout this chapter.
2   See the memoirs of General Maitland H. Wilson, *Eight Years Overseas* (London: Hutchinson, 1950) pp. 129, 158–9. Another commander critical of Lampson's relations with Faruq was Air Chief Marshal Sir Sholto Douglas, AOC (Air Officer Commanding) Middle East. See William Sholto Douglas, *Years of Command* (London: Collins, 1966) pp. 184, 197–202, 244–5. Douglas went so far in his attempt to rectify relations between the monarch and the British as to become a frequent companion of Faruq on visits to Cairo nightclubs.
3   Ali Maher was Chief of the Royal Cabinet in 1935 and 1937, and prime minister in 1936, 1939, 1942 and again in 1952, both before and after the coup by the Free Officers.
4   Barrie St Clair McBride, *Farouk of Egypt* (London: Robert Hale, 1967) pp. 100–1.
5   M. E. Yapp, *The Near East Since the First World War* (London: Longman, 1991) p. 55.
6   See Elie Kedourie, *Politics in the Middle East* (Oxford: Oxford University Press, 1992) pp. 181–2.
7   Yapp, *The Near East*, pp. 55–6.
8   Alaa al-Din Al-Hadidy, 'Mustafa Al-Nahas and Political Leadership', in Charles Tripp (ed.), *Contemporary Egypt: Through Egyptian Eyes* (London: Routledge, 1993) pp. 73–8.
9   Killearn Diary, Middle East Centre, St Antony's College, Oxford, 14 May 1938, p. 90.
10 Killearn Diary, 4 September 1939, p. 169; minute by D. V. Kelly, 23 September 1939, FO 371/23337, J4837/21/16.
11 Lampson to FO, 3/9/39, FO 371/23368, J3518/3369/16 and Annual Report for 1939, FO 371/24632, J582/582/16, 22 February 1940, f. 205.
12 Cab 65/1, War Cabinet conclusions 13(39), 12 September 1939.
13 Lampson to Halifax, 8 October 1940, Review of Political Situation during Last Five Months, J2227/92/16, FO 371/24627, ff. 87–90; also Killearn Diary, 17 June 1940.
14 Killearn Diary, 17 June 1940, pp. 150–2, printed in T. Evans (ed.), *The Killearn Diaries 1934–46* (London: Sidgwick Jackson, 1972), pp. 119–22. The embassy, together with the military chiefs, were prepared to introduce British martial law if necessary, and to replace Faruq on the throne with his pro-British uncle Prince Mohamed Ali, the heir apparent. Killearn Diary, 30 May 1940, pp. 125–6: conference with Generals Wavell and Wilson and Air Chief Marshal Longmore, and June conferences, 23 June 1940, p. 162.
15 Lampson to Halifax, 8 October 1940, Review of Political Situation during Last Five Months, J2227/92/16, FO 371/24627, op. cit.
16 Minute by Thompson, 30 September 1940, J2079/92/16, FO 371/24626. The cabinet decision was taken on 13 June 1940, Cab 65/7.
17 Lampson to Eden, 3 January 1941, J164/18/16, FO 371/27428.
18 Lampson to Eden, 29 April 1941, Review of Political Developments in Egypt during Last Three Months, J1509/18/16, FO 371/27430, f. 126: among the dozen deputies who abstained from voting was Sidqi, who urged that contacts be maintained with the Axis and that 'there should be no pro-British propaganda or insults to the Germans and Italians in the Egyptian press and broadcasts'. See also Lampson to Eden, 17 April 1941, J1431, FO 371/27483, which reported on the Egyptian prime minister's statement in parliament on 14 April.
19 Lampson to Eden, 29 April 1941, Review of Political Developments during Last Three Months, J1509/18/16, FO 371/27430, f. 128.
20 Ibid., f. 125. See also Lampson to Eden, 28 January 1941 (Review of Political Situation in Egypt during Last Four Months) J352/18/16, FO 371/27428: Ali Maher, who chose to stay in the country, even if it meant being under house arrest, was also involved with the Young Men's Muslim Association.
21 Lampson to Eden, 23 September 1941, Review of Political Situation during Last Five Months, from 29 April J3265G, FO 371/27433, ff. 77–83.
22 Lampson to FO, 31 October 1941, J3459, FO 371/27434.
23 Lampson to Eden, 23 September 1941, op. cit., J3265G, FO 371/27433, f. 83. See also Peter Mansfield, *The British in Egypt* (London: Weidenfeld & Nicolson, 1971) p. 274.

Lampson and the wartime control of Egypt

24 Minute by Smart, 20 January 1942, 284/2/42, FO 141/837.
25 Lampson to Eden, 21 January 1942, 284/3/42G, ibid.
26 Eden to Lampson, 2 February 1942, 1/7/42G, FO 141/829.
27 See *The Memoirs of Lord Chandos* (London: The Bodley Head, 1962) pp. 275–6. Oliver Lyttelton, later Viscount Chandos, was minister of state in Cairo at the time, and supported Lampson's position in the Middle East Defence Committee, despite the initial reluctance of the military.
28 See Gabriel Warburg, 'Lampson's Ultimatum to Faruq, 4 February 1942', *Middle Eastern Studies*, 11, 1 (January 1975) pp. 24–5, and Mansfield, *The British in Egypt*, p. 278.
29 Lampson to Eden, 11 February 1942, 1/42/42. FO 141/829. The Wafd won 231 seats out of 264. Mansfield, *The British in Egypt*, p. 279. The Wafd held 81 of the 146 seats in the Senate.
30 *Islamic Societies – Reports by British Intelligence and the Egyptian Police*, Review of the History of the Ikhwan Muslimin (included in Security Summary Middle East No. 103 of 10 December 1942), 305/37/42, FO 141/838. The ban on Muslim Brotherhood meetings was effected in September 1942.
31 Charles Tripp, 'Ali Mahir and the Politics of the Egyptian Army', in Tripp (ed.), *Contemporary Egypt*, p. 65.
32 Field Marshal Lord Wilson of Libya, *Eight Years Overseas 1939–1947* (London: Hutchinson, 1950) p. 129. See also pp. 158–9.
33 Memorandum by General R. O. Stone, 20 April 1943: *Some Military Considerations in Connection with the Present Political Situation*, 1/4/43G, FO 141/855.
34 See J. C. B. Richmond, *Egypt 1798–1952* (London: Methuen, 1977) p. 205; Lukasz Hirszowicz, *The Third Reich and the Arab East* (London: Routledge & Kegan Paul, 1966) pp. 241–3; Tripp, *Contemporary Egypt*, pp. 65–6.
35 *Review of the Foreign Press*, 19 June 1942, pp. 299–300, and 17 July 1942, pp. 345–6; P. J. Vatikiotis, *The History of Egypt* (London: Weidenfeld & Nicolson, 2nd edn, 1980) pp. 351–2.
36 Minute by Smart, 20 April 1942, 1/152/42, FO 141/829.
37 Minute by Smart, 5 October 1942, 1/253/42, FO 141/829.
38 FO to Cairo, 12 April 1943, 1A/14/43, FO 141/855. The reference is to the internment of suspected fifth columnists, and to the government's efforts to maintain calm among the population at large when Rommel's forces were closest to Egypt in the summer of 1942.
39 General Wilson failed to mention in his memoirs, pp. 158–63, Churchill's personal telegram instructing him to support the Ambassador. See Evans, *Killearn Diaries*, entries for 27 April 1943 and 2 May 1943, which reproduced a telegram from Churchill to General Wilson, and 26 November 1943. See also Killearn Diary, 3–7 May 1943, and Laila Amin Morsy, 'Indicative Cases of Britain's Wartime Policy in Egypt, 1942–44', *Middle Eastern Studies*, 30, 1 (January 1994) p. 105.
40 Morsy, 'Britain's Wartime Policy in Egypt'.
41 Lampson to FO, 1 February 1943, 'Review of the Political Situation during Past Four Months', 1/5/43, FO 141/855.
42 Vatikiotis, op. cit., p. 353.
43 Cited in Evans (ed.), *Killearn Diaries*, p. 294, personal telegram to Lampson, 18 April 1944.
44 War Cabinet meetings of 19 and 20 April 1944, Cab 65/42. The minister of state, Walter Moyne, had supported the line taken by General Paget and his military advisers. See Morsy, 'Britain's Wartime Policy in Egypt', p. 112.
45 Faruq dismissed al-Nahas shortly after the conclusion of a conference of Arab states at Alexandria. The conference had discussed the form Arab unity should take, and had agreed a protocol known as the Alexandria Protocol. See Chapter 3 by Michael Thornhill in this volume.
46 Evans (ed.), *Killearn Diaries*, entry for 9 October 1944, pp. 314–15.
47 Mansfield, *The British in Egypt*, p. 282.
48 See Wm Roger Louis, *The British Empire in the Middle East 1945–1951* (Oxford: Clarendon Press, 1984), pp. 17–21. See Chapter 1 (Nicholas Owen) and 4 (Rodney Wilson) in this volume.

7

Egypt 1945–52:
The uses of disorder

CHARLES TRIPP

INTRODUCTION

Egyptian public life in the years following the Second World War and prior to the military *coup d'état* of 1952 has often been characterized as disorderly, violent and chaotic. There is some truth in this. However, a closer examination of the political violence and disorder that have figured so widely in descriptions of this period reveals a more intricate and in some respects stylized pattern of public behaviour than may have been imagined. The demonstrations, public disorders and occasional riots which erupted during these years throw some light on the structures, both symbolic and material, of the political world in which they were occurring. In doing so, they help to explain the nature of the arena in which successive Egyptian governments had to strive for authority, but more particularly for credibility with their peers, with the palace and, to some degree, with the British government.

Public disorder is both a phenomenon and a powerful image, almost a metaphor. As such it acts as a form of language between those concerned, communicating fears of social chaos and the breakdown of hitherto-accepted conventions of political behaviour. More than that, however, demonstrations, rallies and other manifestations of 'direct action' provide the participants with important forms of expression, directing their anger or support and thus publicly involving them in a political world from which they would otherwise be largely excluded. They are being given the opportunity to make their mark and, in doing so, to enter into the shaping of the history of the polity, at least in theory. In reality, of course, it may serve to deflect them from having any effective role in the making of that history, except as part of some more powerful actor's strategy.

In Egypt during the first half of the twentieth century public disorder of this kind always had a role to play. For Egyptian nationalists of whatever party, it was a key element in the vernacular language of the

Egypt 1945–52   113

argument against British domination. It was also assumed to undermine the confidence of either the British or the king in the government of the day. Under certain circumstances, these tactics were largely successful.[1] The features sustaining, and, it could be argued, encouraging, this particular form of political activity were various. Some had been part of public life in Egypt since before the British occupation of 1882. Other rules had been implanted as a direct result of the British occupation or had developed since 1922. Here the British military occupation and all that it implied had been decisive in ordering a certain kind of public life.

However, it had not been the sole factor of importance. Demographic changes in the urban–rural balance of the population, as well as in its generational composition, had contributed to the ways in which political action was to be structured, especially in the introduction of the idea of national politics, based on mass participation. Equally, the new forms of economic life had demanded new forms of organization and of association, and these too had helped to shape the setting in which occurrences of public disorder were to be projected as significant harbingers of change.

The consequences of these changes had been evident during the 1930s.[2] In the period following the ending of the Second World War, similar conditions existed. However, there were added factors that influenced the nature of public disorder during this period. These heightened the symbolic resonance of such disorder, but they also altered the terms under which it took place. One such factor, important particularly in the symbolic realm, was the emergence of a broad, if notoriously fragmented, communist movement in Egypt. The onset of the cold war and the well-developed anxieties of much of the elite about the unknown power of organized labour, lent to communism a particularly threatening character. This threat, illusory though it may have been, had a powerful grip on the imagination of those who saw themselves as the principal actors in Egyptian public life and contributed directly to the symbolic power of public disorder during the period.[3]

Another factor was the entry of the Muslim Brotherhood on to the political stage as an actor in its own right. As an image of unmeasured power and potential menace, the Brotherhood was quite as potent as the communist movement in colouring the imaginations of the political elite. However, as a distinctly indigenous outgrowth of Egyptian society, it was thought, not without justification, to be amenable to the forms of patronage that enmeshed all other organizations in Egyptian public life. In short, there was an ambiguity about the Brotherhood (which in part reflected stresses and strains within the organization itself) that made it a fitting player in the game of staged public disorder that was being used to such effect in Egyptian politics during these years.

114 *Demise of the British Empire in the Middle East*

Finally, the question of the Egyptian army's allegiance to the government of the day and to the Crown took on new importance. In a game where public disorder was being actively encouraged as a means of discrediting rival factions and communicating the sense of menace and impending social breakdown necessary for the transfer of power, it became ever more important to ensure that the ultimate coercive sanction in the state – the Egyptian armed forces – should be prepared to do the bidding of those who sought to profit from social disorder.

This intensified established forms of political patronage in the officer corps, but also encouraged the aspiring radical organizations to cultivate dissent in this arm of the state. Many of the officers who were to overthrow the monarchy had been made aware of the potential political role of the armed forces by one or other of these influences – sometimes by both. They were also concerned about the problem of social disorder, but from their perspective the king and the established politicians were part of the problem. Given the structural basis of the stylized disorders that had prevailed in Egyptian politics since the development of the nationalist movement in the early twentieth century, this was a fairly accurate assessment.

AL-NUQRASHI, SIDQI AND THE MUSLIM BROTHERHOOD, 1945–49

In symbolic terms, demonstrations operated on two levels. The first lay in the highly charged issue that was used as the pretext for bringing people on to the streets to demonstrate. The second was in showing up the inadequacy of the government of the day, both in its commitment to the issue in question and in its capacity to maintain order should the demonstrations become riots. This ensured that the governments themselves became engaged in the ambivalent task of controlling demonstrations and disorders not simply by suppressing them, but also by sponsoring them. This was particularly the case of those which occurred in connection with the troubled relationship with Britain or over the question of Palestine. These occasions allowed the government of the day and its opponents to play out the roles appropriate to these highly charged issues, while at the same time vying with one another for control of the streets in order to appear the more authentic voice of the mass of the population.

This was first seen on a large scale in early November 1945, following the abolition of martial law and in connection with a series of strikes and demonstrations throughout the Arab world against the Balfour Declaration. These events display some of the features that were to govern similar events in the future. Lacking any form of mass party

Egypt 1945–52 115

organization of his own and anticipating widespread Wafdist protests against his government, the prime minister, Mahmud Fahmi al-Nuqrashi Pasha, had taken the precaution of cultivating the Muslim Brotherhood. This limited the impact of the Wafdist demonstrations of that summer and helped the government to control labour unrest.[4]

The growing agitation over the question of Palestine could not be ignored by al-Nuqrashi and his government, just as they could not ignore the agitation over the position of Britain in Egypt. Al-Nuqrashi intended to exploit these themes to his own advantage and in doing so both to pre-empt the Wafd and its allies, as well as to impress upon the British the necessity of renegotiating the terms of the 1936 Anglo–Egyptian Treaty in Egypt's favour. In this scheme, the Muslim Brotherhood was exceptionally useful, as it had the capacity to control large numbers on the campuses and on the streets of Cairo in particular. Furthermore, Hassan al-Banna had unequivocally declared the readiness of his organization to play a full part in Egyptian political life.[5] For his part, al-Nuqrashi assisted the Brotherhood financially. He also forbade the police from using firearms in any circumstances to keep order and gave official sanction for those demonstrations he thought would be useful, much to the consternation of the police.[6]

On the anniversary of the Balfour Declaration, 2 November 1945, an unprecedented closure of businesses, schools, government offices and workshops took place and a massive demonstration was organized at al-Azhar. Some of this initiative came from the Wafd, but the scale of the organization, the initial tolerance shown by the police, and al-Nuqrashi's determination to address the gathering crowds suggest government encouragement. Al-Nuqrashi was seeking to turn these events to his advantage, restating his commitment to the cause of Palestine and pre-empting the efforts of his political opponents to capture the streets.

This was not altogether successful. Encouraged by the small numbers of police present, looters began attacking shops in the Sharia al-Azhar and the Mousky. After initial confusion, the Cairo police moved in and restored order. In another part of town the Ashkenazi synagogue in Sharia Faruq was attacked. Nevertheless, these disorders were also rapidly dealt with and the main body of demonstrators assembled in front of the Abdin Palace and then dispersed.[7] Wafdists and others sought to prolong the disorders, but the police were prepared and moved rapidly to prevent crowds from forming and thus maintained order. The same precautions were taken on the following day when a series of attacks was made on shops in the European section of Cairo, which were intended to embarrass the government. The police moved in rapidly and succeeded in preventing serious disorder.[8]

116   *Demise of the British Empire in the Middle East*

These events bring out a number of themes that are of significance in the analysis of civil disorder during this period. In the first place, there was the desire of the government to stay ahead of the game, preventing its political opponents from mobilizing effective numbers around some highly symbolic and emotive issue. To do this, the government used its powers of patronage to win over some at least of those organizations which had the capacity to bring people out on the streets. In addition, full, if rather ambiguous, use was made of the police and the security forces both to allow certain kinds of manifestation and to suppress others, depending on the identity rather than the actions of the demonstrators. At the same time, it was clear that the government's opponents tried to use the situation to their advantage, injecting an element of violent disorder, trying to turn the demonstrations away from the question of Palestine, which the government had successfully appropriated and extending the disorder beyond the time that the government had allocated. The government's opponents seem to have hoped to create a situation that the authorities would have found much harder to control without resort to a more determined and potentially controversial use of force.

Although al-Nuqrashi succeeded in avoiding these traps in November 1945, he was less successful in doing so when the next major eruption of public disorder took place, in February 1946. By this stage, the context had changed significantly, restricting his options and making public disorder a much more effective means of undermining his government. Al-Nuqrashi was facing problems within his coalition government, particularly from Makram Ebeid and his party, al-Kutla. This had begun as a commonplace dispute about cabinet positions, but had developed into the more serious question of the attitudes of al-Nuqrashi and Ebeid towards the possibility of renegotiating the terms of the Anglo–Egyptian Treaty.[9] It was, consequently, against the background of the perennially troublesome question of Anglo–Egyptian relations and of a divided cabinet that the political drama was to play itself out.

The Wafd had every interest in promoting the most uncompromising position on national issues in order to maintain pressure on the government. These views were being echoed within the cabinet, particularly by Ebeid and the members of al-Kutla. The barely suppressed tension simmered throughout January 1946, while the Egyptian government awaited the crucial British reply to their note of December 1945, formally requesting the opening of talks to re-negotiate the Anglo–Egyptian Treaty. When that reply arrived it received an unfavourable response from most of the Egyptian political world and al-Nuqrashi's opponents claimed that this was due to the initially feeble request that he had sent in December. Only the government press tried to cast the British reply

Egypt 1945–52 117

in a favourable light and, even so, it was noticeable that the al-Kutla press (in theory, supporters of the government) was as hostile as the opposition papers.[10] Apparently thwarted by the British, no longer the master of his own cabinet, and rapidly losing the confidence of the king, al-Nuqrashi was in a particularly vulnerable position.

It did not take long for his opponents to exploit this situation through the use of civil disorder. On 8 February 1946, the Muslim Brotherhood, signalling the end of their relationship with al-Nuqrashi, organized a demonstration of protest at Al-Azhar. There was no serious disorder, but on 9 February 1946 the Wafd, now collaborating with the Muslim Brotherhood, organized a march of 6,000 or so students from the campus of Fuad I University in Giza to the Abdin Palace (a traditional site for such demonstrations). Al-Nuqrashi, having lost his hold on the students through the break with the Muslim Brotherhood, could only rely on the police to prevent the demonstration from developing into more serious disorders in the centre of town. He was aware of the fact that he was losing the confidence of the palace and that King Faruq might use the apparent inability of his government to maintain order as a pretext for his dismissal. Equally, he was aware of the profit which Ebeid and others in his cabinet may have hoped to derive at his expense from any outbreak of serious disorder. Under these circumstances he reversed his orders of November 1945 and authorized the police to use all possible means to prevent the demonstration from reaching the Abdin Palace. These orders resulted in the police's attacking the demonstrators on the Abbas bridge across the Nile and then opening the bridge itself, leading to the death and injury of a number of the student protesters.

If al-Nuqrashi had thought that this show of force would secure his position, he was soon proved wrong. The king, who visited the campus of the university the following day, sought to distance himself from the methods of the police and from the government, which appeared to have sanctioned such methods. Not only the opposition press but also the al-Kutla papers attacked the police for the excessive violence used. On 11 February 1946, a large student demonstration marched on the Abdin Palace to mark the king's birthday, but, in a strange reversal of the previous situation, was this time afforded police protection. Within a couple of days, Ebeid and his three al-Kutla colleagues had resigned from the cabinet in protest at the way in which the demonstration of 9 February had been handled and the next day the king delivered the *coup de grâce* and asked al-Nuqrashi to resign.[11]

Al-Nuqrashi had fallen victim to the dynamics of civil disorder. His position was such that the demonstration of 9 February would have precipitated his downfall whether or not the police had used such exceptionally brutal methods to suppress it. In this case, as in others, it

118 *Demise of the British Empire in the Middle East*

was not the scale of the disorders that mattered, so much as the interpretation that could be placed upon it by those who were seeking to undermine him for other reasons. Having lost the immediate power over such manifestations that his earlier patronage of the Muslim Brotherhood had given him, al-Nuqrashi was without the necessary resources to extricate himself from this dilemma.

His successor as prime minister, Ismail Sidqi Pasha, had no intention of finding himself in a similar situation and was quick to see what could be achieved through the patronage of the very organizations which had turned against al-Nuqrashi. Sidqi made conciliatory gestures both towards the Muslim Brotherhood and towards Young Egypt.[12] As in 1945, the Muslim Brotherhood, joined this time by Young Egypt, was urged to form a rival organization to the Wafd and to ensure that the focus of demonstrations remained Egypt's 'national aspirations'.[13] This prevented Sidqi's many opponents from exploiting the situation to his disadvantage and acted as a useful backdrop to the initiation of talks with Britain about the future of the Anglo–Egyptian relationship.

Accordingly, Sidqi ordered that no force should be used by the police to suppress the large demonstrations planned for 21 February 1946, announced as 'Evacuation Day'. Throughout Cairo, there were demonstrations and a number of attacks on prominent British civilian establishments, such as the Anglican cathedral and the bishop's house. Most conspicuously, however, the crowds of demonstrators gathered in front of that potent symbol of British military occupation, the Kasr al-Nil barracks in the centre of Cairo. It was there, in confused circumstances, that the greatest violence took place when British troops opened fire on the crowds of demonstrators, killing over 20 Egyptians and wounding many more.[14] Despite British warnings of further action by their forces and despite his promises to prevent future demonstrations, Sidqi allowed more manifestations to take place, believing that he had control of the major part of the demonstrators and possibly finding it useful that the British military presence should be the focus of the demonstrators' anger.[15]

Inevitably, in view of the deaths in Cairo, this anger found a focus when 4 March was declared a day of mourning for those killed. A general strike was proclaimed by the various committees representing the Wafd and the communist organizations on one side and the Muslim Brotherhood and Young Egypt, on the other. The day was marked by demonstrations throughout Egypt, but only in Alexandria were there severe disorders. British naval and military establishments in the town were attacked by crowds of demonstrators and in the ensuing violence two British soldiers were killed, as well as a number of Egyptian civilians. On this occasion, however, Egyptian police and army units took an

Egypt 1945–52   119

active part in suppressing the rioting, although apparently rather late in the day. Sidqi had realized that it could be dangerous for his government if the British were to bear the brunt of the disorders. He was to receive an unequivocal warning to this effect from the British ambassador when he was told that a repetition of the events of 21 February and 4 March might lead the British military authorities 'to assume control and restore order'.[16]

As a way of maintaining control of the situation while a delegation was formed to negotiate with Britain, Sidqi extended his patronage of the Muslim Brotherhood. At the same time, he abandoned Young Egypt and had Ahmad Husayn arrested, having presumably come to the conclusion that they were too unreliable and volatile an element to be useful. Sidqi reportedly regarded the 'danger of serious student disorders as a trump card in discussions with Britain, so he [was] interested in maintaining an atmosphere of tension'.[17] When Sidqi's own control of the process was threatened, as in the attempted march by students at Faruq I University in Alexandria at the end of April, he had no qualms about authorizing the police to fire on the demonstrators and ordering the army to occupy the university campus.[18]

A similarly forceful response awaited other attempts by the government's opponents to disrupt public order during the summer of negotiations with Britain. Where the government could not rely on the strength of its ally, the Muslim Brotherhood, to help keep demonstrations within acceptable limits, the police and the army were deployed to ensure no opportunity for civil disorder presented itself.[19] In many situations, however, it seemed that the weight and, indeed the armament, of the Brotherhood was a serious obstacle to any party trying to organize against the government.[20] At the same time, the succession of attacks on British service personnel and on institutions related in some way to the British presence in Egypt were not regarded by Sidqi as matters of much urgency.[21]

More preoccupying for Sidqi at the time was the spectre of labour unrest. Stimulated by falling living standards as inflation took hold, as well as by growing unemployment in the post-war recession, workers in a variety of occupations had begun to organize for protection in official and unofficial unions during 1945. This was particularly the case among the greatest concentrations of industrial workers at the Shubra al-Khaima and Mahalla al-Kubra textile factories. Those workers in Shubra al-Khaima, in particular, situated close to Cairo and working for largely foreign-owned enterprises, became the targets for cultivation by a variety of political forces in the capital. Most obviously, the communist organization HAMTU (*Al-Haraka al-Masriyya li-l-Tahrir al-Watani* [The Egyptian Movement for National Liberation]), the communists in the

Al-Fajr al-Jadid (New Dawn) group, as well as the increasingly articulate left wing of the Wafd formed into *Al-Tali'a al-Wafdiyya* (The Wafdist Vanguard) established links with the workers' organizations of Shubra al-Khaima and elsewhere. They organized around specific grievances, often by means of direct action, such as sit-ins, marches and one-day strikes. However, they also drew numbers of the workers into the nationalist demonstrations of the day.[22]

For Sidqi, this was useful, insofar as it helped to swell the numbers of demonstrators, but he was concerned that they would lend themselves to communist or other organizations that advocated a revolutionary change in Egyptian society and in the Egyptian polity. This was disorder of a more fundamental and more menacing kind than the theatre of the streets that had hitherto dominated images of disorder in Egypt. The fears it provoked were well captured in the wording of the draft law that Sidqi submitted to parliament at this time, by which he wished to impose heavy penalties on those found guilty of 'founding revolutionary societies with the object of overthrowing one class and raising another, overthrowing social and economic regimes, overthrowing any of the basic political institutions of the state'.[23]

Accordingly, Sidqi deployed a twin strategy to deal with the possibility of workers' unrest, as he had done in other cases of threatened civil disorder. On the one hand, he encouraged the Muslim Brotherhood to extend their influence into the trades unions, particularly in Shubra al-Khaima. This was particularly the case during the wave of strikes that hit the textile industry during May 1946. On the other hand, he used the routine methods of arrest and intimidation. These tactics appear to have succeeded in thwarting the threatened general strike of 25 June 1946. Using this as a pretext, Sidqi then launched a thorough campaign of repression against all movements of the left, whether communist, fellow-travellers or part of the Wafdist Vanguard. Scores of people were arrested in July 1946 and a large number of publications and organizations were closed down. Although pamphleteering and other forms of activity could not be halted entirely, it was nevertheless noticeable that there was a fall in the number of strikes and many of the links that had joined political movements of the left to the workers' organizations were severed.[24]

The kind of social revolution and reordering of Egyptian society advocated by the communist movement in Egypt was more fundamentally menacing by nature and for that very reason Sidqi had little difficulty in acting forcefully and effectively to suppress it. It did not command the numbers that could be mobilized around other more emotive causes and there was no ambiguity across the Egyptian elite, much as they might differ on other matters, about the need to deal

Egypt 1945–52 121

resolutely with social unrest of this kind. Even the leadership of the Wafd, represented by such people as Mustafa al-Nahas, Fuad Serag al-Din or Muhammad Salah al-Din, were uneasy about the activities of the Wafdist Vanguard when these went beyond simply bringing out the workers on the streets in support of the leadership's position.

However, on the question of the relationship with Britain, as Sidqi was to discover, the situation was quite different. The faltering negotiations in Egypt and Sidqi's decision to leave for London for private negotiations with the British foreign secretary, Ernest Bevin, angered much of the political elite, many of whom had been represented on the original negotiating team. In these circumstances, Sidqi was vulnerable to the effect that public demonstrations and disorder might have on confidence in his own capacity to govern. Consequently, Sidqi took measures to pre-empt hostile action: members of student committees were arrested and charged with planning sabotage; the opening of the schools and universities was postponed until mid-November; substantial pay increases were granted to the police to stiffen their resolve in the suppression of anticipated civil disorder; large sums of money were distributed among the urban poor to persuade them not to join in the student demonstrations and thus to prevent more general rioting.[25]

These measures were insufficient, however, to prevent the eruption of public demonstrations and disorder in November when the universities reopened and Sidqi had returned to Egypt with the controversial results of his conversations with Bevin. The issue of the Sudan and the unity of the Nile Valley, in particular, became a rallying cry for the growing number of opposition forces and was the slogan under which the students now organized themselves into the National Front of Students of the Nile Valley. Ominously for Sidqi's prospects of controlling the streets, this Front was joined by the Muslim Brotherhood. Responding to pressures within the Brotherhood and reacting adversely to Sidqi's apparent willingness to come to terms with Britain, Hassan al-Banna had begun to distance himself from the government in October 1946. Demonstrations organized by the Brotherhood in Cairo and elsewhere had been easily dispersed by the police, but the talks which then started between al-Banna, the Wafd, Young Egypt and the Watanists, effectively deprived Sidqi of the kind of control he had enjoyed earlier in the year in his dealings with the demonstrators.[26] Sidqi was, in effect, thrown back into the position which had been forced on al-Nuqrashi in February.

However, the prospects of a bloody confrontation between the security forces and the demonstrators were now much increased. Since the beginning of the year, there had been reports of the widespread availability of weapons and in particular the ease with which students

122   *Demise of the British Empire in the Middle East*

were able to acquire revolvers and hand grenades. Under the auspices of the Muslim Brotherhood and of Young Egypt these weapons were being used in the training of their respective paramilitary formations – and in the case of the Muslim Brotherhood this appeared to be officially tolerated while it was under Sidqi's protection.[27] In the demonstrations of November 1946, some of the students turned the guns and explosives they had acquired on the police. This resulted in violent disorders, with large numbers of casualties on both sides. Sidqi ordered the closure of the universities, but the disorders continued, possibly encouraged by the fact that Sidqi had lost the backing of a wide spectrum of the political elite. Furthermore, the king's confidence in his ability to govern and to negotiate a successful outcome with the British was ebbing fast.[28] Faced with this situation and the continuing disorders, Sidqi resigned in early December, in circumstances not dissimilar to those that had unseated al-Nuqrashi earlier in the year. Ironically, he was now succeeded by al-Nuqrashi as prime minister.

For his part, al-Nuqrashi fell back on a tactic that he himself had used before with some success and made conciliatory moves towards the Muslim Brotherhood, releasing large numbers of those arrested in the recent disturbances and inducing al-Banna to break off his talks with the Wafd and others.[29] Nevertheless, members of the Muslim Brotherhood were suspected of involvement in a series of bomb attacks in December on targets with British connections. This may have been an indication that al-Banna was finding parts of his organization, notably the Secret Apparatus, hard to control. Alternatively, it may have been that he did not see such activities as bound by any agreement he might have reached with al-Nuqrashi about discouraging more widespread and more public forms of civil disorder. At any event, it was noticeable that the hostile demonstrations and disturbances that followed al-Nuqrashi's appointment as prime minister came chiefly from Wafd-inspired organizations, and it was not long before Wafdist and Brotherhood contingents were clashing on the campuses and on the streets of Cairo, as in the days of Sidqi's patronage.[30] For his part, al-Nuqrashi, realizing that the negotiations with Britain were on the verge of breaking down, sanctioned numerous demonstrations in January 1947. These served as a prelude to the official breaking off of the talks and to the Egyptian government's placing of its case before the Security Council of the United Nations later in the year.

This initiated a period of curiously intimate but also troubled relations between al-Nuqrashi and the Muslim Brotherhood, which was to end in 1948 with the dissolution of the organization and the assassination of al-Nuqrashi himself. As far as widespread public disorder was concerned, it was important for al-Nuqrashi to keep the

Egypt 1945–52   123

Muslim Brotherhood on his side as a counter-weight to the Wafd on the campuses and on the streets and as a check on the reviving influence of various communist organizations among the industrial workers. This appears to have been achieved during 1947, marked by Hassan al-Banna's expulsion of his deputy Ahmad al-Sukkari from the Brotherhood, accusing him, among other things, of cultivating close relations with Serag al-Din and the Wafd.[31] The formation of the communist-dominated HADITU (*Al-Haraka al-Dimuqratiyya li-l-Tahrir al-Watani* [The Democratic Movement for National Liberation]) in June 1947 foreshadowed a wave of strikes, most serious of which were those in the textile industry in the autumn at Shubra al-Khaima, but also at Mahalla al-Kubra. The significance of the latter was that the enterprises were wholly Egyptian owned and this, for the Muslim Brotherhood, was an inappropriate target for industrial action. Consequently, it appeared that, as in the preceding year, the Brotherhood was encouraged by the government to counter the propaganda of HADITU – a task it undertook with some success.[32]

In effect, the government granted to the Brotherhood a licence to prepare for more violent forms of action in its recruitment and training of the paramilitary formations of *Al-Jawwala* (The Rovers). These had been started some years before by the Muslim Brotherhood and the assistance granted to them in training and supplying these groups had always been a measure of the condition of relations between the Brotherhood and the government of the day.[33] However, unknown to the government, the Brotherhood was also organizing covertly, through the Secret Apparatus (*Al-Jihaz al-Sirri*) for more selective and directed forms of violence. In 1947, with the departure of al-Sukkari, al-Banna appointed the head of the Secret Apparatus, Salih Ashmawi, as his deputy.

For al-Nuqrashi, the Brotherhood was seen chiefly as an instrument to be used in the game of fomenting or discouraging civil disorder. In order to stay ahead on the national question, which the Wafd and others were always willing to exploit, al-Nuqrashi employed two strategies during 1947. The first was the ultimately fruitless one of taking the Egyptian dispute with Britain before the United Nations. In some measure, this removed the issue from the sphere of domestic politics and relieved the government for a brief period of responsibility to be seen to be doing more for the national cause. The second strategy, however, was to encourage the belief that, should Egypt fail to gain satisfaction of its national demands from negotiations with Britain or from the UN, the government would be prepared to use direct action to pursue the struggle, in the form of guerrilla attacks on British installations. To this end, during 1947, the government either tolerated

124 *Demise of the British Empire in the Middle East*

or actively supported the arming and training of the Muslim Brotherhood's paramilitary formations. The Nile Valley Liberation Committee, which included members of the Brotherhood and others, announced that it would be recruiting 'Liberation Battalions' throughout Egypt and that Egyptian army officers would be involved in their training.[34]

There was a strong element of theatre in these proceedings, since al-Nuqrashi would have been well aware of the danger to his own government of trying to launch effective guerrilla warfare against the overwhelming British military presence in Egypt. By the end of 1947 the British military had almost entirely withdrawn to the cities and camps along the Suez Canal and the British Military Mission to the Egyptian army had come to an end. Nevertheless, the number of British troops in the country was still very large and the possibility of a British reoccupation of Cairo and the Delta was kept alive in many sections of the press. Nevertheless, al-Nuqrashi found it useful to encourage a belief in the value of active resistance in order to keep organizations such as the Muslim Brotherhood on his side and to suggest symbolically that he was deeply committed to the defence of the nation's rights by any means possible. The mounting tension over the UN debate on Palestine in the autumn of 1947 saved al-Nuqrashi from having to put these commitments to the test. He could instead direct the attention of the Muslim Brotherhood and others to the cause of Palestine, thereby avoiding the predicament in which the Wafd government was to find itself in the latter part of 1951.

Consequently, shortly after the Security Council's effective shelving of the Egyptian question in September 1947, agitation began on the question of the defence of Palestine. In October, recruiting offices were opened by the Muslim Brotherhood and others seeking volunteers for the struggle to defend Arab Palestine and soon the first Brotherhood 'Liberation Battalion' went on public display with official approval.[35] By December 1947, it was not always possible to prevent demonstrations on the Palestine question from deteriorating into rioting, particular after the strength of feeling caused by the November decision of the UN on partition. Nevertheless, as in 1945, al-Nuqrashi sought to stay ahead of the game by permitting those demonstrations that would rebound to his credit as a 'struggler' on behalf of Palestine, while banning those that he thought might be exploited by his political opponents. When it appeared that the latter had successfully turned a march to their advantage, he had no compunction about using force to prevent disorder.[36] Furthermore, when the Wafd tried to refocus attention on the outstanding questions of Anglo–Egyptian relations and the apparent ineffectiveness of the government, al-Nuqrashi could rely on the Muslim Brotherhood and the police force to prevent this from

Egypt 1945–52 125

escalating. His control over the press, meanwhile, limited the more general impact of such demonstrations.[37]

However, during 1948, more ominous patterns of disorder began to show themselves, suggesting that the government would have to face some of the unforeseen consequences of its own actions. They also prefigured some of the circumstances that would contribute to the overthrow of the regime as a whole in 1952. The first of these developments was the strike by police officers from 4–6 April 1948. This seems to have been due chiefly to the professional grievances of police officers and was precipitated by the government's routine neglect. In Cairo, there was little disturbance and the army was called in simply to guard the principal buildings and to deter any thought of disorder. In Alexandria, however, whether through Wafdist influence or for other reasons, the police demonstrations gave way to general rioting. The army was called in to suppress the disorders, leading to clashes between army units and police officers, which resulted in a large number of deaths and scores of injuries.[38]

The principal significance of these events was twofold. Firstly, the government had clearly taken the police force and the acquiescence of its officers for granted. This was a dangerous oversight in a political game where the encouragement and the suppression of civil disorder played so important a part in determining the fate of governments. The events in Cairo, but more particularly in Alexandria, demonstrated how vulnerable the government was to mutiny from this quarter. The government's deployment of the Egyptian army as a means of escaping from the consequences of this eruption, pointed to the second factor of significance. Initially, it was said that the king had forbidden the use of the armed forces precisely because he believed that al-Nuqrashi had brought the situation upon himself and should now face up to the consequences. However, he reportedly relented once the seriousness of the rioting in Alexandria became apparent.[39] The fighting that followed resulted in the two major branches of the state's security apparatus firing on each other.

The thoughts of both parties go unrecorded, but it seems probable that some at least among the army officers began to wonder about the competence of a government that had allowed such disorder to erupt. In the light of the events of 1952, it may well be that such a spectacle fed into the mutinous thoughts that were already forming within the officer corps of the army itself. Although unremarked by al-Nuqrashi and others in the political elite at the time, the officer corps constituted a new audience before which the game of civil disorder was to be played out. They were not simply observers, however. As participants in the maintenance of order and as potential targets when order broke down,

126   *Demise of the British Empire in the Middle East*

the army officers' thoughts were also coloured by concern that incompetent political leadership might lead to the kinds of disorder that betokened deeper social conflict. After the violence of the events in Alexandria this was further illustrated graphically by the violence connected with the strike and sit-in of male nurses at the Kasr al-Aini hospital on 7 April, which the communist movements sought to exploit and the army was called in to suppress.[40] In this respect, the new patterns of disorder were beginning to create new rules, which the old elite did not yet realize were to change the game fundamentally.

The second ominous development was the violence of the campaign launched by the Muslim Brotherhood during the summer of 1948. The Brotherhood had continued to enjoy official sanction in the training and despatch of units to the Palestine front during 1948. They had taken an active part in operations, even before the entry of the Egyptian army into the war in May, and continued to play a role in certain areas of the front during the following six months. These activities were clearly encouraged and supported by the government, which had provided the Brotherhood with the necessary military equipment.

More uncertain was the degree to which the government condoned a series of devastating bomb attacks organized by the Muslim Brotherhood against Jewish targets in Cairo. In the first of these, two bombs exploded in the Jewish quarter of al-Gamaliyya, destroying a number of houses and killing nearly 50 people.[41] During the following months, a series of similar attacks was carried out. No arrests were authorized at the time and, furthermore, the authorities appeared to turn a blind eye to the obvious possession of explosives by the Muslim Brotherhood.[42] Despite the very considerable powers granted to the prime minister under martial law (declared in May 1948), which he had used to arrest large numbers of communists and Wafdists, little was done against the Muslim Brotherhood. The suspicion must arise, therefore, that these attacks may have been tolerated by the government of al-Nuqrashi as a theatrical, if bloody accompaniment to the war in Palestine. Such a demonstrative use of violence and disorder had been seen before and may have been intended to symbolize the danger of the 'enemy within' – a useful myth to propagate when the military campaign was clearly running into difficulties.

However, al-Nuqrashi's contemplation of the potential consequences of a defeat in Palestine led him to re-examine the potential danger of the Muslim Brotherhood. Having used his powers under martial law to the full, by the autumn of 1948, al-Nuqrashi had little to fear from the Wafd's or the leftist groups' capacity to create disorder. Much of the communist movement was turned against itself on the controversial

Egypt 1945–52 127

question of the establishment of the state of Israel and the security services had in any case detained hundreds of those associated with the movement. By contrast, the Muslim Brotherhood was still at large and was well armed. Periodic discoveries of Muslim Brotherhood arms and explosives caches had been made, and the involvement of members of the Brotherhood in acts of assassination and intimidation unconnected with the Palestine question indicated that al-Banna saw himself as a major political player, heading an organization that would not hesitate to use violence to achieve its own aims.

With the series of defeats suffered by the Egyptian forces following the Israeli offensives of October 1948, the government looked ever more vulnerable in its handling of the Palestine campaign. It is in these circumstances that the security authorities began to move against the Muslim Brotherhood. During these investigations the extent and the nature of the Brotherhood's Secret Apparatus came to light, leading to the arrests of members of the Brotherhood and the brief detention of Hassan al-Banna.[43] For some in the Brotherhood, this was an unexpected turn of events. The reported reaction of one of those arrested in connection with the spate of bombings captures well the mood of indignation and suggests the encouragement hitherto given by the government to the activities of the Brotherhood.[44]

While the investigations were continuing, the Muslim Brotherhood tried to take the issue to the streets and organized large-scale and violent demonstrations on the emotive issues of Palestine and Sudan at the end of November. This led to a closure of Cairo University, but when it was reopened further demonstrations erupted on 4 December 1948, during which Salim Zaki, the Commandant of the Cairo Police, was killed. The police responded in kind and many casualties resulted.[45] The violence of this event and the threatened escalation of such violence with all that it implied for the disruption of public order, confirmed al-Nuqrashi in his determination to crush the Muslim Brotherhood. It also suggested that the Brotherhood was a challenger of the established order, using the threat of civil disorder for its own purposes. It seemed, therefore, to be playing by different rules, making it doubly dangerous.

Accordingly, within a few days, after having ensured that Egyptian army units first surrounded and neutralized the Brotherhood battalions on the Palestine front, al-Nuqrashi issued a proclamation ordering the dissolution of the Muslim Brotherhood and the seizure of its assets. At the same time, a report was issued by the Ministry of the Interior listing the alleged criminal activities of the Brotherhood, dating back to July 1946.[46] This was accompanied by extensive arrests of members of the Brotherhood and by intensive searches for the weapons and explosives that made the Brotherhood such a potentially dangerous player in the game of public disorder. The Brotherhood contemplated fighting the dissolution order by legal means and reportedly began to prepare a case which drew on documents proving that it was the government of al-Nuqrashi that had supplied the organization with the arms and ammunition in the first place.[47]

Whether authorized by al-Banna or not, some members of the Muslim Brotherhood had a different idea of how to fight their dissolution and one of their number assassinated al-Nuqrashi on 28 December 1948. The new prime minister, Ibrahim Abd al-Hadi, ordered further arrests of members of the Brotherhood and a series of violent incidents occurred as members of the Secret Apparatus of the Brotherhood took on the forces of the state which were now turned fully against them. Al-Banna sought unsuccessfully to dissociate himself from these events, reportedly alarmed at what the Secret Apparatus had become and eager to achieve a reconciliation with Abd al-Hadi. The latter, however, had other ideas and almost certainly with his authority, backed up by the palace, plans were reportedly drawn up by the undersecretary of state at the Ministry of the Interior, the chief of the CID and the Prime Minister's office for the assassination of al-Banna. In late January 1949, the police unit which had hitherto accompanied al-Banna for his protection was withdrawn and on 12 February 1949 he was gunned down in central Cairo.[48]

Unsurprisingly, no one was ever charged with his murder. As the authorities had possibly hoped, the disappearance of al-Banna threw the Brotherhood into confusion. Hundreds more members of the Brotherhood were arrested and in May the prime minister received parliamentary approval for the extension of the martial law legislation for a further year. This had followed further discoveries of arms caches belonging to the Brotherhood and by an alleged attempt by members of the Brotherhood to assassinate the prime minister.[49] The Muslim Brotherhood, by revealing itself as an organization that was prepared to use violence to achieve ends that seemed to encompass the elimination of senior members of the political elite, had overstepped the line of acceptable behaviour. It was manifestly not simply an organization that intended to remain subservient to its sponsors. Consequently, it felt the full force of the state deployed against it, eliminating it for some time as a threat to social order. Indeed, during 1949, with the Wafd now scenting the possibility of a return to power and the Muslim Brotherhood effectively neutralized, there was little incentive for the encouragement of civil disorder, even though the controversy of the defeat in Palestine and the unresolved question of British evacuation and the future of the Sudan remained very much alive.

Egypt 1945–52 129

THE LAST WAFDIST GOVERNMENT, 1950–52

Much the same situation obtained with the formation of the new Wafdist government, following the general elections of January 1950. Demonstrations were held periodically, but largely in support of the dominant faction of the Wafd and, as such, there was little incentive to stage public displays of civil disorder. A memorandum on the condition of public security, presented to the new government in January 1950 by the Special Section of the Ministry of the Interior, took a markedly relaxed view of the threats to public order. Only on the subject of the communist threat did the report suggest that there might be dangers in the future. Even here, however, it was suggested at the time that the Special Section might have been exaggerating the danger in order to secure funds and support from the new government.[50]

The Wafd government came to power with a large number of expectations among the general public about its capacity both to alleviate the economic situation of many and to realize Egypt's national goals, defined primarily as the final withdrawal of all British forces from the country and the unification of Egypt and Sudan. These expectations were also visible within the party itself where factions had formed during the previous years of opposition around leading individuals, but also around differing ideas about the direction in which the party should be heading. In such circumstances, although the party leadership could feel confident of controlling the immediate situation, there was a danger that the government would not be able to achieve as much as expected on either front and would therefore be faced by the combustible mixture of external opposition allied with dissident factions within the party. It was perhaps for this reason that al-Nahas went out of his way to conciliate the king during 1950, hoping to remove a factor that had bedevilled previous Wafdist governments. It was also possibly a necessary precaution in dealing with any eruption of civil disorder that the Wafd's opponents might have been tempted to organize in an effort to shake al-Nahas' hold on power.

The opportunity to do so was provided by the faltering of the Wafd government's negotiations with Britain on the question of military evacuation. By the autumn of 1950 it was becoming clear that British intransigence would not allow the Wafd to deliver at an early date the promised complete evacuation. In these circumstances, the utility of demonstration and disorder increased for government and opposition alike. Consequently, these months were filled by competing attempts by the Wafd government and its opponents, particularly the Saadists, to control the streets. Fuad Serag al-Din, the Wafdist minister of the interior, was determined to lay on demonstrations in support of the government and, in particular, in support of the points that the government was trying to get across to the British government concerning the renegotiation of the Treaty.

As on previous occasions, the mass demonstrations were organized to symbolize the fact that the nation stood firmly behind the Wafd government's position and was steadfast in demanding Egypt's national rights. They were staged to coincide with the meeting of the minister of foreign affairs, Muhammad Salah al-Din, with Ernest Bevin, to impress upon the latter the seriousness of the situation and the need for urgent action, since inaction was equally corrosive of the government's authority. Officially, demonstrations were banned, but unofficially Serag al-Din had issued instructions that they were to be allowed. This was further to give the impression that, despite the best endeavours of the Egyptian government's security forces, the force of public opinion was such that it could not be contained. However, in all this, it was crucial, if the government was not to suffer adverse reactions from the British, or indeed from the palace, that the demonstrations should not become serious disorders. To this end, strenuous efforts were made by the government to ensure its control of the demonstrations from within and not simply through an increased police presence.[51]

Ibrahim Abd al-Hadi, leader of the Saadists, on the other hand, was among the opponents of the Wafd actively seeking to encourage the demonstrators to attack cinemas, European business establishments and foreign embassies. It was thought at the time that they were attempting to place the Wafd in a dilemma similar to that which had brought down the government of al-Nuqrashi in February 1946: if the disorders occurred, they would weaken the Wafd's claim that it could maintain public order (a key element in the background to the possibility of British military withdrawal from Egypt); if, on the other hand, the government acted on its promise to break up all demonstrations by any means possible, violence would ensue and the scale of casualties would be considerable.[52] In the event, the various methods employed by Serag al-Din were sufficient to prevent the demonstrations from developing into full-scale civil disorders.

However, as the more violent demonstrations of January 1951 indicated, this was a difficult undertaking. It was complicated in this case by the fact that the people on whom Serag al-Din had hitherto relied to ensure demonstrations were turned to his advantage, had allied themselves with the leftist opposition to Serag al-Din within the Wafd. Their intention seemed to have been, therefore, as much to embarrass him as to place the government itself in a quandary. This dispute evidently gave the opponents of the Wafd considerable

Egypt 1945–52   131

leverage, although effective deployment of the security forces ensured that there was no escalation of the disorders.[53]

As the Wafd government's term of office continued, with nothing to show for its negotiations with Britain, pressures on the government increased. In these circumstances, the question of civil disorder arose once more, especially in view of the fact that the government's good relations with the king had broken down and a more familiar wary mutual suspicion had begun to reassert itself. Demonstrations could be used both to show up the inadequacy of the Wafd government on this and on other fronts, and to provide an occasion for provoking the kinds of disorders which the king had used previously as a pretext for dismissing governments. The violent demonstrations of late August 1951 marking the anniversary of the signature of the 1936 Anglo–Egyptian Treaty showed that disorder was never far below the surface. However, they also indicated that the Ministry of the Interior was well able to keep the situation under control. In part this may have been due to the public re-emergence of the Muslim Brotherhood and its consequent need for a degree of official patronage as it took its case for the restoration of its property through the courts.[54]

The Wafd government's decision on 8 October 1951 to abrogate the 1936 Anglo–Egyptian Treaty and the 1899 Condominium Agreement on Sudan gave the impression that it had now seized the initiative. The Wafd had symbolically reappropriated its role as leader of the most intransigent element in the nationalist movement and was now committed to putting pressure on Britain through direct action to grant the demands for evacuation and unity of the Nile Valley, which the British had rejected in the course of negotiations. In view of the respective resources at the disposal of the Egyptian and the British governments, this was going to be an unequal struggle.

However, it was clear that the Egyptian government did not have a military strategy in mind at the time, whether based on regular or irregular formations. It was in these circumstances, therefore, that the symbolic forms of direct action became important, although, as became apparent, even these could have real and violent consequences. For the Wafd government, it was imperative that it should remain in control of the demonstrations, since it was only too well aware of the possible consequences for its own position of the breakdown of order. Consequently, the government's security forces maintained control and even the violence associated with the large demonstrations of October was described at the time as artificial in comparison with the events of 1947 and 1948.[55]

The Muslim Brotherhood, although conspicuous in the demonstrations, echoed the government's repeated assertion that disorder would

132   *Demise of the British Empire in the Middle East*

be against the national interest. In part, this may have been due to the concern at the time that Britain was looking for a pretext to reoccupy much of Egypt. The situation in the cities of the Canal Zone, where the British military forces were asserting increasing *de facto* control, tended to bear this out.[56] However, the acquiescence of the Muslim Brotherhood may have been due also to the influence of the newly elected Supreme Guide, Hassan al-Hudaybi, as well as to the feelers that were reportedly being extended to the Brotherhood by the Wafd government.[57]

The government continued its efforts to bring all aspects of the 'demonstrative struggle' under its control. This involved principally the recruitment, arming and dispatch to the Canal Zone of 'Liberation Battalions' (*Kata'ib al-Tahrir*), which were ostensibly dedicated to a guerrilla war of liberation against the British forces stationed there. Begun in October in the first enthusiasm of the abrogation of the Treaty, these battalions were initially organized by various groups and parties, in particular the Muslim Brotherhood and the Socialist Party (formerly the Young Egypt Party) of Ahmad Husayn. The government did not want to suppress this apparently popular manifestation of anger against the British and thought that the theatricality of the recruitment and dedication of these groups could serve much the same symbolic purpose as the demonstrations of the time. On the other hand, as with the demonstrations, they were clearly apprehensive about the possibility that the groups might come under the control of the Wafd's opponents and might be used therefore to embarrass and undermine the government.[58]

The massive demonstrations of November 1951 to mark 'National Struggle Day' passed off peacefully. They seemed to show that Serag al-Din's twin tactics of putting a strong police presence on the streets and of bribing those who might have been tempted to turn the event into one of more general disorder had worked. He used the occasion to announce that the government would now take on the responsibility of organizing and training the Liberation Battalions.[59] This angered some, and may have contributed to the violent demonstrations that erupted in Cairo and Alexandria in early December 1951. Called in protest against a clash between British forces and Egyptian police in the Canal Zone, the demonstrations developed into widespread anti-government disorders in which clashes with the police left a substantial number of casualties on both sides. The Muslim Brotherhood reportedly played a large part in these disorders and it may have been in part a response to the pressure that al-Hudaybi was under both from within the organization and from the government to 'commit the Muslim Brotherhood to battle'.[60] Unwilling to take any further chances in view of the deteriorating situation in the Canal Zone, Serag al-Din promptly banned all further demonstrations throughout Egypt. The ban was

*Egypt 1945–52*133

strictly enforced, except in the cases of Wafdist-inspired demonstrations. In addition, he introduced measures to ensure tighter control of the Liberation Battalions.[61]

These now played a more active part in attacking British forces in the Canal Zone. Whether officially organized by the government or by the Muslim Brotherhood and others with government support, the Liberation Battalions closely co-operated with the police and particularly with the units of the *Baluk al-Nizam* (Auxiliary Police) drafted into the Canal Zone at the beginning of the crisis. The role of the police was heightened by the strategy of the government. Not only did they facilitate the operations of the Liberation Battalions and help to enforce the labour and trade boycotts of British military installations, they were also expected by Serag al-Din and the government to confront the British forces directly. In this respect, they stood in for the Egyptian army, which was carefully kept out of any direct confrontation with British troops.[62]

This strategy, useful as it was for the government, placed the police in an invidious position. They were clearly no match for the British armed forces, who were deeply suspicious of them after the clashes of November 1951. In early December, a police unit came to the assistance of some Egyptian civilians who had attacked a British army unit and as a result suffered a number of casualties. A few days later, the police were ordered by Serag al-Din to prevent the British military authorities from demolishing the hamlet of Kafr Abduh even if it meant fighting to the last man. However, faced by overwhelming British force, the police units withdrew. A similar incident at Al-Hamada, where the police surrendered to the British forces rather than fight against impossible odds, led to the court-martialling of their commanding officer. Consequently, when, in January 1952, the British military authorities finally decided to act against the Auxiliary Police in Ismailiyya by demanding the surrender of their weapons and their expulsion from the Canal Zone, it was not surprising that Serag al-Din ordered them to resist, even though they were outnumbered and outgunned. The result was the death of over 50 policemen, with scores more wounded in the battle that ensued on 25 January 1952.[63]

The government was facing mounting pressure to escalate the struggle in the Canal Zone at the time, in the absence of any other strategy. The Muslim Brotherhood was becoming more actively involved and Ahmad Husayn of the Socialist Party came out in strong criticism of the government, calling for its overthrow and helping to organize demonstrations in which for the first time for some years firearms were used against the police. Sensing that the government was losing the initiative on the streets and concerned lest the hostility of the Socialist

134   *Demise of the British Empire in the Middle East*

Party indicated covert palace sponsorship, as on previous occasions, the government had ordered the closure of all schools and universities for a week, beginning on 21 January 1952.[64] It was in the midst of these events that the aforementioned incident had occurred in Ismailiyya and, given these preoccupations, it appeared that Serag al-Din and the Wafd government were prepared to sacrifice the Auxiliary Police as a symbol of their own steadfastness and resolve.

The next day, on 26 January 1952, in Cairo, the Auxiliary Police staged a mass demonstration of protest in front of the Abdin Palace. Some went to the university to encourage the students to demonstrate, in protest not only against the British action in Ismailiyya, but also against the government. In some cases they were joined by the regular police, who had been threatening strike action over pay and conditions for some weeks. Since the Auxiliary Police were the main force responsible for the suppression of riots, this mutiny effectively deprived the government of its usual defence against serious disorder. In fact, it was reported at the time that Serag al-Din had given explicit orders that the demonstration was to be allowed to run its course and Abd al-Fatah Hassan Pasha (minister of social affairs) had even addressed the demonstrating policemen in an attempt to win them over to the side of the government, promising that he would soon join them in the streets. Abd al-Fatah Hassan had also reportedly entered into clandestine negotiations with Ahmad Husayn (possibly on behalf of Serag al-Din) the night before to persuade him to stage an anti-British demonstration of limited scope that day as a follow up to the theatrical if bloody events in the Canal Zone.[65] It appeared, as was suggested at the time, that Serag al-Din had wanted a controlled form of protest demonstration that would deflect the anger of the police and others towards the British and away from the government.

In fact, with the ending of the demonstration by the Auxiliary Police at midday a very different kind of disorder erupted and developed into the events that have come to be known as the 'Burning of Cairo'. Organized groups of men started to appear and carried out apparently prearranged arson attacks on a large number of buildings in central Cairo. Many of these, but by no means the majority, had some association with the British presence in Egypt, commercial or otherwise. These organized gangs were soon joined by crowds on the look out for an opportunity to loot or, as in the case of many of the members of the Muslim Brotherhood involved in the rioting, intent on destroying hated symbols of Western affluence and corruption. Not only were the rioters unchecked by the police, but in many cases they were joined and led by policemen. Furthermore, it was reported that senior police officers

Egypt 1945–52 135

on the spot were conspicuous by their inaction. The Assistant Commander of the Cairo Police was reported as having said tolerantly 'Let the boys have their fun' when asked at the time why he was doing nothing to prevent the arson and looting.[66]

Eventually, the Egyptian army was called in to restore order, but not before the arson and looting had continued for nearly five hours in the centre of Cairo, causing a large number of deaths and a great amount of damage. Serag al-Din was later to claim that he had tried to get the army on to the streets earlier to restore order, but had been prevented from doing so by the king, who had, through the Chief of Staff, Haydar Pasha, suggested that this was a political matter. In other words, it appeared that the king, by now at odds with the Wafdist government, was determined to use the pretext of the riots to dismiss al-Nahas – the very situation which Serag al-Din had been trying to avoid.[67] The following day, after martial law had been declared, the king dismissed the Wafd government and entrusted Ali Maher with the formation of a new administration.

To say that the king exploited the situation of civil disorder to dispose of the Wafd government is not to say that he organized it. In fact, it seems certain that the initial arson attacks were organized by members of the Socialist Party and other associates of Ahmad Husayn. It is possible that they were working in the knowledge that they had the approval of the political opponents of the Wafd government, who would then exploit the situation they had created. However, as a member of the Muslim Brotherhood was later to state, 'the [Socialist] Party had had so much help from Serag al-Din in the form of money, arms, incendiary equipment and police protection that organizing events on 26 January had not been difficult. Right up to the end Serag al-Din had been stupid enough to believe that these facilities would be used in the Canal Zone. He had expected and wanted a riot in Cairo on 26 January, but only a "normal riot".'[68]

Serag al-Din had played the game of public disorder and lost disastrously. In part this was because he had overestimated the degree to which his methods allowed him to control the crowds under the tense circumstances of the time. In part it was because he had effectively provoked a mutiny of the very police force that was intended to protect public order and thus the credibility and authority of the Wafd government. He had thus provided the opportunity for all those forces opposed to the Wafd government to seize the moment – the Socialist Party, the Muslim Brotherhood and others by rioting, and the king by withholding the use of the armed forces and finally by holding the Wafd government ultimately responsible for the disorder.

CONCLUSION

It was remarkable, but also significant that the disorders and violence of January came to an abrupt end after the fall of the Wafd government. Ali Maher, the new prime minister, assisted by the king's nominee Murtada al-Maraghi as minister of the interior, ensured that there would be no further public disorder. All demonstrations were confined to the campus of the university; the campaign against the British forces in the Canal Zone was called off and the Liberation Battalions were transferred to the Ministry of War, where they were brought under tight control and effectively neutralized; the Cairo police force was purged; a motorized riot-control force was established – in short, Ali Maher made the most of his powers under Martial Law to restore order and public confidence in the stability of the regime.[69] Despite the rapid turnover of prime ministers during the following six months,[70] caused largely by their disagreements with King Faruq, there were no serious disorders, merely a few demonstrations of a very limited nature.

In large measure, this was because it no longer seemed very useful to any of the principal players to encourage serious disorder. Al-Hilali's pursuit of the members of the former Wafdist administration kept them off balance. It is also possible that the events of January 1952 had shaken the Wafdist leaders' belief in their capacity to maintain control of civil disorder. The Muslim Brotherhood was experiencing a barely suppressed internal dispute about the merits of violence as a means of achieving their ends. Al-Hudaybi and some of the other leaders were discouraging thoughts of violent action, while the advocates of the use of force were retreating into the covert world of the Secret Apparatus. Meanwhile, Ahmad Husayn had shown his hand in January and, together with many of his party's members, he had been detained under the provisions of martial law. In May 1952, Ahmad Husayn and five other members of the party were indicted for instigating the riots of 26 January.[71]

Unbeknown to most of the participants, the game had moved out of the symbolic realm of staged public disorders. However, in a number of important respects the encouragement of such disorders had helped to set in motion currents within the armed forces that were to contribute to the Free Officers' *coup d'état* of July 1952. In the first place, the ambivalence of the Wafd government towards the 'liberation struggle' against the British in the Canal Zone had created feelings of resentment within the officer corps. The Wafd's strategy of maintaining control of the streets and some vestige of nationalist credibility through the raising of Liberation Battalions and their deployment in sporadic fashion against the British, while the Egyptian army was kept well out of the

Egypt 1945–52 137

fight, appeared to younger Egyptian army officers to be placing them in a deeply humiliating position.[72] These feelings of resentment appear to have been compounded, as far as the Free Officers were concerned, by the deployment of the armed forces to suppress civil disorder in Cairo in January. The continued reliance on the armed forces during the months that followed to sustain martial law and to prevent further disturbances seemed a perversion of their duty: rather than taking on the British, they were being ordered to discipline their compatriots. According to later accounts by some of the Free Officers this was an important factor in causing them to think of carrying out a *coup d'état*.[73]

No less important and indeed crucial for the sequence of events that precipitated the *coup d'état* itself, was King Faruq's determination to use his powers of patronage to ensure that he retained personal control of the armed forces. This, too, could be said in some measure to have been an outcome of the encouragement of civil disorder and of the possibility that the king himself would increasingly become the object of hostile demonstrations. At various times during the preceding years slogans hostile to the king and to the dynasty had been raised. It seemed only a matter of time before the game of demonstration and disorder, which had been used hitherto largely to impress upon the king the incompetence of the government of the day, would be used to threaten him directly. In such circumstances, it seemed all the more important that the king should be able to rely on the personal loyalty of the officer corps, above and beyond its allegiance to him as monarch. At the same time, the palace was aware that there were currents of disloyalty in the officer corps, motivated in part by the same animosities that caused students, workers and others to demonstrate on the streets of Cairo and Alexandria.[74] In 1952, the king's attempt to root out suspected disloyalty and to place his protégés in positions of command, whether in the Officers' Club or in the Ministry of Defence, finally persuaded the Free Officers that they would have to launch their coup immediately or suffer the consequences of discovery.[75]

It could be argued, therefore, that the Free Officers acted both in response to the symbolic power of the staged disorders of the time, and as a result of the structural logic of the uses of disorder within Egyptian politics. Symbolically, the disorders conveyed the image of a system unable, indeed unwilling, to handle the aspirations of the thousands who had come out on the streets at various times to demonstrate their rejection of the *status quo*. For much of the elite this was not so much a lost message, as an irrelevant one. Their game was, after all, more intimately concerned with the preoccupations of a narrow circle of the powerful. However, for those officers who were close to the political movements that had been so instrumental in organizing the disorders,

138　　　　　　　　　*Demise of the British Empire in the Middle East*

the very theatricality of the demonstrations represented a willingness on the part of the powerful elite that had devised the rules of this game to sacrifice those whom they had encouraged and to deploy the armed forces to save the situation when things failed to go according to plan. Patronage was the instrument intended to keep the officers subservient to the principal players and beneficiaries of this game. Like others before them, the officers became aware of their exploitation at the hands of the establishment.

However, as they showed in July 1952, they were able to do something decisive about it, relying on the power of organized armed force and on general disillusionment with the regime that they had come to overthrow. As the following years made abundantly clear, the young officers had also learned lessons about the importance of the politics of demonstration and disorder from the old regime and some of them became even more adept at managing the theatre of mass politics. Nevertheless, the most skilled practitioner among them, Gamal Abd al-Nasir, was quick to appreciate that street theatre was no substitute for a firm and unchallenged hold on the state security services.

NOTES

1　In other cases, as the Wafd discovered in 1937 and Ali Maher and his allies discovered in 1941–42, they could backfire disastrously. Muhammad Husayn Haykal *Mudhakkirat fi al-Siyasa al-Misriyya, Part II 1937–1952* (Cairo: Matba'a Misr, 1953) pp. 45–58 and 218–26.
2　J. P. Jankowski, *Egypt's Young Rebels – 'Young Egypt' 1933–1952* (Stanford, CA: Hoover Institution Press, 1975) pp. 21–7, 38–40; R. P. Mitchell, *The Society of the Muslim Brothers* (London: Oxford University Press, 1969) pp. 15–32; C. Tripp, *Contemporary Egypt: through Egyptian Eyes* (London: Routledge, 1993) pp. 55–67.
3　See Tariq al-Bishri, *Al-Haraka al-Siyasiyya fi Misr 1945–1952* (2nd edn) (Cairo: Dar al-Shuruq, 1983) pp. 75–91, 208–25.
4　Smart to FO, 1 November 1945, FO 371/45928 J3955/3/16.
5　Bowker to FO, 3 October 1945, FO 371/45926 J3402/3/16.
6　Russell Pasha to Bowker, 12 November 1945, FO 371/45928 J4078/3/16.
7　Fitzpatrick (Cairo City Police) to al-Nuqrashi Pasha, 4 November 1945; Fitzpatrick to Russell Pasha, 11 November 1945; Killearn to Bevin, 18 November 1945 – all in FO 371/45928 J4078/3/16.
8　In Alexandria the disturbances associated with the demonstrations and looting were more violent and resulted in the deaths of at least one policeman and five civilians – British Embassy Situation Report (AGD/DMcC), 2 November 1945, FO 141/1009 24/1/45. See also Fitzpatrick to al-Nuqrashi Pasha, 4 November 1945, FO 141/1009 24/38/45. This is the copy of the report that he sent to the British Embassy and on which he had written by hand the comment, 'I am strongly of the opinion that this raid was organised by a master mind to embarrass the present Government'. The fact that a certain number of those who were arrested proved to be workers from Shubra al-Khaima who were on strike at the time and that they had apparently come well equipped to break shop windows, etc., suggested a certain forethought and organization.
9　Killearn to Bevin, 5 January 1946, FO 371/53330 J143/57/16; Killearn to Bevin, 2 February 1946, FO 371/53330 J487/57/16.
10　Killearn to Bevin, 9 February 1946, FO 371/53330 J582/57/16.
11　Bowker to Bevin, 16 February 1946, FO 371/53330 J670/57/16.

Egypt 1945–52   139

12 Bowker to FO, 18 February 1946, FO 371/53282 J689/39/16; Bowker to FO, 18 February 1946, FO 371/53282 J766/39/16.
13 H. Erlich, *Students and University in Twentieth-Century Egyptian Politics* (London: Frank Cass, 1989) pp. 156–7.
14 Bowker to FO, 23 February 1946, FO 371/53330 J802/57/16; Russell Pasha to Cairo Embassy, 22 February 1946, FO 371/53288 J1125/39/16; P. J. Vatikiotis review article, 'The New Western Historiography of Modern Egypt', *Middle Eastern Studies*, 27, 2 (April 1991) pp. 324–5.
15 Bowker to FO, 22 February 1946, FO 371/53282 J771/39/16; Bowker to FO, 1 March 1946, FO 371/53286 J925/39/16.
16 FO to Cairo Embassy, 9 March 1946, FO 371/53287 J1012/39/16. For the events in Alexandria see Killearn to FO, 4 March 1946, FO 371/53286 J964/39/16; Bowker to FO, 5 March 1946, FO 371/53287 J1003/39/16.
17 Thistlethwaite (Box 500) relaying report from security-services representative in Cairo, 27 March 1946, FO 371/53289 J1416/39/16.
18 Campbell to FO, 5 May 1946, FO 371/53331 J1992/57/16.
19 Campbell to FO, 14 June 1946, FO 371/53331 J2700/57/16.
20 Campbell to FO, 18 April 1946, FO 371/53331 J1737/57/16; Campbell to FO, 9 July 1946, FO 371/53305 J3052/39/16; Campbell to FO, 12 July 1946, FO 371/53331 J3080/57/16.
21 Campbell to FO 13 May 1946, FO 371/53331 J2139/57/16; Jenkins (DSO) to Cairo Embassy, 12 June 1946, FO 371/53304 J2879/39/16; Campbell to FO, 22 June 1946, FO 371/53331 J2813/57/16; Campbell to FO, 17 July 1946, FO 371/53307 J3186/39/16; Campbell to FO, 20 July 1946, FO 371/53307 J3181/39/16; Campbell to FO, 22 July 1946, FO 371/53307 J3186/39/16. Eventually, after a series of discoveries and denunciations, most of the group responsible were arrested, Campbell to FO, 3 August 1946, FO 371/53309 J3420/39/16.
22 J. Beinin and Z. Lockman, *Workers on the Nile* (Princeton, NJ: Princeton University Press, 1987) pp. 310–42.
23 Campbell to FO, 12 July 1946, FO 371/53306 J3098/39/16.
24 Beinin and Lockman, *Workers*, pp. 348–50; Campbell to FO, 12 July 1946, FO 371/53331 J3080/57/16; Campbell to FO, 12 July 1946, FO 371/53327 J3066/53/16; Bowker to FO, 21 October 1946, FO 371/53327 J4464/53/16.
25 Bowker to FO, 14 October 1946, FO 371/53314 J4237/39/16; Campbell to FO, 11 October 1946, FO 371/53331 J4263/57/16; Bowker to FO, 25 October 1946, FO 371/53331 J4450/57/16; Shotter (Box 500) to FO, 13 January 1946, relaying DSO report for November 1946, FO 371/62961 J283/12/16.
26 Bowker to FO, 16 October 1946, FO 371/53315 J4314/39/16; Thistlethwaite (Box 500), 10 February 1947, relaying DSO report for December 1946, FO 371/62990 J722/13/16; Erlich, *Students*, pp. 160–1.
27 Jenkins DSO report, 9 March 1946, FO 371/53327 J1565/53/16; Bowker to FO, 11 March 1946, FO 371/53288 J1256/39/16; Campbell to FO, 22 June 1946, FO 371/53303 J2833/39/16; Campbell to FO, 7 August 1946, FO 371/53309 J3487/39/16.
28 Bowker to FO, 30 November 1946, FO 371/53331 J5075/57/16.
29 Thistlethwaite (Box 500), 10 February 1947, relaying DSO report for December 1946, FO 371/62990 J722/13/16.
30 Bowker to FO, 13 December 1946, FO 371/53332 J5330/57/16; Bowker to FO, 20 December 1946, FO 371/53332 J5430/57/16; Campbell to FO, 28 December 1946, FO 371/53332 J5504/57/16.
31 Mitchell, *Muslim Brothers* p. 53; Mahmud Abd al-Halim, *Al-Ikhwan al-Muslimun – Ahdath Sana'at al-Ta'rikh*, Part I (Alexandria: Dar al-Da'wa, 1979) pp. 475–81.
32 Beinin and Lockman, *Workers*, pp. 352–8, 375–82; T. Y. Ismael and Rifa'at El-Said, *The Communist Movement in Egypt 1920–1988* (Syracuse, NY: Syracuse University Press, 1990) pp. 59–62.
33 Mitchell, *Muslim Brothers*, pp. 32, 39–48.
34 Bowker to FO, 6 September 1947, FO 371/62993 J4351/13/16.
35 Bowker to FO, 18 October 1947, FO 371/63021 J5178/79/16; Mitchell, *Muslim Brothers*, pp. 55–7.
36 Campbell to FO, 9 December 1947, FO 371/63021 J6107/79/16; Campbell to FO, 20 December 1947, FO 371/63021 J6377/79/16.
37 Chapman Andrews to FO, 20 January 1948, FO 371/69210 J411/68/16.

140   Demise of the British Empire in the Middle East

38   Campbell to FO, 5 April 1948, FO 371/69210 J2324/68/16; Campbell to FO, 5 April 1948, FO 371/69210 J2326/68/16; Campbell to FO, 6 April 1948, FO 371/69210 J2364/68/16; Campbell to FO, 7 April 1948, FO 371/69210 J2468/68/16; Summerhayes (Consul-General, Alexandria) to Campbell, 7 April 1948, FO 371/69210 J2689/68/16; Watson to Heron (FO), 13 April 1948, FO 371/69210 J2765/68/16.
39   Campbell to FO, 7 April 1948, FO 371/69210 J2468/68/16.
40   Watson to Heron (FO), 13 April 1948, FO 371/69210 J2765/68/16.
41   Chapman Andrews to FO, 20 June 1948, FO 371/69210 J4305/68/16.
42   Mitchell, *Muslim Brothers*, pp. 63–4; Campbell to McNeil (FO), 3 December 1948, FO 371/69212 J7886/68/16.
43   Campbell to McNeil (FO), 3 December 1948, FO 371/69212 J7886/68/16.
44   A report from one of the British security-service representatives alleges that the arrested member of the Brotherhood told the state prosecutor: 'I am surprised that you arrest us for blowing up Jewish shops when the government was encouraging us to do so. More than this – the authorities used to return to us all explosives found when we alleged that they were destined for Palestine. But it now seems that the government wishes to hide other crimes for which we are not responsible', 'Old Man' to Cairo Embassy, 30 November 1948, FO 141/1271 172/58/48.
45   Campbell to FO, 4 December 1948, FO 371/69211 J7749/68/16; Campbell to FO, 5 December 1948, FO 371/69211 J7782/68/16.
46   Extract from *Le Journal d'Egypte*, 9 December 1948, in FO 141/1271 172/63/48.
47   *Le Journal d'Egypte*, 20 December 1948, in FO 141/1271 172/73/48; FO 141/1271 172/77/48.
48   Security-services representative to Tomlinson (Cairo Embassy), 14 February 1949 and 17 February 1949, FO 371/73463 J1633/1015/16.
49   Report of meeting at the British Embassy, Cairo to discuss internal security, 16 February 1949, FO 141/1370 517/2/49G; Campbell to FO, 30 April 1949, FO 371/73464 J3686/1015/16; Campbell to FO, 6 May 1949, FO 371/73464 J3783/1015/16 The alleged attempt on Abd al-Hadi's life was so inefficiently carried out and came so fortuitously a few days before parliament had to decide on the question of martial law that some doubt must remain as to whether it was a genuine attempt to assassinate the prime minister.
50   Special Section memorandum, 12 January 1950, FO 141/1391 1019/1/50.
51   Campbell to FO, 16 November 1950, FO 371/80349 JE1016/66; Sansom reports of 24 November 1950 and of 25 November 1950, FO 371/80349 JE1016/71.
52   Sansom reports of 24 November 1950 and of 25 November 1950, and Wardle-Smith to Allen (FO) 5 December 1950, FO 371/80349 JE1016/71.
53   Chapman Andrews memorandum, 22 January 1951, and Stevenson to FO, 12 February 1951, FO 141/1434 1013/2/51G.
54   Stevenson to FO, 26 August 1951, FO 371/90115 JE10110/25; Stevenson to Morrison, 5 September 1951, FO 371/90115 JE10110/26; Mitchell, *Muslim Brothers*, pp. 82–4.
55   Stevenson to FO, 9 October 1951, FO 371/90115 JE10110/28; Stevenson to FO, 10 October 1951, FO 371/90116 JE10110/31; Stevenson to FO, 16 October 1951, FO 371/90116 JE10110/35; Kemp (Acting Consul-General, Alexandria), 12 October 1951 and Stevenson to Morrison, 26 October 1951, FO 371/90118 JE10110/88.
56   Stevenson to FO, 19 October 1951, FO 371/90116 JE10110/45; Stevenson to Morrison, 26 October 1951, FO 371/90118 JE10110/88; General Erskine to Stevenson, 16 October 1951, FO 141/1439 1041/2/8/51G; Consul (Port Said) to Cairo Embassy, 17 October 1951, FO 141/1439 1041/2/49/51G.
57   Mitchell, *Muslim Brothers*, pp. 85–9; Stevenson memorandum, 25 October 1951, FO 141/1440 1041/2/108/51G.
58   C-in-C, Middle East to Ministry of Defence, 27 October 1951, FO 141/1440 1041/2/135/51G; Morris report, 7 November 1951, FO 371/90119 JE10110/106.
59   Stevenson to FO, 13 November 1951, FO 371/90118 JE10110/99; Stevenson to FO, 13 November 1951, FO 371/90118 JE10110/113; Serag al-Din was reported to have paid Ahmad Husayn a very substantial sum of money in part to win over the Socialist Party, in part to act as a counter to his Wafdist colleague, Salah al-Din, who was busy cultivating the Muslim Brotherhood – Morris report, 7 November 1951, FO 371/90119 JE10110/106.
60   Stewart memorandum, 4 December 1951, FO 141/1450 10112/3/51G; Stevenson to FO, 3 December 1951, FO 371/90120 JE10110/147; Chancery to African Department, 6 December 1951, FO 371/90122 JE10110/195.

Egypt 1945–52 141

61 Stevenson to FO, 6 December 1951, FO 371/90120 JE10110/155; Stevenson to FO, 8 December 1951, FO 371/90121 JE10110/177.
62 Stevenson to FO, 20 December 1951, FO 371/90123 JE10110/218.
63 Rapp (BMEO) to FO, 30 November 1951, FO 371/90120 JE10110/143; Stevenson to FO, 3 December 1951, FO 371/90120 JE10110/147; Stevenson to FO, 3 December 1951, FO 371/90120 JE10110/149; Report of the British Embassy Committee of Enquiry into the Riots in Cairo on 26 January 1952, p. 3, FO 371/96873 JE1018/86.
64 Stevenson to FO, 21 January 1952, FO 371/96870 JE1018/5; Stevenson to FO, 26 January 1952, FO 371/96870 JE1018/6.
65 Report of the British Embassy Committee of Enquiry into the Riots in Cairo on 26 January 1952, pp. 3–4, 33–4, FO 371/96873 JE1018/86.
66 Report of the British Embassy Committee of Enquiry into the Riots in Cairo on 26 January 1952, pp. 4–15, FO 371/96873 JE1018/86. Imam Bey had spent much of his time in the Political Police and was regarded as a protégé of Serag al-Din. This reinforced the view that none of the usual government orders had been issued to counter the possibility of riots. See Russell Pasha report, 5 February 1952, Report of the British Embassy Committee of Enquiry into the Riots in Cairo on 26 January 1952, Appendix B, p. 44 FO 371/96873 JE1018/86.
67 Hamilton memorandum on conversation with 'Former Interior Person', 13 February 1952, FO 141/1453 1011/15/52G; Murray memorandum on conversation with Gallad Pasha, 7 February 1952, FO 141/1453 1011/21/52G.
68 Chancery to African Department, 18 February 1952, FO 371/96872 JE1018/78.
69 Stevenson memorandum, 7 February 1952, FO 141/1453 1011/15/52G; Stevenson to FO, 2 March 1952, FO 371/96873 JE1018/98; Stevenson to Eden, 10 March 1952, FO 371/96874 JE1018/92.
70 Ali Maher's government fell in the first week of March, to be succeeded by Nagib al-Hilali, whose adminstration lasted until late June, when he was replaced by Husayn Sirri, who resigned on 20 July to give way to al-Hilali once again. The Free Officers' *coup d'état* of 23 July restored Ali Maher to the premiership.
71 Stevenson to FO, 13 May 1952, FO 371/96875 JE1018/152 The trial began in the second half of May, but was suspended for some weeks by the July *coup d'état*. It resumed in September 1952, but was suspended again in November, when the defendants were released without bail. In April 1953 all charges were dropped.
72 Stevenson to FO, 8 December 1951, FO 371/90121 JE10110/172.
73 Kamal al-Din Rif'at, *Harb al-Tahrir al-Wataniyya* (Cairo: Dar al-Kitab al-Arabi li-l-Taba'a wa-l-Nashr, 1968) pp. 158–75; Abd al-Latif al-Baghdadi, *Mudhakkirat*, Vol. 1 (Cairo: Al-Maktab al-Misri al-Hadith, 1977) pp. 44–5.
74 There had long been a tradition of pamphleteering within the Egyptian armed forces, presumably as a way of communicating grievances without being traceable. This was not a very conspiratorial way of proceeding, but it gave some indication to the authorities of the nature of the currents of dissent within the armed forces and often allowed them to act accordingly. See Kellar (MI5) to FO, 20 November 1945, FO 371/45928 J4006/3/16, enclosing pamphlet from the 'National Liberation Movement of Egypt – Army Division Section'; also Killearn to FO, 11 January 1946, FO 371/53327 J268/53/16, enclosing a translation of the leftist and anti-monarchical pamphlet *Al-Haqiqa*; see also Hoda Gamal Abdel al-Nasir, *Britain and the Egyptian Nationalist Movement 1936–1952* (Reading: Ithaca Press, 1994) Appendices 12, 13, 14, 15, 18, 20, 21, 22, pp. 311–34.
75 J. Gordon, *Al-Nasir's Blessed Movement: Egypt's Free Officers and the July Revolution* (Oxford: Oxford University Press, 1992) pp. 49–52.

8

Britain and the Egyptian problem, 1945–48

JOHN KENT

At the end of the Second World War the British position in the Suez Base, formalized under the 1936 Anglo–Egyptian Treaty, was already a problem. It was a problem British policy-makers first had to address in the context of the strategic and power-political changes brought about by the Second World War. Inevitably, preserving a position in Egypt became linked to a number of issues central to Britain's position as a world power and to the nature of informal empire. Thus the practical questions associated with the maintenance and role of what was the largest military base in the world, with installations outside the areas authorized by the 1936 treaty and with troops far in excess of the permitted 10,000, actually involved more general concerns.

There is now a substantial body of literature on the Egyptian base, which has examined its significance for Anglo–Egyptian relations.[1] The tendency has been to portray the policy of the British governments in terms of the well-known reformist initiatives linked to the retreat from empire which, in the Middle Eastern case, were apparently first revealed at the conference of officials arranged by Bevin in September 1945.[2] This established the British Middle East Office, in order, among other things, to promote the social and economic development of the region. With Bevin's natural commitment to the under-privileged in Egypt, as elsewhere, this could have provided the basis for the development of a new Anglo–Egyptian relationship in sharp contrast to the old regime of pashas and court followers which surrounded King Faruq and had often been supported and manipulated by the British.

However, while looking forward to a new social and economic order in Egypt linked to the end of old-fashioned exploitative capitalism, Bevin was also a dedicated imperialist eager to re-establish Britain as a great world power and as a post-war equal to the United States and the Soviet Union.[3] This meant not only resisting Soviet attempts to expand their power and influence in the Dardanelles and the Mediterranean,

Britain and the Egyptian problem, 1945–48

but also preserving Britain's position as the dominant regional power in the Middle East.

Another tendency has been to link the preservation of a British military role in Egypt and the Middle East to the strategic importance of the region in any future war with the Soviet Union.[4] Much less has been written on how the practical constraints produced by Britain's post-war military and economic weakness affected policy to Egypt (thus revealing the true motives of decision-makers) and to Middle Eastern defence. In particular, the linkage between Egyptian policy and strategic planning has not been fully explored, with too many planning documents taken at face value and too little attention given to the perceptions of Great Power status and prestige, which were the main considerations of British policy-makers in the post-war period.

In 1945, the linkage between world-power status, defence strategy and policy to Egypt was revealed in the growing hostility between Britain and the Soviet Union. As the military assumed the Soviet Union could be the only possible enemy in any future global war, they defined the Middle East's importance as an area from which strategic bombing raids could be launched on the Soviet Union, and which it was necessary to defend in order to avoid any threat to the African continent. Sub-Saharan Africa, along with the British Isles, the Western hemisphere and the Antipodean dominions, was regarded as a main wartime support area. Yet the original source of the idea (the PHP [Post Hostilities Planning] paper of early 1945) of Egyptian airfields being used for strategic bombers was looking forward to the post-1955 period.[5] It was an early example of the British tendency to plan for a future period in the hope that the resources would be available to implement the plans.

In the immediate post-war years British Lincoln bombers could hardly reach the Soviet Union from the Middle East. As modified Lancasters the Lincolns were unsuitable for strategic bombing of Soviet targets as they could fly no higher than 19,000 feet. Moreover, the trials in 1946 revealed a large number of problems,[6] and by 1948 it was accepted that British bombers would not be used in a strategic role against the Soviet Union.[7] As one RAF policy-maker pointed out, the B-29 was the only allied aircraft that could hit essential targets in Russia.[8] Unfortunately, the American B-29s required longer runways than those available in Egypt before 1951.[9]

Given that intelligence estimates predicted the Soviets would not be capable of waging global war before the end of 1956, the short-term need to prepare for a war with the Soviet Union was less important than the need to be perceived as the leading regional power in the Middle East. This was deemed to depend on exclusive British responsibility for the defence of the region through which ran one of the key symbols of

British imperialism – the Suez Canal. The first threat to this came not from the military might of the Soviet Union but from the wartime deputy prime minister who became the head of the post-war Labour government in the summer of 1945. In 1944, Attlee, in his capacity as chairman of the Suez Canal Committee, had suggested international arrangements for the defence of the Suez Canal Zone. Such ideas were not acceptable to the Conservative members of the committee and the matter was referred to the cabinet.

In preparation for this, Foreign Secretary Anthony Eden and Sir E. Grigg, later Lord Altrincham, the minister resident in the Middle East, submitted memoranda for the cabinet.[10] For Eden, Middle East defence responsibilities had to remain exclusively in British hands because the defence of the region was 'a matter of life and death to the British Empire'.[11] Lord Altrincham also saw the Middle East as a 'region of life or death consequence for the British Empire' because of its oil and communications and its importance for Britain's Great Power status. Most important of all, it was deemed to be an area in which the 'British political method must make good if the British way of life is to survive'.[12]

These ideas of status and Britishness were of greater importance as determinants of Middle Eastern policy and informal empire than the more practical issues of defending the Middle East or attacking the Soviet Union. The defence of the Middle East, as will be seen, eventually came to be regarded as impossible in the period being examined here. But this harsh reality was not accepted, as the consequences of accepting it would have involved a radical rethink of Britain's role in the Middle East and its status as a world power. The questions of status and prestige and Britain's leading regional role were also more important determinants of Egyptian policy than any desire for social and political change or economic development, and they quickly became entangled in Anglo–Soviet rivalry in the Straits and the Mediterranean. The fact that at Potsdam the Soviets were demanding bases in the Straits and justifying this in relation to the British base in the Suez Canal Zone was a source of difficulty for British policy-makers. The Suez base was ostensibly geared to the defence of an important international waterway, but the passage between the Black Sea and the Mediterranean was an equally important international waterway. The British could not accept Soviet bases there because they feared it would produce greater Soviet influence in the Middle East and eastern Mediterranean.

To make matters worse, it was difficult for the British to claim that whereas the Turks were opposed to any Soviet bases in the Straits, the Egyptians were quite happy with the British presence in the Suez Canal Zone. The issue of British withdrawal had been raised by the Watanists, a small and uncompromising nationalist party, in January 1945. The

Britain and the Egyptian problem, 1945–48 145

Egyptians then raised the question of treaty revision at the San Francisco conference to establish the United Nations held between April and June 1945.[13] Thus it was vital but difficult for the British to secure their position in the Middle East through a new defence agreement with Egypt. This became an urgent problem once the formal Egyptian request to renegotiate the 1936 treaty, with a view to securing the evacuation of British forces, was made on 20 December 1945.

For the British the problem of finding suitable collaborators who would accept whatever future military requirements Britain might have in Egypt was already well in evidence. Moreover, the lack of any mass-based political movement[14] made Bevin's ideas of a partnership in the development sphere somewhat impractical, even if Britain, like the USA, had been amply blessed with economic resources. In addition, Egyptian politics was extremely factional, with many groups and individuals eager to exploit nationalist issues such as the British presence in Egypt for narrow political advantage.

What the British ideally wanted at the beginning of 1946 was a political party that believed in collaboration in the implementation of social reform and the preservation of a British role in the defence of the Middle East, which required a base in the Canal Zone. As no such party existed, securing collaborators to negotiate a new treaty guaranteeing British rights in the Canal Zone became important. There were a number of different possibilities, but the choice was complicated by the fact that it was not clear whether a nationalist coalition, including the Wafd, would be a better long-term prospect for securing Britain's needs than a small faction more eager to make an agreement that might ultimately prove unpopular.

The obvious idea of using the Wafd was highly problematic. The Wafd had been installed in power by British tanks in February 1942 much to the dislike of King Faruq, who was averse to al-Nahas, the Wafd leader. This had tarnished their nationalist credentials, which had only been regained in 1945, when, after refusing to participate in the January elections, they had orchestrated an anti-British propaganda campaign.[15] The alternative to the Wafd was King Faruq and whatever palace government he could form. But Faruq was an indolent and ineffective monarch, who was personally corrupt and who spent much time in the gambling dens of Europe. He did, however, have the power to appoint prime ministers, to dismiss governments, to veto legislation and to prorogue the parliament, which consisted of an elected Chamber of Deputies and a Senate, whose members were mostly royal appointees.

Under the wartime coalition government in 1945, the Foreign Office had inclined to favour King Faruq despite the mutual animosity between the king and the British ambassador, Lord Killearn. Killearn believed Faruq and the Egyptian prime minister, al-Nuqrashi, to be hopeless and dangerous.[16] Disagreements between the Foreign Office and the ambassador arose as early as June 1945 over whether to press for the return of the Wafd or to support King Faruq. Killearn favoured the Wafd, but the Foreign Office's desire to work with Faruq won the day despite the doubts of Prime Minister Attlee. The permanent under-secretary, Sir A. Cadogan, justified the Foreign Office's position on the grounds that the time was not right for the return of the Wafd and that action that might precipitate a crisis should be avoided until the political situation in Egypt was clearer. The Foreign Office doubted if a more reasonable successor to al-Nuqrashi could then be found and Cadogan believed that there was no reliable candidate who would co-operate with Britain.[17]

The question for the Labour government was whether the lack of viable collaborators other than King Faruq would continue to dictate a policy of securing British requirements in Egypt through a corrupt monarchy; or whether greater efforts would be made to establish a new basis for an Anglo–Egyptian partnership, based on a common commit-ment to social and economic reform and the defence of the Middle East. In other words, would the need to preserve an informal empire in the Middle East and secure facilities in the Canal Zone be given the same priority as they had been under the wartime coalition government?

In the general sense these questions were largely answered at Potsdam and the London Council of Foreign Ministers in September 1945, where the main Anglo–Soviet disputes focused on the eastern Mediterranean. More specifically, the commitment to reform, as opposed to imperial defence, was undermined by the Treasury as much as the Egyptian situation. By 1947, development plans were essentially geared to British colonies, as it was believed they could make the biggest contribution to relieving Britain's post-war economic difficulties. These centred on the dollar gap produced by the fact that the United States was the major source of capital equipment and consumer goods much needed by war-ravaged European economies, which could not produce the exports to pay for them. Thus, in March 1947, the Treasury asserted that 'until 1951 it must be assumed that there would be no additional help for the Middle East beyond those limited resources released out of sterling balances; and even these could only be used for development if import controls were employed to make sure that sterling releases did not finance an adverse balance of payments account'.[18]

Yet the confirmation that imperial needs in Egypt would dictate a policy of collaboration with King Faruq came before the economic crisis ended any hope of Britain's gaining credit from economic assistance to Egypt. It resulted from a number of events following the British reply

Britain and the Egyptian problem, 1945–48   147

to the Egyptian demand for the evacuation of British troops. The Foreign Office foresaw difficulties in any negotiations because: (1) the Egyptian government contained no representatives of the largest political party – the Wafd; (2) there was enmity between the king and the Wafd; and (3) the prime minister and minister of foreign affairs were temperamentally unfitted to undertake such important negotiations.

Consequently, while the British government were anxious to avoid interference in Egypt's internal affairs the issues were so important that it would be necessary to voice British anxieties about the existing government to the king, whose influence was deemed to be keeping it in power.[19] The embassy in Cairo was therefore asked to press Faruq to establish a new government containing the Wafd, or if not, a more broadly based coalition.[20]

In the meantime the instructions sent to Cairo referred to the need for a bilateral defence agreement based on the fact that the Commonwealth and individual Middle Eastern states had a common interest in the security of the region. Only through the military and economic protection of a Great Power could Egypt survive an attack, and therefore Egypt should provide assistance to Britain, as in the Second World War, in order to secure such protection. The Egyptians were to be told that this would involve Britain's stationing the minimum forces for a wartime establishment necessary for the defence of the Middle East and for the air defences needed to prevent bombing raids on Egypt. In addition to these instructions on defence, the embassy were also informed that the political articles of the 1936 treaty, which were out of date, could now be renegotiated.[21]

The British note aroused widespread hostile comment in Egypt and on 4 February, the anniversary of the surrounding of the Abdin Palace by British tanks in 1942, there were a number of anti-British demonstrations. One Egyptian newspaper published a cartoon of Egyptian tanks bombarding the British embassy, and the Chamber of Deputies suspended its session for five minutes as a sign of mourning. In this anti-British atmosphere where Faruq stood to benefit from hurt Egyptian national pride, the Wafd could attack the king and al-Nuqrashi's unrepresentative government only by condemning the proposed treaty negotiations as incompatible with Egyptian sovereignty. On 11 February, Lord Killearn, a supporter of al-Nahas not the king, reported that the situation was not conducive to successful treaty negotiations. He was then replaced, with King George approving the name of the new British ambassador on 14 February. By introducing a new British ambassador and a new Egyptian government under Sidqi Pasha, it was hoped that progress on a new Anglo–Egyptian agreement over the base could be made. It was geared very much to co-operation

148   *Demise of the British Empire in the Middle East*

with and through King Faruq. Killearn's replacement, Sir R. Campbell, was told before leaving for Egypt in March that it had been decided to work with King Faruq as the chief element of continuing stability and not to attempt to force al-Nahas into power.[22]

Before the new ambassador arrived in Egypt, on 21 February, further attacks on British establishments in Cairo occurred which, according to the embassy, led to troops firing in self-defence. The Egyptians claimed that the incident was sparked by a British army lorry's driving into a crowd with fatal consequences, and that subsequently 50 people were killed or wounded by the British. In these circumstances Sir R. Campbell soon became convinced that if any agreement was to be achieved it would have to be based on the peacetime evacuation of the Egyptian base.

Sir R. Campbell's views were at odds with the instructions sent to Killearn and were also soon in conflict with the views of the Commanders-in-Chief (Cs-in-C), Middle East, on what peacetime arrangements were necessary in the Canal Zone. The Cs-in-C argued that some 5,000 troops and 300 aircraft would be needed.[23] Yet, despite the frequent claims about the importance of defending the Middle East, the military had no plans drawn up to do so, on which force requirements in Egypt could be based. The Cs-in-C were assessing what would be necessary to maintain an important British presence and an effective operational base in Egypt, not what the force requirements for defending the Middle East would be. This fact is crucial in understanding how relations with Egypt and the British presence in the Canal Zone were initially related to defence planning. Moreover, consideration of the Cs-in-C's views also sheds light on the relationship of military thinking to the foreign-policy requirements that the embassy were addressing. The Middle East Cs-in-C's paper on military requirements in Egypt did not reach the COS (Chiefs of Staff) until 23 March and was not considered by them until 27 March. By then, the Cs-in-C, having seen the embassy's criticisms,[24] had changed their views on the need for a permanent peacetime presence in the Suez base. In order to facilitate the beginning of treaty negotiations, they were prepared to accept a phased with-drawal of British forces, but evacuation was deemed to be dependent on a satisfactory settlement of the regional security problem.[25] Thus by the time the COS began to discuss the views of the Cs-in-C these had in fact changed, and the issue central to their concerns now was the regional security problem.

The regional security problem was not the imminent threat of a Russian attack, which the military believed was unlikely to come before the end of 1956,[26] but the preservation of exclusive British responsibility for the defence of the Middle East. This matter of life and death was now threatened by the Egyptians as well as by Prime Minister Attlee's

Britain and the Egyptian problem, 1945–48 149

opposition to a continued British presence in the region. Attlee had challenged the strategic value of attempting to defend the Middle East as early as 1945 in the context of the debate on the future of the Italian colonies.[27] In early 1946, as the COS sought desperately to justify the strategic importance of the Middle East rather than determine what forces would be necessary to defend which areas within it, on 2 March, Attlee produced a paper for the Defence Committee challenging the desirability and the practicality of maintaining Britain's military position in the Middle East, to which Bevin then responded.[28]

Discussion by the Defence Committee on the importance of defending the Middle East was then postponed until the COS had produced an overall assessment of the strategic position of the British Commonwealth. As a further complication, at the Defence Committee on 27 March, Bevin, who had been considering the possibility of leasing the base, rejected Sir R. Campbell's view that the Egyptians would want Britain to evacuate Egypt completely. The Foreign Secretary argued that the question of evacuation turned on the ultimate location of Britain's Middle Eastern forces and that discussions with the Egyptians should be delayed until the COS reported on his and the prime minister's memos (DO(46)40 and 27) on Mediterranean strategy[29] which were discussed on 5 April.[30]

In the meantime Bevin suggested, more in line with the embassy's views, that the delegation be authorized to state British policy at the outset as (1) the complete evacuation from Egypt of all British combat troops (as opposed to those troops maintaining the base); (2) the maintenance by Egypt, with British collaboration, of naval, land and air-administrative and air-defence organizations; (3) obtaining permission for the transit of troops and aircraft, and securing the maintenance requirements of the transit organization; (4) the creation of a regional headquarters to be located in the Canal Zone; and (5) the provision of equipment for the Egyptian forces. The cabinet supported the idea of offering the evacuation of combat troops at the outset of negotiations subject to the views of the COS.[31]

The snag now was the military's insistence that combat troops should not include the air squadrons deemed necessary for the defence of the base. In the light of the COS views the British delegation sent to conduct the talks was instructed to negotiate on the basis of Bevin's five points with the qualification that, if possible, combat troops should not include the fighter squadrons.[32] As a last resort the delegation might agree to their withdrawal as soon as the Egyptian air force had reached sufficient strength to provide a peacetime garrison, and provided British control over long-range bomber bases would be retained for many years to come.[33]

150   *Demise of the British Empire in the Middle East*

The leader of the British delegation, the secretary of state for air, Lord Stansgate, soon became convinced after his introductory meeting with Sidqi that an offer of full and complete evacuation would have to be made at the outset if the discussions were to make any progress.[34] The COS were reluctant to accept this, but when Major-General Jacob of the British delegation returned to explain the advantages and disadvantages, the COS came round.[35] The prospect of disorders to accompany those in Palestine, and the delegation's belief that the offer of evacuation would secure Egyptian co-operation and the required peacetime facilities, influenced the COS decision. In addition, there was the possibility of troops going to Palestine and Cyrenaica as part of a general redeployment of Middle Eastern forces. Finally, with the cold war developing in the wake of the conflicts over Soviet bases in the Straits, the Soviet claim to a trusteeship of Tripolitania and the disputed presence of Soviet forces in Iran, it was important for the British imperial image not to be tarnished. Thus the cabinet was able to endorse the Defence Committee's recommendation to offer total evacuation and a phased withdrawal over five years.[36]

The subsequent negotiations between 9 and 22 May proved at best a disappointment for the British given that Sidqi, the new prime minister, was seen as an improvement on al-Nuqrashi. The Egyptians refused to accept a lengthy British withdrawal period of five years, and argued that the required wartime facilities should not be incorporated formally into the treaty but subject to more informal arrangements of the kind made between friendly and independent sovereign states; this was not acceptable to the Foreign Office[37] or to the military.[38] The other bones of contention were the Egyptian reluctance to grant facilities, if the British perceived a threat of war, and the areas in which an outbreak of war would automatically produce the reactivation of the base.

For the Egyptians it was important to establish the principle of consultation over mutual assistance in times of war and over the use of the base; this was seen as the essential basis of co-operation between any fully independent states. For the British the importance of the negotiations lay in securing rights in Egypt rather than establishing the principle of partnership.[39] The latter would ostensibly threaten Britain's ability to defend the Middle East but would certainly undermine Britain's claim to regional hegemony and Great Power status. The promise of evacuation had not smoothed the way to the British obtaining what they regarded as their military rights to defend the empire.

This key question of what was required in the Middle East to defend the Commonwealth/empire continued to preoccupy policy-makers at the same time as the negotiations with the Egyptians ran into difficulties in May 1946. The COS produced a paper on strategic requirements in

Britain and the Egyptian problem, 1945–48   151

the Middle East, which was discussed by the Defence Committee on 27 May. The paper was not detailed enough to satisfy Attlee in terms of the requirements in the Middle East, where there were still a large number of uncertainties. It proved impossible for the Defence Committee to endorse the COS report, and Attlee commented that the whole position in the Middle East required re-examination. The prime minister wanted to know which areas Britain had to defend in the region and what would be Britain's wartime and peacetime requirements to defend them. Attlee was trying hard to inject an element of realism into military thinking about the Middle East, but, although the COS produced a revised and detailed report, the issues were never addressed in precisely the way Attlee required. The COS still preferred to concentrate on why the Middle East was so important for British defence strategy, including its strategic bomber bases and oil, even though they acknowledged they would be unable to defend all the Middle East oil fields. What they were still not doing was defining what could be defended and what was required to do this.[40]

With the Anglo–Egyptian negotiations deadlocked, Bevin attempted to overcome Egyptian concerns about any apparent subservience by removing the provision and administration of base facilities from the treaty and placing them in the hands of a joint defence board. The board would also recommend when it was necessary for the base to be reactivated.[41] The COS were opposed to this second major concession and argued that the geographical position of Egypt made it vital for the defence of the Commonwealth, and that what they were demanding from the Egyptians in terms of security needs was insignificant compared with the security measures taken by the Soviets in the Baltic and Balkan states.[42] The cabinet decided, however, to override the COS and pursue the negotiations on the lines of Bevin's proposals for a joint defence board. As Attlee stated, there was no more justification for arguing that Britain had to have base facilities in Egypt because they were necessary for the empire's security than for demanding bases from Britain's continental allies.[43]

When Stansgate returned to Egypt on 7 July for a second round of talks, it soon became evident that Britain's agreement to exclude the provision of base facilities and the administrative arrangements for them from the treaty had not solved the problem. The issue of sovereignty over the Sudan had now to be addressed, along with the differences over the conditions for reactivation and the timing of the evacuation. The Cs-in-C and the delegation saw no objection to the Egyptian proposals on the latter issues. However, in London, there was a determination to ensure the base's availability if Turkey, Greece or Persia were attacked,[44] whereas the Egyptians did not want to be involved in a war that did not directly threaten them or other members of the Arab League. This lay behind the dispute over the Egyptian article 2 (British article 5) of the proposed treaty, which Stansgate felt was unnecessary.[45] On 10 July, a new Egyptian draft was received, which required that the two powers consult in order to decide on common action to deal with any aggression against Egypt or adjacent countries. The revised British draft made no provision for governmental consultation and stipulated military action by both powers in the event of war involving Britain or Egypt or endangering their security in Egypt and neighbouring territories.[46]

Stansgate believed that Britain should accept the Egyptian draft of article 2, agree to withdraw all naval forces by 31 March 1947 and to evacuate completely within three years.[47] In the Foreign Office, R. G. Howe was not inclined to accept the Egyptian article 2, but it was not yet clear whether that, the status of the Sudan or the evacuation period was of greatest significance for the Egyptians.[48] The COS, in contrast to their earlier stance, came out on the side of Stansgate to the extent that they believed an agreement with Egypt was essential. In their view, a failure to conclude an agreement would lead to disturbances in Egypt when Britain lacked the necessary forces to impose its will on the Egyptians. On the other hand, while Stansgate wanted to end the negotiations because delay would increase suspicions of British reluctance to withdraw, the COS saw no objection to continuing the negotiations, despite the opportunity this would give to opposition politicians in Egypt.[49]

In the light of these disagreements the prime minister put the issue to the cabinet, which agreed that the negotiators should demand an evacuation period of three years, accept the Egyptian draft of article 2 if necessary, and avoid any inclusion in the Sudan protocol of anything implying recognition of Egyptian sovereignty over the Sudan.[50] Bevin, who was not present at the cabinet on 1 August, refused to accept his colleagues' decision and wrote to Attlee requesting that the decision be ignored and that the Egyptian version of article 2 be rejected by the delegation in Egypt.[51] Instead Bevin proposed yet another draft of article 2 with an additional paragraph that could be used by Stansgate in further negotiations.

The issue of whether there should be consultation before reactivation and the areas of conflict that would justify reactivation produced a series of irate telegrams between Bevin and Stansgate in July and August 1946. Stansgate became ever more convinced that such issues were not sufficiently important to jeopardize the chances of an agreement, which he believed would become more difficult to achieve with the passage of time; if Britain was going to stand firm, Stansgate believed it should do so on the Sudan issue not on article 2.[52] However Bevin believed

Britain and the Egyptian problem, 1945–48

article 2 was a matter of principle and that the Egyptians, like market traders, were setting a high initial price in the expectation of some hard bargaining. For their part the Egyptians claimed that the British would not be content with the kind of treaty normally concluded between independent states, but wanted exceptional clauses 'due to a state of mind which has prevailed for many years'.[53]

By 21 August the talks were deadlocked over article 2 and the Egyptian wish to have some reference to the unity of the Nile valley under the Egyptian crown, which Bevin explicitly ruled out.[54] This, according to Stansgate, was now probably the vital issue, but the British could not fully accept the modifications to article 2, and in early September the Egyptian delegation was still producing redrafts of the latest British draft.[55] Bevin then decided that there was no possibility of a compromise on article 2. A draft treaty was presented on 17 September as the final British offer and duly rejected by the Egyptians.[56]

When Bevin had first considered the Anglo–Egyptian talks earlier in the year he had refused to accept the Egyptian position on article 2 and the evacuation protocol. This was in contrast to Stansgate, who wanted to make concessions on these issues in order to be able to deal with the Sudan question. By October, Bevin's determination to get a satisfactory article 2 was such that he was prepared to abandon his previous insistence on avoiding any reference to Egyptian sovereignty over the Sudan, on the assumption that if such a concession was made the Egyptians would accept the British position on article 2 and the evacuation timing.[57]

In the event Bevin was proved wrong to the extent that while the concession on the Sudan may have influenced Egyptian acceptance of the three-year evacuation period, it did not win acceptance of any of the previous British drafts of article 2 despite five meetings with Sidqi, who visited London in October 1946. In essence, the British were forced to accept the main substance of the Egyptian case on article 2 as put forward earlier in the year.[58] Later, Stansgate would imply that the delay on the base issue aroused Egyptian suspicions that the British were stalling on evacuation, which then hardened attitudes on the Sudan question. It was the Sudan that eventually prevented any ratification of the final Bevin/Sidqi-agreed draft of a new Anglo–Egyptian treaty.[59]

The issue of King Faruq's right to be recognized as King of Egypt and the Sudan was a complex question, which had a significant effect on Anglo–Egyptian relations but will not be dealt with in detail here. Disagreements on this question led not only to the failure to secure ratification of a new treaty but to the fall of Sidqi on 9 December 1946 and his replacement by al-Nuqrashi. As al-Nuqrashi announced his intention to refer the matter of the British presence in Egypt to the UN,

154   *Demise of the British Empire in the Middle East*

it was clear that the policy of relying on Faruq had not worked.[60] Sir Orme Sargent was one of the advocates within the Foreign Office of abandoning the policy of working with Faruq and minority governments in favour of co-operation with the Wafd; he was also in favour of reverting to a policy of intervention in Egyptian politics to bring this about. Sargent, like the ambassador and the oriental counsellor in Cairo, believed that in Egypt and in the post-war world in general there was a feeling that Britain was displaying weakness; this had to compensated for by tough policies designed to show that Britain meant business and to win the respect of the Russians, Egyptians and anyone else who believed that the British Empire could be taken advantage of.[61]

One way of being tough was to enforce Britain's rights under the 1936 treaty, although of course Britain was contravening it in a number of ways. The movement of troops in and out of Egyptian territory without passports and the non-payment of tax by service vehicles, which were authorized by the treaty, were issues on which Bevin wanted a hard line taken. The problem was that antagonizing the Egyptians was seen as a risky business by the military and the problem would increase as Britain reduced its forces in the Canal Zone to the 10,000 troops permitted by the treaty.[62] The cabinet took no decision on the enforcement of treaty rights, which left the decisions in the hands of the men on the spot.[63] As time was increasingly to show, the desire to take a tough line with the Egyptians was not matched by a military or economic capacity to do so with impunity.

The British survived the Egyptian complaints to the UN without a condemnatory resolution, but pressure to reduce the numbers of troops in Egypt to the levels permitted by the treaty increased. As Attlee commented to Bevin:

> I cannot see how the fact of our needing a Commonwealth base in the Middle East gives us any ground for demanding that the base should be in Egypt, a sovereign state. We have no case to retain more troops than we are allowed under the Treaty. Our only defence is the difficulty of removal in the time at our disposal. COS must press on with alternative arrangements.[64]

However, by early 1947, Attlee had abandoned his struggle to change the military's determination to make the defence of the Middle East one of the three pillars of British defence policy; this only increased the significance of the facilities in the Canal Zone.[65] Egypt's importance also increased because of the decision in September 1947 to leave Palestine, which had previously been deemed essential for the British military position in the Middle East. And there was the continuing uncertainty about a British base in Cyrenaica, because in 1947 the Council of Foreign Ministers' deputies had been unable to agree on arrangements for the

Britain and the Egyptian problem, 1945–48   155

ex-Italian colonies. Finally, by the end of 1947, the Americans were expressing an interest in facilities in Egypt. Bevin also saw a possibility of receiving US aid for the region if the importance of Britain's role there could be demonstrated.[66]

In addition to the growing importance of Egypt in 1947 it became clear that the military were retreating from their 1946 decision to evacuate Egypt in peacetime. By the summer of 1947 the COS had informed the Foreign Office that the assumptions about requirements in Egypt on which the Bevin–Sidqi draft agreement had been based no longer held good.[67] Thus, even though King Faruq seemed keen to reopen talks, there appeared to be little chance of any future agreement, as the military were no longer thinking in terms of the complete evacuation offered in 1946. To try and get round this problem and to avoid having to renegotiate the 1936 treaty, Bevin, albeit on the assumption that Cyrenaica would ultimately be available, proposed simply reducing the British peacetime presence in Egypt to about 1,000 men, but leaving the other treaty provisions in force until a regional defence arrangement could supersede the 1936 treaty.[68]

The military planners' desire to retain a peacetime military presence in the Canal Zone stemmed from a belief that the key to the defence of the Middle East lay in an ability rapidly to establish British forces in Egypt and operate effectively from the base on the threat of war; this in turn required a nucleus base in peacetime.[69] Such ideas were reinforced in 1948 by the 'Intermezzo' study of Middle Eastern defence strategy based on estimates of British and Soviet force levels in 1957–58. Its main conclusions were that it would be possible to prevent a Soviet advance to the Mediterranean and the Persian Gulf only by an all-out policy of air interdiction on enemy lines of communication; that would require airfields in Egypt and other Mediterranean states and a main base in Egypt on the outbreak of war to provide support facilities for the air forces.[70]

Despite the fact that the embassy had made it clear in 1946 that a British offer of evacuation was a *sine qua non* of any agreement, in January 1948, Bevin discussed several ways of breaking the deadlock with officials in the Foreign Office and with the ambassador in Cairo; they included leasing the areas in which Britain would retain facilities and the provision of weapons and training to make the Egyptians feel they were being treated as equals.[71] The ambassador believed that all that mattered was the Egyptians' willingness to permit re-entry. If they granted re-entry rights then Britain would not need a treaty. If they were unwilling to do so, then any treaty provisions would have little value. Consequently, the embassy was more inclined to favour a general agreement rather than the securing of specific rights.[72]

The Foreign Office was determined to secure specific military rights in Egypt if these were required by the COS, because the ostensible reason for having a peacetime military presence in Egypt was related to the importance of defending the Middle East. Yet at the start of 1948 no plans, to which force levels in Egypt should in theory have been related, had been drawn up to defend the Middle East. Ironically, as the military were insisting on maintaining forces in Egypt, they were also embarking, albeit reluctantly, on a new initiative, which would ultimately undermine the primacy of Middle East defence in British global strategy. This was the idea of military co-operation in the defence of western Europe as part of Bevin's idea of Western Union, which, along with a Middle East Union, would constitute part of the Third Force that was to be the first aim of British foreign policy between January 1948 and October 1949.[73]

This forced the military to plan for the defence of western Europe, which they knew was impossible and led them to insist on the involvement of the Americans in western European defence co-operation. The immediate consequence of this was the first emergency British global-war plan,[74] codenamed 'Doublequick', which in turn produced the first emergency plan for the defence of the Middle East, codenamed 'Sandown'.[75] 'Sandown' revealed that the defence of the Middle East was also impossible in the short term. It stated: 'Because of the need to concentrate all available land forces to meet the land threat to Egypt, the Allies cannot undertake any major subsidiary operations. Certain areas will therefore be left without Allied forces or with inadequate support.' These included the oil-producing areas and so 'plans for the destruction of oil installations and the Trans-Persian railway' would be put into effect. 'The object of the land operations will therefore be to impose the maximum delay on the enemy as far from the Egypt base as administrative resources will allow. The operations will consist of a series of delaying and harassing actions by mobile forces. ... A prepared defensive position will be constructed on the general line Jericho–Ramallah–North of Tel Aviv'.[76] In short, the British had to have peacetime base facilities in Egypt in order to defend the base in Egypt, given that so little of the rest of the Middle East was to be defended.[77]

Moreover, in order to do this the COS were now requiring 20,000 troops in Egypt in peacetime.[78] And they were also acknowledging the difficulties surrounding the Anglo–American strategic offensive, which it was believed would not be big enough to attack targets in the Soviet Union and halt the Soviet offensives in Europe and the Middle East. The British strategic bomber force was deemed to have too short a range to deliver an effective offensive into Russia. Its prime task, for which it was also deemed quite inadequate, was to prevent an enemy build

Britain and the Egyptian problem, 1945–48 157

up in western Europe and slow the Russian advance into the Middle East.[79]

The British military therefore wanted facilities in Egypt to carry out tasks that they could not perform. This was clearly an inadequate rationale for the kind of Egyptian policy they were pursuing. In a sense the military requirements were irrelevant, yet they were influencing the approach taken to negotiations with Egypt. They had allowed the offer of evacuation to go ahead and had subsequently produced the insistence on a peacetime presence in the Suez Canal Zone. Yet the real needs were to a large extent political, even though forces that could not defend the Middle East and its oil fields could perform more limited cold war duties. More importantly such forces could justify a military presence geared less to viable operational plans than to the maintenance of Britain's status and prestige in the Middle East and to Britain's role as a world power. This was what informal empire, military strategy and the Egyptian problem were really all about. Unfortunately, there was no solution in sight, given Britain's economic and military weakness and the lack of any Egyptian political groupings prepared to collaborate on British terms, which had become more demanding by 1948.

NOTES

1 See E. Lerman, 'British Diplomacy and the Crisis of Power in Egypt: the Antecedents of the British Offer to Evacuate 7 May 1946', in K. M. Wilson (ed.), *Imperialism and Nationalism in the Middle East: The Anglo–Egyptian Experience 1882–1982* (London: Mansell, 1983); Wm Roger Louis *The British Empire in the Middle East 1945–51* (London: Mansell, 1988) Ch. 6; Wm Roger Louis, 'The Tragedy of the Anglo–Egyptian Settlement of 1954', in Wm Roger Louis and R. Owen (eds.), *Suez 1956: the Crisis and its Consequences* (Oxford: Oxford University Press, 1989); R. Ovendale 'Egypt and the Suez Base Agreement', in John W. Young (ed.), *The Foreign Policy of Churchill's Peacetime Administration* (Leicester: Leicester University Press, 1988); John Kent, 'The Egyptian Base and the Defence of the Middle East 1945–54', *Journal of Imperial and Commonwealth History*, 21, 3 (1993); and H. Rahman, *A British Defence Problem in the Middle East: The Failure of the 1946 Anglo–Egyptian Negotiations* (Reading: Ithaca, 1994). M. J. Cohen, *Fighting World War III from the Middle East: Allied Contingency Plans 1945–1954* (London: Frank Cass, 1997).
2 H. Rahman, *A British Defence Problem*, pp. 17–22.
3 On this, see John Kent *British Imperial Strategy and the Origins of the Cold War 1944–49* (Leicester: Leicester University Press, 1993) especially Chs. 2 and 3.
4 See M. J. Cohen, *Fighting World War III*.
5 Cab 81/46, PHP(45)10, 27 March 1945; See BDEEP series A, Vol. 2, R. Hyam (ed.), *The Labour Government and the End of Empire, Part 3* (London: HMSO, 1992) for documents on the discussions relating to defence strategy which were based on the concept of main support areas containing the manpower and raw materials deemed necessary to win the next war, as they had been in the Second World War.
6 See AIR 20/7097.
7 DEFE 5/11 COS(48)110, 18 May 1948.
8 AIR 20/7097, R. M. Foster (ACAS (P)) to Sir Arthur Sanders (Vice Chief of the Air Staff), 29 September 1948.
9 It was not until late 1948 that the British accepted that work would have to commence on extending the runways in Egypt. There was then an argument with the Americans

158   *Demise of the British Empire in the Middle East*

over who should pay, which was not resolved until the spring of 1949, when Britain agreed to cover the initial work at Abu Sueir, FO 371/69286A, no. 6615, Alexander to Cripps, 5 October 1948; DEFE 4/16, COS 138(48)2, 27 September 1948; FO 371/73552, no. 3630, minute by M. N. F. Stewart, 19 May 1949. The programme, which was delayed by the troubles in the wake of the abrogation crisis, was eventually done in two stages with the Americans eventually agreeing to provide half the money, AIR 20/8544, J. Whitworth Jones to General F. H. Griswald (USAF, S. Ruislip), 24 November 1952.

10   Owing to the end of the wartime coalition in May 1945 and the creation of a Conservative caretaker government, the matter was never discussed by the full cabinet.

11   Cab 66/65, WP(45)256, 'Defence of the Middle East', War Cabinet memorandum by Eden, 13 April 1945.

12   Cab 66/67, CP(45)55, 'Imperial Security in the Middle East Area', War Cabinet memorandum by Lord Altrincham, 2 July 1945.

13   Rahman, *A British Defence Problem*, pp. 35–6.

14   The Wafd was largely composed of landowners, financiers, lawyers and other middle-class groups, although it could exert some influence over the lower classes, where social deference was strong.

15   Rahman, *A British Defence Problem*, p. 33.

16   FO 141/1043, no. 19, Cairo tel. 1180, 30 May 1945.

17   FO 371/45921, no. 2054, minute by Sir A. Cadogan, 30 June 1945.

18   T 236/1274, Treasury memorandum: 'Economic Policy in the Middle East', March 1947.

19   Cab 80/99, COS(46)8, 12 January 1946.

20   Rahman, *A British Defence Problem*, p. 41.

21   Cab 129/6, CP(46)17, 'Revision of the Anglo–Egyptian Treaty of 1936', memorandum by Bevin, 18 January 1946.

22   FO 371/53304, no. 2955, Cairo tel. 1183, 2 July 1946.

23   Cab 80/100, COS(46)95, annex, memorandum by the Commanders-in-Chief Committee, Middle East, for the COS Committee, 27 March 1946.

24   FO 141/1081, no. 7, despatch no. 350 from R. J. Bowker to Bevin on the military requirements in Egypt of the Commanders-in-Chief, Middle East, 10 March 1946.

25   FO 371/53289, no. 1309, Cairo tel. 548, 25 March 1946.

26   The British military, like their American counterparts, did not believe the Soviets would start a major war in the 1940s. A strategic summary considered by the COS on 31 October 1947 concluded that Russia was not yet ready to undertake an offensive war. Britain's military strategy was defined as preventing the spread of hostile influences in peacetime because any such spread would make future operations in wartime more difficult. In order to carry out such a task it was deemed vital that Britain's prestige throughout the world should be maintained, especially in the Middle East, DEFE 4/8, COS 134(47)3, 31 October 1947, JP(47)139, 31 October 1947, annex II. The only military danger was war breaking out by accident and in that case the Chief of the Naval Staff and the Chief of the Air Staff believed the Soviets would be likely to draw back or retreat eastwards rather than attack westwards, DEFE 4/11, COS 39(48), COS Committee minutes, 17 March 1948.

27   The debate between Attlee, on the one hand, and the COS and Bevin, on the other, has been well covered. See especially the pioneering work by R. Smith and J. Zametica, 'The Cold Warrior: Clement Attlee Reconsidered 1945–47', *International Affairs* 61, 2 (1985) and John Kent, *British Imperial Strategy*, Chs. 3 and 5. For a good selective documentary coverage see R. Hyam, *The Labour Government and End of Empire*.

28   Cab 131/2, DO(46)27, 'Future of Italian Colonies', memorandum by Attlee for the Defence Committee, 2 March 1946; Cab 131/2, DO(46)40, annex, note by Bevin for the Defence Committee, 13 March 1946.

29   Cab 131/1, DO 9(46)3, 27 March 1946, 'Egypt – Withdrawal of Troops from Cairo and Alexandria', Defence Committee minutes; Cab 131/2, DO(46)4, 'Strategic Position of the British Commonwealth', memorandum by the COS for the Defence Committee, 2 April 1946.

30   Cab 131/1, DO 10(46)2, 'Strategic Position of the British Commonwealth', Defence Committee minutes, 5 April 1946.

31   Cab 128/5, CM 33(46)4, 'Egypt', Cabinet conclusions on the offer to evacuate British troops at the start of negotiations, 11 April 1946.

Britain and the Egyptian problem, 1945–48   159

32 Cab 131/1, DO 12(46)2, 'Revision of Anglo–Egyptian Treaty', Defence Committee minutes, 15 April 1946.
33 FO 371/53291, no. 1659, FO tels. 718 and 719, 16 April 1946.
34 FO 371/53292, no. 173, Cairo tel. no. 713 from Lord Stansgate to Bevin, 22 April 1946.
35 Cab 79/47, COS 64(46)9, 24 April 1946; Cab 131/1, DO 14(46)2, 'Revision of the Anglo–Egyptian Treaty', Defence Committee minutes on the offer of complete evacuation, 24 April 1946.
36 Cab 128/5, CM 37(46)1, 'Egypt', Cabinet conclusions on the offer to evacuate Egypt, 24 April 1946.
37 FO 371/53296, no. 2172, FO tel. no. 960, 16 May 1946.
38 Cab 131/1, DO 17(46)1, 'Strategic Requirements in the Middle East', Defence Committee minutes on the problems in Egypt, Palestine and Cyrenaica, 27 May 1946.
39 The text of the first British draft treaty pertaining to their rights is indicative of the extent to which they were seeking collaboration between equals. 'The High Contracting Parties agree that in the event of a war involving either of them, or of imminent menace of war, or of apprehended international emergency, their respective armed forces will take the necessary measures in close co-operation with each other, and that British forces of all arms shall receive all facilities and assistance, including the use of Egyptian ports, roads, railways, airfields and telecommunications, in accordance with the Egyptian system of administration and legislation. The Egyptian government will take all the administrative and legislative measures, including the establishment of martial law and effective censorship, necessary to render these facilities and assistance effective.' FO 371/53295, no. 2158, 15 May 1946.
40 Cab 131/1, DO 17(46)1, 'Strategic Requirements in the Middle East', Defence Committee minutes on the problems in Egypt, Palestine and Cyrenaica, 27 May 1946.
41 Cab 129/10, CP(46)219, 'Revision of Anglo–Egyptian Treaty', Cabinet memorandum by Bevin, 5 June 1946.
42 Cab 129/10, CP(46)224, 'Revision of Anglo–Egyptian Treaty', report by the COS to the cabinet on the implications of developments since December 1945, 7 June 1946.
43 Cab 128/5, CM 58(46), 'Anglo–Egyptian Negotiations', cabinet conclusions on the continuance of negotiations, 7 June 1946.
44 FO 371/53306, no. 3140, FO tels. 3 and 4, 18 July 1946.
45 FO 371/53306, no. 318, Alexandria tel. no. 17 from Lord Stansgate to Bevin on article 2 of the proposed treaty, 21 July 1946.
46 On these issues see FO 371/53305, no. 3050 for the Egyptian draft; Cab 84/83, JP(46)140, 16 July 1946; FO 371/53305, no. 3076, Alexandria tel. 9, 14 July 1946; FO 371/53306, no. 3138, Alexandria tel. 10, 17 July 1946.
47 FO 371/53308, no. 3299, Alexandria tel. 33, 25 July 1946.
48 FO 371/53308, no. 329, minute by R. G. Howe, 29 July 1946.
49 FO 371/53308, no. 3332, Alexandria tel. 39 from Lord Stansgate to Attlee, 29 July 1946; Cab 79/50, COS 119(46)1, COS Committee minutes, 30 July 1946.
50 Cab 128/6, CM 76(46)7, 'Anglo–Egyptian Treaty Negotiations', cabinet conclusions on the instructions to the British delegation, 1 August 1946.
51 FO 371/53309, no. 3519, minute by Bevin to Attlee, 4 August 1946.
52 FO 371/53308, no. 333, FO tel. 30 from Bevin to Lord Stansgate, 5 August 1946; FO 371/53309, no. 3412, Alexandria tel. 46 from Lord Stansgate to Bevin, 6 August 1946; FO 371/53308, no. 3333, FO tel. 33 from Bevin to Lord Stansgate, 7 August 1946; FO 371/53310, no. 3579, Alexandria tel. 48 from Lord Stansgate to Bevin, 8 August 1946; FO 371/53309, no. 3412, FO tel. 34 from Bevin to Lord Stansgate, 8 August 1946; FO 371/53309, no. 3466, Alexandria tel. 54 from Lord Stansgate to Bevin, 10 August 1946; FO 371/53309, no. 3498, Alexandria tel. 56 from Lord Stansgate to Bevin, 12 August 1946; FO 371/53309, no. 3495, draft telegram 490 from Bevin (Paris) to Lord Stansgate, 13 August 1946.
53 FO 371/53310, no. 3606, Alexandria tel. no. 75 from Lord Stansgate to Bevin, 21 August 1946.
54 FO 371/53310, no. 3639, FO tel. 68, 26 August 1946.
55 FO 371/53311, no. 3752, Alexandria tel. 113, 3 September 1946.
56 FO 371/53311, no. 3772, FO tel. no. 106, 12 September 1946.
57 FO 371/53314, no. 4213, conclusions of FO meeting in Paris with embassy officials to discuss the Anglo–Egyptian Treaty, 4–5 October 1946.

160   *Demise of the British Empire in the Middle East*

58   FO 371/53317, no. 4634, record of the fifth and final meeting between Bevin and Sidqi, appendix, 25 October 1946.

59   FO 371/62942, no. 723, letter from Lord Stansgate to Bevin, 8 February 1947.

60   FO 371/62969, no. 1653, minute by Sir O. G. Sargent to Attlee, 3 April 1947.

61   FO 141/1187, no. 28A, memorandum by Sir W. Smart, 2 April 1947; FO 371/62969, no. 1653, minute by Sir O. Sargent to Attlee, 3 April 1947.

62   FO 371/62970, no. 2064, minute by J. P. E. C. Henniker to Bevin, 24 April 1947.

63   Cab 128/9, CM 38(47)1, cabinet conclusions on the enforcement of treaty rights, 22 April 1947.

64   PREM 8/837, minute by Attlee to Bevin, 10 August 1947.

65   It is not entirely clear why Attlee changed his mind although it has been suggested that the COS had threatened to resign if their views on the Middle East were not accepted. See R. Smith and J. Zametica, 'The Cold Warrior'. The other two pillars were the defence of the UK and the defence of the sea communications between Britain and the other main support areas.

66   T 236/1274, minute by E. W. Playfair, 19 May 1947. At the same time, Bevin was 'opposed to the adoption of a combined Anglo–American policy for the Middle East as this area was primarily of economic and strategic interest to the United Kingdom'. DEFE 4/8, COS 144(47)1, COS Committee Minutes, 21 November 1947. This has to be borne in mind when assessing the Pentagon talks on the Middle East in the autumn of 1947, which covered political and economic aspects as well as military ones and were geared to agreement on general principles; they were certainly not geared to detailed strategic planning or to a combined Anglo–American Middle East policy. For details of the Pentagon talks see *Foreign Relations of the United States* (hereafter *FRUS*), 1947, (Washington, DC: Government Printing Office, 1976) Vol. V, pp. 485–627.

67   DEFE 4/6, COS 97(47)6, 30 July 1947, Annex II.

68   DEFE 4/8, COS 141(47)2, COS Committee Minutes, 14 November 1947; FO 371/69192, no. 598, minute by Bevin to Attlee, 15 December 1947.

69   DEFE 6/3, JP(47)10, 'Middle East Defence – Military Requirements in Egypt', report by the JPS to the COS, annex, 6 August 1947.

70   DEFE 5/11, COS(48)111, 'Staff Study "Intermezzo"', report by the Commanders-in-Chief, Middle East to the COS, 13 May 1948.

71   FO 371/69192, no. 255, 'Egypt and Sudan', note of a FO meeting with Bevin, 10 January 1948; FO 371/69192, no. 554, 'Egypt', note of a FO meeting with Bevin on future talks with the Egyptians, 20 January 1948.

72   FO 371/69174, no. 1685, minute by M. R. Wright, 27 February 1948.

73   See John Kent, *British Imperial Strategy*, Ch. 6; John Kent and John W. Young 'British Policy Overseas: The Third Force and the Origins of NATO. In Search of a New Perspective', in B. Heuser and R. O'Neill (eds.), *Securing Peace in Europe* (London: Macmillan, 1992); John Kent and John W. Young, 'British Defence Planning and the Concept of Western Union, 1947–48', in R. Aldrich (ed.), *British Intelligence, Strategy and the Cold War, 1945–1951* (London: Routledge, 1992).

74   Emergency plans were drawn up to prepare for war in the next 12 months with the forces available at the time. 'Doublequick' was not an Anglo–American plan but a British one drawn up in the light of information supplied by the Americans about their basic deployments in global war at the joint planning talks in April 1948. There were a number of differences between 'Doublequick' and the first US global-war emergency plan codenamed 'Halfmoon' including reference to the plans for the evacuation of Europe, which the Americans refused to change despite a British request. Subsequently, consultations produced combined plans incorporating the elements of the separate national plans. Fully integrated planning never took place in the 1940s and early 1950s because the Americans always refused to supply the vital information on the exact role of the Strategic Air Command, which was responsible for the US strategic nuclear arsenal. The British therefore were never sure what was targeted for nuclear destruction. In addition, after 1949, there were important Anglo–American disagreements about the concept of how to fight global war.

75   See Chapter 2 in this volume by M. J. Cohen.

76   DEFE 4/16, COS 145(48)2, report by the JPS to the COS, 7 October 1948, (JP(48)106), annexes, 11 October 1948.

Britain and the Egyptian problem, 1945–48   161

77 In 1950, when the British review of Middle East strategy was advocating the defence of the Inner Ring on a line in southern Turkey the US military were critical of this because it defended so little of the Middle East and, in their view, amounted to a defence of Egypt. DEFE 5/25, COS(50)416, draft of comments by the US joint planners on the British review of Middle East policy and strategy, 19 October 1950.
78 DEFE 5/12, COS(48)191, 23 August 1948.
79 DEFE 5/9, COS(48)210, 16 December 1948.

9

Discord or partnership? British and American policy toward Egypt, 1942–56

PETER L. HAHN

Historians of the Anglo–American relationship during and after the Second World War have debated whether competition or co-operation characterized that relationship. Some scholars have perpetuated the view of Winston Churchill that the two powers enjoyed a harmonious 'special relationship' by developing a close political-military partnership that was instrumental in defending the interests of the Western democratic world against Nazi Germany and the Soviet Union. Revisionist scholars have stressed that beneath the veneer of collaboration against the Axis and Soviet Russia lay deep rivalries and disagreements over tactical military planning, British imperialism, commercial concessions, and policy toward Europe, Asia and the Middle East.[1]

This chapter will examine whether the USA and Britain, while maintaining and expanding their global united front against common adversaries, remained united or divided in their policies toward Egypt. It will suggest that the USA and Britain consistently maintained a close partnership on behalf of their joint resistance to the Nazi menace and Soviet communism in general and on behalf of their common strategic interests in the Middle East in particular. To be sure, there were moments when tactical differences generated friction that threatened to dissolve the partnership, but the bonds of friendship ran sufficiently deep to survive such quarrels.

COMPETITION AND CONCILIATION, TO 1945

In the Second World War era, the USA and Britain worked as strategic allies during times when they faced considerable security risks. Britain had politically, militarily and economically dominated Egypt since the late nineteenth century. Facing the prospect of Italian expansion in 1936, Britain and Egypt negotiated a Treaty of Preferential Alliance that

British and American policy toward Egypt 163

authorized Britain to occupy Egypt and defend it from foreign aggression. From 1940–42, Axis forces repeatedly threatened to overrun Egypt, tempted by the prizes of the Suez Canal and the vast British military base in the Canal Zone. In early 1942, after German troops invaded Egypt and threatened Alexandria, British authorities in Cairo decided to take drastic action to assert their control of the country. On February 4, they surrounded the Abdin Palace with tanks to force a reluctant King Faruq to name a prime minister suitable to their interests. With firm control of Cairo, the British army repulsed the Germans at the Battle of El Alamein in November 1942 and together with American forces expelled Axis forces from Africa in May 1943.[2]

Prior to the Second World War, the United States lacked official interests in Egypt, but early in the war it came to appreciate the importance of British power in the Canal Zone as a barrier against Axis capture of the oilfields and lines of communication in the Middle East. While some American officials disliked the high-handed display of power by Britain in the 4 February 1942 incident at Abdin Palace, the Roosevelt administration, reeling from the Japanese attack on Pearl Harbor, explicitly endorsed the British action. Under-Secretary of State Sumner Welles refused to criticize the British action because Egypt was 'clearly within the British sphere of influence'. In fact, well before the February incident, President Franklin D. Roosevelt had encouraged Prime Minister Winston Churchill to defend the Suez Canal and provided Lend-Lease supplies to British forces stationed in the Canal Zone.[3]

In contrast to this American support of the British military presence in Egypt, an Anglo–American commercial rivalry developed in Egypt once the danger of Axis conquest passed with the victory at El Alamein. State Department officials had covetously eyed trade potential in Egypt since the 1930s. 'I can see large benefits from the political, economic and financial standpoints', Minister to Egypt Alexander C. Kirk advised in October 1941, 'of developing American–Egyptian relations … as a possible impetus to a larger postwar trade in this entire area.' By 1944–45, American officials were protesting at British trade restrictions and promoting their own commercial ambitions in the Middle East.[4]

The end of the world war accentuated Anglo–American rivalry. State Department officials downplayed Roosevelt's wartime partnership with Britain and underscored his sympathy for national independence of Middle East peoples. 'It is our intention to revert as quickly as possible, following the conclusion of hostilities', they advised the new president Harry S. Truman, 'to the historic policy of the "Open Door" and equality of opportunity' in the region. US policy toward Egypt, NEA officials advised in August 1945, 'centers chiefly about securing non-discriminatory treatment for American interests and furnishing to Egypt all

164

Demise of the British Empire in the Middle East

proper economic assistance with a view to maintaining order and stability in this strategic part of the Near East'. In the atmosphere of Anglo–American tension caused by discordant views on Europe, the Soviet Union and Palestine, Truman approved a policy of challenging British hegemony in the Middle East. 'The Americans are commercially on the offensive in the Middle East', Foreign Secretary Ernest Bevin remarked. Britain would 'not make any concession that would assist American commercial penetration into a region which for generations has been an established British market'.[5]

FORGING AN ANGLO–AMERICAN PARTNERSHIP, 1946–50

In the late 1940s, cold war considerations gradually forced American officials to suspend their challenge to British hegemony in the Middle East, shelve their sensitivity to Egyptian aspirations for national independence, and align their own policy with Britain's. As the cold war escalated in 1946–47, American and British officials realized that they shared common strategic aims in the Middle East. The two powers collaborated in opposing perceived Soviet expansionism in Iran and Turkey, and as they confronted the Soviets on other fronts they concluded that mutual co-operation was essential to their success. British and American military strategists who planned hypothetically for war against the Soviet Union considered it imperative to maintain the British military-base facilities in Egypt. American contingency war plans codenamed PINCHER (March 1946), MAKEFAST (autumn 1946), BROILER (August 1947) and CRASSPIECE (November 1949), posited that a massive Western strategic air offensive from Egyptian airfields against vital targets in the Soviet Union would be an essential component of victory. The importance of airfields in the Cairo–Suez region, the US Joint War Plans Committee declared, 'can hardly be over-emphasized'.[6]

British planners agreed that the base in Egypt was the 'keystone' of regional defense, and after the Labour government in London withdrew from India, Greece and Palestine the importance of the base in Egypt soared. Especially after abandoning the Palestine mandate, the Foreign Office concluded that to leave Egypt would attract Soviet penetration of the Middle East and 'heighten the probability of world war in which we would be massacred'. 'Egypt is the key', the COS (Chiefs of Staff) explained in January 1947, 'to the whole position of the Middle East in its relations to the defence of the Commonwealth'. British war plans like SANDOWN of August 1948 and SPEEDWAY of December 1948 affirmed that Egypt was a vital base for a strategic air offensive

British and American policy toward Egypt 165

against the Soviet Union. 'The strategic key to this area [the Middle East] is Egypt', Bevin told the cabinet, 'to which there is no practical alternative as a main base'.[7]

In 1948–50, mounting cold war tensions over the Berlin blockade, the Chinese communist revolution, the Soviet explosion of an atomic device, and the Korean War accentuated the strategic value of Egypt. A strategic air offensive against the Soviet Union remained the cornerstone of American and British contingency war plans through 1952. Even as the deployment of long-range aircraft diminished the importance of Cairo–Suez as a primary staging area, the base remained vital as a post-strike landing site for medium-range bombers launched from the British Isles to attack industrial targets in the southern Soviet Union.[8]

In light of these strategic factors, American officials in several ways endorsed the preservation of the British base in Egypt. US officials first demonstrated a new willingness to back the British during Anglo–Egyptian negotiations to revise the treaty of 1936. These negotiations began at Egyptian request in 1946 and continued sporadically for nearly a decade. In the first round, Egyptian Prime Ministers Mahmoud al-Nuqrashi and Ismail Sidqi insisted on unconditional British withdrawal from their homeland and sought American endorsement of their position. British officials considered it essential to maintain a working base, and thus offered at a maximum to withdraw all combat forces from Egypt, provided they retained the right to leave behind air-defense units and maintenance technicians who would keep the base operational, and the right to reoccupy the base in the event of war. Given the strategic importance of the British presence in Egypt, US officials intervened in the negotiations on Britain's behalf by encouraging Egypt to submit to Britain's terms. Egyptian criticism of the USA for taking Britain's side deterred American officials from pursuing the matter, but they refused Egyptian appeals for help in achieving unconditional British evacuation of Egypt and they remained privately sympathetic to Britain even as the Anglo–Egyptian talks stalemated short of any meaningful agreement.[9]

American support for Britain wavered slightly but remained strong during debates in the United Nations Security Council on the Anglo–Egyptian stalemate. When Egypt appealed to the Security Council to order Britain to evacuate Egypt, the British initially asked the USA for its full support, but once the Soviet Union threatened to intervene in the dispute to counterbalance American involvement, officials in London and Washington agreed that the USA should remain on the sidelines. Concerned about the dangers of antagonizing Egyptian nationalism, American officials privately encouraged the British to make a compromise settlement. While British evacuation of Egypt would raise

166 *Demise of the British Empire in the Middle East*

'serious questions involving the security of that area', NEA officials noted, 'in view of the intensely nationalistic feeling in Egypt, this Gov[ernmen]t has not wished to take [a] position [which] would further complicate our relations with the peoples of the Near East'. Thus they sought some compromise settlement that would preserve essential British interests, while recognizing the aspirations of Egyptian nationalists. Frustrated by 'the spineless attitude adopted by the State Department', Bevin briefly considered making concessions under American pressure, but ultimately he remained firm with Egypt, whose appeal to the Security Council died of neglect. Reluctantly, American officials went along with the British plan.[10]

During the Anglo–American consultations, known as the Pentagon Talks, of October 1947, American officials shed their ambivalence between British security interests and Egyptian national aspirations, and gave full support to the maintenance of British base rights in Egypt. Bevin arranged the talks with the hope of reaching a 'gentlemen's understanding' on common Anglo–American policy toward Egypt, Palestine, Greece and Cyrenaica. Prior to the talks, Pentagon strategists persuaded State Department officials such as Loy Henderson to shelve their abiding concern with Egyptian nationalism and recognize that 'regional security and stability' depended on the British presence in Egypt. In light of mounting cold war tensions in Europe, the enormous demands on American resources in Europe and Asia, and Britain's traditional dominance of the Middle East, in October 1947 US officials resolved that 'it is our strong feeling that the British should continue to maintain primary responsibility for military security in that area'. At the talks, American and British negotiators jointly agreed that 'the British should have the right to maintain [in Egypt] ... certain strategic facilities ... during peacetime in such a condition that they could be effectively and speedily used in case of an immediate threat to the security of the Middle East and [the] right of re-entry in order to make full use of these facilities' in wartime. American officials would endorse indefinitely the British presence in Egypt, even in the absence of British concessions to Egyptian nationalism.[11]

Furthermore, US officials sided with Britain in 1948–49 when Bevin attempted, without success, to negotiate with Egypt a deal that would end the base impasse on terms consistent with British security. US officials endorsed Britain's position, and refused Egyptian entreaties to encourage Britain to withdraw unconditionally from Egypt. On the other hand, American officials refrained from becoming Britain's full partner in maintaining the base in Egypt. To signal Egypt that he enjoyed complete American backing, Bevin encouraged the USA to send a high-ranking military officer to Fayid to participate in the talks and to join

British and American policy toward Egypt 167

Britain in participating in a new defense plan for Egypt. 'The moment has now come' for American participation in Middle East defense, Bevin observed privately. 'It will have a profound general effect if we can secure it.'[12]

While some Pentagon officials and ambassador to London Lewis W. Douglas favored fulfilling Bevin's request, the JCS (Joint Chiefs of Staff) and Secretary of State Dean G. Acheson decided to reject it in May 1949 for two reasons. First, they wished to avoid alienating Egyptian leaders, who were profoundly angered by US policy toward Palestine, and to 'restore the cordial relations' that the US and Egypt enjoyed before 1948. Second, they concluded that the USA simply lacked the resources to incur additional major commitments to regional defense. 'We wanted the British to hang on in the Middle East as long as possible', Assistant Secretary of State George McGhee recalled. 'We didn't want to have to replace them.' American officials also refused Britain's request for permission to divulge to Egypt the American plans to use Canal Zone airbases in war. Britain should seek to maintain its control of Egyptian airbases 'under the guise of potential British use'.[13]

In late 1949 and early 1950, American and British officials reaffirmed their close security partnership in Egypt. Policy-makers in the State and Defense Departments agreed that Anglo–American objectives in the Middle East were 'now substantially the same'; the Foreign Office recognized that 'co-operation between London and Washington in regard to the Middle East is extremely close'; and McGhee and Michael Wright of the Foreign Office jointly reaffirmed the conclusion to the 1947 Pentagon talks. Ever sensitive to Egyptian nationalism, McGhee succeeded at instilling some of his concern in Wright. 'It was not sufficient just to ward off Communism in the Middle East', he cautioned Wright. 'It was essential to assist the peoples of the Middle East to improve their living standards and social and political institutions and to acquire self-respect.' Wright conceded that 'nationalism and communism should not be fought together', and the two men agreed that 'it must be our common aim to align the forces of nationalism in the Middle East against communism and to guide them into channels friendly to the Western Powers'. Wright's acknowledgment notwithstanding, when British–Egyptian base negotiations resumed in early 1950, American officials endorsed to Egyptian officials the view that the British presence in Cairo–Suez enhanced Egyptian security against Soviet attack.[14]

The agreement by the United States and United Kingdom, in conjunction with France, to issue a Tripartite Declaration on the Middle East in May 1950 illustrated the depth of Anglo–American understanding. The Tripartite Declaration originated in the issue of arms supply to Middle East states. In late 1949, to induce Egyptian concessions on the

168   *Demise of the British Empire in the Middle East*

base issue, Britain resumed arms shipments to Arab powers, including Egypt. Israel complained that such arms supply threatened its national security, and pro-Israel members of Congress, labor unionists and civic leaders in the USA pressured Truman and Acheson either to force the British to stop arming the Arab states or to arm Israel in kind. Initially, the NSC (National Security Council), meeting in the absence of Truman, endorsed the British arms supply as conducive to Western security interests and dismissed Israeli complaints of insecurity as unfounded. But Truman, sensitive to the pro-Israel pressure, rejected the council's advice. Truman's position compelled the State Department to conceive of a declaration by the three Western powers that they would make future shipments of arms to Middle East states dependent on their declarations of non-aggression. If the signatories found any regional state preparing to 'violate frontier or armistice lines', the three would 'immediately take action, both within and outside the United Nations to prevent such violation'. British officials immediately warmed to the declaration the moment the Americans proposed it on 12 May. 'This is an important development of which it seems important to take advantage', Bevin explained to Prime Minister Clement Attlee. 'Such assurances [of non-aggression] taken together would almost amount to an internal non-aggression pact in the Middle East.' British officials also welcomed the implied American commitment to Middle East stability and the tone of Anglo–American co-operation that permeated the document.[15]

THE KOREAN WAR ERA: TESTING OF THE ANGLO–AMERICAN PARTNERSHIP

The outbreak of war in Korea tested American confidence in Britain's policy of firmness toward Egypt for two interrelated reasons. First, American officials anticipated that the Soviet Union would attempt to penetrate the region politically or even militarily. Second, officials in Washington also calculated that nationalism, if unsatisfied, would undermine Western ability to defend the region against Soviet encroachments, in peace or war. While the British remained determined to hold their strategic facilities in the Canal Zone despite Egyptian protests, American officials were torn between recognition of the abiding strategic value of the British base and fear that that base might become inaccessible in the absence of concessions to Egyptian nationalism.

On the one hand, US officials remained aware after the outbreak of war in Korea of the strategic value of British occupation of the Canal Zone. In early July 1950, State Department officials declared privately, that 'we have never sought, nor do we intend, to undermine the special

British and American policy toward Egypt 169

treaty position which Britain enjoys in Egypt'. When Egyptian ambassador Mohammed Abdul Rahim asked McGhee to pressure the British to evacuate Egypt unconditionally, McGhee replied that in light of Korea 'Russian aggression in the Near Eastern area' now seemed possible, in which event 'it would be essential to our common strategic interests to have the British on the spot.' In October 1950, McGhee agreed with Bernard Burrows of the Foreign Office that 'the Egyptian base would also be essential in the event of a localized Korean type of conflict in the Middle East'.[16]

On the other hand, American officials became very concerned in late 1950 that Egypt's rising anger toward the Western powers – stemming from British occupation of the Canal Zone and from American policy toward Israel – would render the British base in Egypt worthless. American prestige in Cairo hit a 'low ebb', State Department officials observed. If the Soviets invaded, the Arab states might prove 'unable or unwilling to resist and would be obliged to submit' to Moscow.[17]

In late 1950 and early 1951, American officials expressed these concerns to the British and encouraged policy-makers in London to reconsider whether Gaza, Iraq or Cyrenaica might provide a suitable alternative base to Egypt. 'Both the UK and the US will stand to lose if a compromise solution is not found' to the Anglo–Egyptian base dispute, Wells Stabler, Officer in Charge of Egyptian Affairs, observed, 'which will give some satisfaction to Egyptian national aspirations.' Special Assistant to the NEA, Samuel K. C. Kopper added that 'throughout the Arab world, ultra-nationalist elements may ... form a greater threat to the maintenance of a pro-Western orientation than the communists'. State Department officials encouraged Britain to make concessions to the Egyptians, who were 'at a point of decision as to whether to cast their lot irrevocably with the West, to remain neutral, or to drift into the Soviet orbit'.[18]

In early 1951, with the Egyptians threatening to abrogate the 1936 treaty and applauding the nationalist revolution in Iran, McGhee concluded that the gain in solving the Anglo–Egyptian impasse 'would outweigh the present advantages of the British position' in Egypt. He urged Britain 'to reach a mutually satisfactory agreement [with Cairo] which takes into account ... Egyptian national aspirations' as well as 'the vital question of security' in the region, by inviting Prime Minister al-Nahas to London for talks and resuming arms deliveries to Egypt. In June, Stabler even advised the British to consider leaving Egypt on the reasoning that 'the base might become a liability rather than an asset. Certain grave difficulties would ensue if Britain had to "dig in" in the Canal Zone'. This advice 'extremely disturbed' British officials. 'While we are ready to make any reasonable concession to Egyptian national

170   *Demise of the British Empire in the Middle East*

aspirations, we are not prepared to give up our essential defence requirements in order to reach an agreement.'[19]

To reconcile their conflicting desires to preserve the British presence in Egypt and to mollify Egyptian nationalism, in early 1951 American officials launched a policy initiative involving a greater American commitment to the defense of Egypt and the Middle East. McGhee, in particular, envisioned a greater American role in regional defense as a means to break the Anglo–Egyptian deadlock. He hoped, for example, that an Anglo–American offer to Egypt to join a trilateral security pact 'would give the Egyptians opportunity to say that the end result was a joint defense agreement with two great world powers and Egypt, all on an equal basis.' 'Unless a new element', such as American participation, 'is injected into the picture', State Department officials told their Pentagon colleagues, 'the British will be unable much longer to withstand ... the demand for evacuation.'[20]

Although Pentagon officials initially refused to sanction American participation in a Middle East pact, they eventually went along with a similar idea to help solve a thorny Anglo–American dispute that surfaced in 1951 over naval commands in the Mediterranean. American officials favored establishing an American command in the western Mediterranean and attaching it to NATO's southern flank. Britain proposed establishing a single British command over the entire Mediterranean, and through it integrating the forces of the USA and of Turkey, which joined NATO in 1951. Exhaustive negotiations between US and British officers failed to produce any agreement on this issue, and in May 1951 Foreign Secretary Herbert Morrison commented that 'delay and argument over this question' were 'in danger of poisoning Anglo–United States relations'. In May 1951, British officials proposed the establishment of a Middle East Command (MEC) with a British supreme commander, affiliated with NATO, and charged with planning regional defense. State Department officials seized on the idea not only as a way to resolve the argument over naval commands but also to add a 'new look' to the Anglo–Egyptian deadlock. The Pentagon agreed reluctantly to join a command that would achieve these purposes.[21]

When the USA agreed to recognize the MEC as a British command, Britain submitted to American pressure to invite Egypt to join MEC as a charter member as a means to resolve the base dispute. Morrison agreed to admit 'Egypt as a partner in a new Allied Middle East Command, in return for which she would be expected to make available to the Allied Command ... those minimum facilities which she still refuses to grant to us'. This idea 'seems at present to offer the only basis upon which the negotiations can be prolonged'. Together with French and Turkish officials, Morrison and Acheson discussed the terms of the

British and American policy toward Egypt   171

MEC and Egypt's role in it in August and September 1951. In early October, the four Western governments jointly proposed to Egypt that the command be established in Cairo with Egyptian participation. In the context of burgeoning Egyptian nationalism, Prime Minister al-Nahas declined the proposal and instead pushed through the Egyptian parliament bills that unilaterally abrogated the 1936 treaty.[22]

The MEC had promised to reconcile British and American interests in Egypt, and its categorical rejection by Egypt, conversely, placed American and British policy on a collision course once again. Incensed by the abrogation, the British redoubled their determination firmly to maintain their occupation of Egypt. Violence wracked the Canal Zone, as the Egyptians challenged British rule through a campaign of guerrilla attacks and sabotage, and as the British, especially after Churchill returned as prime minister on 26 October 1951, staunchly defended their position. Tension steadily escalated until a major battle between British soldiers and Egyptian police on 25 January 1952 left 42 Egyptians and four British dead. The next day, mobs of angry Egyptians protested in the streets of Cairo, burning some 750 buildings and killing 26 Westerners.[23]

As the violence flared, American officials conceded that Britain had the right to defend itself but began to doubt the wisdom of Britain's firmness in Egypt. 'We are ... prepared to give our full diplomatic and political support', Acheson told the British, 'to measures necessary (but which do not go beyond what is necessary) for the purposes of protecting the Suez Base and keeping the Canal open.' Yet as the turmoil escalated, American officials came to fear that 'Egypt is rapidly going down the drain and ... will soon be lost unless the trend is soon reversed'. Therefore, Acheson pressed the British to accept a so-called 'package deal', in which the Western powers would make certain concessions to Egypt, such as recognizing Faruq as king of the Sudan as well as Egypt, in exchange for Egyptian co-operation with the MEC. But Churchill rejected the package deal as a retreat that would weaken British credibility and prestige throughout the Middle East and instead encouraged the USA to send combat forces to help Britain defend the Canal Zone.[24]

Frustrated by Churchill's attitude, State Department officials advised the NSC to consider taking steps to placate Egyptian nationalism even if those steps led to a complete break with Britain. Pentagon officials disagreed, arguing that British air bases in Cairo–Suez remained vital in Western war plans. In light of Pentagon views, Acheson gently pressured the British to concede. 'I am greatly disturbed by the situation in Egypt', he told Foreign Secretary Anthony Eden. 'I fear that unless the situation is changed substantially in the immediate future, opportunity

172   *Demise of the British Empire in the Middle East*

for negot[iation]s with moderate elements will have been lost.' Eden rejected even this modest appeal, saying 'I am disposed to let the Egyptians stew for the present.'[25]

The Egyptian revolution of July 1952 introduced another element of tension into Anglo–American policy in Egypt. Although both London and Washington initially welcomed the new government headed by General Mohammed Neguib and Colonel Gamal Abd al-Nasir, they soon divided over arms-supply policies. In late 1952 American officials moved to supply Egypt with military aid. Such aid would strengthen Neguib against his younger and more nationalistic colleagues, induce Egypt to co-operate with the Middle East Defense Organization (MEDO) (a revised form of the MEC), and entice Egypt to settle with Britain. British officials criticized the American plan. They feared that arms from the USA might only encourage the Egyptians to turn stubborn in talks with Britain, and they feared that if those talks collapsed and violence resumed, Egyptians might attack British soldiers with American weapons.[26]

Anglo–American tension over Egypt increased even more after President Dwight D. Eisenhower and Secretary of State John Foster Dulles took office in Washington in January 1953. Having personally witnessed evidence of extreme nationalism during a visit to Cairo in early 1953, Dulles declared in July that the MEDO was 'on the shelf' and he shifted the focus of US regional security planning from Egypt to the northern tier states of Turkey, Iraq and Iran. In view of this shift of focus, Eisenhower and Dulles became more determined to facilitate an Anglo–Egyptian base settlement that would arrest the rise of Egyptian nationalism. They decided to press the British to make concessions, limited only by their general desire to maintain the Anglo–American alliance and by lingering Pentagon concerns with preserving maximum possible access to Egypt in wartime.[27]

Eisenhower's decision to pressure Britain resulted in a sharp rise of tension between the two allies in early 1953. Churchill, under fire from some of his 'backbenchers', about 40 ultra-conservative members of his own parliamentary party, refused to make any concessions to Egypt. His aides told Evelyn Shuckburgh that he 'thought we should sit on the gippies and have a "whiff of grapeshot"'. Eisenhower, by contrast, expected his British counterpart to make some concessions to Egypt. In March 1953, he refused to endorse a British outline for settlement because it offered nothing to Cairo; he refused to promise that he would withhold military aid to Egypt before a base agreement was reached; he refused Churchill's request, designed to counter the backbenchers' criticism, that a prestigious American military officer participate in British talks with Egypt; and he refused to endorse Britain's negotiating

British and American policy toward Egypt 173

position before the talks began. So angry were British officials at the American position, Ambassador Winthrop Aldrich warned from London, that the Anglo–American alliance might be in jeopardy. As a consequence, Eisenhower relented slightly, and wrote to Neguib encouraging him to recognize that British military presence in Egypt contributed to Egypt's security.[28]

Soon thereafter, however, Dulles concluded that the situation in Cairo was 'most dangerous' and might trigger a shift in the country's outlook to neutralism or even alignment with the Soviets. 'From Foster's personal observation', Eisenhower wrote Churchill, 'I have come to the conclusion that some step should be made soon to reconcile our minimum defense needs with the very strong nationalistic sentiments of the Egyptian Government and people.' In a harshly worded reply, Churchill blasted Eisenhower for refusing to endorse the British effort to provide regional defense and for encouraging Egyptian resistance to British demands. Although concerned by the 'veiled threat' in the message, Eisenhower and Dulles remained firm, and in July 1953 Churchill privately called Eisenhower 'weak and stupid' and expressed regret that he had been elected.[29]

Tensions over the base issue were exacerbated by a dispute over prospective American arms sales to Egypt. Dulles offered to sell Egypt tanks, mine detectors, radios and ammunition valued at $11 million. In deference to British concerns, he withheld from the offer any weapon that might be used by guerrillas against British forces, but in early May 1953 he indicated that he would consummate the deal despite British protests. Anglo–Egyptian talks deadlocked days later, however, forcing American officials to reconsider the arms sale. 'The issue contains more dangers for our relations with Britain than any other single issue I [can] think of', James Bonbright, deputy assistant secretary of state for European affairs, commented. 'If the base negotiations break down and guerrilla warfare starts with Egyptians shooting British soldiers with American ammunition, the results could be catastrophic' for the Anglo–American alliance. When Churchill urgently pleaded for a suspension of the deal, Eisenhower reluctantly agreed to 'drag our feet for a while'. The reversal on the arms sale illustrated American consistency in placing the alliance with Britain over Egyptian national aspirations when the two conflicted.[30]

Although they retreated on the arms sale to Egypt, American officials worked hard in 1953 and 1954 to mediate an Anglo–Egyptian base settlement. 'We are not "backing" either Britain or Egypt', Dulles told Ambassador to Cairo Jefferson Caffery in summer 1953, as Anglo–Egyptian talks resumed in Cairo. 'In certain respects we share the British position. In other respects we share the Egyptian position.' Under

174   *Demise of the British Empire in the Middle East*

American mediation, rapid progress was made toward compromise on the major features of a base settlement. In November 1953, however, the talks collapsed over the seemingly innocuous matter of what type of uniforms the British base technicians would wear. Although both powers were stubborn on this issue, Dulles held the British accountable for the impasse. To force their hand, he threatened in late 1953 to release a promised economic-aid grant of $25 million in January 1954 with or without a base agreement. Churchill asserted that such aid would stiffen Egyptian stubbornness, reveal Anglo–American divergence, and 'have a serious effect on Anglo–American relations'. When Dulles informed Eden that he was 'in deadly earnest' about releasing the aid, Eden privately commented that such a move 'will be deadly to Anglo–American relations'. As in the case of the proposed arms sale, Churchill appealed to Eisenhower to overrule Dulles. As before, Eisenhower relented. Again, when confronted by irreconcilable interests, American officials chose to preserve the Atlantic alliance at the expense of their objectives in Egypt.[31]

In early 1954, perhaps influenced by the strain in Anglo–American relations, Eden conceived of a means to break the deadlock with Egypt. Britain would duck the issue of uniforms by having civilian contractors in civilian dress maintain the base. Encouraged by Eisenhower, Churchill reluctantly accepted this provision. With American backing, British and Egyptian officials then quickly hammered out a formal base treaty, initialled in July and signed in October, that provided for the withdrawal of British troops from Cairo–Suez by June 1956.[32]

CO-OPERATION AND CONFLICT, 1954–56

The Anglo–Egyptian base treaty of 1954 removed a central point of contention in Anglo–American relations in Egypt and renewed, for a brief period, close Anglo–American co-operation in Egypt. In 1954–55, US and British officials collaborated in formulating the so-called 'Alpha plan', a comprehensive outline for a permanent peace settlement between Egypt and Israel. When Eden suggested a joint effort to solve this problem, Dulles immediately agreed, and officials from both governments promptly devised what Shuckburgh called 'a full blueprint for settlement'. Eden and Dulles co-ordinated their presentations of the plan to Egyptian and Israeli leaders in early and mid-1955, but their efforts came to naught. A rising crescendo of violence along the Egyptian–Israeli frontier in 1955 undermined the Alpha plan by spoiling whatever atmosphere of Egyptian–Israeli peacefulness might have existed.[33]

British and American policy toward Egypt 175

Eden and Dulles also co-ordinated their reactions to the Soviet–Egyptian arms deal of September 1955. They resolved to strengthen the northern-tier arrangement, to continue to promote the Alpha plan, and to prevent additional Soviet incursions into the Arab world, in part by offering Egypt joint funding of the Aswan dam. By early 1956, both powers had tired of al-Nasir's criticism of the Baghdad Pact as an instrument of Western imperialism and his efforts to undermine British influence in Jordan. With Britain in the lead, the Western states had resolved by March 1956 to distance themselves from Cairo. Eden conceived a plan to limit al-Nasir's influence through political, economic and propaganda means, and he explored the feasibility of removing al-Nasir from power through covert operations. The Americans adopted a similar policy, code-named 'Omega', to 'let Colonel Nasser realize that he cannot cooperate as he is doing with the Soviet Union and at the same time enjoy most-favored-nation treatment from the United States'. The Americans apparently stopped short of endorsing covert operations, perhaps out of fear that no suitable alternative leader existed.[34]

In light of their anti-al-Nasir strategies, British and American officials agreed that they should shelve their plans to provide aid for the Aswan dam. Rather than abruptly terminate the offer, they would let it 'wither on the vine' to avoid provoking al-Nasir into retaliatory measures such as accepting Soviet aid for the dam. Members of Congress determined to stop the Aswan deal, however, threatened to limit Eisenhower's general prerogatives in foreign aid dispensation, and Dulles felt compelled to terminate the aid offer on 19 July. Dulles' action 'will suit us very well', Foreign Secretary Selwyn Lloyd agreed, and he promptly withdrew Britain's aid offer as well.[35]

Cancellation of the Aswan dam aid offers prompted al-Nasir to nationalize the Suez Canal Company in late July. That action provoked the Suez Crisis, during which American and British differences over Egypt became more pronounced than at any other time in the post-war period, if not in history. British officials considered nationalization a dire threat to their economic, strategic and political interests, and they immediately resolved to recover control of the canal company, by force if necessary. 'The Egyptian has his thumb on our windpipe', Eden observed, and he informed Eisenhower that Britain, in conjunction with France, intended to initiate hostilities against Egypt in order to secure 'the removal of Nasser'. Despite US opposition to such action, British officials grimly determined to move ahead with the attack on Egypt without informing their US counterparts. With France and Israel, they hatched a covert plan of collusion in which Israel would attack Egypt, providing a pretext for Britain and France to send military forces into the Suez Canal region.[36]

176   *Demise of the British Empire in the Middle East*

Eisenhower took the very different view that nationalization of the canal company was a regrettable action but certainly not a cause for war. A British assault on Egypt, he reasoned, would provoke Anglophobia around the world, recommit British forces to indefinite occupation of the Canal Zone, and incite other Arab powers to retaliate by curtailing the supply of oil to the West. Endorsing the use of force, he told the NSC on 31 August, 'might well array the world from Dakar to the Philippine Islands against us'. An Anglo–American schism on the issue 'would be extremely serious', he added, 'but not as serious as letting a war start and not trying to stop it'. To head off war, Eisenhower and Dulles worked hard from August to October to find a political settlement to the crisis. They publicly demanded a peaceful settlement, organized two international conferences at London to seek a compromise solution to the question of canal control, and promoted Anglo–Egyptian discussions at the United Nations.[37]

When war broke out on 29 October, the gap between the USA and Britain widened. To halt the Israeli–Egyptian fighting, Eisenhower sought a UN ceasefire resolution. True to the collusion plan, Britain instead issued an ultimatum to Egypt and Israel to pull back from the Canal, and, when Egypt refused, on 31 October British and French warplanes bombed Egyptian military airfields, a preparatory step to an invasion. Dulles called the ultimatum 'as crude and brutal as anything he had seen ... [and] utterly unacceptable'. 'The French and British do not have an adequate cause for war', Eisenhower declared. He did not 'see much value in an unworthy and unreliable ally and ... the necessity to support them might not be as great as they believed'. The Anglo–French bombardments, Eisenhower declared, were 'the damnedest business I ever saw two supposedly intelligent governments get themselves into'.[38]

Eisenhower decided to halt the Anglo–French attack because in his judgment it threatened vital Western interests throughout the developing world. 'How could we possibly support Britain and France if in so doing we lose the entire Arab world?' he asked. American action to stop the attack would prevent the Soviets 'from seizing a mantle of world leadership through a false but convincing exhibition of concern for smaller nations'. Eisenhower imposed financial and oil sanctions on Britain and France to force them to halt their attack. He welcomed the British and French acceptance of a ceasefire on 6 November but stubbornly maintained the sanctions until both powers pledged to withdraw from Egypt in December. As a result of Eisenhower's actions, Anglo–American strain intensified. Ill feelings were accentuated when Eisenhower agreed to receive Eden and French premier Guy Mollet in Washington in early November but then rescinded the offer, at Dulles' advice, as long as the two European armies remained in Egypt. In late

British and American policy toward Egypt 177

November, 100 Conservative Party stalwarts signed a resolution that American policy 'is gravely endangering the Atlantic Alliance', but Eisenhower refused to soften his stance until Britain agreed to leave Egypt.[39]

In the end, however, the Anglo–American tension remained, as Dulles observed, 'a violent family squabble, but not one which was likely to end in divorce'. Both Britain and the USA recognized the need to repair their relationship at the NATO ministers' meeting that opened on 10 December 1956. State Department officials considered the meeting 'the most important one ever held', and British officials found it 'urgently necessary' to restore 'satisfactory political relations' with Washington. At the meeting, the NATO partners affirmed their friendship. Relations also improved after Eden departed London on 23 November for medical convalescence in Jamaica and resigned the prime ministry on 9 January 1957. Already in secret contact with cabinet ministers Richard A. (Rab) Butler and Harold Macmillan, Eisenhower welcomed Macmillan's ascent to Number 10 Downing Street, and declared his hope of renewed Anglo–American partnership. Eisenhower's defense of Egypt had strained but not broken the alliance.[40]

CONCLUSION

The USA and Britain formed a partnership with regard to Egypt during the Second World War and the early cold war. The USA implicitly endorsed British imperialism in Egypt during the 4 February 1942 incident. Commercial rivalry briefly revived in the late years of the world war, but in the late 1940s the USA consistently supported Britain in its conflict with Egypt over the maintenance of the British base in Egypt. In the early 1950s, the Tripartite Declaration, the Middle East Command, the Alpha Plan, the Aswan dam aid offer and the Omega initiative all bore the imprint of Anglo–American co-operation. To be sure, British and American officials occasionally sparred over certain issues, such as Acheson's 'package deal' proposal and Dulles' desire to award Egypt military and financial aid over British objections, born of America's lingering desire to pacify Egyptian nationalism.

But in all such cases American officials relented to British desires and held back from taking steps that might have irreparably ruptured the Atlantic alliance. Only during the Suez Crisis of late 1956 did American officials withhold their usual endorsement of British policy in Egypt and implement an anti-British policy. But the Americans were concerned more with the tactics, rather than the aims, of British policy. British and American officials eventually overcame the strain produced during the crisis and reaffirmed their partnership.

178 *Demise of the British Empire in the Middle East*

The close Anglo–American relationship in Egypt originated in common security objectives. It was not coincidental that the partnership originated in 1941–42, when both powers were worried at the prospect of Nazi domination of the Middle East, and that it waned temporarily in 1943–45, when threats to regional security diminished. As the cold war generated new concerns with Middle East security after 1946, American officials suspended their sensitivity to Egyptian national aspirations and consistently sided with Britain in its negotiations with Egypt on control of the Canal Zone base. Even after the strategic value of Egypt diminished in 1953, US officials refrained from breaking completely with Britain in order to promote Anglo–American harmony in the cold war. Even as the Suez Crisis revealed Anglo–American conflict over Egypt, the two powers remained in agreement that a united front would serve their common security interests in the cold war. Despite the depth of mutual anger during the Suez War, the alliance survived.

NOTES

1 Works that endorse the 'special relationship' thesis include John Baylis, *Anglo–American Defence Relations, 1939–1980: The Special Relationship* (New York: St Martin's, 1981), and D. Cameron Watt, *Succeeding John Bull: America in Britain's Place, 1900–1975* (Cambridge: Cambridge University Press, 1984). Revisionists who document Anglo–American rivalry include David Reynolds, *The Creation of the Anglo–American Alliance, 1937–1941: A Study in Competitive Cooperation* (Chapel Hill: University of North Carolina Press, 1982); Terry H. Anderson, *The United States, Great Britain, and the Cold War, 1944–1947* (Columbia, MI: University of Missouri Press, 1981); Christopher Thorne, *Allies of a Kind: The United States, Britain, and the War Against Japan* (New York: Oxford University Press, 1981); Wm Roger Louis, *Imperialism at Bay: The United States and the Decolonization of the British Empire, 1941–1945* (London: Oxford University Press, 1984); and Robert M. Hathaway, *Ambiguous Partnership: Britain and America, 1944–1947* (New York: Columbia University Press, 1981).

2 Alexander Kirk to Cordell Hull, 21 January, 1, 4 February 1942, *Foreign Relations of the United States* (hereafter FRUS), *1942* (Washington, DC: Government Printing Office, 1963) Vol. 4, pp. 63–7. See also Charles D. Smith, '4 February 1942: Its Causes and Its Influence on Egyptian Politics and on the Future of Anglo–Egyptian Relations, 1937–1945', *International Journal of Middle East Studies*, 10 (October 1979) pp. 453–79.

3 Welles to Murray, 5 February 1942, *FRUS, 1942*, Vol. 4, pp. 69–70. See also Roosevelt to Churchill, 2 April 1941, 18 March 1942, in Manfred Jonas *et al.* (eds.), *Roosevelt and Churchill: Their Secret Wartime Correspondence* (New York: Dutton, 1975) pp. 137–8, 194–6; Kirk to Hull, 2 August, 7 September 1942, *FRUS, 1942*, Vol. 4, pp. 86–7; memorandum for the record by Esposito, 6 December 1944, Records of the Army Staff, Record Group (RG) 165, OPD 475.7, case 224, National Archives and Records Administration (NARA), Washington, DC (hereafter RG 165, with appropriate filing designations).

4 Kirk to Hull, 15 October 1951, *FRUS, 1941* (Washington, DC: Government Printing Office, 1959) Vol. 3, p. 314. See also John A. DeNovo, 'The Culberston Mission and Anglo–American Tensions in the Middle East, 1944–1945', *Journal of American History*, 63 (March 1977) pp. 913–36.

5 State Department policy statement, 16 April 1945, Harry S. Truman Papers (President's Secretary's Files), Subject File: cabinet Series, box 159, Harry S. Truman Library, Independence, Missouri (Truman Library) (hereafter PSF with appropriate filing designations); NEA policy statement, 'Egypt', 30 August 1945, General Records of the

British and American policy toward Egypt 179

Department of State, RG 59, 711.83, NARA (hereafter RG 59); and memorandum by Bevin, 17 September 1945, Records of the Cabinet Office, Cab 129/1, CP(45)174, Public Record Office (PRO), Kew, London (hereafter Cab 128 or 129 with appropriate filing designations). See also memorandum by Henderson, 13 November 1945, *FRUS, 1945* (Washington, DC: Government Printing Office, 1969) 8, p. 14.

6   JWPC 450/3, 10 March 1946, Records of the Joint Chiefs of Staff, RG 218, CCS 092 USSR (3-27-45), section 7, NARA (hereafter RG 218 with appropriate filing designations). See also JPS 789 (PINCHER) 2 March 1946, US Department of Defense, Joint Chiefs of Staff, *Records of the Joint Chiefs of Staff, Part 2: 1946–1953: Soviet Union* (Washington, DC: University Publications Microfilm) reel 1 (hereafter *RJCS*); 'Air Plan for MAKEFAST, n.d. (autumn 1946), RG 165, ABC 381 USSR (2 March 1946), section 3; JCS 1725/1, 1 May 1947, in Thomas H. Etzold and John Lewis Gaddis (eds.), *Containment: Documents of American Policy and Strategy, 1945–1950* (New York: Columbia University Press, 1978) pp. 302–11; JSPG 496/11, 18 December 1947, *RJCS: Soviet Union*, reel 4; CRASSPIECE, JCS 1844/46, 8 November 1949, *RJCS: Soviet Union*, reel 5.

7   Memorandum by the COS, 2 April 1946, Records of the Defence Committee, Cab 131/2, DO(46)47, PRO (hereafter Cab 131 with appropriate filing designations); memorandum by Dixon, 8 January 1947, Records of the Foreign Secretary's Office, FO 800, ME/47/2, PRO (hereafter FO 800 with appropriate filing designations); memorandum by Chiefs of Staff, 23 January 1947, Records of the Chiefs of Staff Committee, DEFE 5/3, COS (47)5(O), PRO (hereafter DEFE 4 or 5 with appropriate filing designations); and memorandum by Bevin, 19 October 1949, Cab 129/37, CP(49)209. See also Air Staff Plan SANDOWN, 21 August 1948, Records of the Royal Air Force, AIR 8/1602, PRO (hereafter AIR 8 with appropriate filing designations); and digest of Plan SPEEDWAY, 16 December 1948, Records of the Prime Minister's Office, PREM 8/745, PRO (hereafter PREM 8 or 11 with appropriate filing designations).

8   JSPC 684/40, 2 June 1948, Records of the Army Staff, RG 319, P&O 686 TS, case 1, NARA (hereafter RG 319 with appropriate filing designations); memorandum by Maddocks, 4 February 1949, RG 319, P&O 686 TS, case 9; Air Force COS to JCS, 26 March 1949, RG 319, P&O 463 ME TS, case 6/2; memorandum for Secretary of State for Air, 9 May 1949, and minutes of meeting, 13 May 1949, Cab 131/8, DO(49)13:5; and Johnson to Acheson, 19 May 1949, and PPS/56, n.d. (4 August 1949), *FRUS, 1949* (Washington, DC: Government Printing Office, 1976) Vol. 1, pp. 300–11, 368–77; and NSC 47/2, 17 October 1949, PSF, Subject File: NSC Series, box 193.

9   Minutes of meetings, 4 February, 18 March 1946, Cab 128/5, CM 11(46)3 and CM 25(46)4; and memorandum of conversation by Acheson, 20 April 1946, and Byrnes to Tuck, 24 May 1946, Tuck to Byrnes, 11 June 1946, and memorandum of conversation by Wadsworth, 16 December 1946, RG 59, 741.83.

10 Marshall to Johnson, 8 August 1947, *FRUS, 1947* (Washington, DC: Government Printing Office, 1971) Vol. 5, pp. 787–90; Bevin to Cadogan, 11 August 1947, Political Correspondence of the Foreign Office, FO 371, 62979, J3756/12/16, PRO (hereafter FO 371 with appropriate filing designations). See also Bevin to Sargent, 25 April 1947, FO 371/62970, J1924/12/16; Marshall to Douglas, 1 May 1947, *FRUS, 1947*, Vol. 5, pp. 769–70; Henderson to Marshall, 9 July 1947, Douglas to Marshall, 16 July 1947, and Jernegan to Fales, 8 September 1947, RG 59, 741.83; and memorandum of conversation by Lascelles, 17 July 1947, FO 371/62877, J3430/12/16.

11 Douglas to Marshall, 1 September 1947, State Department policy memoranda, n.d. (early October 1947), NEA memoranda, n.d. (early October 1947) *FRUS, 1947*, Vol. 5, pp. 321–3, 513–22, 543–44; and US–UK agreed minute, n.d. (16 October 1947), FO 800/476, ME/47/17.

12 Bevin to Campbell, 5 February 1949, FO 800/457, Eg/49/6. See also PPS/23, 24 February 1948, *FRUS, 1948* (Washington, DC: Government Printing Office, 1976) Vol. 5, pp. 655–6; and Douglas to Acheson, 12 July 1949, Patterson to Acheson, 19, 23 July, 2 August 1949, and Holmes to Acheson, 30 August 1949, RG 59, 883.20.

13 Memorandum by Merriam, 13 June 1949, *FRUS, 1949*, Vol. 6, pp. 31–9; George C. McGhee, *Envoy to the Middle World: Adventures in Diplomacy* (New York: Harper & Row, 1983) p. 53; and JSPC 877/73, 20 September 1949, RG 319, P&O 600.1 TS, section 1, case 8. See also Acheson to Holmes, 17 February 1949, *FRUS, 1949*, Vol. 6, pp. 194–5.

14 NSC 47/1, 1 September 1949, Records of the National Security Council, RG 273, NARA (hereafter RG 273 with appropriate filing designations); minutes of meeting, 14

180   *Demise of the British Empire in the Middle East*

November 1949, and agreed minutes of meeting, 14 November 1949, FO 371/75056, E14770/1026/65. See also memorandum by Collins, 10 April 1950, Records of the Office of the Secretary of Defense, RG 330, CD 6-6-7, NARA (hereafter RG 330 with appropriate filing designations); and memorandum of conversation by Acheson, 13 April 1950, Dean G. Acheson Papers, Secretary of State Series, box 64, Truman Library (hereafter Acheson Papers with appropriate filing designations).

15   Tripartite Declaration Regarding Security in the Near East', Department of State *Bulletin*, 5 June 1950, p. 886; and Bevin to Attlee, 12 May 1950, FO 800/477. See also Foreign Office Paper, 30 July 1949, FO 371/75056, E14565/1026/65; memoranda of conversation by Acheson, 10, 28 March 1950, Battle to Acheson, 14 April 1950, Acheson Papers, Secretary of State Series, box 64; NSC 65, 28 March 1950, and Lay to Truman, 31 March 1950, PSF, Subject File: NSC Series, box 207; and memorandum for the President, 7 April 1950, ibid., box 220.

16   NEA policy statement, 5 July 1950, RG 59, 611.74; memorandum of conversation by Stabler, 17 July 1950, RG 59, 641.74; and memorandum of conversation by Howard, 24 October 1950, *FRUS, 1950*, Vol. 5, pp. 230–3.

17   Paper by Stabler, 24 October 1950, RG 59, 780.5.

18   Stabler to McGhee, 14 December 1950, statement by Kopper, 28 December 1950, and paper by Kopper, 27 December 1950, *FRUS, 1950*, Vol. 5, pp. 330–2, 271–8, 11–14. See also memorandum of conversation, 19 September 1950, FO371/80383, JE1055/55.

19   Minutes of meeting, 2 May 1951, *FRUS, 1951* (Washington, DC: Government Printing Office, 1982) Vol. 5, pp. 113–20; State Department aide-memoire, 21 May 1951, RG 59, 641.74; and draft cable to Elliott, 14 August 1951, and minutes by Bowker, 11 August 1951, FO371/90136, JE1051/177. See also Morrison to Attlee, 27 June 1951, FO 800/636, Eg/51/8.

20   Matthews to Marshall, n.d., *FRUS, 1950* (Washington, DC: Government Printing Office, 1978) Vol. 5, pp. 326–8; and Matthews to Marshall, 11 December 1950, RG 330, CD 092.2 (Egypt) 1950. See also James to Edmonds, 28 October 1950, FO 371/80480, JE12211/1; and approved summary of conclusion, 23 October 1950, *FRUS, 1950*, Vol. 3, pp. 1686–9.

21   Minute of meeting, 7 June 1951, Cab 131/10, DO(51)15:1; minutes of meeting, 21 May 1951, DEFE 4/43, COS(51)84:1; and PPS paper, 23 May 1951, *FRUS, 1951*, Vol. 5, pp. 144–8. See also NSC 47/4, 6 March 1951, PSF, Subject File: NSC Series, box 212; minutes of meeting, 24 May 1951, and UK record of meeting, 8 June 1951, *FRUS, 1951*, Vol. 3, pp. 523–4, 528–33.

22   Memorandum by Morrison, 27 July 1951, Cab 128/19, CM39(51)4. See also Morrison to Acheson, 15 August 1951, *FRUS, 1951*, Vol. 5, pp. 372–6; Acheson to Morrison, 30 August 1951, and Acheson to Caffery, 8 October 1951, RG 59, 641.74; Dorsz to McGhee, 5 October 1951, RG 59, 780.5; Morrison to Acheson, 12 October 1951, and Morrison to Attlee, 12 October 1951, PREM 8/1388; and 'Text of Four-Power Proposal', Department of State *Bulletin* 25 (22 October 1951) pp. 647–8.

23   Morrison to Attlee, 12 October 1951, FO 800/469, ME/51/15; Caffery to Acheson, 24 October 1951, 18 December 1951–4 February 1952, and Gifford to Acheson, 30 October 1951, RG 59, 641.74.

24   Acheson to Gifford, 17 October 1951, RG 59, 641.74; minutes of meeting, 12 December 1951, *FRUS, 1951*, Vol. 5. pp. 434–7; and Acheson to Gifford, 14 December 1951, RG 59, 641.74. See also memorandum by Churchill, 6 January 1952, FO 800/807, ME/52/3; and minutes of meeting, 9 January 1952, *FRUS, 1952–1954* (Washington, DC: Government Printing Office, 1986) Vol. 9, pp. 1746–9.

25   Acheson to Eden, 31 March 1952, FO 800/768, Eg/52/30; and Eden to Stevenson, 13 July 1952, PREM 11/91. See also summary of discussion, 23 April 1952, and NSC 129/1, 24 April 1952, RG 273; and Bradley to Lovett, 25 June 1952, RG 330, CD092 (Egypt) 1952.

26   Caffery to Acheson, 20 August 1952, RG 59, 774.00; Churchill to Eden, 26 August 1952, PREM 11/392; State Department aide-memoire, 5 November 1952, and Caffery to Acheson, 21 November 1952, RG 59, 780.5; Acheson to Lovett, 11 December 1952, RG 330, CD 091.3 Egypt; US aide-memoire, 10 December 1952, FO 371/96897, JE10345/46; and Byroade to Acheson, 3 January 1953, RG 59, 774.5MSP.

27   Circular cable by Dulles, 30 July 1953, RG 59, 780.5. See also memorandum of discussion, 1 June 1953, Dwight D. Eisenhower Papers (Ann Whitman File): NSC Series, box 4, Dwight D. Eisenhower Library, Abilene, Kansas (Eisenhower Library) (hereafter Whitman File with appropriate filing designations); memorandum by Dulles,

British and American policy toward Egypt 181

'Conclusions on Trip', n.d. (May 1953), John Foster Dulles Papers, box 73, Princeton University, Princeton, New Jersey (hereafter Dulles Papers with appropriate filing designations); Hankey to Eden, 5 August 1953, PREM 11/485; and memorandum by H. P. Smith, 26 August 1953, RG 330, CD 092(Egypt)1952.

28   Shuckburgh diary, 30 January 1953, in Evelyn Shuckburgh, *Descent to Suez: Diaries, 1951–56* (New York: Norton, 1987) pp. 75–6. See also Churchill to Eden, 6 January 1953, PREM 11/392; Eden to Churchill, 16 January 1953, FO 800/770, Eg/53/6; Eden to Churchill, 9, 10 March 1953, FO 800/771, Eg/53/46; Eisenhower to Eden, 16 March 1953, and Eisenhower to Churchill, 19 March 1953, Whitman File: International Series, boxes 15–16; Eisenhower to Neguib, 24 March 1953, RG 59, 774.13; and Eisenhower to Churchill, 7 April 1953, PREM 11/486.

29   Dulles to Eisenhower, 17 May 1953, Whitman File: Dulles–Herter Series, box 1; Eisenhower to Churchill, 10 June 1953, and Dulles to Eisenhower, 15 June 1953, Whitman File: International Series, box 16; and Colville diary, 24 July 1953, in John Colville, *Fringes of Power: 10 Downing Street Diaries, 1939–1955* (New York: Norton, 1985) p. 672. See also, Churchill to Eisenhower, 12 June 1953, PREM 11/485.

30   Bonbright to Raynor, 9 May 1953, *FRUS, 1952–1954*, 9, pp. 2063–4; Eisenhower to Churchill, 8 May 1953, Whitman File: International Series, box 16. See also Eden to Makins, 26 January 1953, PREM 11/392; Dulles to Caffery, 9 February 1953, RG 59, 774.00; Byroade to Dulles, 19 February 1953, RG 59, 780.5; and Eden to Makins, 4 May 1953, PREM 11/395.

31   Dulles to Caffery, 22 July 1953, RG 59, 641.74; Eden to Dulles, 17 November 1953, FO 371/102843, JE11345/8; memorandum for the file by Merchant, 16 December 1953, RG 59, 641.74; and minute by Eden, (16 December 1953), FO 371/102843, JE11345/9. See also Dulles to Aldrich, 12 November 1953, RG 59, 641.74; Churchill to Eisenhower, 22 December 1953, PREM 11/699; and Eisenhower to Churchill, 23 December 1953, Whitman File: International Series, box 17.

32   Memorandum of conversation, 12 April 1954, Dulles Papers, White House Memoranda Series, box 1; minutes of meetings, 22 June, 7 July 1954, Cab 128/27, CC 43(45)1 and 47(54)2; and Stevenson to Eden, 11–31 July 1954, PREM 11/702.

33   Shuckburgh diary, 7 March 1955, *Descent to Suez*, p. 252. See also memorandum of conversation by Dulles, 14 February 1955, Dulles to State Department, 24 February 1955, Byroade to Dulles, 6 April, 16, 17, 20 May 1955, *FRUS, 1955–1957* (Washington, DC: Government Printing Office, 1989) Vol. 14, pp. 53–4, 70, 144–5, 188–92; Powers to Radford, 18 August 1955, RG 218, CJCS (Radford), 091 Egypt; and State Department report, 12 September 1955, IR 7042, RG 59, Records of the Research and Analysis Branch.

34   Dulles to Eisenhower, 28 March 1956, Whitman File: Diary Series, box 13. See also minutes of meeting, 20 October 1955, Cab 128/29, CM 36(55)1; Dulles to Eisenhower, (October 1955), Whitman File: Dulles–Herter Series, box 4; Hoover to Humphrey, 14 December 1955, White House Central File [WHCF] (Confidential), box 70, Eisenhower Library (hereafter WHCF with appropriate filing designations); Eden to Eisenhower, 26 November 1955, PREM 11/1177; memorandum of conversation by Russell, 26 October 1955, *FRUS, 1955–1957*, Vol. 14, p. 655; minute by Eden, 3 November 1955, PREM 11/859; Eisenhower diary entry, 10 January 1956, Whitman File: Diary Series, box 9; Lloyd to Trevelyan, 25 March 1956, FO 371/118861; Shuckburgh diary, 1, 3, 12, 13 March 1956, *Descent to Suez*, pp. 339–41; and unsigned message to Washington, 3 April 1956, *FRUS, 1955–1957* (Washington, DC: Government Printing Office, 1989) Vol. 15, pp. 448–9.

35   Selwyn Lloyd, *Suez, 1956: A Personal Account* (London: Cape, 1978) p. 69; Lloyd to Makins, 19 July 1956, FO 371/119056, JE1422/230. See also memorandum of conversation by Allen, 19 July 1956, *FRUS, 1955–1957*, Vol. 15, pp. 863–4.

36   Eden quoted in Hugh Thomas, *Suez* (New York: Harper & Row, 1967) p. 476; and Eden to Eisenhower, 5 August 1956, PREM 11/1098. See also minutes of meeting, 27 July 1956, Cab 128/30, CM 56(54); and Eden to Eisenhower, 27 July 1956, and minutes of Lloyd–Pineau meeting, 29 July 1956, PREM 11/1098; minute by Lloyd, 24 October 1956, FO 800/725; and minutes of meetings, 18, 24 October 1956, Cab 128/30, CM 71(56)4 and CM 73(56)7; and Anthony Eden, *Full Circle: The Memoirs of Sir Anthony Eden* (London: Cassell, 1960) pp. 518–21, 564.

37   Minutes of meeting, 31 August 1956, Whitman File: NSC Series, box 8. See also minutes of cabinet meeting, 27 July 1956, Whitman File: Cabinet Series, box 7; memorandum of

182 *Demise of the British Empire in the Middle East*

conversation by Goodpaster, 28 July 1956, Whitman File: Diary Series, box 16; and memorandum of conversation by Dulles, 30 July, 12 October 1956, Dulles Papers, Telephone Conversation Series, boxes 5, 11; Makins to Lloyd, 31 August 1956, FO 371/119124, JE 14211/1267; memorandum of conversation by Rountree, 8 September 1956, *FRUS, 1955–1957* (Washington, DC: Government Printing Office, 1990) Vol. 16, pp. 439–40; and Makins to Lloyd, 4 September 1956, PREM 11/1121.

38 Memoranda of conversations, 30 October 1956, Whitman File: Diary Series, box 18; Eisenhower quoted in Robert A. Divine, *Eisenhower and the Cold War* (New York: Oxford, 1981) pp. 85–6. See also Dixon to Lloyd, 30 October 1956, PREM 11/1105; and Eisenhower to Eden, 30 October 1956, and Eden to Eisenhower, 30 October 1956, PREM 11/1177.

39 Summary of discussion, 1 November 1956, Whitman File: NSC Series, box 8; and Eisenhower to Dulles, 1 November 1956, Whitman File: International Series, box 19; Nutting, *No End of a Lesson*, p. 154. See also memorandum of conversation by Goodpaster, 30 October 1956, Whitman File: Diary Series, box 19; Hoover to Aldrich, 27 November 1956, WHCF (Confidential), box 82; minutes of meetings, 29 November, 1 December 1956, Cab 128/30, CM 91(56)1 and CM 96(56)1.

40 Summary of discussion, 30 November 1956, Whitman File, NSC Series, box 8; minutes of meeting, 27 November 1956, Cab 128/30, CM 89(56)2. See also memorandum of conversation, 20 November 1956, Whitman File: International Series, box 15; record of conversation by Lloyd, 10 December 1956, PREM 11/1107; memorandum of conversation by Goodpaster, 15 December 1956, Dulles Papers, White House Memoranda Series, box 4; and Alistair Horne, *Harold Macmillan*, Vol. 1, *1894–1956* (New York: Viking, 1989) pp. 452–60.

PART 4

DEGREES OF ACCOMMODATION WITH BRITAIN

10

The decline of British influence and the ruling elite in Iraq

MICHAEL EPPEL

The status of the ruling elite of traditional notable families in Iraq, which had prevailed since the establishment of that country in 1921, was undermined by the rise of new social forces, and especially the Westernized middle strata (*effendiyya*).[1] Politicians from among the conservative ruling elite, whose interest lay in preserving the *status quo*, had no solutions for the economic and social distresses of the *effendiyya* and the poorer strata whose numbers were growing steadily in the cities. The conservative politicians, who mobilized nationalist sentiment as a means of enlisting the support of the *effendiyya* in the cities and the creation of a common denominator for the heterogeneous population of Iraq, had no answer to the *effendiyya*'s own radical nationalist-ideological moods and messages, which included more and more demands for socio-economic and political changes. At the same time, the decline in British influence in Iraq and in the Middle East in general, accompanied by Britain's decreased ability to defend the regime that it had established in 1921 and the elite that it had helped to reinforce during the 1920s,[2] played a role in the creation of conditions under which that elite was removed from power, and the Hashemite monarchy was overthrown in 1958. The fall of the monarchy in the coup led by Abd al-Karim Qassem in July 1958 marked the end of the historical chapter of British rule and influence in Iraq. Between 1941 and 1958, Britain went from total control to the loss of all its influence and standing in Iraq.

The difference of opinion between Britain and Iraq with regard to the limitations on Iraq's independence imposed by the various articles of the British–Iraqi treaty of 1930 acted as a catalyst for anti-British nationalist unrest, which reached its zenith with the rise of Rashid Ali al-Gaylani's nationalist government to power in April 1941. The hostilities between Britain and Iraq the following month marked the peak of a wave of anti-British nationalism which had developed in Iraq since the British conquest following the Second World War.[3] This wave had gained strength during the 1930s, in the wake of political radicalization, increased social unrest, and the growing influence of nationalist-authoritarian-Fascist trends in the Middle East. The al-Gaylani government enjoyed the support of a group of anti-British nationalist officers, headed by Salah al-Din al-Sabbagh, who, since 1937, had become the main focus of power in Iraq.

Iraqi anti-British nationalism stemmed not only from objection to Western dominance and to the limitations placed by Britain on Iraq's independence, but was fuelled also by economic distress, social tensions and the identity crises and frustrations among the social groups and strata that had been increasingly exposed to modernization and Westernization.

Following the conflict and the suppression of the nationalist forces that had supported the al-Gaylani government, Britain resumed full control of Iraq. Britain restored the Hashemite monarchy and reinforced the control of the conservative elite, on which it had based its own status in Iraq.[4] However, Britain failed to change the basic conditions, or to halt the processes and tensions that had undermined its status in that country.

The al-Gaylani government and the nationalist supporters had been perceived by many members of the *effendiyya* and the poorer urban strata as a popular nationalist uprising (the 'Rashid Ali Movement'). Their ejection only increased hatred for Britain as a colonialist oppressor. The myths that had grown up around the anti-British revolt of 1920 and had become the foundation of Iraq's nationalist heritage now gained an additional chapter – the myth of the 'Rashid Ali Movement' as a popular anti-British nationalist movement. Both chapters of the central modern myths behind Iraqi nationalism centred on events in the struggle against Britain.

In addition to intensifying the hatred of Britain, the outbreak of violence in 1941 affected the stability of the regime and the socio-political structure in Iraq, which hitherto had constituted the basis for Britain's position in Iraq. The 'Rashid Ali Movement', though headed by politicians and army officers, most of whom belonged to or were affiliated with the conservative ruling elite, gravely damaged the status of that elite as well as that of the royal house. The status of the major politicians of the ruling elite declined, and their nationalist image, which they had taken such care to foster in the 1920s and 1930s, was severely weakened.

Nuri al-Sa'id, the architect of the British–Iraqi treaty of 1930, Regent Abd al-Ilah, Jamil al-Midfa'i, Tawfiq al-Suwaydi and other senior politicians, who fled Iraq in March–April 1941 and returned in June of that year following the expulsion of Rashid Ali and the nationalist

Decline of British influence and the ruling elite in Iraq 187

officers, were now viewed by large segments of public opinion, especially among the *effendiyya*, as the collaborators and slaves of Britain.[5]

In view of the outbreak of violence, in which the *effendiyya* and the urban masses had played a central role, Nuri al-Sa'id (prime minister between 1941 and 1944) and other senior politicians tended to rely even more on the support of the tribal notables, who were in the process of becoming landowners. The integration of these notables into parliament and various Iraqi state institutions – a process initiated by King Faysal I in the 1920s with British encouragement – was intended to neutralize the Shi'ite threat and to reinforce state control of the tribes.[6] This trend increased after 1941, in order to balance the growing influence of the new, nationalist-oriented urban forces calling for change in the socio-political *status quo*. The percentage of landowning tribal notables and their intimates in parliament rose considerably after 1941, to a figure of 30–35 per cent and more, as against 18–20 per cent in the 1930s.[7] This had the effect of intensifying the conflict experienced by the conservative ruling elite and its politicians: between their need for the *effendiyya* and their increasing dependency on the conservative landowning tribal notables, who opposed the reforms and accelerated modernization that the *effendiyya* and the poorer strata needed so badly.

The *effendiyya*, who were constantly increasing in numbers as the modernization of Iraq continued, viewed Britain not only as the colonialist force that limited Iraq's independence and sought to keep it in a position of weakness and backwardness, but as the mainstay of the elite and its despised conservative politicians.

BRITAIN AND THE SEARCH FOR A CHANGE IN THE SOCIO-POLITICAL
BASES OF THE BRITISH POSITION IN IRAQ

At the close of the Second World War, the status of the ruling elite in Iraq was undermined by the rise of the new social forces and their ever-increasing nationalist, radical and leftist changes and moods. In the inter-Arab arena, Iraq and Transjordan were competing with Egypt and Saudi Arabia for dominance in the Arab League, the Fertile Crescent and primarily in Syria. The question of the British–Iraqi treaty of 1930, which was due to expire in 1957, arose immediately after the war. Negotiations between the parties for a new treaty were to have begun only in 1952.

However, with the end of the war, relations with Britain became a central issue charged with nationalist emotions in the Iraqi political arena.[8] The growing anti-British trends in Egypt and the renewal of

188 *Demise of the British Empire in the Middle East*

Egyptian–British negotiations in 1946 attracted the interest of Iraqi nationalists. Iraqi politicians demanded the opening of negotiations for modification of the treaty, or the conclusion of a new treaty, in which the limitations on Iraq's independence would be removed and its status made equal to that of Britain itself.

Nuri al-Sa'id, Regent Abd al-Ilah, and major pro-British politicians were not happy about renewing discussion of such a sensitive theme; however, in view of Iraqi public opinion and the desire not to lag behind Egypt, they could not resist the demands for a modification of the treaty or for a new treaty altogether.[9] The difficulties which characterized Anglo–Egyptian relations in 1946 also raised hopes among Iraqi politicians, who believed that a hasty resolution of the topics disputed by Iraq and Britain would assure economic aid and military supplies to Iraq, and would thus strengthen its regional position *vis-à-vis* Egypt and Saudi Arabia. This consideration arose in the context of the polarization that occurred between the Egyptian–Saudi and the Hashemite–Iraqi–Transjordanian axes. The questions of Syria's and Palestine's future and the domination of the Fertile Crescent provided the central points in the dispute.

At the end of the First World War, British officials believed increasingly that Britain's continued reliance in Iraq on the narrow conservative elite and its corrupt senior politicians could have dangerous consequences for Britain's status, in view of the social unrest and the rise of the new social forces. Following the establishment of the Labour government in England in 1945 and Ernest Bevin's appointment as foreign secretary, British diplomats became increasingly sensitive to the need to open a channel of communication with the modern middle class then emerging in Iraq and other Arab countries, and to win them over to a more positive attitude toward Britain.[10] This approach, strongly encouraged by Bevin, implied that in the Middle East Britain must stop relying exclusively on the rich, conservative families of the ruling elites of notables, who still sought to preserve the socio-political *status quo* even if this meant holding up economic development and perpetuating the gap between their countries and the West. According to Bevin, if Britain desired a firm position in the Middle East, and wanted to meet the challenge of Soviet infiltration and communist influence and to hold its own against covert competition by the United States, it must find a way to make contact with the new forces calling for social change and economic development – that is, the *effendiyya*.

In view of the weakness of the political forces that reflected the Westernized middle strata, British officials sought out Iraqi politicians who would be able to meet these complex requirements: in other words, to be pro-British on one hand, and popular among the anti-British,

Decline of British influence and the ruling elite in Iraq   189

nationalist *effendiyya* on the other; while at the same time, being capable of achieving economic and political modernization in Iraq and convinced of the rightness of such modernization.[11] Although not all Foreign Office officials or British representatives in the Middle East agreed with this anti-colonialist trend, those who had thought in such terms even before Bevin's days[12] were soon joined by more recent converts won over by Bevin.

One of the few Iraqi politicians who the British hoped would be capable of promoting socio-economic and political reform, while remaining acceptable to the nationalist *effendiyya* and yet being pro-British and a convenient opposite number for dialogue, was the Shi'ite politician Salih Jabr.[13] Jabr, the scion of a modest family, had climbed the state bureaucratic ladder and found his place in the ruling elite by marriage to the daughter of one of the richest landowners in Iraq. He enjoyed the protection and patronage of the conservative politician Nuri al-Sa'id. Jabr did indeed support democratization, integration of young members of the *effendiyya* into the Iraqi state administration, accelerated development and modernization, and socio-economic reform. At the same time, however, the *effendiyya* viewed him as totally identified with the conservative elite and with Nuri al-Sa'id, his patron, the epitome of pro-British conservatism.

On 29 March 1947, a government headed by Jabr – the first Shi'ite prime minister since the establishment of the Iraqi State – was formed in Baghdad. Revising the treaty with Britain and drafting a new one were the prime goals of the Jabr government.[14] Jabr had inherited a situation in which calling for urgent revision of the treaty was the only way of avoiding an immediate and crushing attack by Iraqi nationalists and by those politicians who saw advantage in exploiting the nationalist ferment. Jabr sought to gain for himself the status of the most senior and reliable Iraqi politician with influence in the inter-Arab arena.

The negotiations between Britain and Egypt ran aground in the autumn of 1946. The failure of Egyptian Prime Minister Isma'il Sidqi to ratify the draft of the treaty with Britain led to his resignation and to crises in British–Egyptian relations. The anti-British demonstrations in Egypt and the Egyptian refusal to sign the treaty were quite sympathetically viewed by the nationalist public opinion of the Iraqi *effendiyya*. Jabr feared the effects of British–Egyptian negotiations on the nationalists in Iraq, and intended to exploit the dead end into which they had run in order to pressure Britain into making concessions to Iraq. By using the crisis in Anglo–Egyptian relations, Jabr sought to transform Iraq into Britain's mainstay in the area and to ensure that Iraq would be the first among the Arab states to receive significant military and economic aid. The achievement of military and economic assistance from Britain and

190 *Demise of the British Empire in the Middle East*

the reinforcement of Iraq's position *vis-à-vis* that of Egypt were vital, in light of the polarization and rivalry that prevailed in the inter-Arab arena between Iraq and Transjordan, on one hand, and the Egyptian–Saudi axis, on the other.

Another motive for urgent action had to do with the Iraqi government's anxiety – shared by the ruling elite as a whole – over the question of communism in general and that of Soviet penetration of northern Iraq in particular.[15] This anxiety was increased following several strikes over economic issues between 1945 and 1947, as well as by the growth in communist activity (although this was, admittedly, taken more seriously than it need have been). Moreover, the Iraqi elite was apprehensive about the possibility of a Kurdish revolt assisted by the Soviet Union.[16]

At this time Iraq was in desperate need of economic aid, including food shipments. As a by-product of a new treaty and the resultant stabilization of relations with Britain, Jabr hoped for economic and military aid. The difficulties encountered in their talks about military aid led Jabr to agree in June of that year to postpone the continuation of negotiations until the autumn.

THE PORTSMOUTH TREATY FIASCO AND ITS CONSEQUENCES

In August 1947, contacts on the new Iraqi–British treaty were renewed, under pressure from the Regent and Jabr.[17] Jabr's distress and disappointment mounted when Britain – then undergoing an economic and financial crisis of its own – refused to unfreeze Iraq's currency reserves in British banks and to permit their exchange for gold and dollars. This denied Jabr a political and financial achievement to present to the Iraqi public. He now feared attacks from the 'unholy alliance' of the parliamentary opposition (who would cite the nationalist cause in justification for turning against him)[18] with *al-Istiqlal*-led nationalists of the Baghdad streets (frustrated by their election defeats in March 1947) and communist activists. This was the background for Jabr's statement to the British Chargé d'Affaires in Baghdad, in November 1947, that he was in urgent need of an achievement that he could present to parliament at the opening of its next session, on 1 December.[19]

The Regent and his prime minister, who both hoped that the British would remain in Iraq, wanted Britain to agree to the transfer to Iraq of sovereignty over the British military bases and to remove other conspicuous limitations on Iraq's sovereignty. In 1945, the Regent had been reluctant to renegotiate the treaty with Britain, but now favoured it with considerable vigour. His change of heart was due to the anti-

Decline of British influence and the ruling elite in Iraq

royalist and anti-Hashemite trends emerging in Iraq, primarily under the influence that nationalists and communists were gaining among the *effendiyya* and the masses, but also among the ranks of the opposition in parliament.[20] He arranged for the supply of new weapons and equipment to the Iraqi Army in order to ensure its loyalty. During his visit to London in October 1947, the British informed the Regent of their willingness to reopen negotiations, although, as noted, they were not obliged to do so until 1952.

The Labour government sought to improve Britain's status, not by preserving the colonial empire, but by replacing it with bilateral treaties with its former protectorates within the framework of the British Commonwealth. Bevin thought that Britain should comply with Iraq's desires in the matter of the treaty and should extend military and economic aid to Iraq[21] (as far as it was able at the time). In light of the disappointment over the crisis in relations with Egypt in 1946 and the rising waves of anti-British nationalism among its citizens, Iraq now appeared to Bevin as Britain's mainstay in the Middle East. Iraq, with its petroleum resources, its great economic potential, and its explicitly pro-British leaders – especially Salih Jabr, who was perceived as a representative of the new generation of politicians, and a proponent of reforms and modernization – met British expectations and seemed to be a convenient ally. It was thought that good relations with Iraq might constitute an important basis for strengthening Britain's status throughout the Middle East. The British decision to reopen the negotiations also derived from fear that refusing Iraqi requests would increase nationalist pressure on the government of Iraq.[22]

Britain was prepared to concede a considerable proportion of the Iraqi demands for removal of the limitations on its independence. The true bone of contention, however, was the question of the British bases in Habbaniya and Shuaiba.[23] From Iraq's point of view, the matter of the bases was an emotionally charged subject, which symbolized British military presence and the limitations on Iraqi sovereignty. As Britain saw it, the bases were extremely vital for the protection of the oil fields and the strategic routes in the Persian Gulf and northern Iraq. Even when the empire was in the process of collapse and India, Britain's most important colony, had already been granted independence, Iraq's strategic importance remained unchanged, because of its proximity to the Soviet Union. Eventually, in January 1948, it was agreed that Britain would retain its status in the bases, though it was noted that, when world peace prevailed, the British military presence in Iraq would come to an end and would be replaced by collective security arrangements according to the UN Convention.

The new treaty, signed on 15 January 1948 at Portsmouth, was never

192   *Demise of the British Empire in the Middle East*

ratified. When news of the signature reached Baghdad, the city broke out in violent riots and demonstrations, which led to the dismissal of the Jabr government and to Iraq's withdrawal from the new treaty. The wave of violence, though brought about by anti-British nationalist opposition to the treaty, was caused no less by the economic distress of broad strata of Iraq's population and the frustration of the students and young members of the *effendiyya* who led the riots and demonstrations. Activists of *al-Istiqlal*, the National Democratic Party and the Communist Party played a central role in provoking the riots. The violence in January 1948 – the *wathba* – shook the regime and the ruling elite to their foundations, and gave rise to fears of revolution.[24] However, in 1948, Iraq did not yet have enough of a well-organized opposition to exploit the situation for political gains, let alone in order to seize power. At the head of the opposition parties, whose activity had contributed to the outbreak of riots, were politicians who belonged to or were affiliated with the ruling elite; as such, while they admittedly sought to bring about political changes, they feared that the outbreak of chaos in the streets and the absolute collapse of the regime might threaten the existence of the Iraqi state. The traditional tribal forces were still capable of providing support for the elite politicians. The ruling elite, Britain's mainstay, was able to survive, but was impotent to sign a new treaty with Britain.

The fall of the Jabr government damaged Britain's prestige and frustrated attempts to resolve the various differences between the two states, which would have secured British interests while giving some satisfaction to the nationalist claims in Iraq. But more important, the collapse of the government put an end to any British hope of finding among the Iraqi politicians allies who could be accepted by the new, increasingly anti-British social forces.

After the failure of the Portsmouth treaty and the fall of the Jabr government, British and Iraqi efforts continued with a view to reaching some kind of arrangement on central issues: oil, the economy and security. In 1952, a new agreement was concluded between the government of Iraq and the British-owned Iraq Petroleum Company (IPC), which gave Iraq much better conditions than those of the previous contract. The flexibility demonstrated by the British representatives of IPC, stemmed from the lessons learned during the Mussadeq crisis in Iran the previous year, and of the 1950 Saudi–American agreement for a 50–50 split on oil profits.[25] The British continued to encourage Iraq to allocate resources to development and improvement of its standard of living; to this end, they encouraged the establishment of the Iraq Development Board in 1950.[26] The Iraqi–British moves and agreements were in the framework of relations with the conservative pro-British senior politicians. The

Decline of British influence and the ruling elite in Iraq 193

British abandoned the trend of encouraging new politicians and political forces that favoured development of socio-political and economic change, which might have expanded the base of support of the regime among the *effendiyya* and the poorer strata.

THE ACCELERATED EROSION OF THE SOCIO-POLITICAL CONSERVATIVE FORCES: THE BASIS OF THE BRITISH POSITION IN IRAQ, 1948–58

During the 1950s, British experts and diplomats in Iraq continued to issue warnings that the elite, on which Britain relied so heavily in Iraq, was narrow and composed of politicians and rich families who had a hard time adjusting to the changes on the Iraqi scene and whose status had therefore been undermined. Various memoranda and reports indicated the socio-political processes and tensions, the poverty and social gaps, which were liable to cause the collapse of the regime and the ruling elite.

In 1953, Sir John Troutbeck – British Ambassador to Iraq between 1951 and 1954 – submitted a long and comprehensive report on the socio-political situation in Iraq and the vital need for democratization and socio-economic reforms in order to preserve the stability of the regime. Troutbeck emphasized repeatedly the close relationship between the preservation of political stability in Iraq and the preservation of British interests and British–Iraqi defence arrangements.[27] Another report, by the ethnographer Wilfrid Thesiger, which dealt with the social processes among the tribes and city residents, reflected the erosion in the status of the ruling elite and the landowning tribal notables who had become the main support of that elite.[28]

Despite British awareness of the decline of the ruling elite and the rise of new social forces, no real attempt was made to find new allies. On the one hand, the British had difficulty convincing the conservative Iraqi politicians, primarily Nuri al-Sa'id, to institute socio-economic reforms, implement democratization and expand the scope of party activity. On the other hand, among those politicians and parties in favour of reforms, they found no allies capable of coping with the conservative trends among the elite.

The activity of the opposition parties, which was permitted to resume in 1946, continued sporadically, and was repeatedly banned for certain periods, owing to outbreaks of violence and the fears of the elite. These parties – the rightist-nationalist *al-Istiqlal* and the moderate leftist National Democratic Party – which represented the new social forces, admittedly enjoyed the support of the younger generation of the Westernized middle strata; however, their ability to cope with the dominant conservative trends of the ruling elite, which relied more and more on traditional and conservative sectors of the population (the tribes in general and the landowning tribal notables in particular), was limited. True, it was the activity of those parties, as well as that of the Communist Party, which catalyzed the transformation of socio-political unrest among the students and the *effendiyya*, and mobilized the economic distress of the poorer strata into waves of demonstrations and violent riots (the *wathba* of January 1948, the *intifada* of November 1952, and the renewed rioting of October 1956). However, the opposition parties were unable to translate these outbreaks into concrete political achievements.

The Conservative British government, which came to power in 1951, did not share the ideological outlook that had impelled the Labour government to seek allies among the new social forces. This might have not only encouraged economic development but also socio-political and economic reform, which in turn might have allayed the tension within Iraqi society and halted anti-British nationalist trends.

Despite the evaluation by British diplomats and experts of the danger to the stability of the regime, owing to its conservatism and lack of a broad base of support, the Foreign Office in London emphasized security-related, strategic issues – in other words, the rapid and efficient integration of Iraq into a regional defence alliance to counter the threat of communism, while relying on the conservative, pro-British politicians and elite. The British diplomats – some of whom had conservative views – found it convenient, despite their fears, to conduct bilateral relations with the pro-British conservative senior Iraqi politicians. The latter were well known to His Majesty's Government and believed that their own future, as well as that of their country, and the preservation of the all-important *status quo*, could be assured by means of a treaty with Britain.

In September 1953, a new government was set up in Iraq under Fadhil al-Jamali, a pro-Western nationalist politician from the ruling elite, who believed in implementing controlled reform while enlisting the support of the nationalist students and young members of the middle strata. This government was regarded by British officials with scepticism and suspicion.[29] Al-Jamali aroused certain fears and reservations among the British diplomats, owing to his tendency to strengthen Iraq's ties with the United States and to regard the latter as an ally capable of assisting in Iraq's development and strengthening its regional status. As al-Jamali and his government – which included young technocrats convinced of the necessity for reform – had little political backing and depended on the majority of parliament, which was controlled by Nuri al-Sa'id and the dominant conservative elements

Decline of British influence and the ruling elite in Iraq   195

of the elite, Britain did nothing to strengthen the new government, both because it viewed it as intrinsically weak and because of fear of its liberal, pro-American trends.

Following the fall of the al-Jamali government in April 1954, control in Iraq returned to the hands of the long-standing politician Nuri al-Sa'id (in the first few months – April–August 1954 – the actual prime minister was Arshad al-'Umari, one of Nuri's intimates). Nuri's return to power marked an intensification of Iraqi activity aimed at involving Iraq in a strategic alliance with the West, specifically with Britain, while suspending party-political activity and adopting stringent measures against the opposition.

The exacerbation of the cold war and the risk of a Third World War increased the weight given by Britain to strategic considerations and the involvement of Iraq in a Middle Eastern defence pact. Britain's inability to bring Egypt and other Arab states into a regional alliance with the West, which could constitute a strategic barrier against communist incursion, gave Iraq even more of a key position in the context of regional preparedness. The establishment of a pro-Western defence alliance, which would also involve the northern-tier states of Iran and Turkey, was in line with Nuri al-Sa'id's regional policy, according to which Iraq was slated to play a key role as the link between the Arab League and the non-Arab states in the area, and as the principal mainstay of Britain and the West in the Middle East.[30]

The Turkish–Iraqi treaty of January 1955 and the Baghdad Pact that coalesced during 1955 constituted a British attempt to form a strategic barrier against the Soviet threat, which would enable Britain to cope with the rise of radical trends in the Arab world and to preserve its interests in the region in general and in Iraq in particular. None the less, Britain's attempt to maintain its status in Iraq and the Middle East by setting up a regional framework failed.

True, the Baghdad Pact proved a convenient solution, as it enabled an arrangement to be made with regard to the sensitive issues of preserving British capacity for military intervention in Iraq and constituted an important link in the global strategic array. But what undermined Britain's status in Iraq was not the Soviet strategic threat. Rather, the Baghdad Pact did not provide a response to the challenge of increasingly leftist-nationalist radicalism, whose influence on the new urban social strata throughout the Arab world, and primarily in Iraq, was constantly growing and expanding. The involvement of Iraq in a regional defence alliance with Britain could not stop the social processes that ate away at the status of the ruling elite and the Iraqi regime; nor could it neutralize the rise of those social and political forces inspired by the radical leftist-nationalist atmosphere and the revolutionary regime in Egypt.

196   *Demise of the British Empire in the Middle East*

Britain's reliance on the conservative ruling elite, as well as its alienation from the *effendiyya* and the poorer strata, reduced its influence on the officers of Iraq's army. Admittedly, after the renewed conquest of Iraq by Britain in 1941, those officers who were suspected of anti-British nationalism had been expelled from the army; still, anti-British sentiments continued to flow beneath the surface of the junior and intermediate officer corps. Britain's image as a colonialist power and the mainstay of a reactionary elite which was holding back Iraq's development and preventing any solution for the distress of much of its Westernized middle-stratum population was shared by many of the army officers who originated in that stratum. It was only natural, then, that the *coup d'état* launched by radical nationalist officers under Abd al-Karim Qassem and Abd el-Salam Arif in July 1958 dealt a death blow to the influence of the former Great Power in Iraq.

Britain's status in Iraq was closely related to the fate of the ruling elite, which it had fostered since the establishment of the Iraqi state. That elite, which had become more and more dependent on the conservative landowning elements and the tribal notables, was Britain's sole mainstay in Iraq. The failure of British attempts – especially under the Labour government – to expand its support base in Iraq, encourage development and democratization, and halt the nationalist trends, which identified Britain with the hated elite, was a foregone conclusion. The new social forces were characterized by anti-British nationalist trends. Britain, whose interests and status in Iraq had always been linked to the elite politicians, had no practical way of forming a dialogue with these new forces.

The British attempt to adapt its relationship with Iraq to the new conditions of the cold war by establishing a regional defence alliance, the Baghdad Pact, did not provide a response to the challenges facing the conservative elites in the Arab states and Britain's own status in the Middle East. The close link maintained by Britain with the conservative elite and the regime backed by it in Iraq proved to be a death sentence for British influence and status when the regime fell, dragging the elite down with it, in 1958.

NOTES

1   On the characteristics of the *effendiyya*, or Westernized middle strata, see Michael Eppel, 'The Elite, the *Effendiyya* and the Socio-political Conditions of the Growth of Nationalism and the Diffusion of Pan-Arab Ideology in Hashemite Iraq: 1921–1958', *International Journal of Middle Eastern Studies* (forthcoming).

2   See Peter Sluglett, *Britain in Iraq, 1914–1932* (London: Ithaca, 1976).

3   Walid M. S. Hamdi, *Rashid Ali al-Gailani and the Nationalist Movement in Iraq, 1939–1941* (London: Dart, 1987).

4   Daniel Silverfarb, *The Twilight of British Ascendancy in the Middle East* (London: Macmillan 1994) pp. 12–19.

Decline of British influence and the ruling elite in Iraq 197

5 Ibid.
6 Hanna Batatu, *The Old Social Classes and Revolutionary Movements of Iraq* (Princeton, NJ: Princeton University Press, 1978) pp. 31–2, 99–110.
7 Ibid., p. 103.
8 See, e.g., *al-Zaman* (Baghdad), 2 January 1945. 'Parliamentary and Press Campaign for Revision of the Anglo–Iraqi Treaty of Alliance', 5 February 1945, in Stonehewer Bird (British Ambassador to Iraq) to FO, no. 241, 8 July 1945, PRO/FO/371/45303/E/5420.
9 Busk (Baghdad) to FO, no. 35, 5 September 1946, PRO/FO/371/52402/E/906.
10 Bevin to Eyres (Damascus), 15 January 1947, PRO/FO/371/52365/E/12303.
11 Wm Roger Louis, *The British Empire in the Middle East, Arab Nationalism, the United States and Postwar Imperialism* (Oxford, Clarendon Press, 1983) pp. 315–17.
12 See comments by C. W. Baxter, Head of the Foreign Office Eastern Department, on 7 March 1945, on letter from Cornwallis (Baghdad), PRO/FO/371/42329/E/1531.
13 Louis, *British Empire in the Middle East*, p. 321. Michael Eppel, *The Palestine Conflict in the History of Modern Iraq* (London: Frank Cass, 1994), pp. 160–1.
14 *The Cabinet Programme of H. Saleh Jabr, Baghdad, April 10, 1947* (Baghdad Government Press, 1947).
15 British Intelligence Report, Iraq and Persia, Tribal and Political Review for the Year 1946, PRO/FO/371/52321/E/4248.
16 Busk (Baghdad) to Wright (FO), 1 September 1947, PRO/FO/371/61594/E/8789. Thompson (Baghdad) to Bevin, 26 September 1945, PRO/FO/371/45295/E/7495.
17 Busk to FO, no. 712, 1 August 1947, PRO/FO/371/61592/E/7328.
18 Busk to FO, no. 278, 31 July 1947, PRO/FO/371/61592/E/7156.
19 Busk to FO, no. 1049, 7 November 1947, PRO/FO/371/61596/E/10448G.
20 Busk to FO, no. 278, op. cit. Outward Telegram from Commonwealth Relations Office, Top Secret, no. 807, 19 November 1947, PRO/FO/371/61596/E/10554.
21 Bevin to Hugh Dalton, 15 October 1947, PRO/FO/371/61595/E/9513. Memorandum by Bevin, CP(47), 277, 3 October 1947, Cab 129/21.
22 Louis, *British Empire in the Middle East*, p. 328.
23 Silverfarb, *Twilight of British Ascendancy in the Middle East*, pp. 132–4.
24 Eppel, *The Palestine Conflict*, pp. 173–7. Silverfarb, *Twilight of British Ascendancy in the Middle East*, pp. 141–55.
25 Matthew Elliot, *Independent Iraq, the Monarchy and British Influence* (London, New York: Tauris, 1996) p. 32. Stephen Hemsley Longrigg, *Oil in the Middle East: A Political, Social and Economic History* (London: Oxford University Press, 1968) pp. 189–91.
26 Gerwin Gerke, 'The Iraq Development Board and British Policy, 1945–1950', *Middle Eastern Studies*, 27 (1991) pp. 231–55.
27 Troutbeck (Baghdad) to Churchill, no. 108, 22 June 1953, PRO/FO/371/104665/EQ/1016/32.
28 'The Mass Movement of Tribesmen from Amara Liwa to Baghdad and Basra', by W. Thesiger, 18 July 1955, in Embassy (Baghdad) to Levant Department, 5 August 1955, PRO/FO/371/115748/VQ/1015/11.
29 Michael Eppel, 'The Fadhil al-Jamali Government in Iraq, 1953–1954: The Last Attempt at Changes and Reforms in the Conservative Regime Before the Revolution', *Journal of Contemporary History* (forthcoming).
30 On Nuri al-Sa'id's view of Iraq's regional role, see a report of his conversation with Syrian politician Sa'adallah al-Jabiri, al-Istiqlal (Baghdad), 5 October 1946. Troutbeck (Baghdad) to FO, 31 August 1954, PRO/FO/624/241.

11

British rule in Jordan, 1943–55

ILAN PAPPÉ

THE KINGDOM OF ABDALLAH, KIRKBRIDE AND GLUBB

In July 1920, Britain was granted a mandate over Palestine, which included Transjordan. Transjordan was the geographical term used to describe the southern parts of the Ottoman province of Damascus. This was a barren and scarcely populated land, which had been a marginal area and, until the late 1880s, had lain outside the control and authority of the central government. The northern parts of the country were inhabited by tribes subsidized by the Turks in order to keep them away from the pilgrimage route to Mecca, which passed through Transjordan. The tribes and the land came under British control during the First World War. A number of Arabic-speaking officers were sent as representatives of the mandatory government established in Palestine by the summer of 1920. One of these officers was Alec Kirkbride, who would be instrumental in shaping the Anglo–Transjordanian relationship until the early 1950s.

In January 1921, the Amir Abdallah arrived at the southern border of Transjordan. Abdallah had been promised by the British, as part of their overall war agreement with his family, the Hashemites, the throne of Iraq, but had to give it up after Faysal, his brother, had been moved to Baghdad from Damascus, which had become French, as a result of contradictory promises made by the British to both the French and the Hashemites during the First World War. Abdallah was asked to stay in the Hijaz, as foreign minister in the little kingdom the British carved out for his father. This proved to be an unsafe place to stay in, as the Saudis were about to take over. The imminent fall of his father's kingdom led Abdallah to declare his intention to redeem Syria, or at least the southern parts of it, that is, Transjordan.[1] It was Winston Churchill's reshuffling of the local pawns that eventually installed Abdallah in Amman as the head of a local sheikdom, which would become an independent kingdom in 1946.

Thus, from its very inception, Transjordan was closely tied to the

British rule in Jordan, 1943–55 199

British Empire in the Middle East; a connection secured by a bilateral defence treaty signed in 1928 in the face of Arab condemnation of its servitude. This treaty would be revised, every now and then, so as to allow Transjordan the appearance of being an independent entity, without affecting seriously the basic British interests in the country. These interests included a British right to use Transjordanian territory as a base and employ the country's army as a tool for regional British operations or in the event of a more global war. Thus, for instance, in 1941, Abdallah's army was sent to help Britain quell an anti-British revolt in Baghdad. This army, the Arab Legion, was considered a significant component in the post-Second World War scenarios, prepared by the British Chiefs of Staff and which simulated a possible confrontation with the USSR in the Middle East.[2]

The Anglo–Transjordanian alliance was one of the cornerstones of Britain's Middle Eastern policy. British interests in Jordan were looked after by General Glubb Pasha, who became the Chief of the General Staff of the Arab Legion and by Sir Alec Kirkbride, the British resident and later ambassador until 1952 (as noted, Kirkbride had arrived in Transjordan before Abdallah and by 1920 had already represented the British in the country). Kirkbride and Glubb occupied positions similar to that of a high commissioner in the empire, and, like Lord Cromer before him, Kirkbride's modest title, 'resident', did not reflect his real power in the kingdom. But whereas Cromer had been in Egypt at the peak of the empire, Kirkbride enjoyed an exceptional position, far exceeding that expected of a diplomat representing a diminishing empire after the Second World War. His colleagues in the rest of the Arab Middle East did not fare so well. They were facing a growing hostility at a time when Britain became the indisputable enemy of national movements all over the Arab world.

Kirkbride's position was strengthened in the years 1928–45, mainly due to the close personal friendship he had developed with Abdallah. There were a few occasions on which the two men were found to disagree, but all in all it was an harmonious relationship. Abdallah's relationship with the government in London, however, was more problematic. A particularly tense moment came when, in 1941, the Amir's grandiose dream of becoming the King of Greater Syria was revealed (Greater Syria included Lebanon, Transjordan and Palestine). The scheme was rejected by everyone concerned, including Winston Churchill, who in 1921 had supported Abdallah. The government eventually followed the advice of its foreign secretary, Anthony Eden, who suggested staying aloof and letting the scheme fall due to universal Arab rejection. This policy was pursued, but only once did Glubb Pasha deviate from it. When, in July 1947, Abdallah seriously contemplated the overthrow of the Syrian government, as part of his scheme to install himself as King of Syria, Glubb firmly objected to using the Arab Legion for that purpose and the plan collapsed.[3] However, notwithstanding this episode, there was little reason for any resentment in London and generally Transjordan proved itself to be Britain's most loyal ally in the Middle East.

Transjordan was valuable to Britain for two reasons: first, for its apparent loyalty in an area where ever since the 1920s nationalism had become more and more anti-British; and then for its proximity to Palestine. Kirkbride, and for that matter Abdallah, could play an important role in formulating Britain's regional policy because of Transjordan's ability to intervene in Palestine's affairs, according to British interests. But it was only in the 1940s that Transjordan became a major British concern. Up to 1943, policy-makers in London regarded the sheikdom as a remote and marginal base within the British infrastructure in the Arab world. It was the deteriorating situation in Palestine, and the diplomatic impasse there, that elevated Transjordan's value in London's eyes.

Since 1937, British officials had regarded Transjordan as an integral part of a future solution for the Palestine question. In that year, for the first time, British representatives raised the possibility of annexing Arab areas in Palestine to Transjordan as part of an overall solution. This possibility had been raised by the royal commission of inquiry, the Peel Commission, which had arrived in October 1936 in the wake of the unrest in Palestine. The commission published its recommendations in July 1937, in which it called for the partitioning of Palestine between the Arabs and the Jews. It suggested that most of the areas allotted to the Arabs would be annexed to Transjordan.

These recommendations were reviewed in 1943 in a special cabinet committee searching for solutions to the Arab–Jewish conflict in Palestine. Like the Peel commission before it, this committee recognized the need to partition Palestine between Arabs and Jews. However, this committee did not wish to entrust large areas of Palestine to Transjordanian hands – though it was willing to envisage a joint Egyptian–Jordanian control over the Negev, lest this strategic area should fall into Jewish hands. The committee was not so much interested in enlarging Abdallah's territory as concerned with the need to connect the British Middle Eastern Headquarters in Egypt with the British air bases and oil fields in Iraq. Jordan was merely to serve as a land bridge and was treated as a marginal component in this strategic build up. But the plan was never implemented. A Cairo conference of the diplomatic and military representatives of Britain in the area decided to reject the plan. Winston Churchill, the prime minister, preferred a Jewish Negev, while the

British rule in Jordan, 1943–55 201

Foreign Office objected forcefully to the idea.[4] When Labour came to power, the concept of an Arab Negev was accepted by all – although whether it should be under Egyptian or Jordanian rule remained an open question. It was to Kirkbride's credit that the Foreign Office, and then the government as a whole, not only opted eventually for a Jordanian Negev, but even advocated the Jordanization of as much of Palestine as possible.[5]

Indeed, Kirkbride's, and Abdallah's, most impressive accomplishment came in February 1948 when they persuaded London to reverse its Palestine policy for what would be known later as the 'Greater Transjordan' option. This option was based on the assumption that Britain would have to leave Palestine in an orderly manner and without endangering its own interests in the country and the area. This solution for post-mandatory Palestine envisaged the partitioning of the country between the Zionist movement and the Hashemites. It was not a novel idea, having been mooted ever since the Amir Abdallah had set foot in Transjordan. But until 1948 it had always been only one of many possible solutions to the Palestine conflict explored by policy-makers in London.

Once the decision to leave Palestine was taken (mainly due to domestic pressure, the withdrawal from India and the severe financial crisis in the islands), Britain had to review its Middle Eastern policy in general, and its approach toward the question of Palestine in particular. Palestine's main strategic value, in a post-mandatory era, was its envisaged future role as a battlefield in case of a Third World War. In the years immediately after 1945 such a war was still expected to be fought with conventional arms; hence, the Russians were expected to try, and probably succeed in, occupying the Suez Canal and the oil fields of the Arabian peninsula. Palestine and Transjordan were intended to be a first line of defence, allowing time for more forces to come and reoccupy whatever needed to be taken back. During the last days of the mandate, Egypt was still considered as Britain's principal base and her most important strategic asset in the area. The growing hostility of Egyptian nationalism towards Britain produced war scenarios in the Ministry of Defence, which visualized the reoccupation of Egypt, should it fall to Russian hands, with or without local consent. For this Britain needed at least one co-operative ally and base – which it found in Abdallah and Transjordan.[6]

The 'Greater Transjordan' policy became valid once it was endorsed by the Jewish Agency in the beginning of 1947. It seems that Abdallah did not enter any significant negotiations with the Jewish side until November 1947. Hence, even if he knew about it, Kirkbride must have regarded it as insignificant. In November 1947, Abdallah met the acting head of the Political Department of the Jewish Agency, Golda Meyerson

202 *Demise of the British Empire in the Middle East*

(Meir), and began negotiations in earnest. It seems that he informed Kirkbride of that particular meeting only a month later. The British representative updated Harold Beeley, Bevin's adviser on Palestine, who opposed the notion of annexing Arab Palestine to Transjordan. Beeley recommended a pro-Palestinian policy, that is, supporting the opposition in most of the Arab countries to the UN partition plan and to a Jewish state, and seemed to prefer a continued British presence in Palestine. Abdallah decided to appeal directly to Bevin and the British government in February 1948. He sent his prime minister, Tawfiq Abu al-Huda, to London, supposedly to discuss a new treaty between the two countries, but in reality to discuss with Bevin the extent of the Transjordanian–Jewish understanding over the future of Palestine.[7]

In February 1948, Abu al-Huda succeeded in winning Bevin over to the pro-Hashemite option. The Foreign Office experts were quick to follow suit and prepared a convincing memorandum to the cabinet exploring the strategic benefits for Britain from the creation of a greater Transjordan. Thus, at the beginning of 1948, the British government abandoned all other avenues and adopted the 'Greater Transjordan' option as the only policy towards the Arab–Jewish conflict in Palestine. The arguments were clear: it would be easier to partition the country between two newcomers to the Palestine scene – the Zionists and the Hashemites – than to reconcile the ideological rift between the Zionist movement and the indigenous Palestinian population. Furthermore, it was the only way to safeguard British interests in post-mandatory Palestine: neither the Jews nor the Palestinians were trusted as Britain's sentries in the area.[8]

The Foreign Office and the Colonial Office had little trust, if any, in the Jewish community in Palestine after 1945. Therefore even if the Jewish state proved to be hostile, at least Britain could rely on Transjordan to maintain London's interests in the area. Most experts in Whitehall predicted that the future Jewish state would at best be neutral in its attitude towards the global cold war and at worst pro-communist.[9]

A Palestinian Arab Palestine was totally rejected by the British. The Foreign Office was convinced that such a state would be headed by the ex-Mufti, Haj Amin al-Husayni (it was referred to as a 'Mufti State'). Al-Husayni's leadership of the Arab revolt in Palestine, his involvement in the anti-British and pro-Nazi coup in Iraq in 1941, and his wartime collaboration with Hitler, had all made him an arch enemy of Britain in the area.[10]

Once the shift took place, the British started working energetically for it. The government instructed the British officers in the Legion how to act in case war broke out after Britain's withdrawal from Palestine, in order to help the king implement the annexation of Arab Palestine,

*British rule in Jordan, 1943–55*203

to his kingdom. The officers were instructed to pre-empt a hostile Palestinian reaction to such a move by mobilizing pro-Hashemite elements among the West Bank population.

Britain was instrumental in mobilizing a limited American support for the new policy and checking any antagonistic intervention by the UN. More important, it was quite skilful in anticipating successfully a hostile reaction from countries such as Syria and Egypt, the governments of which were in the early days of 1948 deeply involved in preparing some sort of a military option against the UN partition plan. London's strategy was to encourage a close co-ordination between the two Hashemite sister states. It was decided to allow Iraqi forces to occupy part of Samaria so as to enable the Legion to concentrate on the occupation of the rest of Arab Palestine. In the war itself the Iraqi forces proved to be less loyal than expected. The Iraqi rank and file supported local Palestinian resistance to the Jordanian annexation of the West Bank, but not to the extent of endangering the new regime in this part of Palestine. On the other hand, towards the end of the 1948 war the Iraqis helped the king to deter the Israelis from occupying the West Bank. The Israeli government considered on at least three occasions a takeover of parts of the West Bank.[11]

Indeed, the Israeli endorsement of the 'Greater Transjordan' option was not given wholeheartedly; rather, it was a combination of Israeli suspicions about Hashemite sincerity and Israel's own territorial ambitions. This ambivalence would make the 'Greater Transjordan option' only a basis for a tacit alliance between the two sides and one that was never properly mapped out. But they did negotiate on the basis of the maps provided in the UN partition resolution, which delineated very clearly which part of Palestine should be Arab. The two sides, and for that matter Britain, tacitly agreed that Abdallah would be entitled to carve out of the area allotted to the Palestinians an additional territory for his own kingdom. He eventually did so in the 1948 war, occupying the area known ever since 1949 as the West Bank without one shot being fired. This outcome led this writer and some of his colleagues to conclude that the tacit understanding was adhered to, and that this explains the results of the 1948 war; although this remains a disputed historiographical issue.[12]

British officials in the withdrawing mandatory government, and particular those in the legation in Amman, followed closely the fluctuations in the Hashemite–Jewish negotiations: from their deadlock in April 1948, (following an impressive Jewish success on the ground in the civil war developing in Palestine before the Arab armies entered the country in May 1948) to their successful conclusion in May 1948, when British officers of the Legion met with Hagana (the main Jewish military

204   *Demise of the British Empire in the Middle East*

force) commanders to try to agree on maps of division. The two sides had failed to reach an understanding over the future of Jerusalem, thus they agreed to divide the land but not the city. The city and its environs would become the stage on which the fiercest and bloodiest fighting in the war would take place. In September 1948 the city was divided, under an agreement more or less on the lines suggested by the British officers in May 1948.[13]

One additional concern of the British was the desire for a clean and safe withdrawal from Palestine. They needed the king to ensure that a major Arab attack on Palestine would not take place before the British left Palestine (they also ensured that the Jews would not declare a state of their own before that date). The Arab League and Arab governments, although suspecting Abdallah's policy in Palestine, nevertheless could not go to war without the Legion, the best and most experienced of the Arab armies. The secretary-general of the Arab League, Azzam Pasha, who all along had suspected that the Arab intervention in Palestine would be a fiasco, wanted Abdallah to be a possible scapegoat. This is probably why he suggested that Abdallah should be the titular head of the invading Arab forces that entered Palestine on 15 May 1948. This served Abdallah well, and he altered the original war plans of the League, at the last moment, so that his and the Iraqi contingents would be deployed only where he wanted them – in the West Bank – and would not join forces, as promised in the original plan, with the Syrians in the north and with the Egyptians in the south.[14]

These Jordanian manoeuvres were known to the British and helped them assess correctly the results of the 1948 war and prepare for the future. After the first week of fighting in the 1948 war, whether intentionally or out of necessity, it became apparent that the Legion's operations during the war did not constitute a breach of the Hashemite–Jewish understanding.

When the 1948 war ended, the basic guidelines underlying British policy were validated by the Israeli–Jordanian armistice agreement of 1949, which finalized the partition of post-mandatory Palestine between the Hashemite kingdom of Jordan (Transjordan's title since 1949) and the state of Israel. It would take another year or so before Israel, and in particular Ben-Gurion, would become openly pro-Western, and even longer before he became pro-British. But the transforming pace of the Israeli attitude was quicker than had ever been predicted by the British experts on Palestine. Judging the view from London, one can say that as far as the Foreign Office, and even Bevin, were concerned, following the armistice agreement, Britain's interests seemed secure in post-mandatory Palestine. The chances for a solution in the conflict, however, were as remote as ever. The 'Greater Transjordan' option, none the less,

British rule in Jordan, 1943–55 205

seemed valid to Amman, Jerusalem and London until the later 1960s, when, in hindsight, it was increasingly realized that the option was bound to fail as it totally disregarded the aspirations of the Palestinians. This could not have been acknowledged until the 1960s because of the weakness of the Palestinian national movement. Towards the end of the 1960s, the PLO transformed the movement into a force potent enough to keep the conflict alive, recruit pan-Arab support, pursue guerrilla warfare against Israel and to destabilize the Hashemite regime in Amman.

Ignoring the Palestinian side of the story not only affected the chances of solving the conflict, but also had implications for British policy in the Middle East as a whole. The tighter Britain's reliance on Jordan seemed to be, the more hostile the neighboring Arab countries became towards the Hashemite kingdom. Kirkbride was fully aware of the general Arab allegations made at the time, and had persuaded London to terminate the British mandate over Jordan, grant it independence in 1946 and conclude a new treaty in 1948 with more formal independence for Jordan. But the clauses in the new treaty allowing British interference in Jordan's internal and external affairs were too obviously in Britain's favour. More importantly, British officials seemed to think that such a neo-colonialist practice would easily be accepted by whoever represented Arab nationalism in Jordan or elsewhere.

The experts on Arab nationalism in the Foreign Office underrated the intensity of anti-British feelings across the Arab world, and found it difficult to acknowledge the existence of such feelings in Jordan. They derided the genuine desire of Arab politicians to win independence – a desire that they regarded as a rhetorical means for gaining political power. They attributed requests for withdrawal to either communist incitement or personal fanaticism, and reported to their superiors that in most cases these positions stemmed from sheer personal opportunism. It seemed, as comes out so clearly from the attitude of the British Chief of the Imperial Staff, General Slim, during the Anglo–Egyptian negotiations in 1949–51, that the British considered the Arabs as unequal and junior partners in future alliances. Furthermore, the British apparently deluded themselves that this inequality was natural and totally acceptable to their Arab interlocutors.[15]

This was worse in the case of Jordan. British officials, and particularly those at the Ministry of Defence, regarded Jordanian officers as incompetent and did not inform them even about matters relating to Jordan's security. Thus, for instance, when the two sides declared proudly in 1948 that from now on direct British control over the Jordanian army would cease, London sent a secret directive to senior

British officers in Jordan informing them that the Jordanian army was still an integral part of British military forces in the Middle East.[16] Even without being aware of this directive, leaders and spokesmen of the Egyptian national movement knew, from their own experience, that there was no genuine British interest in evacuating any of its bases in the Middle East. The portrayal of Jordan as Britain's puppet thus continued with great force even after the conclusion of the new Anglo–Jordanian defence treaty.

Attempts to replace colonial control with defence treaties had failed totally. They were rejected not only by opposition movements in the countries concerned, but also by the governments of the day. The same treaty accepted by Abdallah in 1948 had already been rejected by the Iraqi parliament earlier in the year. The rejection took place a month before the same draft treaty was offered to Tawfiq Abu al-Huda in London. Bevin thought that the unpopularity of the Iraqi government, and not that of the treaty, had produced the rejection. Hence the same terms were offered to Jordan.[17] At the time the Jordanian consent seemed to be not the exception that proved the rule, but rather a positive development portending future successes.

'KIRKBRIDE WOULD NOT LAST FOREVER': THE END OF ABDALLAH'S RULE

It was in the nature of pragmatic British policy-making to appreciate that neither Kirkbride nor Abdallah would live forever. Therefore, in 1948, steps were already being taken to prepare for the post-Abdallah and post-Kirkbride period in Jordan. 'Kirkbride would not last forever', the ambassador at Amman reported, and suggested sending an Arabic-speaking potential successor for himself to establish a close relationship with the heir apparent, Prince Talal.[18] British officials, and Kirkbride in particular, were highly disappointed by the character and behaviour of Talal, who had already displayed anti-British feelings during the Second World War. In the event, no one was sent and Talal would not remain in power long enough to become a problem. The real problem for Britain in post-1948 Jordan lay not in personalities but in demographic realities on the ground and the strengthening of anti-British nationalism in the neighboring Arab countries.

The annexation of Palestine's West Bank to Jordan had turned the kingdom into a state with a predominantly Palestinian population.[19] It could easily turn into what the British called the 'Mufti State', should the Hashemite regime fall. It was Kirkbride's and Glubb's task to ensure that the annexation did not lead to this undesirable result. Abdallah did

British rule in Jordan, 1943–55

207

not help. He was eager to accelerate the *de jure* annexation and make it public; this violated Arab League decisions, which insisted on maintaining military rule in liberated Palestinian areas (as the Egyptians themselves did in the Gaza Strip, which they had occupied in 1948). Moreover, Abdallah desired to accompany the process by democratizing the kingdom; that is, following the unification of the two banks of the river Jordan in April 1950 with free elections. It was mainly Kirkbride's pressure, and Glubb's actions on the ground, that prevented potential anti-Hashemite Palestinians from participating in these elections. None the less, the April 1950 elections created a Jordanian legislature with a Palestinian majority and one which was more receptive than the dynasty to pan-Arabist pressures. This parliament would become the basis for the emergence of more national governments in 1956 and, henceforth, for bringing about the end of British rule, although not that of the Hashemite dynasty, in Jordan.[20]

After the elections of 1950, for the first time in Jordan's history, members of parliament made anti-British remarks: calling for the total withdrawal of Britain from the Arab world. Kirkbride was alarmed; but London was not, though it would be in 1954, when words turned into stones thrown at British institutions in Amman, and General Glubb was forced to leave the country.

The parliament also succeeded in foiling Abdallah's attempt to conclude a separate peace treaty with Israel in February 1950. On this at least, Kirkbride saw eye to eye with the parliament. He was content with the *de facto* agreement with Israel and saw no reason for antagonizing the Arab world any further. He valued the American *de facto* recognition, given at the beginning of 1949, and the UN endorsement (given by the UN mediator Bernadotte before his assassination in September 1948) as far more important than an official treaty with Israel.[21] The Arab League had already taken some steps against Jordan's annexation of the West Bank; mainly the restoration of an independent Palestinian representation in this Arab regional organization. This 'Palestine Department' served Haj Amin al-Husayni as a basis for anti-Hashemite activities in Jordan, leading to an abortive coup to overthrow, and possibly assassinate, Abdallah in 1949 (with the help of Arab officers in the Legion), and culminating in Abdallah's assassination in July 1951.

In Kirkbride's eyes, the most alarming step Abdallah had taken was to allow a committee of Palestinians and Jordanian jurists to prepare a new constitution for the kingdom. We can now safely say that had not Abdallah's grandson, Husayn, suspended this constitution in 1956, Jordan might have become a constitutional monarchy. Where he could, Kirkbride did all he could to prevent what he termed the 'Palestinization of Jordan'. One of his successes was to persuade the Foreign Office not

208   *Demise of the British Empire in the Middle East*

to accept Abdallah's offer to settle in Jordan as many Palestinian refugees as possible. Kirkbride convinced Whitehall to accept the Israeli concept of resettling most of the refugees in Iraq and Syria. He also persuaded the king not to include more than three Palestinian ministers in the various cabinets he established.[22]

Kirkbride's superiors in London brushed aside his gloomy predictions about the effect Palestinization would have on Jordan. It was only a matter of time before Palestinians 'would see things the way the King did',[23] wrote the head of the Eastern Department. But of course they did not. At least not the followers of Haj Amin al-Husayni, who murdered the king in July 1951. As Kirkbride had predicted, Abdallah's death strengthened Jordan's pan-Arabist orientation. But, contrary to his predictions, it did not Palestinize it. As he himself put it: Jordan 'was no longer in a fearlessly independent position within the Arab League.'[24] What he meant was that, without Abdallah, Jordan was no longer totally committed to Britain. Kirkbride left shortly after Abdallah's death. The Foreign Office looked forward to business as usual and saw no threat to Anglo–Jordanian relations in the wake of the king's death.

'ALL THE INDICATIONS SO FAR ARE THAT JORDAN IS FORTUNATE IN HER RULER': HUSAYN'S EARLY YEARS

Abdallah's death was followed by a long period of instability in Jordan's history. Talal's reign was short and after his removal in 1953 (probably because of mental illness, but possibly as a result of local and British intrigues) the very young King Husayn took power with the help of senior and pro-Hashemite politicians. Husayn impressed the Foreign Office as a mature man for his age. 'He was at first bored', wrote Geoffrey Furlonge, the veteran head of the Eastern Department, who succeeded Kirkbride in Amman, 'but seems to be settling down, which process will be accelerated if a suitable bride can be found for him.' But apart from that, 'All the indications so far are that Jordan is fortunate in her ruler.'[25] Three years later very few officials would still subscribe to this view.

The main concern in 1953 was the high tension on the Israeli–Jordanian border, to the point that the Jordanian government invoked the Anglo–Jordanian defence treaty in January of that year. Amman wanted London to curb the Israeli retaliations on Jordanian territory taken against Palestinian infiltrators. In February, the Jordanian government, now in charge of affairs in the kingdom in the lull between Abdallah and Husayn, surprised General Robertson, the British commanding officer in the Middle East, by requesting a more permanent and larger British military presence in the country. The Jordanians

British rule in Jordan, 1943–55 209

wanted British reinforcements in case of an Israeli attack, even on the West Bank. But in 1949, the British government had already decided, without informing the Jordanians, that the Anglo–Transjordanian treaty would be invoked only if Transjordan proper was attacked.[26] An Israeli decision to release blocked mandatory accounts and grant them to Jordan a month later improved the atmosphere and Britain was not asked to do what it could not do, that is, to undertake military action against Israel.[27] The treaty would be invoked again that year after the Qibya massacre – an Israeli retaliation for a murderous attack by Palestinian infiltrators against an Israeli family near Tel Aviv. The Israeli operation turned into a merciless revenge resulting in the death of 53 Palestinians. In this most inappropriate circumstance, a US mediator, sent to try and co-ordinate water utilization in the Jordan valley, naturally failed.

The professional civil servant, unlike the foreign secretary, saw some 'blessing' in the tension on the border. It had improved Jordan's image in the Arab world, without, so it seemed, undermining Britain's position in the kingdom.[28] However, Jordan's image in the Arab world was not improved so long as British forces remained stationed there. Everywhere else in the Arab world, national governments struggled to secure the departure of British soldiers from their countries. In Jordan they were still present in great numbers.

How to keep Jordan as a base and yet make it appear an independent kingdom continued to trouble the British. Different and opposing British interests were displayed on this question. The army wanted to expand the British military presence in Jordan, particularly when it appeared inevitable that British forces would have to leave Egypt. On the other hand, the Foreign Office worried about the possible implications of such a move on Jordan's image in the Arab world.[29] The crux of the matter was the Jordanian government's, and later King Husayn's, ambivalence on the question. It seems that the Hashemite rulers had a more inflexible attitude to the Anglo–Jordanian agreement. In their eyes, it existed only to protect the regime against the danger of being toppled from within or in case the country was attacked by Israel. These deliberations led nowhere. British forces were not increased until 1958, when British paratroops temporarily came to assist the king, but this episode is beyond the scope of the present chapter.

Stabilizing the Israeli–Jordanian border thus became an urgent British interest; but this did not necessarily mean brokering a comprehensive peace. It was the Americans who prodded Britain to take a more active role in the peace talks. In 1953, John Foster Dulles came to London to suggest a new approach to the conflict. The Americans recommended inducing the Arab countries to give up some of their demands by

210 *Demise of the British Empire in the Middle East*

inviting them to join a pro-Western defence treaty. The Foreign Office had their reservations: it had been tried in 1951 and failed. The Arab leaders did not mix defence issues or global-war considerations with their struggle against Israel: the only compensation they desired was from Israel.

The Americans introduced another channel through which they thought peace might be made. They hoped to persuade the Arab countries to give up the idea of repatriating the Palestinian refugees by offering financial aid for their resettlement. This deal was accepted in principle only by the Syrians. In addition, Damascus also wanted minor rectifications on the Israeli–Syrian border, which the Israelis were reluctant to make. Other Arab leaders were unwilling to give up the principle of repatriation. Britain advocated that Syria should be the new homeland for the Palestinian refugees, fearing that otherwise the onus would be on Jordan, which already hosted the largest number of refugees. To that end, Britain wanted Washington to exert pressure on Israel to meet Syrian demands. But when Dulles met Eden in March 1953 he told him and the Foreign Office experts on the region that it was Britain's task to 'get Israel and the Arab states to make peace'.[30] British officials did not share this view. They regarded Israel as the intransigent party in the conflict. Therefore it was Israel that had to be forced, by American pressure, to make concessions that would bring about a peaceful solution to the conflict.

A year later, in 1954, Washington persisted in its efforts to involve Britain in the diplomatic efforts; but on both sides of the Atlantic it was realized that far greater problems for Britain's and the West's position in the area lay ahead. Their source was Gamal Abd al-Nasir.

THE WAR AGAINST AL-NASIR

Already in 1953, British officials became aware of a growing Egyptian involvement in Jordanian affairs. Jordan was chosen by al-Nasir as one of the first test cases of his ability to liberate monarchic and traditional regimes from Western influence, or, as he saw it, from Western imperialism. After consolidating his regime in 1954, he focused his attention on the two Hashemite kingdoms.

Al-Nasir not only initiated, he also reacted. After all, he was willing to reach a *modus vivendi* with the West, provided it did not force him to become hostile to Soviet policy in the region and it did not compel him to modify his policy *vis-à-vis* Israel or the conservative Arab regimes. British efforts in 1954 to induce King Husayn to back Iraq's attempt to lead the Arab world on to a pro-Western path were perceived by al-Nasir

British rule in Jordan, 1943–55　　　　　　　　　　　　　　　　　　　211

as a provocative act against his policies. Indeed, under strong British influence, in 1954 Baghdad was seeking potential members for a pro-NATO alliance in the Middle East.

In 1954, none the less, Britain and al-Nasir were not engaged in open warfare. These were the early days of the 'Arab cold war' and al-Nasir had only just begun to achieve a firmer grip over Egyptian domestic politics. His rejection of the British offer to the Hashemites to join a pro-Western pact was thus cautious. Al-Nasir explained to the Iraqi prime minister, Nuri al-Sa'id, that Egypt could not endorse such a policy as long as British soldiers were stationed on Egyptian soil. Al-Nasir's pressure in 1954 proved to be effective for only a few months. Nuri al-Sa'id soon decided to lead the way to a pro-Western alliance in the area.[31] Al-Sa'id desired the financial benefits promised by the West, and genuinely feared a Russian invasion in northern Iraq. In spring 1954, he signed bilateral pacts with Pakistan and Turkey. Britain joined these pacts in the spring of 1955, and its entrance turned the series of treaties into a regional alliance – the Baghdad Pact – against which al-Nasir felt compelled to act. NATO gave its immediate blessing to the new alliance and thus involved all the regional countries concerned in the global cold war.

In London as well as in Baghdad, Jordan's participation in the new formation seemed essential for the success of the pact. The Foreign Office asserted that the only way to ensure Husayn's adherence was to allay the king's fears of a possible hostile Egyptian reaction. In the days following the inception of the Baghdad Pact, therefore, British diplomats did their best to seduce al-Nasir to join in, by supporting Egypt's territorial demands of Israel. Together with American experts, they devised the Alpha plan, a comprehensive peace plan for the Palestine question, which offered Egypt part of the Negev – large enough to connect Egypt with Jordan – in return for a peace treaty with Israel. The idea of a land bridge was meant to serve the Baghdad Pact, no less than to satisfy Egyptian territorial ambitions (in addition, they promised to pressure Israel on the question of the refugees).[32]

Al-Nasir, it seems, was facing a double-edged British policy. On the one hand, he had ample reason to suspect the Baghdad Pact as an anti-Nasirite move; on the other, he was supported by the British in his basic demands on the Palestine question. It seems to us that he was justified in suspecting the first move as being more authentic and more indicative of British ambitions in the area than the latter. In the summer of 1955, he decided to challenge the move by trying to win over political support for his policies in Jordan.

Al-Nasir claimed in retrospect that he did not seek an open confrontation with Britain over Jordan's fate. He felt betrayed by Eden, who had promised him that only Iraq would be asked to join NATO's defence plans. British documents corroborate this recollection. According to official British accounts from 1955, al-Nasir and Eden had indeed reached such an understanding in April 1955. In return for Britain's promise not to include Jordan in the Baghdad Pact, Eden had demanded an Egyptian commitment to refrain from any further anti-British propaganda against the Baghdad Pact, and al-Nasir had agreed.[33] It seems that neither side adhered to the understanding. However, until the autumn of 1955, both sides kept a low profile in their attempts to win Jordan over to their respective side. This is why British dispatches to the Jordanian government in the summer of 1955 urged it to adopt a neutral position towards the Baghdad Pact. It seems that at first Husayn was quite enthusiastic about the pact and was willing to join it.

But Husayn must have found it difficult to comprehend British advice during these turbulent months of 1955. Britain was sending ambiguous messages to its only remaining ally in the Arab world. When Glubb Pasha pleaded with London to raise the British subsidy for the national guard and the Legion, which were the necessary tools for the king to maintain his grip over the country, he was rejected. Husayn did not hesitate and by 1954 had already asked for an increased subsidy, even when such a request complicated his own position in the kingdom. Other subsidies, such as from the Saudis, were also undermining his authority. Glubb deemed that a doubling of the annual British support was essential for keeping the national guard as an effective tool.[34]

The relative calm in London, to be replaced dramatically by panic in 1955, was due also to the improvement in Israeli–Jordanian relations in 1954. The Palestinian infiltrations, which had been the main cause for the tense situation on that border, were declining in 1954. However, when the crisis with Egypt developed, so did that with Israel. Palestinian unrest in the West Bank was growing with the Nasirite intervention on the domestic scene in Jordan; this unrest spread and endangered both Husayn and the British position in Jordan.

THE BEGINNING OF THE END OF BRITISH RULE IN JORDAN:
THE CRISIS OF 1955–56

After positive reports on Jordan's situation in 1954, 1955 seemed suddenly to be a very bad year for Britain's interests and policy. In September 1955, the tone of British correspondence and probably of the oral consultations with the king altered. He was advised to abandon his neutrality. The Egyptian–Czech arms deal, struck during that month, was seen by the British government as a declaration of war, a cold one

British rule in Jordan, 1943–55   213

at least. The Foreign Office was totally surprised by the arms deal, and the panic, which struck the diplomats also affected the politicians. Al-Nasir became the 'Hitler' of the Middle East. Eden and Macmillan employed discourses and images that unnecessarily harmed Western relations with the Egyptian leader.

The British were surprised, partly because their man in Amman, Charles Duke, was busy with the nitty-gritty of the personal struggle in domestic politics inside Jordan, and did not pay attention to more long-term processes, as Kirkbride had done. As a British representative, Duke was still quite influential, although he may not have enjoyed Kirkbride's prestige and stature. He was a decisive factor when decisions concerning the priming or the timing of elections in Jordan were made. Duke's main success was in convincing the king to move from one prime minister to the other, throughout the troubled year of 1955, without free elections.[35]

As late as August 1955, Duke reported that the main problem in Jordan was the power struggle between the cabinet and the parliament over amendments to the Jordanian constitution (or, put differently, it was a struggle about who would be running the country's affairs). A bemused Duke seemed to think that this was quite irrelevant when he and the king were the masters of the game. The king, however was nervous about this continued internal strife for power. In fact, he became ill due to it and had to receive a series of injections to calm him down and enable him to sleep through the long and blustery nights of August 1955. Indeed, he would need them for the next month or so.[36]

The British discovered that most of the opposition groups in Jordan, the Muslim Brotherhood, the Palestinian *Ba'ath* and the communists, were all aligned in one way or another to Egypt. The Egyptian connection with the local *Ba'ath* branch, although originally a Syrian creation, was particularly close. The *Ba'athis* were active in organizing anti-British demonstrations and preparing long petitions calling for British withdrawal from Jordan. The *Ba'ath* and a smaller group, the National Socialist party, were behind the public show of support for Egypt's arms deal with the Eastern Bloc.[37] The Communist Party was in close contact with the Egyptian consul in Jerusalem and was thus also under al-Nasir's influence. The Muslim Brotherhood in the East Bank was quite independent, but the branches in the West Bank were guided by the movement's leaders in Egypt. However, the latter alliance was short lived. Al-Nasir soon found himself in direct confrontation with the Brotherhood in Egypt, which in return improved Husayn's relationship with it.

Al-Nasir was acting on two levels. He conducted official negotiations with Husayn, on the one hand, and encouraged opposition groups to exert pressure on the king, on the other. On the official level, al-Nasir invited Husayn to join Egypt, Syria and Saudi Arabia in a regional defence pact. It is impossible to know how far he wanted to go: to change Jordan's policy or its regime. He sent two delegates to Amman that year to add weight to his pressure on the king. Major Salah Salem (whose junior title did not reflect his senior position) and Fieldmarshal Abd al-Hakim Amer, who sought to strengthen Egypt's ties with the opposition groups, particularly with the young Arab officers in the army, hoping to establish them as another 'free officers' corps, which had succeeded so well in toppling the old regime in Egypt (and would serve as a model for future Arab coups and revolutions).[38]

The most alarming part of the story for London was the fact that Amer came uninvited. Britain responded, or rather 'retaliated', with a visit of one of its own generals. In December, shortly after Amer's visit, General Sir Gerald Templer, Chief of the Imperial General Staff, also visited Amman. He came with a mandate to negotiate Jordan's accession to the Baghdad Pact. Templer's visit was in fact the first official British invitation to Jordan to join the new pact. Hitherto, the official negotiations had been conducted by the Turks, who had sent their president and an impressive entourage to persuade Jordan. This had not swayed the government or the king of Jordan. The government did not, in any official communiqué, reject the idea of the pact, but it demanded a proper Anglo–Jordanian dialogue in which Jordan's conditions for entry would be discussed: these included an increase in military and financial aid (apparently quite beyond Britain's capacity in 1955). Templer came, so he believed, just to negotiate the terms of entry; in the event, he arrived when it was already clear to many in the Hashemite court that entry to the treaty might bring down the dynasty altogether.

Wise political leadership would have not entrusted a military man with such a sensitive mission. Sending a general for a delicate political mission was utterly wrong; Templer was, *ex officio*, a bad choice for conducting such negotiations. This was a typically hasty decision, characteristic of British policy-making ever since panic had stricken the Foreign Office when it realized that Jordan was no longer a 'loyal' ally. Templer's visit aggravated an already charged and tense situation.

Husayn was positive in general, so it seems, in his conversations with Templer, informing him of his consent to be part of the pact. However, he insisted that time was needed to prepare public opinion. Templer encountered a particularly hostile attitude from the prime minister, Said al-Mufti, whom Duke had saved when King Husayn had wanted to sack him earlier.[39] As a result of the visit, four Palestinian ministers resigned and al-Mufti was encouraged by the third Egyptian visitor that year, Anwar Sadat (Egyptian minister of state at the time) to follow suit.

British rule in Jordan, 1943–55 215

Before that, al-Mufti declared the termination of the negotiations. Husayn had to change his tactics.[40]

In the beginning of 1956, a new prime minister was appointed, Hazza al-Majali. He was a young, inexperienced pro-Hashemite politician, who made a public commitment to prepare for Jordan's entry to the new pact. The opposition gathered momentum as a result of the declarations and even senior government officials took to the street. More ministers resigned, and Husayn had to dissolve the parliament and the government. This wave of unrest, in the wake of Templer's visit, threatened to bring down Husayn. Al-Nasir need not have done much more than he already had done before that visit. It was clear now that the public mood developing after Templer's visit would not enable the king to join the pact.

Nowhere in the British analysis of the problem is there evidence of any recognition of the possible anti-British turn that Arab nationalism took in Jordan. Events were explained by a conspiracy theory. The only question dealt with was why the Egyptians had been so successful. Duke attributed it to their propaganda abilities, and the charisma of al-Nasir among Palestinians (according to this view, not al-Nasir the anti-Western champion had attracted popularity, but al-Nasir the anti-Israeli had mobilized Jordanian support). Duke explained that the Czech arms deal was acclaimed, since it provided arms with which Israel could be fought. 'Everything in this country is judged by the touchstone of Palestine and Israel, and it is here that Great Britain is regarded as having failed her Jordanian friends, and our prestige and influence have suffered in consequence.'[41] This was indeed true to a certain extent and was manifested in the political discourse used by the opposition in its condemnation of the Baghdad pact. But in hindsight it seems that Duke failed to appreciate that his own and Glubb's presence in Jordan were in fact the main problem for both Palestinians and Arab nationalists in Jordan.

The crisis reached a climax in January 1956. Husayn dissolved his government and postponed the scheduled elections, thereby contributing to the already existing agitation. Thousands of demonstrators took to the streets during the first week of January. Institutions and targets that had never come under attack before were attacked: the prime minister's office was one of them, ministers' cars was another. British and American establishments were besieged and attacked with molotov cocktails and stones. The riots extended to the country at large. Americans had not been a target before in Jordan, so it 'must have been a communist inspiration'[42] concluded a shocked American representative in Amman, quoted in a British document (like that of the British, their analysis of the motivating force behind Arab nationalism was

216   *Demise of the British Empire in the Middle East*

particularly trite). A senior British officer in the Legion lost his life in these disturbances, an ominous sign that Jordan was no longer a safe haven for British soldiers.[43]

In the midst of the crisis came a renewed Saudi offer to replace the British subsidy by an Arab one. After hesitating for a few months, the king decided to accept the offer. This was a clear indication of the decline of Britain's position in Jordan: it signalled the readiness of Husayn to do without Britain. British officials on the spot and at home provided an instant analysis of the crisis. It was a shallow analyis, because, as we now know with hindsight, the crisis was a prelude to the inevitable end to the British empire in Jordan and in the Middle East as a whole. The superficiality of this analysis contrasts with Kirkbride's astuteness, in 1951, in predicting more or less this same course of events. On the other hand, Duke resorted to conjectural explanations rather then discerning long-term processes. The most curious part of his report is the way he attributed the unrest to Husayn's unpopularity, resulting from his misbehaviour towards his newly wedded wife, princess Dina al-Awn.[44]

All in all, Duke was highly impressed by the king. 'He bore himself courageously and steadfastly in the crisis, and it appeared that for the first time he was rising to his responsibilities on the political plane.' Husayn was particularly skilful in dividing the opposition. He hit the weakest, the refugees, arrested the communists, and left the *Ba'ath* activists at liberty. Husayn was dissuaded at the last moment by Duke and Glubb from imposing an emergency military rule and invoking the Iraqi–Jordanian defence pact. But London was more attuned to the king's suggestion, and officials in the Foreign Office played with the idea of the Legion's taking over the West Bank and the Iraqi army the Eastern bank should the need arise.[45] These officials must have realized that such a move would be totally rejected by Israel, who had made it clear that it would consider any such moves as a *casus belli*; and yet this point does not appear in the British documents.

With the appointment of a new prime minister, Samir al-Rifa'i, the stormy crisis appeared to subside. The Foreign Office reported to the cabinet that the king had succeeded in restoring order without the need for British intervention.[46] Samir al-Rifa'i now declared that Jordan would not join the Baghdad Pact.

Its unpopularity growing steadily, the British army was about to lose control over the Legion. British officers in the Legion had taken a direct part in quelling the demonstrations. The Jordanian press reported that they had been trigger happy and had fired shots when their Jordanian subordinates had refused to do so. A secret report to the Chief of the Imperial General Staff in April 1956 by the Commander in Chief of the British Middle East HQ stated that only after British officers had ordered

British rule in Jordan, 1943–55 217

them to do so had the Legion soldiers opened fire on demonstrators, and in many cases had refused to do so. These events were still fresh in the public collective memory when the final act in the end of British rule in Jordan took place.[47]

'THE HOMELAND IS OURS, THE ARMY IS OURS'[48]

In March 1956, two months after the crisis had supposedly ended, Husayn shocked the British by moving dramatically towards independence. In that month, he dismissed Glubb Pasha as chief of his army and sent him home. This was followed, in April 1956, by a gradual expulsion of British officers from the Arab Legion. Sir Alec Kirkbride was called in as a saviour and dispatched to Jordan, but to no avail. In May 1956, Husayn began negotiations for a defence pact with Egypt, which was followed, ironically, by an abortive attempted coup by pro-Nasirite Arab officers in the Legion to topple him – all of which led a disappointed Evelyn Shuckburgh, the head of the Levant department, to write, 'I am beginning to wonder whether our investment there is worth while. It costs us approximately 12 million pounds a year, for which we get no adequate military or political return.'[49]

The investment, however, was not able to prevent social and economic deprivation, mainly among the Palestinians in the West Bank, who were discriminated against, and the refugees, who refused to integrate. Although Jordan as a national economy prospered by its association with Britain, which compensated for its lack of any natural resources, it was, none the less, as Duke put it, an 'artificial prosperity'. The subsidy was not large enough to allow long-term planning. The main problem was the inability to induce the Americans to invest in Jordan. This is probably why the king turned to Arab subsidies, a move that also had its political price.

All over the Middle East the feeling was that the British empire in the Middle East had come to an end. A humiliating reminder of this state of affairs was the stoning of Eden's car in Bahrain in March 1956, more or less on the day that Husayn dismissed Glubb. It seems that since 1954 Husayn no longer felt that he was getting the *quid pro quo* he deserved for being loyal to Britain, while the other Arab countries were celebrating both independence and an impressive arms build-up. In 1958, Husayn would call in the British he had expelled in 1956 to save him from yet another pro-Nasirite threat, but this temporary revival of the Anglo–Jordanian alliance would not change the new political reality in Jordan. To all intents and purposes the 35 years of British rule in Jordan came to an end in 1956.

218 *Demise of the British Empire in the Middle East*

NOTES

1 This explanation for Abdallah's move to Transjordan is given in Mary C. Wilson, *King Abdallah, Britain and the Making of Jordan* (Cambridge, 1987) p. 44.
2 This scenario was offered in a large exercise called 'Intermezzo'. PRO, FO 371/68378, E4319, Notes on Intermezzo. See also the introduction in Ilan Pappé, *Britain and the Arab–Israeli Conflict, 1948–1951* (London and New York, 1988) p. x.
3 PRO (Public Record Office Documents), FO 371/68403, E300 and E2001, Glubb's and Kirkbride's memoranda, December 1947. See also Ilan Pappé, 'Sir Alec Kirkbride and the Anglo–Transjordanian Alliance', in John Zametica (ed.), *British Offiicals and the British Foreign Policy, 1945–1950* (Leicester, 1990) pp. 125–6.
4 Ilan Asia, *The Core of the Conflict; The Struggle for the Negev, 1947–1956* (Jerusalem, 1994) (Hebrew) pp. 28–9.
5 Ibid.
6 See Note 2 on Intermezzo.
7 PRO, FO 371/68818, E1901, Brief for Bevin's meeting with Tawfiq Abu al-Huda, 6 February 1948. See also Pappé, Britain, pp. 9–15.
8 On the Transjordan option see Pappé, *Britain*, pp. 74–114.
9 Ibid.
10 See Pappé, Britain, pp. 13–14 for a more detailed discussion.
11 On the Iraqi role see Ilan Pappé, *The Making of the Arab–Israeli Conflict 1947–1951* (London and New York, 1992) pp. 127–8, 137–40 and 183–4 on their role towards the end of the war.
12 For a most elaborate discussion on the meaning of the understanding see the preface and conclusion to Avi Shlaim, *The Politics of Partition: King Abdallah, the Zionists and Palestine, 1921–1951* (Oxford, 1990). A recent contribution to the debate on the collusion has appeared in 'Debating Israel's History with Benny Morris, Ilan Pappé, Avi Shlaim and Efraim Karsh', *Middle East Quarterly*, 3,3 (September 1996) pp. 50–5.
13 Report on the meeting in May can be found in PRO FO 371/68852, E6008, Amman to London, 8 May 1948.
14 I discuss this at length in a chapter titled 'The Arab World Goes to War, Or Does It' in *The Making of the Arab–Israeli Conflict*, pp. 102–34.
15 Wm Roger Louis, *The British Empire in the Middle East, 1945–1950* (Oxford, 1984) p. 578.
16 See PRO, FO 371/68818, E2994, throughout March 1948.
17 This comes out in a correspondence between Tawfiq Abu al-Huda and Ernest Bevin in PRO FO 816/113, 20 March 1948.
18 PRO FO 371/68864, E13842, Kirkbride to Burrows, 21 October 1948. See also Robert Bolitho, *The Angry Neighbours: A Diary of Palestine and Transjordan* (London, 1957) pp. 118–19.
19 There are two important sources for the number of Palestinians: the first is S. G. Thicknesse, *Arab Refugees: A Survey of Resettlement Possibilities* (London, 1949) and the UN Economic Survey Mission Final Report. According to both, the Eastern Bank population was 450,000, out of which 225,000 were Palestinians, and another 400,000 Palestinians resided in the West Bank. On top of this, Jordan hosted 400,000 refugees in the West Bank and 100,000 in the East Bank.
20 See Pappé, 'Sir Alec Kirkbride', for full discussion of Kirkbride's role.
21 See Kirkbride's views in PRO FO 371/82715, E1015/18, Amman to London, 6 March 1950.
22 PRO, FO 371/82706, E1017/2, Kirkbride to Bevin, 2 August 1950.
23 PRO, FO 371/82716, E1053/2, Furlonge to Kirkbride, 30 November 1950.
24 PRO, FO 371/98856, Annual Report for Jordan for 1951.
25 PRO, FO 371/110873, E141974, Annual Report for Jordan 1953, 25 January 1954.
26 PRO FO 371/104231, E141974, Amman to London, 16 February 1953.
27 Ibid.
28 Annual Report for Jordan for 1953, op. cit.
29 PRO, FO 371/104231, E141974, Memo by the Chiefs of Staff, 6 February 1953.
30 Minutes in ibid.
31 John Campbell, Defense of the Middle East, Problems of American Policy (New York, 1958) pp. 53–4.
32 PRO FO 371/11580/31, Foreign Office Minute, 11 April 1955.

British rule in Jordan, 1943–55   219

33 Uriel Dann, 'The Foreign Office, the Baghdad Pact and Jordan', *Asian and African Studies*, 21, 3 (November 1989) p. 248. The British ambassador in Cairo felt that al-Nasir was later betrayed by Selwyn Lloyd when the latter promised that Jordan would not join the pact; see the ambassador's memoirs, Humphrey Trevelyan, *The Middle East in Revolution* (London, 1970) p. 56. David Carlton, one of Eden's biographers, felt that in this case al-Nasir was almost entitled to stage an all-out confrontation and propaganda war against Britain; David Carlton, *Anthony Eden* (London, 1981) p. 392.
34 PRO, FO 371/115638, E141801, Foreign Office Memo, 11 August 1954.
35 Foreign Office Memo, 10 August 1954, ibid.
36 Ibid.
37 PRO, FO 371/121461, E141801, Duke's Annual Report for 1955, 6 January 1956.
38 P. J. Vatikiotis, *Politics and the Military in Jordan* (London, 1967) p. 122.
39 Annual Report for 1955, op. cit.
40 PRO, FO 371/121461, E141801, Annual Report for 1955, 6 January 1956.
41 Ibid.
42 PRO, FO 371/121464, E141974, Amman to London, 12 January 1956.
43 Ibid..
44 Annual Report for 1955, op. cit.
45 PRO, FO 371/121463, E141801, Foreign Office Memoranda from 10 and 11 January 1956.
46 Ibid.
47 *Aahar Saaa*, Amman, 4 January 1956.
48 *Al-Difa*, 5 March 1956.
49 PRO, FO 371/121466, E141974, 12 May 1956.

12

Britain and the Palestine question, 1945–48: The dialectic of regional and international constraints

AVRAHAM SELA

INTRODUCTION

By the end of the Second World War in Europe the 'Palestine question' was high on the agenda of the Western Powers, assuming a new urgency and international momentum. This narrowed significantly Britain's freedom of decision-making on the issue. Britain's mandate in Palestine had indeed reached a dead end, owing, above all, to the impact of the Holocaust on public opinion in the West, which manifested itself in support of the vigorous Zionist claim for a Jewish state. The constraints on British decision-making on Palestine were aggravated further by the growing intervention of US President Harry S. Truman in favor of the Zionists, who now came out into open revolt in Palestine. Financially exhausted by the war, Britain was now dependent on the United States for its own economic rehabilitation.

Britain's post-war imperial weakness and its implications were not immediately recognized by all British decision-makers. Indeed, British policy in Palestine after the war reflected the tension between the two main approaches at Whitehall: the 'little England,' economic-based approach, represented by Prime Minister Attlee; and a conservative, strategically oriented approach, advocating the preservation of British hegemony in the Middle East through the construction of a regional defence system, represented by Foreign Secretary Bevin and the Chiefs of Staff.[1]

The apparent success of Zionist propaganda and diplomatic efforts in the United States toward the end of the war triggered deep concern among Arab regional actors, followed by intensive diplomatic action on behalf of the Palestinian–Arab cause. The Arab governments insisted that Palestine should become a unitary independent state where Jews would constitute a permanent minority, threatening that acceptance of

Britain and the Palestine question 221

the Zionist claims would ruin the Arabs' friendly relations with the United States.[2]

The intensifying Arab involvement in the Palestine issue interacted strongly with the rising popular demands in Egypt and Iraq for full national independence and revision of their treaties with Britain. Indeed, if any single major consideration had persisted in Britain's Palestine policy since the mid-1930s it was an awareness of the growing nature of the Palestine question as an all-Arab and all-Muslim issue. This meant that any political measure concerning Palestine had to serve Britain's interests in the Arab Muslim world.

London's diplomatic efforts to reconcile those contradictory pressures and reach a practicable settlement to the Palestine conflict, described by one historian as a 'policy of procrastination and delay',[3] merely underlined the impasse that the mandate had reached. Britain's policy on the Palestine question remained ambivalent, representing a constant effort to reduce the damage to its regional and international position. Thus, although Britain's policy on Palestine tended to take a pro-Arab direction, this tendency, as noticed by Albert Hourani, 'was crossed by another: the desire to be innocent, to appear to world opinion as blameless and impartial. The clash of these tendencies gave British policy its erratic and confused nature.'[4]

Indeed, Britain's decision to relinquish the mandate, effectively sabotaging the United Nations' partition resolution and paving the road to its failure, turned into an abandonment of its Arab allies while also deepening the Jewish community's perception of Britain as 'perfidious Albion'. Finally, it was the Palestinian–Arab disaster and the humiliating defeat of the Arab states in the 1948 war that dealt a death blow to Britain's stature in the Arab Middle East.

PALESTINE AS A REGIONAL ARAB ISSUE

The regional constraints on Britain's handling of the Palestine question were rooted deeply in the formative period of the contemporary Arab Middle East. Between the two world wars, the Palestine Question was a major driving force in the formation of pan-Arab nationalism, in conjunction with socio-political changes in the Fertile Crescent countries and Egypt and their struggle for national liberation. Encapsulating Islamic, Arab nationalist and anti-Western sentiments, the Palestine cause became a core political and moral theme in Arab public life. The defence of Palestine was thus presented as an Islamic and pan-Arab national duty.

The intensifying Arab–Zionist conflict in Palestine, particularly in the wake of the 1929 riots, became increasingly instrumental in the political struggle for power and, as such, a constant issue on both Arab domestic and regional agendas. The process represented a convergence of interests, though not of identical political goals, of the Palestinian–Arab community, ambitious Arab political elites striving for regional power, and their opposition movements, which, in turn, entangled Britain's posture in the Middle East in an unresolvable contradiction.[5] Britain's close alliance with the Hashemite rulers of Iraq and Transjordan was a source of inter-Arab tension and suspicion at London's role in advancing these clients' ambitions, particularly Abdallah's aspirations in Palestine and Syria.[6] The linkage between Britain's mandatory role in Palestine and regional Arab politics was highlighted by the increasing use of the Palestine issue as a rallying theme in anti-government and anti-British campaigns waged by radical political movements, especially in Iraq and Egypt.[7]

By and large, the Arab states' involvement in the Palestine conflict, culminating in the invasion of Palestine by their regular armies in mid-May 1948, was the result of domestic popular pressures stemming from strong hostility to foreign domination and solidarity with the Arabs of Palestine. In Egypt, as well as in the newly independent states of the Fertile Crescent, domestic political and economic difficulties proved overwhelming. Growing militant religious, nationalist and communist opposition led to an increasing inclination of the ruling elites to espouse the Palestine issue as an indispensable source of legitimacy.

Palestine thus came to serve as a focus of regional Arab politics, stirred by supra-state pan-Arab and Islamic networks and political movements. The Palestine question was indeed unique in enhancing common Arab action and crystallizing the regional system's nucleus—institutionalized in the foundation of the League of Arab States in March 1945. With the foundation of the League, the Palestinian national movement – still exhausted by the 1936–39 revolt, with its political leaders detained or in exile – lost any effective representation of its own cause. The question of Palestine thus became a collective Arab issue supervised by the Arab League.[8]

The regionalization of the Palestine question was encouraged by Britain whose mandatory policy, under the impact of the revolt of 1936–39 and growing Italian and German agitation in the Arab countries, assumed an increasingly regional rationale, tightly linked to British imperial considerations. The change reflected the Foreign Office's growing perception that the Palestine conflict had become a central issue on the agenda of Arab and Muslim societies in the Middle East as well as among the Muslims of India, leading to a shift in the centre of gravity of decision-making on the issue from the Colonial to the Foreign Office. Henceforth, Britain's mandatory policy tended to

Britain and the Palestine question 223

assume a clear pro-Arab nature in order to secure the 'good will' of the Arabs as a guarantee of Britain's imperial interests and stature in the Middle East.[9]

Britain encouraged Arab rulers to play an official role in the Palestine question in co-ordination with its policy, hoping thereby to mitigate violence against its policy. In the May 1939 White Paper Britain undertook to consult with the Arab governments before making any change in that policy.

IN SEARCH OF A LONG-TERM SOLUTION

With the end of the war in Europe British officials in the Middle East maintained that their country's stature in the region was at its peak due to victory, as well as to the White Paper policy in Palestine, and the role played by Britain in securing Syria's and Lebanon's independence and in excluding France from the Levant. The preservation of those achievements, in addition to creating a regional defence system through new or revised bilateral treaties with each of the Arab states, seemed to be linked more than ever before with the settlement of the Palestine question. The architects of Britain's Middle East policy tended to portray the Palestine question as a 'focus of Britain's policy', and the 'pillar of Britain's strategic interests' in the region.[10]

Yet Britain's regional policy suffered from inherent contradictions. Apart from the Hashemite regimes, which perceived the alliance with Britain to be vital for their survival – and for which they were held in contempt by their Arab rivals – other ruling elites were obsessed with obtaining complete national liberation and sovereignty over their territories in peace and war times. However, not only were Arab officials unable to separate Palestine from their own quest for national liberation, but Britain's decision-makers misperceived the growing popular militant pressures on the Arab ruling elites, which strictly limited their freedom of manoeuvre regarding relations with the former colonial power as well as on Palestine.[11]

At the same time, even before the war came to its end, Britain was confronted with a determined Zionist leadership, which had adopted a claim for the establishment of a Jewish state over the whole of mandatory Palestine, and a growing anti-British Jewish terrorism, which threatened to expand into a full-blown Jewish rebellion if immigration were stopped. However, Britain's main concern was the possible negative impact of Zionist influence in the United States on Anglo–American relations. This was especially acute in view of strong American public support for the removal of all British restrictions on

224 *Demise of the British Empire in the Middle East*

immigration to Palestine of Holocaust survivors. In the view of pro-Arab British officials the growing Zionist impact on American public opinion and party politics 'poisoned Britain's relations with the United States'.[12] Moreover, the intensified public manifestations of American solidarity with the Zionist aspirations in Palestine in 1944–45 aroused the Arab governments' fears and agitation, renewing their political efforts on behalf of the Palestinian cause.[13]

Under these circumstances, and British economic dependence on the United States by the end of the war, the continued *status quo* in Palestine under the White Paper was no longer optional. Yet Britain's quest for a realistic long-term solution during the next four years proved futile. In January 1944, the cabinet had approved the special Cabinet Committee's recommendations for partition, the establishment of a Jewish state and annexation of Arab Palestine to Transjordan. But these recommendations, which had never been official, or public, met the same fate as the Peel Commission's partition plan of 1937. Once again, it was the Foreign Office and the military echelon that led the campaign against partition, perceived to be ruinous to Britain's imperial and regional interests.[14]

A proposal submitted in April 1945 by Edward Grigg, the minister-resident in Cairo, for the establishment of a British trusteeship over Palestine under United Nations' supervision, was also rejected by the government, mainly on grounds of anticipated Arab objection to any withdrawal from the White Paper and the constitutional promises it included.[15]

The Foreign Office and the Chiefs of Staff maintained that a partition of Palestine would generate severe Arab violence in the region, which would destroy friendly Arab–British relations, and undermine Britain's vital interests in the Middle East. These were defined in terms of communications, oil and strategic bases, which could be preserved only by securing the 'good will' of the Arabs. Another source of concern was the anticipated penetration of the United States and Soviet Union in the region after the war, and the Arab states' drive toward unity.[16]

The Foreign Office's objection to partition won the full endorsement of Britain's military commanders, heads of civil administration and diplomatic echelons in the Middle East, who, in 1944–45, regarded even the slightest deviation from the White Paper as a disaster for Britain's interests in the region. It was estimated that, in view of the anticipated violence of both Arabs and Jews to partition or of Jews to a continuation of the White Paper policy, at least another division would be needed in Palestine. Such a level of reinforcement seemed unrealistic as long as the war continued, or, during the year after, owing to the need to secure the occupied European territories.[17]

Britain and the Palestine question 225

Towards the end of the war, Churchill advocated placing part of the responsiblity for the Middle East – including a long-term settlement of the Palestine problem – on the American government. The Labour government also strove to win the support of the United States for a settlement in Palestine, in order to mitigate Zionist pressures and to legitimize Britain's Palestine policy in the United States.[18]

Based on the State Department's position this tendency realistically assumed that there was a British–American consensus on the need to resolve the Palestine problem in a way that would preserve Western interests in the Middle East, especially in view of the post-war Soviet threat. To Whitehall's chagrin, however, the American input became affected increasingly by President Truman's pro-Zionist intervention, which frustrated repeated British attempts at co-ordination with Washington. Indeed, as Bevin's biographer commented, 'The Jewish demands and the Arab reaction were predictable; direct intervention by the American President was not.'[19]

Although unable to arrive at any practical long-term policy in Palestine, a short-term policy was urgently needed. The White Paper's Jewish immigration quota was about to be exhausted in July 1945, and the problem of Europe's Jewish survivors could not be ignored. Under the new Labour government two long-term solutions were considered. A proposal for 'provincial autonomy', which had deep roots in the Colonial Office, suggested partition of the country into separate Arab and Jewish autonomous provinces, with possible federal unity in the future. The second solution, suggested by Bevin, was the establishment of a federal union under Abdallah's throne, comprising three units: Arab and Jewish units in Palestine, according to the Cabinet Committee's scheme, and Transjordan. Both proposals, however, were eventually rejected. While the first one seemed to perpetuate the partition of the country, and was therefore rejected by the Arabs, the second was rejected by both the Jews, who refused to be ruled by an Arab prince, and Ibn Saud, whose hostility to Abdallah left no doubt as to his anticipated rejection of such scheme.[20]

In September, shortly after the advent of Attlee's Labour government, a conference chaired by Foreign Secretary Bevin, comprising Britain's representatives in the Middle East and officials of the foreign and colonial offices, approved a temporary continuity of the White Paper's policy on immigration, maintaining an average quota of 1,500–2,000 immigrants per month, until a long-term solution to the Palestine question was reached. The decision reflected a clear British preference to confront the outraged response of the Zionists and the Yishuv, over running the risk of wide-scale riots in the Arab world and among the Muslims of India.[21]

226   *Demise of the British Empire in the Middle East*

The decision to adhere to the White Paper policy coincided with the position advocated by the Foreign Office and the 'Middle East Defence Committee' since April 1944, to preserve Britain's control of Palestine and to reject both Zionist and Arab claims. The Labour government resolved that if it was decided to suspend further Jewish immigration, Britain would submit the Palestine question to the United Nation's Trusteeship Committee. However, Bevin maintained that an approach to the United Nations should be accompanied by specific recommendations, which, in addition to being acceptable to both Arabs and Jews as well as to the United States, would secure the defence of British interests in the Middle East. In other words, the ideas considered by the Foreign Office and the Chiefs of Staff assumed, or at least envisioned, that control over Palestine would be retained anyway.[22]

Paradoxically, President Truman's pressure on London to allow the immigration of 100,000 displaced Jewish persons from Europe gave the British government a pretext for a further delay of the decision on a long-term policy in Palestine. London could hardly underestimate Truman's pressures, especially in view of its need for Washington's financial assistance, and its strategic co-operation in containing Soviet encroachment into Europe and the Middle East. Yet the American President's intervention provided Bevin with the opportunity to try to secure an American endorsement for Britain's Palestine policy by establishing an Anglo–American Committee of Enquiry (AACE) on Palestine. The gulf between the two powers was demonstrated by their different interpretations of the committee's terms of reference, intended to satisfy their respective clients.[23]

The establishment of the AACE came less than a month after the Jewish national leadership had taken an unprecedented decision to wage a violent struggle against Britain, in collaboration between the national command of the Hagana, and the IZL (Irgun Zvai Leumi [National Military Organization]) and Lehi (Lohamei Herut Israel [Israel Freedom Fighters]) 'dissident' groups. Britain's decision to prefer American-backed diplomatic means over forceful disarmament of the Yishuv reflected Whitehall's concern about the American public response to a violent repression of the Yishuv – for which, in any case, Britain was hardly ready militarily – and an evaluation that the American administration would ultimately endorse its Palestine policy. The British decision was accompanied by an acknowledgement of the need to allow continued Jewish immigration. The growing effort of Jewish illegal immigration orchestrated by the Hagana constituted a growing moral as well as military burden on the British government. Moreover, the growing number of detained illegal immigrants at Atlit camp (near Haifa) triggered concerns lest the Hagana try to release them by force.[24]

Britain and the Palestine question

BEVIN'S FUTILE DIPLOMACY

The Jewish armed struggle came to a halt for the period of the AACE's work. On the Arab side, despite an Iraqi attempt to impose a collective Arab boycott of the AACE, the Arab League discussions of the issue were concluded with a rather non-committal announcement on 5 December. British officials interpreted it as informal acquiescence in a six-month prolongation of Jewish immigration to Palestine according to the White Paper's quota in return for British adherence to that document, and a continued Arab–British dialogue concerning Palestine.[25]

It is noteworthy that the League's decision was approved without the delegates of the newly established Palestinian Higher Arab Committee (HAC), owing to their late arrival in Cairo. However, the official response of the Palestinian–Arab leadership to Bevin's announcement on the AACE clearly demonstrated the former's disagreement with the Arab League's position. The HAC rejected any further Jewish immigration and American involvement in shaping the future of Palestine, and claimed an exclusive right to be the 'ultimate ruler' on the Palestine question.[26] Indeed, the collective Arab position remained unequivocally opposed to any further Jewish immigration into Palestine. To balance their collaboration with the AACE, the Arab governments decided to impose, as of 1 January 1946, a full economic boycott on the Jewish community in Palestine, as an indication of their determination to curtail its development.[27]

The impact of the Palestinians on the Arab governments was indeed undeniable when Bevin appealed to the latter to accept the cabinet's decision of 1 January 1946 – before it was published – on prolongation of Jewish immigration (1,500 per month), for the period of the AACE's work. Despite the Arab governments' understanding approach to the British appeal, none was willing to approve such a decision, especially in view of the American Congress' resolution of 17 December 1945 in support of immediate and wide-scale Jewish immigration to Palestine. Yet the early inclination of the Arab governments to refer Bevin's request to the Arab League, indicating the collective nature of the matter, came to an end once the HAC announced its utter rejection of the cabinet's decision. Hence, with the announcement of the cabinet decision in late January on continued Jewish immigration the Arab governments responded officially in a tone identical to the HAC's. In Lebanon, Syria and Iraq, special parliamentary sessions denounced the British government, presumably to enhance their own domestic legitimacy.[28]

While the Arab governments and the HAC – now led by Jamal al-Husayni, who had been released from British detention – opted to collaborate with the AACE, all Palestinian–Arab parties other than the Husaynis demanded to boycott the AACE, so that the issue would be referred soon to the United Nations where the Arabs would be treated even-handedly. The intense public debate within the Palestinian–Arab community over the AACE reflected the split that had affected the HAC in late March as a result of Jamal al-Husayni's attempt to secure his party's domination through enlarging the number of HAC members. It was also a protest against the Arab League's policy on Palestine and in support of the Husayni faction. By and large, the Arab governments' testimonies repeated the familiar attitude regarding Palestine, emphasizing that it must remain Arab. The only exception was the Palestinian–Arab demand, voiced by Jamal al-Husayni and Ahmad Hilmi, that Britain withdraw its forces from Palestine as soon as possible, admitting that this would lead to an armed showdown and solution of the conflict by force. This demand, which came in response to a similar claim by David Ben-Gurion, Chairman of the Zionist Executive, clearly indicated the growing militancy in both parties and the understanding that the dispute would be decided in Palestine itself.[29]

Bevin's gain was indeed no more than a short-lived relief, as indicated by the frustrating responses of the parties concerned to the AACE's recommendations announced in early May. As expected, the Zionists rejected the Committee's main recommendation, namely, that Palestine should remain a unitary, bi-national, state. Even though the Committee had approved President Truman's request for the immediate immigration of 100,000 Jews into Palestine, it was far from meeting the Zionist essential claim for free Jewish immigration to Palestine. The Committee's recommendations came to be perceived as a blow to the Zionists, especially because, in April, Britain and Egypt had started negotiations on the latter's demand for a revision of the 1936 Anglo–Egyptian Treaty and a total evacuation of British troops from Egypt. This, and Prime Minister Attlee's announcement on 9 May that British forces would be evacuated from Egypt, left the impression that Britain had decided to turn Palestine into its main strategic base in the Middle East.[30]

In June, the Jewish armed struggle against the British mandate was renewed, accompanied by intensified efforts at illegal immigration, settlement activity and propaganda. Soon these efforts and their impact on Anglo–American relations began to influence British public opinion, parliament and even the cabinet, reinforcing the view that Britain should rid itself of the 'thankless' duty in Palestine by returning the mandate to the United Nations and withdrawing altogether.[31]

Just how polarized the Jews and Arabs were was demonstrated by the vigorous rejection of the AACE's recommendations throughout the Arab world, blurring the boundaries between domestic and regional,

Britain and the Palestine question 229

or popular and official spheres. The protests, strikes, demonstrations and militant proclamations all combined to create a sense of crisis. Once again the Palestine question demonstrated its overwhelming rallying power in Arab politics. Apart from rejecting the immigration of 100,000 Jews into Palestine, and the abolition of restrictions on land sales to Jews, the Arabs were particularly bitter about the AACE's recommendation that Palestine should become neither a Jewish nor an Arab state. The Arabs argued that with continued Jewish immigration and land purchases a Jewish state would be inevitable.[32]

The collective Arab response to the AACE's recommendations was consolidated at an Arab summit conference at Inshas, Egypt (28 May) and at the Arab League Council's session convened in the Syrian resort town of Bludan (8–12 June). These meetings indicated an escalation in the level of Arab commitment to the Palestinian–Arab cause. The Inshas summit undertook, for the first time, to support the Arabs of Palestine 'by all possible means', in addition to making an unequivocal commitment to extend financial support.[33] Yet the Arab response was affected markedly by Britain's pro-Arab position and reservations in regard to the AACE's recommendations. In fact, the Arab governments strove to reach a consensus with Britain that would help London to retreat from the Committee's recommendations. This was indicated by the intimate consultations between Arab leaders and British officials during the Bludan meeting, particularly with Brigadier Clayton, whose presence in Bludan was not a secret.[34]

The Bludan conference rejected Jamal al-Husayni's demand to prepare for an armed rebellion, which would entail financial and military assistance to the Arabs of Palestine. However, in view of the growing Jewish armed struggle, the conference recommended that the Arab governments 'encourage popular support of material and human resources for the defence of the Arabs of Palestine', which would be sponsored by 'Committee(s) for the Defence of Palestine', to be established in each Arab country. The option of appealing to the United Nations, strongly advocated by the HAC, was not endorsed, owing to doubts about its chances of success. The preference was for co-ordination with Britain. It was therefore decided to request that Britain end the mandate and enter into negotiations with the Arab governments on the future of Palestine in accordance with the United Nations' Charter. Although the word 'trusteeship' was purposely omitted – to prevent misunderstanding about the Arabs' being willing to accept less than the full independence of Palestine – the Arab request to begin negotiations on Palestine clearly referred to articles 79–80 of the UN Charter.[35]

The Bludan conference completed the process of undertaking

collective Arab responsibility for the Palestine question, and specified the instruments for implementing this duty. Although a new HAC was appointed, the authority to allocate financial and other Arab resources for the Palestine cause was entrusted officially to a newly established 'Palestine Committee' within the Arab League, headed by the Secretary-General Azzam and members of each of the Arab states and the HAC.[36] This structure was meant to enhance the Arab states' control over the Palestinian issue, especially in view of the HAC's intentions to shift to armed rebellion, which would bring them into confrontation with Britain and entangle them in domestic turmoil. However, in the absence of direct control over the Palestinian–Arab community itself, the Arab League's authority was bound to remain limited, encouraging frustration and inter-Arab disagreements.

The collective Arab memorandum to Britain and the United States adopted a threatening tone regarding any attempt to implement the AACE's recommendations. The threat included a hint of applying economic sanctions, namely, an embargo on oil supplies to Britain and the United States, and encouragement of volunteers from the Arab countries to support the Arabs of Palestine. Despite this demonstration of unity, the Arab coalition was divided deeply by competition over contradictory goals and priorities, which would make any compromise on Palestine impossible. Hence, the Arab League Council came under strong Iraqi pressure to adopt resolutions threatening specific economic and political sanctions against Britain and the United States in case of implementation of the AACE's recommendations. The Iraqi proposal met with strong reservations from most Arab delegates, who feared that such a threat would harm their own interests. The disagreement was settled finally by accepting the Iraqi demand but keeping it secret – although the resolutions on sanctions and 'popular' military and financial support to the Arabs of Palestine were reported informally to the British government.[37]

Even before the official publication of the AACE's recommendations, most British cabinet members, including Prime Minister Attlee, were sceptical about their possible implementation, because of the evident need to impose them by force on both Jews and Arabs and Britain's strategic constraints in this regard. The gloomy state of the mandate was best reflected by the cabinet's consensus that implementation of the Committee's recommendations would lead to both Arab and Jewish revolts and to irreparable rupture between Britain and the Arab states. Bevin was alone in his hope of obtaining American political, military and financial co-operation in their full implementation, which he conceded would be vital for disarming the Jewish military organizations. Bevin also objected to returning the mandate to the United Nations, arguing

Britain and the Palestine question 231

that it would enable the Soviet Union to intervene in the Palestine conflict.[38]

In May, London and Washington indeed agreed to hold joint discussions of 'experts' on the implementation of the AACE's recommendations, the result of which would become a basis for consultations with the Arab and Zionist parties. Yet, while the American administration insisted on the early implementation of the recommendation on the 100,000 Jewish immigrants, Britain's priority was to conclude an agreement with the Egyptian government on the revision of the 1936 treaty, before new suggestions on Palestine were presented to the Arabs. It was Bevin's assumption that it would be easier to win Egypt's consent to the implementation of the AACE's recommendations after its own national claims had been met. Indeed, the key question from a British viewpoint was how to proceed with diplomacy on Palestine without undermining its regional interests.

However, despite disenchantment with the mandate, the Chiefs of Staff, with the Foreign Office's backing, continued to insist on retaining a British military presence of two divisions in Palestine, as a part of any future solution. Moreover, the cabinet's unilateral decision of 6 June to evacuate British troops from Egypt (though not from the Canal Zone), in spite of the Chiefs of Staffs' objections, made Palestine even more crucial to Britain's strategic interests in the Middle East. The advocates of a continued presence in Palestine suggested repeatedly that it would be impossible to enforce a solution unacceptable to either the Jews or Arabs. These considerations and the successful repressive measures taken against the Yishuv's political leadership and military infrastructure on 29 June 1946 underpinned the British suggestion of a 'provincial autonomy' plan at the 'experts' talks as a solution that was not an alternative to the mandate, and which coincided better with British interests in the Middle East. The 'experts' talks resulted in an agreed plan of 'provincial autonomy' which the British Cabinet approved immediately, later to be known as the 'Morrison–Grady Plan'.[39]

The plan was intended to secure long-term British domination of Palestine. It proposed dividing the country into four districts – Arab, Jewish, Jerusalem and the Negev. While the Negev was to remain under direct British control, the first three districts were to be administered by local autonomous administrations, whose powers would include municipal and civil affairs, land sales and immigration. The districts were to be subordinated to a central government headed by a high commissioner. The central government was to be in charge of foreign and financial affairs, and security. The main advantage of the plan was its ambiguity and its possible development toward either direction

232 *Demise of the British Empire in the Middle East*

advocated, respectively, by the Foreign and Colonial Offices: a bi-national unitary state, or partition.[40]

Apart from the fact that the plan was rejected by both Jews and Arabs, the main blow it sustained came from Washington, where President Truman, under strong Zionist and partisan pressure, and with an eye on the approaching elections to Congress due in November, refused to adopt it. None the less, the British cabinet decided to promote the plan as a basis for consultations with Jews and Arabs, whose consent would enable a British trusteeship regime to be established.[41]

The cabinet's decision was affected apparently by the dramatic change in Zionist policy in the summer of 1946. On 5 August, the Jewish Agency, meeting in Paris, decided by a decisive majority to support partition and the establishment of a 'viable Jewish state' in part of Palestine. The harbingers of this change were apparent in the private meetings held by Weizmann, Ben-Gurion and Shertok with the AACE in Jerusalem the previous March, during which the Jewish delegates presented a map with the desired Jewish state, comprising the Peel Plan plus Jerusalem and the Negev. The timing of the official change in the Zionist policy, however, reflected a sense of despair, fear of a violent confrontation with Britain, and loss of White House support, following the British comprehensive military crack-down on the Yishuv's leadership and military infrastructure on 29 June 1946 ('Black Saturday') – which in turn provoked the blowing up of the King David Hotel (22 July) by the IZL. Above all, however, it was the 'Morrison–Grady' plan and its perceived danger to Zionist aspirations that determined the change in the Zionist programme.[42]

In the summer of 1946 a temporary convergence of circumstances seems to have triggered a growing support among British and American senior officials in the Middle East as well as in Washington for the idea of partition, assuming that if Britain and the United States collaborated on such a scheme, Arab resistance would not constitute an obstacle. Such a solution appeared to High Commissioner Cunningham, for example, as preferable to provincial autonomy, which would have caused a confrontation with both Jews and Arabs. However, the Foreign Office and Chiefs of Staff remained unmoved in their objection to partition.[43]

But the abyss between Arab and Jewish positions remained as unbridgeable as ever. While the Zionist Executive regarded the plan as a formula for creating an independent Palestinian state in which the minority status of the Jews would be perpetuated, Arab policy-makers suspected it as being nothing but a prelude to partition. Moreover, they announced that they would neither meet nor negotiate with the Zionists. Even before the London Conference convened on 9 September

Britain and the Palestine question 233

at the St James' Palace, the Arab delegations rejected the provincial autonomy plan as a basis for negotiations.[44]

The absurdity of the conference was manifested by the absence of the parties directly concerned, who boycotted the meeting; the HAC, for not being allowed to determine its own delegates, and the Zionist Executive, in protest against the mass arrests of the Yishuv's leaders (though British officials did hold informal contacts with Zionist leaders during the conference). According to Britain's request, the Arab delegations submitted their own plan for a unitary Palestinian state, in which the Jewish community would be recognized constitutionally as a political minority. Jewish immigration would be entirely halted and only Jews with at least 10 years' residence would be recognized as citizens.[45]

The Arab plan, submitted without prior consultation with the HAC, led to the latter's bitter criticism of the Arab governments. At the next session of the Arab League Council, Jamal al-Husayni argued that the Arab governments misrepresented the Palestinian–Arab attitude, accusing them of doing too little to ensure that the HAC be invited to London and be granted the right to choose its own representatives.[46]

In June 1946, the Mufti al-Hajj Amin al-Husayni returned to the Middle East after a long absence in Nazi Europe and, by the Bludan resolutions, re-established his official position as the HAC's president. Henceforth, the Mufti focused his activity on restoring his own authority and reorganizing the HAC, on the assumption that a military showdown with the Jews was imminent. For the short run, however, the main impact of his return (even though he was not allowed into Palestine and forced to operate from Egypt and Lebanon) was the stiffening of the collective Arab attitude on Palestine. His reputation as a bitter enemy of Britain, a holy man and symbol of the Arab struggle for national liberation, especially among the newly emerging urban middle class in the Arab countries, explains his influence on Arab decision-makers, who perceived him as a potential threat to their domestic stability.

Another element of extremism injected into the collective Arab position was Syria's and Saudi Arabia's concerns that Britain was heading towards a partition that would allot the Arab part of Palestine to Transjordan, which in May 1946 had been granted independence under Abdallah's kingship. Indeed, by the summer of 1946 Abdallah's relations with his Syrian neighbours deteriorated, owing to the Hashemite king's proclamations of his aspiration to unify 'Greater Syria' under his own throne and his support of opposition groups in Syria. The perceived threat to Syria pushed its regime to increasing identification with Iraq's extremism on Palestine. Indeed, in the summer of

1946, the Jewish Agency reached an informal understanding with Abdallah that in the event that Palestine was partitioned he would not interfere with the establishment of a Jewish state, while the Jews would be indifferent to the fate of the Arab part of Palestine, understanding that it would be annexed to Transjordan.[47]

In late October, the prospects for a negotiated settlement in Palestine seemed worse than ever. On top of the poor results of the London conference, on 4 October, the eve of the Jewish Day of Atonement, Truman repeated his claim for massive Jewish immigration into Palestine and endorsed a solution based on a compromise between the Morrison–Grady plan and partition of Palestine.[48] Truman's declaration, which was understood as support of a Jewish state, further undermined Bevin's chances of reaching a negotiated settlement that would grant the Jews less than a state. Against this backdrop, Bevin presented three options to the cabinet in case Britain reached no agreed settlement with the Arabs and Jews:

1. Imposing a solution on one of the parties – an option dismissed by the Chiefs of Staff on military grounds.
2. Relinquishing the mandate and withdrawing from Palestine, which would seriously affect Britain's stature in the Middle East.
3. Partition and the merger of the Arab part with Transjordan.[49]

In November and December 1946 it had become obvious to the cabinet that the only practical option for Britain was to return the mandate to the United Nations, the implications and implementation of which became a matter for discussion at the Colonial and Foreign Offices. The main issues on the agenda were whether or not to accompany the approach to the United Nations with specific recommendations, and if so, whether Britain should endeavour to secure a trusteeship under UN auspices or seek swift withdrawal from Palestine. A major question was the prospects of either option securing endorsement by the United Nations. Given the attitudes of the parties concerned it was unavoidable to refer the Palestine mandate to the United Nations if Britain wanted to retain its presence in the country. Otherwise, there was a danger that the Arab states might appeal to the United Nations to undertake the role of trustee of Palestine, as the party directly concerned with this territory.[50]

In early 1947, it became clear to the British that there was no chance of reaching an agreed solution between Jews and Arabs in the second phase of the London Conference. In effect, the deliberations at this stage meant reaching an agreement with either party, while mitigating the other's objections so as to allow Britain to refer the issue to the United Nations with a recommendation that would win that organization's

Britain and the Palestine question 235

support and secure continued British domination over Palestine. Indeed, the cabinet strove to refrain from referring Palestine to the United Nations without recommendations. Not only would it be tantamount to an admission of failure, but it would also pave the way for Soviet infiltration of Palestine, if the United Nations opted for a multinational trusteeship.[51]

As in the case of the Peel Commission's recommendations of 1937, the Colonial and Foreign Offices were divided over the desired outcome. Although the prospects for winning the United Nations' support for partition by a two-thirds majority seemed poor, the cabinet was convinced by Colonial Secretary Creech-Jones to discuss a draft resolution of partition, which had enjoyed wide support within the Labour Party and among some cabinet members. In contrast, the Foreign Office persisted in its adherence to a pro-Arab solution, of a bi-national unitary state, with a limited Jewish immigration acceptable to the American administration.[52]

In the cabinet's discussion, which ended in mid-February, Attlee, Bevin and Lord Alexander, the defence secretary, together with the Chiefs of Staff, adhered to their rejection of partition on grounds of Britain's economic, military and political interests in the Middle East. With the collapse of the Bevin–Sidqi agreement on the revision of the 1936 Anglo–Egyptian Treaty, and the intention to withdraw from India, Palestine appeared to be even more vital than before to the existence of British military bases and logistic facilities in the region. That Palestine was the only substitute for Egypt the General Staff was willing to consider was manifested by the December 1946 decision to transfer an additional British division from Egypt to Palestine.[53]

Notwithstanding the majority support for partition in the cabinet, Bevin managed to extract a resolution that would allow him to resume talks with both Jews and Arabs without a commitment to a specific plan. Bevin's decisive weight in the cabinet regarding Palestine was highlighted by Creech-Jones' withdrawal of his own proposal and his acceptance of the foreign secretary's position. Ultimately, partition was not officially suggested to either of the parties concerned. However, the Arab and Jewish positions in the second phase of the London Conference illustrated how far from reality had been the cabinet's assumptions. Instead, on 7 February, the cabinet approved Bevin's plan for a bi-national unitary state in Palestine.[54]

The talks conducted by the foreign and colonial secretaries (formally) with the Arab delegations, and (informally) with the Zionist Executive led by Ben-Gurion, demonstrated the unbridgeable gap not only between the disputed parties but also between each of them and the British government. Under the HAC's pressure the Arab states stiffened

236 *Demise of the British Empire in the Middle East*

their attitude, rejecting unequivocally any manifestation of self-governing Jewish government in Palestine or any further Jewish immigration. They reiterated their rejection of the provincial autonomy proposals, whether according to the 'Morrison–Grady Plan', or Bevin's idea of a bi-national unitary state, presented to them on the day it had been approved by the cabinet.

The Jewish delegates, on the other hand, insisted on their ambiguous claim for 'a viable Jewish state', which even in its minimal version, would include a large Arab population (300–400,000) compared with the contemporary Jewish population of 650,000. Indeed, even Creech-Jones, a strong supporter of partition, perceived such a resolution as impracticable. Ben-Gurion's implied willingness to allow Britain to maintain military bases in the Jewish state left unmoved the Foreign Office and Chiefs of Staff, whose main concern was to ensure the support of the Arab states. In fact, the value of a British military base in the Jewish state seemed worthless in view of the Arab uproar that this was anticipated to provoke.[55]

THE DECISION TO WITHDRAW

During the winter of 1947 Britain was in a deep economic crisis. This catalyzed the cabinet's decisions on substantial cutbacks in overseas commitments. Within one week (14–20 February) the cabinet decided to refer Palestine to the United Nations without any recommendations; to cease, as of 31 March, all economic and military assistance to Greece and Turkey; to withdraw military forces from Greece; and to transfer responsibility in India to local government no later than June 1948. Obviously, in this gloomy atmosphere the cabinet could not adopt a policy that would have led Britain to a violent confrontation in Palestine, even with one of the parties. Indeed, the deliberations in the cabinet revealed growing criticism of Bevin's Palestine policy, which seemed hesitant and contradictory and which, after 18 months of delays and procrastination in decision-making, ended in impasse.[56]

Speaking in parliament on 25 February, Bevin bitterly blamed President Truman for the failure of the London Conference, and expressed his hope that the disputing parties would be more willing to come to an understanding in view of the British decision. It is quite clear that at this stage Bevin still perceived the decision to refer Palestine to the United Nations as a tactical, hence reversible, step. This was clarified to parliament by Creech-Jones, namely, that Britain was not relinquishing the mandate but looking for advice on how to implement it. Bevin apparently hoped that the Arabs and Jews would ultimately prefer an

Britain and the Palestine question 237

agreed solution which would leave the initiative in his hands. Bevin's criticism of Truman constituted another appeal to the American Administration to share the burden of settling the Palestine dispute without risking Soviet involvement. In any case, the Foreign Office predicted that the chances of securing the required two-thirds support for a pro-Zionist partition resolution were very meagre. Failure to do so would result in the UN's backing Britain's policy as defined in the 'Bevin Plan'.[57]

Bevin's wishful expectations, however, were soon frustrated by the Arabs, Jews and President Truman whose positions remained unmoved, leading to inevitable inertia in the United Nations. None the less, this course of events could hardly have come as a surprise to Whitehall, because even those who perceived the decision to refer Palestine to the United Nations as a tactical measure had been fully aware of the risks and uncertainties it involved concerning British interests there.

The decision to resort to the United Nations in fact indicated that the politicians, in contrast to the Chiefs of Staff, did not regard a continued British military presence in Palestine so essential as to dictate their policy, but as one subordinate to Britain's regional Arab policy. In adopting this course of action, the cabinet was well aware of the possibility that the resort to the United Nations could lead to withdrawal from Palestine and to the end of the mandate. From mid-February 1947, official spokesmen reiterated their government's preference to relinquish the mandate rather than to impose a United Nations' resolution unacceptable to the Arabs and Jews and contradictory to Britain's conscience.[58]

Britain submitted the Palestine question to the United Nations officially only on 2 April. It requested the convention of a special session of the General Assembly to discuss the establishment of an inquiry committee on Palestine, the findings of which would be brought before the regular, annual session of the General Assembly in September. The Arab governments repeated their loathing of another committee of inquiry whose recommendations might be contradictory to the Arab interest, insisting that the issue be discussed by the General Assembly itself. Under the HAC's pressure, the collective Arab attitude was defined in terms of a clear demand that the General Assembly should confine itself to discussing the end of the British mandate and the recognition of Palestine's independence as a unitary state. As a fall-back position, the Arabs insisted that they be represented in the committee of inquiry and that its terms of reference be confined to future constitutional aspects, without referring to the Jewish question.[59]

Despite initial American reservation at the lack of British recommendations, the Special Session of the General Assembly rejected all

238   *Demise of the British Empire in the Middle East*

the Arab demands and threats to quit the session and boycott the committee. The final resolution, supported by the American and Soviet delegations, resolved to establish an *ad hoc* committee of inquiry with authority to handle the issue in all its aspects, including the issue of Jewish displaced persons in Europe. Practically, however, only the HAC boycotted the United Nations Special Committee on Palestine (UNSCOP).[60]

The summer of 1947 witnessed intensified Jewish terrorism conducted by the IZL and Lehi against British military and police personnel in Palestine, and growing illegal Jewish immigration sponsored by the Hagana, which led to violent clashes between the immigrants and British authorities. Britain's inability to repress Jewish terrorism, owing to its military weakness and lack of clear policy, became a growing burden on the mandatory government, eroding its control of the situation. In fact, by the eve of the publication of UNSCOP's recommendations, the British military and civil administrations in Palestine were concerned mainly with defending themselves within confined security zones, increasingly isolated from the local population. For the first time since the end of the war, the impact of Palestine on Britain's parliament and public opinion was discernible, indicating the futility of continued British presence in Palestine under these circumstances.[61]

The UNSCOP report, published on 31 August, recommended, unanimously, the termination of the British mandate and granting Palestine independence. However, the committee's members were divided as to the desirable solution. The majority recommended the partition of Palestine and the establishment of Jewish and Arab states after two years of transition, during which Britain should continue to govern the territory under UN auspices. Jerusalem and its surroundings were to become *corpus seperatum* under international trusteeship. The majority plan offered the Jewish state favourable territorial boundaries, enabling 150,000 Jewish immigrants into the proposed Jewish area during the transitory period. The Arab and Jewish states were to sign a formal economic union and mutually to guarantee minority rights in their own state before independence.

The minority plan recommended that Palestine become an independent federal state, following a transitory period of three years. During this period, Jewish immigration would be decided according to the economic absorption capacity, defined by a committee consisting equally of Jewish, Arab and UN members. The federal legislature would comprise two houses, one based on parity and the other on the relative proportion of the total population of Jews and Arabs. Legislation would require a majority vote of both houses. Cases of deadlocked legislation would be arbitrated by a five-member body with an Arab majority. The

Britain and the Palestine question 239

roles of head of state and his deputy would be shared by the two peoples.[62]

UNSCOP's report was another blow to the British, following the General Assembly's special session in which the Soviet Union unexpectedly supported partition (although the significance of this new attitude was grasped fully only in October 1947). On 20 September, the British cabinet unanimously adopted Bevin's unequivocal recommendation that the mandate be ended and Britain's forces be withdrawn from the country as early as possible. The final nature of the decision was reflected by the British refusal to prolong its responsibilities under the mandate, in the absence of a UN resolution on the Palestine problem. Britain's intentions were reiterated by the Colonial Secretary's announcement of 26 September to the UN General Assembly that in the absence of a resolution agreed to by both Arabs and Jews, his government would not take part in its implementation and would withdraw its military forces and administration from Palestine.[63]

This announcement was received with scepticism by both Arabs and Jews, being interpreted as an attempt to coerce them to reach a compromise. Indeed, Bevin hoped that the decision and announcement of Britain's policy on Palestine would force the disputed parties to arrive at an understanding in order to prevent chaos and civil war. However, this did not affect the British decision to end the mandate. Bevin asked British missions in the Middle East to examine carefully any indication of willingness to reach a compromise, with the intention of playing a mediating role to Britain's benefit.[64] The results of this search for moderation ended with yet more frustration as both Arabs and Jews had become, as of late September, increasingly involved in binding announcements of intentions, and preparations, in view of the impending military showdown.[65]

The cabinet's decision of 20 September was taken over the objections of the Chiefs of Staff, whose assumptions about Palestine's crucial strategic significance remained unaltered. The cabinet's decision was eased by the UN Security Council's rejection of Egypt's demand to declare the Anglo–Egyptian Treaty of 1936 null and void, removing the threat to Britain's strategic bases at the Suez Canal.

Even though the colonial secretary's announcement of 26 September was subject to various interpretations, it signalled to the military and civil authorities in London and Palestine that they might begin planning the withdrawal from Palestine. The withdrawal schedule, published on 13 November, set 1 August as the end of the operation. The British withdrawal plan from south to north was a matter of concern to the Syrian regime, which feared a takeover of Palestine by the Arab Legion as a first step in implementing Abdallah's 'Greater Syria' scheme.[66]

240   *Demise of the British Empire in the Middle East*

In October, the reports and evaluations from Jerusalem and Amman strengthened the Foreign Office's conviction that King Abdallah and the Jewish Agency were about to agree on partitioning Palestine between them. The main problem faced by the foreign secretary was how to prevent the anticipated negative reactions of the Arab states toward Abdallah, and to Britain itself as the power that had colluded in this agreement. No less important was the need to prevent a clash of interests between Britain and Abdallah in the event of the latter's entanglement in hostilities with the Yishuv. Given Abdallah's image as an archetypical British stooge, his financial dependence on Britain's subsidy and the British command of his Arab Legion, any such contingency could confront Britain with American and international pressure to cease its financial aid to Jordan and to withdraw the British officers serving in the Arab Legion. These considerations resulted in the conclusion that Abdallah should be unofficially encouraged to reach agreement with the Jews, while officially maintaining Britain's non-committal policy on the Palestine conflict.[67]

Whatever role the prospects of an agreed partition of Palestine between the Jewish state and Abdallah played in consolidating Britain's final decision to end the mandate and withdraw its forces, the seemingly solid co-operation between these two protagonists of partition proved to be fragile and short-lived. Indeed, in October and November Abdallah seemed to be the only power capable of intervening militarily in Palestine. However, the rapid deterioration of events in Palestine into a civil war following the UN partition resolution of 29 November, and the Arab world's reactions thereon, dragged the Hashemite king into the fray against his best interests, diminishing his capacity to act independently in disregard of the collective Arab policy on Palestine. As Abdallah succinctly explained his position to Golda Myerson in their secret meeting on 11 May 1948: 'Earlier, I was one. Now I am one of five.' What has been termed irreverently as 'collusion', was in fact the only chance of preventing a costly war and the disastrous results for the Palestinians.[68]

Despite the intensified violence in Palestine and political agitation in the Arab world, Bevin continued to seek an agreed Arab–Jewish solution based on his own plan or on UNSCOP's minority plan, in which the Jews would give up their demand for a separate state. This approach might explain Britain's stiffening position against the imposition of partition during the General Assembly's deliberations in the course of October and November 1947, and in fact until the end of the mandate. Britain reiterated that it would neither take part in a UN force assigned to this mission nor allow any UN authority to operate in Palestine as long as the mandate was in force.[69]

Britain and the Palestine question 241

Bevin's approach was unchanged by the General Assembly's partition resolution (by a two-thirds majority) on 29 November. Britain itself refrained from proposing a withdrawal from the partition resolution, so as not to appear to be acting against the UN resolution or against the United States, which had played a key role in supporting the partition plan. However, Bevin continued inexorably with his efforts till the end of the mandate to solicit the State Department to effect a withdrawal of the administration's support for partition, explaining that the violent Arab resistance to such a resolution would be most harmful to Anglo-American interests in the Middle East.[70]

Britain's apparent objection to the partition of Palestine, and especially its announced decision to prevent the UN Commission on implementation of the partition from entering Palestine before 15 May (the date for ending the mandate), was interpreted by the Arabs as a tacit encouragement to escalate their objection to partition, even violently. Some reports suggested that British officials in the Middle East had unofficially advised the employment of Arab volunteers as a ploy to undermine partition.[71]

The temporary boost to British prestige in the Arab world led the Hashemite regimes to seek a revision of their strategic relations with Britain. This prestige, however, was short-lived and fragile. In the course of 1947 and early 1948 Egypt grew resentful toward Britain over the impasse that prevailed in the efforts to revise the 1936 Treaty. The suspension of the January 1948 Anglo–Iraqi agreement, shortly after its signing at Portsmouth, was another manifestation of how vulnerable and shaky Britain's position in the Arab states had become even without the thorny issue of Palestine.

Britain's policy of withdrawal from Palestine was in practice impartial towards both the parties concerned, giving utmost priority to a swift and secure evacuation of equipment and personnel strictly as planned. However, in the Arab and Jewish memory, Britain has been portrayed as betraying them by allying with the adversary. The collapse of the unofficial Arab military effort, and massive exodus of 250,000–300,000 Palestinian–Arabs from their homes before the official end of the mandate, when Britain was still the responsible government, was depicted in Arab historiography as the epitome of its mandatory role: sponsoring the demographic, economic and military growth of the Jewish community in Palestine until the it was strong enough to defeat the Palestinian-Arab community. In Arab restrospect, the final stage of the mandate seemed nothing but the creation of a shield behind which the Zionists managed to implement partition and to drive out most of the Palestinians from the areas they had captured.[72]

Indeed, during the last two months of the mandate the Arab

242   *Demise of the British Empire in the Middle East*

temporary appreciation of Britain's objection to partition faded rapidly along with the failure of the Arab unofficial military effort in Palestine. Moreover, Britain's initiative at the Security Council, which led to the 29 May resolution on applying an embargo on war materials to the Middle East, although meant to help the Arabs, in fact, turned into another fiasco for its Middle East policy. The embargo, implemented strictly by Britain, in fact harmed most those very allies – Jordan, Iraq and Egypt – who were not only unprepared for a lengthy and costly war, but were obliged by their treaties with Britain to purchase war arms and ammunition only from the latter. By contrast, the Jewish state managed to acquire large quantities of arms and ammunition during the war, to enlarge its armed forces and their proficiency, and to initiate decisive operations against each Arab military sector separately. Thus, in the summer of 1948, Britain's refusal to supply its Arab allies with arms, ammunition and spare-parts resulted in growing Arab hostility to the United Kingdom for betraying the Arab cause and letting the Arabs down, and approaches of some Arab leaders to the Russians.[73]

CONCLUSION

'British policy in the whole Middle East stands or falls, in every sense, by what happened in Palestine',[74] was maintained succinctly by Albert Hourani shortly after the Palestine war. In retrospect, there is little doubt that *nakbat filastin* (the Catastrophe of Palestine), as the results of the war came to be known in the Arab world's political ethos, epitomized their frustrated hopes and collective grievances in contemporary history. As such, the Palestine disaster was to remain a major destructive and radicalizing force in Arab societies and politics, which accelerated the decline of Britain in the Middle East.

Britain's repeated efforts at reaching a reasonable solution agreed by the two communities in dispute could not overcome the national and religious sentiments that motivated their political aspirations and mutual alienation. It might be instructive to compare the cases of Palestine and India, which were both partitioned through civil war in the very same year, 1948. Contrary to the case of India, with which Attlee and some of the cabinet members were personally involved, the drawn-out and volatile decision-making process on Palestine was affected by the lack of any direct familiarity of the ministers involved with the territorial and communal realities of Palestine. Even in India, where the two communities shared a long common history and elements of Indian identity, Britain's efforts to maintain Indian integrity and unity failed. This was much more difficult to achieve in the case of Palestine, given

Britain and the Palestine question 243

the utter denial of Jewish political rights in Palestine maintained by the Arab–Muslim world.

While the option of an imposed solution had not been considered regarding India, Bevin's calculations and efforts to secure American support for his policy in Palestine were all linked to the concept of the coercion of the Jews, or at the least ensuring the Arab states' acquiescence. Compared with the delayed, interrupted and unilateral implementation of partition in Palestine (by the Yishuv), the division of India, once agreed upon by the two main contenders in May 1947, proceeded with speed and determination, although the consequent inter-communal bloodshed claimed a much higher toll than the whole 1948 Palestine war.[75]

NOTES

1   Wm Roger Louis, *The British Empire in the Middle East 1945–1951* (Oxford: Oxford University Press, 1984) p. 107; Michael J. Cohen, *Palestine and The Great Powers 1945–1948* (Princeton, NJ: Princeton University Press, 1982) pp. 34–6 (henceforth, *Palestine*).

2   See for example, *Foreign Relations of the United States, 1944*, Vol. 5 (Washington DC: Government Printing Office, 1965) pp. 565–70, 578–80, 590–8, 604–10, 612–14, 616–19, 621, 638–40, 648–9, 652–4 (henceforth, *FRUS, 1944*); Ahmad al-Shuqairi, *Arba'un 'Aam fi al-Siyasa al-'Arabiyya wal-Dawliyya* (Beirut: Dar al-'Awda, 1969) (in Arabic) p. 230; *al-Misri*, 10 August 1944.

3   Gabriel Cohen, 'Mediniut Britanya 'Erev Milhemet Ha'atzmat'ut', in Yehuda Wallach (ed.), *Hayinu Keholmim* (Tel Aviv: Massada, 1985) (in Hebrew) p. 72 (henceforth, 'Britain's Policy').

4   Albert Hourani, 'The Decline of the West in the Middle East', *International Affairs*, 29, 2 (April 1953) p. 167.

5   Avraham Sela, 'The 1929 Wailing Wall Riots as a Watershed in the Palestine Conflict', *The Muslim World*, 84, 1–2 (January–April 1994) pp. 60–94.

6   Ahmed M. Gomaa, *The Foundation of the League of Arab States* (London: Longman, 1977) pp. 8–14; Yehoshua Porath, *In Search of Arab Unity 1930–1945* (London: Frank Cass, 1986) pp. 148–58.

7   This was especially salient in response to the revised treaties Britain signed with Egypt (October 1946) and Iraq (January 1948), see for example, Muhammad Mahdi Kubba, *Mudhakkirati fi Samim al-Ahdath 1918–1958* (Beirut: Dar al-Tali'a, 1963) (in Arabic) pp. 225–7; Alan Bullock, *Ernest Bevin, Foreign Secretary 1945–1951* (Oxford: Oxford University Press, 1985) p. 507; Louis, *The British Empire*, pp. 334–46; a 'post-mortem' analysis (Top Secret) attached to a letter from Burrows, 4 July, 1948, PRO, FO371/68385/E4371.

8   Elie Kedourie, *Islam in the Modern World* (London: Mansel, 1980) pp. 56–7, 78; Porath, *In Search of Arab Unity*, p. 162; Ernest Dawn, 'The Formation of Pan-Arab Ideology', *International Journal of Middle Eastern Studies*, 20, 1 (1988) p. 69; Barry Rubin, *The Arab States and the Palestine Conflict* (Syracuse: Syracuse University Press, 1981) pp. 23–184.

9   On the crystallization of this perception in the late 1930s, see Kedourie, *Islam in the Modern World*, pp. 69, 114 ff.

10 Grigg to Eden: 27 June 1945, FO371/45378/E4711, and 29 June, *ibid.*, E4775; Secretary of the Colonies, Hall, to the cabinet, 1 September 1945, FO371/45379/E6744.

11 Campbell to Foreign Office, 7 February 1948, PRO, FO371/68384/E1970, and Bevin's response, *ibid.*; memorandum of Wright, 11 October 1948, PRO, FO371/68379/E13309; Kubba, op. cit. pp. 225–7; Louis, *The British Empire*, pp. 334–46.

12 H. Beeley's summary on Britain's policy and the Palestine Question, 1945–1948, attached to his letter to Burrows, March 24, 1949, PRO, FO371/75340/E4121.

13 Cohen, *Palestine*, p. 25.

244   *Demise of the British Empire in the Middle East*

14   On the appointment of the committee and results, see Gavriel Cohen, *Churchill and Palestine* (Jerusalem: Yad Ben-Zvi, 1976) (in Hebrew) p. 68; Porath, *In Search of Arab Unity*, pp. 129–37, 147–8.

15   Grigg to Bevin and Hall, 11 March 1945, FO371/45376/E1716; letter from the Minister-Resident Office to Smart, 11 April 1945, FO371/45377/E2644; Cohen, *Palestine*, p. 14; a joint memorandum of the FO and CO, 11 June 1945, FO371/45377/E3975.

16   Eden's memorandum dated 30 November 1944 (distributed at the end of December 1944), Public Record Office (henceforth, PRO), FO371/45376/E435.

17   Porath, *In Search of Arab Unity,*. 145; Michael J. Cohen, *Retreat from the Mandate* (London: Paul Elek, 1978) pp. 157–9.

18   Cohen, 'Britain's Policy', pp. 28–32.

19   Bullock, *Bevin* p. 48. On the agreement between Whitehall and the State Department, see Cohen, *Palestine*, pp. 50–1, 55–7.

20   Cohen, *Palestine*, pp. 24–7; Minutes of a discussion at the FO, headed by Bevin with participation of Britain's representatives in the Middle East, 6 September 1945, FO371/45379/E6954.

21   Cohen, *Palestine*, pp. 25–6.

22   Cohen, *Palestine*, pp. 23, 27; M. Haron, 'The British Decision to Give Palestine Question to the United Nations', *Middle Eastern Studies*, 17, 2 (April 1981) p. 241.

23   J. C. Hurewitz, *The Struggle for Palestine* (New York: Schoken, 1976) p. 236.

24   Yossef Heller, *bama'avak limdina: hamediniyut hatzionit bashanim 1936–1948* (Jerusalem: Merkaz Shazar, 1985) (in Hebrew) pp. 78, 83; Cohen, *Palestine*, pp. 80–1; Draft Memorandum to the Foreign Secretary, no date (January 1946), PRO, FO371/52503/E200; Bevin to Hall, 12 January, PRO, FO371/52505/E513.

25   Clayton's minute on meeting with Abdul Rahman Azzam, Secretary-General of the Arab League, 19 November 1945, PRO, FO141/1021/129/144/45; Hall to Bevin, 8 January 1946, PRO, FO371/52505/E513; Jami'at al-Duwal al-'Arabiyya, *Al-mahadir al-khitamiyya lijalsat dawr al-ijtima' al-'adi al-thani limajlis al-jami'a 31.10.45–14.12.45* (Cairo, 1949) (in Arabic, henceforth, Arab League, *Second Session*) pp. 127–8, 148, 154–5, 158–9; Trafford Smith to Baxter, 22 December, 1945, PRO, FO371/45396/E10164.

26   The Arab Higher Committee's Memorandum, ISA, 65/5, file 3055; *al-Ahram,*12 December 1945.

27   Arab League, *Second Session*, pp. 101, 127–8, 148, 154–5, 158–9.

28   Memorandum for the Foreign Secretary, no date (January 1946), summarizing the cabinet's considerations and contacts with the Arab governments, PRO, FO371/52503/E200; *FRUS 1945*, pp. 841–2; AHC's decision, 9 January 1946, ISA, 65/5, file 3055; see, for example, Syria's memorandum, enclosed with Shone to Bevin, 14 February 1945, PRO, FO371/52511/E1705; and the Iraq parliament's decisions, Stonehewer-Bird to Foreign Office, 8 February 1946, PRO, FO371/52509/E1176.

29   Husain al-Khalidi to Ahmad Hilmi, 21 February 1946, ISA, 65/5, file 3875; *al-Ahram*, 29 March 1946; Khalil al-Budairi, *Sitta wasittun 'aam fi al Haraka al Wataniyya al Filastiniyya Wafiha* (Jerusalem, 1946) (in Arabic) pp. 107–9; Cunningham to Colonial Secretary, 2 April 1946 (Monthly Summary, March 1946), PRO, FO371/52514/E3175; Azriel Karlibach, *Va'adat Hahakira Ha'anglo-America'it Le'inyanei Eretz-Israel* (Tel Aviv: Manshurat Salah al-Din, 1946) (in Hebrew) pp. 352–66, 454–6, 653.

30   Cohen, *Palestine*, pp. 82–3.

31   Cohen, 'Britain's Policy', pp. 21–6; Bullock, *Bevin*, pp. 254–5, 298–9; Cohen, *Palestine*, pp. 66–7, 78–9; Louis, *The British Empire*, pp. 430–3.

32   For a large body of Arab and Muslim responses, PRO, CO/733/463/75872/132/13; Kubba, pp. 130–1; *Foreign Relations of the United States 1946*, Vol. 7 (Washington, DC: Government Printing Office, 1969; henceforth, *FRUS 1946*) pp. 592–3.

33   Shuqairi, op. cit., pp. 268–9; Jami'at al Duwal al 'Arabiyya, *Madabit Jalsat Dawrat al Ijtima' al Rabi'a Ghair al' Adiyya, 8.6.46–12.6.46* (Cairo, 1946) (in Arabic, henceforth, Arab League, *Fourth Session*), p. 17.

34   Campbell to Foreign Office, 8 June 1946, PRO, FO371/52526/E4523; Shone to Foreign Office, 13 June 1946, PRO, FO371/52314/E5454; 14 June 1946, PRO, FO141/1084/384/30/46.

35   Arab League, *Fourth Session*, pp. 47–9, 54; Sasson to Eliahu (Epstein), 20 June 1946, Central Zionist Archive (henceforth, CZA), S/25, file 451; Howe to Bevin, 3 July 1946, PRO, FO371/52543/E7065. 'Azzam argued that the Arab governments would accept a 10-year

Britain and the Palestine question   245

36 long British trusteeship if its independence afterwards could be assured, Clark to Foreign
    Secretary, 25 June 1946, *FRUS 1946*, pp. 635–6.
36 On the committee and its duties, Arab League, *Fourth Session*, sixth meeting, 12 June
    1946, pp. 12, 73.
37 Arab League, *Fourth Session*, third meeting, pp. 31–43, 56; [Iraq], *Taqrir Lajnat al Tahqiq al
    niyabiyya fi Qadiyyat Filastin* (Baghdad, 1949; henceforth, *Iraq Parliamentary Committee*);
    Kubba, op. cit., pp. 127–8.
38 Discussion at the Cabinet Defence Committee, 24 April 1946, PRO, FO371/52517/E3839;
    Cabinet Conclusions, 3 June 1946, FO371/52527/E5066; Foreign Office to the Ambassador
    in Washington, 18 June 1946, and minute of Harris, 16 May 1946, PRO, FO371/52521/
    E4098.
39 Foreign Office to Washington, 25 July 1946, PRO, FO371/52544/E7157; and to Cairo, 27
    July 1946, ibid.
40 Louis, *The British Empire*, p. 454; Bullock, *Bevin*, p. 300; Beeley's summary on Britain's
    policy and the Palestine Question, 1945–1948, attached to his letter to Burrows, 24 March
    1949, PRO, FO371/75340/E4121.
41 Louis, *The British Empire*, pp. 436–8; Bullock, *Bevin*, pp. 300–1; Beeley's summary, op. cit.
42 Hurewitz, *The Struggle*, pp. 260–1; Yossef Heller, 'me'hashabat hashchora' lahaluka,
    kayitz 1946 kinkudat mifne betoldot hamediniyut hatzionit', *Zion*, 43, 3–4 (1981) (in
    Hebrew), pp. 315–6.
43 Louis, *The British Empire*, pp. 445–6; Bullock's argument – pp. 300, 302 – that Bevin, unlike
    his officials, did not object to such a solution is not supported by the foreign secretary's
    records.
44 For Lebanon and Syria's responses, *al-Ahram*, 24, 27 July 1946; Young to FO, 26 July 1946,
    and FO response to Beirut, 6 August 1946, PRO, FO371/52544/E7164; Clayton to FO, 29
    July 1946, PRO, FO371/52545/E7267; Campbell to FO, 14 August 1946, PRO, FO371/52552/
    E7993.
45 Memorandum from Howe to Sargent, 19 December 1946, PRO, FO371/52567/E12394.
46 Arab League, *Fifth Session* (Cairo, 1947) pp. 60–1.
47 Avraham Sela, 'maga'im mediniyim bein hasochnut hayehudit levein memshalot 'ever
    hayarden umitzrayim bidvar heskem 'al halukat eretz-yisrael, 1946', *Hatzionut*, 10 (1985)
    (in Hebrew) pp. 266–7, 276.
48 *FRUS 1946*, p. 703.
49 Cabinet Conclusions, 25 October 1946, FO371/52563/E10827.
50 Bullock, *Bevin*, pp. 332–3; Louis, *The British Empire*, p. 456. On the development of Britain's
    decision to refer Palestine to the United Nations, see Cohen, 'Britain's Policy', pp. 33–4.
51 US Under-Secretary Acheson's memorandum, 21 January 1947, *Foreign Relations of the
    United States, 1947*, Vol. 5 (Washington, DC: Government Printing Office, 1971; hence-
    forth, *FRUS 1947*), pp. 1008–111; Haron, 'The British Decision', pp. 243–4.
52 Bullock, *Bevin*, pp. 363–5; Louis, *The British Empire*, p. 454; Cohen, *Palestine*, pp. 203–4,
    212–13.
53 On the cabinet's discussions in the winter of 1948 and the views in the Labour Party,
    cabinet and military echelons, Cohen, 'Britain's Policy', pp. 41–53; Bullock, *Bevin*,
    pp. 348–64.
54 Cohen, *Palestine*, pp. 213–14. Bevin's plan suggested a five-year British trusteeship as a
    transitory period toward independence during which the two communities would be
    incorporated in the central government; Jewish immigration of 4,000 per month for two
    years (total of 96,000), after which the number of immigrants would be determined by
    the high commissioner in consultation with an advisory council and in accordance with
    the country's economic absorption capacity for the rest of the trusteeship period; transfer
    of land ownership would be governed by the autonomous provinces, Bevin's letter to
    the American Secretary of State, 7 February 1947; *FRUS 1947*, pp. 1033–5.
55 Cabinet Session, 14 February 1947, PRO, Cab 128/9, pp. 144–7, in Cohen, 'Britain's Policy',
    pp. 55, 60.
56 Cohen, ibid., pp. 66–71.
57 Cohen, *Palestine*, pp. 59–60, 221–2; Louis, *The British Empire*, p. 462, 464–7; Haron, 'The
    British Decision', p. 244.
58 Bullock, *Bevin*, p. 367, 446; Cohen, *Palestine*, pp. 83–4; for a discussion of the British
    decision-making process regarding the withdrawal from Palestine, see *Cathedra*

246 *Demise of the British Empire in the Middle East*

(Jerusalem), Vol. 15 (April 1980) (in Hebrew), with I. Kolath, M. J. Cohen, A. Ilan and G. Cohen, pp. 140–93.

59 Cadogan to Hoo, 2 April 1947, *FRUS 1947*, pp. 1067–8; Campbell to FO, 12 April 1947, PRO, FO371/60874/E3096; minute by Garran, 15 April 1947, FO371/61875/E3112; *al-Ahram*, 4 April 1947; Abdul Rahman Azzam's report to the Arab League, 6 October 1947, 'Jami'at al-Duwal al-'Arabiyya, *Madabit Jalsat Dawr al-Ijtima' al-'Aadi al-Sabi' li-Majlis al-Jami'a 7.10.47–22.2.48* (Cairo, 1948) (in Arabic, henceforth: Arab League, *Seventh Session*) p. 30.

60 *Al-Ahram*, 14 May, 18, 1947; *Filastin*, 17 May 1947.

61 The option of applying martial law over the country was rejected for lack of sufficient forces, Crocker to Cunningham, 13 August 1947, and Cunningham's response, Cunningham's Papers, Middle East Centre, St Antony's College, Oxford, Box 5, file 4, no. 67, 69; *The Memoirs of Field Marshal the Viscount Montgomery of Alamein* (London, 1961) pp. 473–9.

62 *Report to the General Assembly by the United Nations Special Committee on Palestine*, 31 August 1947 (London, 1947) pp. 72–96.

63 Cohen, 'Britain's Policy', pp. 101–7; 112–13; Cohen, *Palestine*, pp. 275–6; Louis, *The British Empire*, pp. 473–5. On the final nature of the announcement of 26 September see Beeley's summary of Britain's Palestine policy 1945–1948, PRO, FO371/75340/E4121.

64 Joint cable of the foreign and colonial secretaries, 3 October 1947, PRO, FO371/ 61882/ E9639; FO to all delegations in the Arab capitals and Jerusalem, 16 October 1947, ibid.; FO to Cairo (and all Middle East delegations), 15 December 1947, PRO, FO371/ 61890/E11262.

65 See, for example, Cunningham's summary of his talks with Dr Husain al-Khalidi and David Ben-Gurion, 2 October 1947, Cunningham Papers, V/1/77.

66 Khaldun Sati' al-Husri, *Mudhakkirat Taha al-Hashimi*, Pt II, 1942–1955 (Beirut: Dar al-Tali'a, 1978) (in Arabic) p. 157; minute by cable, 15 October 1947, PRO, FO371/61886/E10349.

67 See especially Burrows' comprehensive memorandum, 28 November 1947, PRO, FO371/ 62194/E10806, and Kirkbride to Bevin, 22 December FO371/61584/E11734.

68 See, for example, Avi Shlaim, *Collusion Across the Jordan* (New York: Columbia University Press, 1988), especially, pp. 202–4, 208–10, 218–20. For a critique of the 'collusion' literature see Avraham Sela, 'Transjordan, Israel and the 1948 War: Myth, Historiography and Reality', *Middle Eastern Studies*, 28, 4 (October 1992) pp. 623–88.

69 Bullock, *Bevin*, p. 477; Cohen, *Palestine*, p. 296.

70 Memorandum of Burrows, 7 November 1947, PRO, FO371/61888/E10731; FO to Washington, 1 January 1948, FO371/61584/E12400; Conversation of Bevin and Iraqi Prime Minister Jabr, 22 January 1948, FO371/68365/ E121; Bevin to Inverchapel, 19 April 1948, FO371/ 68649/E4887.

71 Houston-Boswell to Attlee (monthly summary, December 1947), 17 January 1948, PRO, FO371/68493/E1216; Report by the 'Orphan', 24 February 1948, CZA, S/25, file 3569; 'Ali Jawdat, *Dhikrayat* (Beirut: Matabic al-Wafa', 1965) (in Arabic) pp. 269–70.

72 Hourani, 'Decline of the West', p. 162; See also A. Sela, 'Arab Historiography of the 1948 War: The Quest for Legitimacy', in Lawrence J. Silberstein (ed.), *New Perspectives on Israeli History* (New York: New York University Press, 1991) pp. 124–54.

73 See for example, unsigned minute, 8 September 1948, PRO, FO371/68379/E12211.

74 Hourani, 'Decline of the West', p. 158.

75 T. G. Fraser, *Partition in Ireland, India and Palestine: Theory and Practice* (New York: St Martin's Press, 1984) p. 127.

Index

Abdallah, King of Transjordan/Jordan, xv, 9, 18, 54, 56, 57, 58, 59, 60, 81, 82, 83, 84, 85, 87, 88, 198, 199, 200–8, 222, 225, 233, 234, 239, 240; assassinated July 1951, xv, 86, 207; negotiations with the Jewish Agency, 201–2

Abdin Palace, Cairo, 115, 117, 134, 147; incident 4 February 1942, xiv, 104, 163, 177

Abu Sueir base, Egypt, 26, 27, 28, 32, 157–8n

Acheson, Dean, US secretary of state, 167, 168, 170, 171, 177

Africa, 5, 8, 11, 23, 65, 72, 143, 163; north Africa, 51, 107; South Africa, 48, 108

air bases, 25, 26, 27, 155, 164, 167, 171

air offensive, attack, 25, 26, 27, 31–2, 65, 143, 156, 164, 165, 176

Al-Alami, Musa, Palestinian Arab leader, 48, 49, 52

Aldrich, Winthrop, US ambassador in London, 173

Alexander, Lord, British defence secretary, 235

Alexandria, Egypt, 48, 95, 118, 119, 125, 126, 132, 137, 138n, 163

Alexandria Protocol, 48, 49, 50, 'Alpha' plan, 174, 175, 177, 211

Amer, Fieldmarshal Abd al-Hakim, 214

America, American, Americans (*see also* United States), xiii, xv, 8, 14, 15, 16, 23, 25, 26, 28, 30, 31, 32, 34, 35, 70, 71, 73, 75, 86, 103, 155, 156, 162–78, 192, 195, 203, 207, 209, 210, 211, 215, 217, 223, 224, 225, 226, 227, 230, 231, 235, 237, 238, 240, 243

American Congress, 168, 175, 227, 232

American–Egyptian relations, 163, 166, 167, 174

American proposed arms sales to Egypt, 173, 174, 177

Amman, Jordan, 57, 58, 59, 85, 87, 88, 198, 203, 205, 207, 208, 213, 214, 215, 240

Anglo–American alliance, allies, xiii, 25, 26, 28, 30, 31, 32, 33, 34, 43, 107, 156, 160n, 162–78, 179n, 223, 225, 228, 241

Anglo–American commercial rivalry, 3, 163, 164, 177

Anglo–American Committee of Enquiry on Palestine, 52, 226, 227, 228, 229, 230, 231, 232

Anglo–Arab relations (see also Arab–British relations), 13, 15, 16, 18, 42

Anglo–Egyptian agreement, xiii, 147

Anglo–Egyptian financial and commercial agreement, 67

Anglo–Egyptian post-1945 negotiations, 16, 51, 53, 86, 89, 99, 103, 115, 116, 121, 122, 130, 131, 145, 147, 148, 149, 150, 151, 152, 153, 155, 156, 157, 159n, 165, 166, 167, 170, 172, 173, 188, 189, 205, 221, 228, 231, 235, 241

Anglo–Egyptian relations, 89, 95, 96, 109, 116, 118, 124, 142, 146, 153, 165, 169, 170, 188, 189, 191

Anglo–Egyptian Treaty, 1936, 16, 86, 97, 105, 131, 132, 142, 147, 154, 155, 162, 169, 239; abrogation, 171

Anglo–Egyptian Treaty, 1954, 174

Anglo–Iranian Oil Company, 10, 65, 73, 74, 75, 76

Anglo–Iraqi post-1945 negotiations, 187, 188, 189, 190, 191, 221, 241

Anglo–Iraqi Treaty, 1930, 86, 87, 185, 186, 187

Anglo–Soviet rivalry, disputes, 144, 146

248   *Demise of the British Empire in the Middle East*

Anglo–Transjordanian/Jordanian alliance, relations, 198–217, 218n
Anglo–Transjordanian treaty, 199, 205, 206, 208, 209
anti-monarchical, anti-royalist, 19, 190–1
Aqaba, 29, 31
Arab, Arabs, xiv, xv, 6, 10, 11, 13, 14, 15, 16, 17, 19, 30, 33, 35, 41, 42, 43, 44, 45, 46, 47, 48, 49, 50, 51, 52, 53, 54, 55, 56, 57, 58, 59, 60, 64, 65, 67, 68, 69, 70, 71, 72, 73, 74, 76, 79, 80, 81, 83, 84, 85, 86, 87, 88, 89, 107, 168, 169, 175, 176, 188, 189, 190, 195, 199, 200, 201, 202, 203, 204, 205, 207, 209, 210, 211, 212, 214, 215, 216, 217, 220, 221, 222, 223, 224, 225, 226, 227, 228, 229, 230–43; Arabism, 80, 90; Arab nationalism, nationalists (*see also* nationalism, nationalists, national movements), xiii, xiv, 8, 11, 14, 76, 80, 83, 86, 90, 205, 206, 215, 221; Arab state system, 79–90; Arab unity, 41, 42, 43, 44, 45, 46, 47, 48, 49, 50, 60, 87, 224; pan-Arab, pan-Arabism, 41, 42, 43, 45, 46, 49, 50, 51, 79, 85, 90, 205, 207, 208, 221, 222
Arab–British relations, 80, 86–90, 224, 227
Arab–Israeli conflict, 17, 60
Arab–Israeli war, 1948, xv, 54, 57, 84, 88, 203, 204, 221; armistice, 59, 82, 85, 204; truce, 59
Arab–Jewish conflict, 200, 202
Arab League, xv, 17, 41, 42, 45, 49, 50, 51, 52, 53, 54, 55–6, 57, 58, 59, 60, 79, 81, 82, 83, 85, 86, 90, 91n, 99, 152, 187, 195, 204, 207, 208, 227, 228, 229, 230, 233; Palestine committee, 207, 222, 230
Arab Legion, Transjordan/Jordan (*see also* Jordan army), 56, 58, 84, 85, 199, 200, 202, 203, 204, 207, 212, 216, 217, 239, 240
Arab–Zionist conflict, 221
Arabian peninsula, 82, 201; Hijaz, 81, 198
Arif, Abd el-Salam, Iraqi leader, 196
Aswan dam, 175, 177
Attalah Pasha, Egyptian Army Chief of Staff, 105
Attlee, Clement, Labour prime minister, 5, 6, 8, 24, 25, 67, 71, 144,

146, 148, 149, 151, 152, 154, 158n, 168, 220, 225, 228, 230, 235, 242
Australia, 5, 23
Axis powers, force (*see also* Germany, Nazi Germany, Italy), 45, 101, 103, 105, 107, 163; pro-Axis, 70, 101, 105
Al-Azhar, Cairo, 97, 115, 117
Azzam, Abdul Rahman, Egyptian politician and secretary-general of the Arab League, 45, 49, 50, 51, 52, 57, 99, 102, 204, 230

B-29 bombers, 26, 27, 143
Ba'ath Party, 213, 216
Baghdad, 11, 69, 74, 189, 190, 192, 198, 199, 211, 212
Baghdad Pact, 1955, 34, 89, 175, 195, 196, 211, 214, 215, 216
Balfour Declaration, 88, 114, 115
Balkans, 67, 151
Al-Banna, Hassem (*see also* Muslim Brotherhood), 102, 105, 115, 121, 122, 123, 127, 128
Ben-Gurion, David, Zionist leader and Israeli prime minister, 204, 228, 232, 235, 236
Bernadotte, Count, UN mediator, 88, 207
Bevin, Ernest, Labour foreign secretary, xiii, 3, 5, 6, 7, 8, 9, 10, 11, 12, 13, 14, 15, 16, 17, 18, 19, 23, 24, 25, 52, 54, 56, 71, 72, 86, 88, 109, 121, 130, 142, 145, 149, 151, 152, 154, 155, 156, 164, 165, 167, 168, 188, 189, 191, 202, 204, 206, 209, 220, 225, 226, 227, 228, 230, 231, 234, 235, 236, 237, 239, 240, 241, 243
Bludan (Syria) summit, 53, 55, 229, 233
Britain, British, xiii, xv, 3, 5, 6, 8, 9, 10, 11, 13, 14, 15, 16, 18, 19, 20, 23, 24, 25, 27, 28, 29, 30, 31, 32, 33, 34, 35, 41, 42, 43, 44, 45, 46, 47, 48, 49, 50, 51, 52, 53, 54, 55, 56, 57, 58, 59, 60, 64, 65, 67, 68, 70, 71, 72, 73, 74, 75, 76, 79, 80, 81, 84, 86, 87, 88, 89, 90, 95–109, 112, 113, 114, 115, 116, 117, 118, 119, 121, 122, 123, 124, 129, 130, 133, 134, 136, 137, 142, 143, 144, 147, 148, 149, 150, 151, 152, 153, 154, 155, 156, 157, 162–78, 185–96, 198–217, 220–43; anti-British, 8, 15, 19, 52, 102, 107, 108, 118, 134, 145, 147, 176, 177, 185, 186, 187, 188, 189, 191, 192,

Index

194, 196, 199, 200, 202, 205, 206, 207, 212, 213, 215, 222, 223; bases (*see also* Suez Base, Suez Canal), 9, 19, 23, 24, 25, 28, 29, 30, 34, 47, 75, 87, 89, 95, 103, 144, 147, 148, 149, 150, 151, 154, 156, 163, 164, 165, 166, 167, 168, 169, 170, 172, 173, 174, 177, 190, 191, 199, 200, 201, 209, 224, 228, 235, 236, 239; Defence Committee, 149, 150, 151; Defence Coordination Committee, Middle East, 34–5; evacuation, withdrawal from Egypt, 51, 89, 128, 129, 130, 131, 144, 145, 147, 148, 149, 150, 152, 153, 155, 157, 165, 166, 169, 170, 206, 209, 228, 231; influence in Iraq, 185–96; Ministry of Defence, 201, 205; traditional alliances, 3, 17

British ambassador in Egypt (*see also* Sir Miles Lampson), 10, 11, 47, 50, 51, 99, 105, 106, 107, 119, 95–109, 145, 146, 147, 148, 149, 154, 155; in Iraq, 55

British Defence Coordinating Committee, Middle East, 30, 31

British Empire (*see also* Imperial), xiii, 3, 4, 5, 6, 7, 8, 12, 13, 15, 24, 45, 67, 71, 72, 100, 109, 142, 144, 150, 151, 154, 191, 199, 216, 217, 220

British Middle East Headquarters in Cairo, 200, 216

British Middle East Office, 3, 9, 12, 13, 17, 18, 142; Development Division, 3, 17, 18

British Military Mission, Egypt, 105, 124

British Petroleum (*see* Anglo–Iranian Oil Company), 74

Caffery, Jefferson, US ambassador to Egypt, 173

Cairo, 11, 13, 27, 33, 47, 51, 53, 55, 56, 58, 59, 69, 87, 88, 95, 96, 115, 117, 118, 119, 122, 124, 125, 126, 127, 128, 132, 134, 135, 137, 147, 148, 154, 163, 164, 165, 167, 169, 171, 172, 173, 174, 175, 227; burning of Cairo, 134, 135, 171; conference, 200; Kasr al-Nil barracks, 118; 'open city', 99, 103

Caliph, Caliphate, 45, 46

Campbell, Sir R., British ambassador to Egypt, 148, 149

'Celery' plan, 30, 31

Chiefs of Staff, British, 5, 9, 16, 24, 26, 28, 29, 30, 31, 32, 34, 148, 149, 150, 151, 152, 154, 155, 156, 164, 199, 220, 224, 226, 231, 232, 234, 235, 236, 237, 239; Joint Planning Staff, 26, 31, 32

Churchill, Winston, Conservative prime minister, 11, 44, 67, 81, 107, 108, 162, 163, 171, 172, 173, 198, 199, 200, 225

Clayton, Brigadier I., 229

cold war, 6, 16, 26, 28, 30, 113, 150, 157, 158n, 164, 165, 166, 177, 178, 195, 202, 211

Colonial Office, 13, 44, 202, 222, 225, 232, 234, 235

Commanders-in-Chief, Middle East, 28, 148, 151

Commonwealth, 29, 31, 32, 147, 149, 150, 151, 154, 164, 191

communism, 5, 6, 15, 167, 190, 194

communists, 6, 10, 30, 118, 119, 120, 123, 126, 169, 188, 190, 191, 192, 193, 195, 202, 205, 213, 215, 216, 222

Committee of Imperial Defence, 44

Conservatives (British), 11, 24, 67, 144, 172, 177, 194

coup d'état, Egypt 1952, 112, 172

'Crasspiece' plan, 164

Creech-Jones, Arthur, colonial secretary, 4, 235, 236, 239

Cripps, Sir Stafford, chancellor of the exchequer, 4, 7, 14

Cromer, Lord, 7, 199

Cyprus, 8, 9

Cyrenaica (*see* Libya), 7, 150, 154, 155, 166, 169

Damascus, 31, 44, 50, 81, 82, 198, 210

development, *see* Middle East social and economic development

Al-Din, Fuad Serag, Wafd minister of the interior, 121, 123, 129, 130, 132, 133, 134, 135

Al-Din, Muhammad Salah, Wafd minister of foreign affairs, 121, 130

disorder, civil and public, 97, 103, 108, 112–38, 150, 152, 192, 194, 215, 229

'Doublequick' plan, 156, 160n

Duke, Charles, British ambassader to Jordan, 213, 214, 215, 216, 217

Dulles, John Foster, American secretary of state, 172, 173, 174, 175, 176, 177, 209, 210

250 *Demise of the British Empire in the Middle East*

Eden, Anthony, Conservative foreign secretary and prime minister, 5, 42, 44, 49, 51, 95, 96, 103–4, 144, 171, 172, 174, 175, 176, 177, 199, 210, 211, 212, 217; Mansion House speech, May, 1941 43, 44, 45
effendis, 97
effendiyya, xiv, 185, 186, 187, 188, 189, 191, 192, 193, 194, 196
Egypt, Egyptian, xiii, xiv, xv, 3, 5, 8, 9, 10, 11, 12, 13, 14, 15, 16, 17, 19, 23, 25, 26, 27, 2 8, 29, 30, 31, 32, 33, 34, 35, 41, 42, 43, 45, 46, 47, 48, 49, 50, 51, 52, 53, 55, 56, 57, 59, 60, 64, 65, 68, 69, 70, 71, 72, 76, 79, 80, 81, 82, 83, 84, 85, 86, 87, 88, 89, 90, 95–110, 112, 113, 116, 119, 120, 121, 122, 123, 124, 129, 130, 131, 132, 134, 137, 142, 143, 145, 146, 147, 148, 149, 150, 151, 153, 154, 155, 156, 157, 162–78, 187, 188, 189, 190, 191, 195, 199, 200, 201, 203, 204, 206, 207, 209, 210, 211, 212, 213, 214, 215, 217, 221, 222, 228, 231, 233, 235, 239, 241, 242; army, xiv, xv, 56, 59, 97, 102, 105, 106, 107, 108, 109, 114, 118, 124, 125, 126, 127, 133, 135, 136, 137, 138, 141n, 149; army officers, 104, 105, 124, 125, 126, 136, 137, 138; Free Officers, xiv, 89, 136, 137, 138, 214; auxiliary police, 133, 134; communist movement, 113, 119, 120, 123, 126, 127, 129; Copts, 106; Delta, 95; democracy, 98, 109; *état de siège* (*see also* martial law), 47, 99; Independents, 100, 101, 102; al-Kutla, independent Wafdist party, 106, 116, 117; labour movement, trade unions, 72, 113, 115; Ministry of the Interior, 127, 128, 129, 131, 136; neutrality, 98–101; parliament, 15, 45, 96, 97, 100, 101, 102, 104, 107, 108, 109, 145, 147, 171; police, police officers, 106, 125, 133, 134, 135, 171; Royal Cabinet, 108; senate, 97, 105; textile industry, 119, 120, 123
Eisenhower, Dwight D., US president, 172, 173, 174, 175, 176, 177
El Alamein, 45, 163
elites, traditional, conservative, xiv, xv, 52, 79, 88, 89, 90, 185–96, 222, 223; political, 85, 86, 88, 113, 120, 121, 122, 125, 126, 128, 137, 138, 222

Far East, 5, 31, 67, 95, 103
Faruq, King of Egypt, xiv, xv, 10, 12, 45, 46, 48, 84, 89, 95, 96, 97, 98, 99, 100, 102, 103, 104, 105, 106, 107, 108, 109, 113, 114, 117, 122, 125, 129, 131, 135, 136, 137, 142, 145, 146, 147, 148, 153, 154, 155, 163, 171; ultimatum to, 104
fascist trends, 186
Faysal, King of Syria, Iraq, 81, 187, 198
Fertile Crescent, 43, 45, 46, 48, 60, 81, 82, 89, 187, 188, 221, 222
First World War, 7, 12, 23, 41, 81, 90, 188, 198
Foreign Office, British, 3, 5, 7, 8, 13, 17, 28, 30, 33, 34, 44, 48, 52, 98, 99, 106, 145, 146, 147, 150, 152, 154, 155, 156, 164, 189, 194, 201, 202, 204, 205, 207, 208, 209, 210, 211, 213, 214, 216, 222, 224, 225, 226, 232, 234, 235, 236, 237, 240
France, French, 41, 44, 47, 49, 50, 74, 79, 81, 86, 99, 167, 170, 175, 176, 198, 223; Free French, 44; Vichy, 43, 44, 103
Fuad, King of Egypt, 96, 97

Gaza, 59, 169, 207
Germany, 43, 45, 65, 70, 98, 99, 101, 109, 163, 222; Nazi Germany, 44, 53, 162, 178, 202, 233
Glubb, General John, 57, 58, 199, 200, 206, 207, 212, 215, 216, 217
Greece, 5, 25, 32, 101, 105, 108, 151, 164, 166, 236
Grigg, Sir Edward (Lord Altrincham), Minister Resident in the Middle East, 144, 224

Al-Hadi, Ibrahim Abd, Egyptian prime minister, 128, 130
Hagana, Jewish Defence Organization, 203, 226, 238
Haifa, 57, 74, 75, 76, 226
Halifax, Lord, British foreign secretary, 3
Hashemite(s), 46, 50, 53, 58, 60, 80, 81, 86, 90, 91n, 185, 186, 188, 198, 201, 202, 203, 204, 205, 206, 207, 208, 209, 210, 211, 215, 222, 223, 233, 240, 241; anti-Hashemite, 46, 48, 80, 82, 83, 191, 207
Hassanein, Ahmad, Chief of the Egyptian Royal Cabinet, 96, 105, 108
Holocaust, 50, 220, 224

Index

Huda, Tawfiq Abdul, Transjordanian prime minister, 88, 202, 206
Husayn, King of Jordan, 86, 207, 208, 209, 210, 211, 212, 213, 214, 215, 216, 217
Al-Husayni, Haj Amin, Mufti of Jerusalem, 53, 56, 57, 58, 59, 60, 202, 206, 207, 208, 233
Al-Husayni, Jamal, Palestinian Arab leader, 227, 228, 229, 233

Al-Illah, Abd, Crown Prince and Regent in Iraq, 82, 87, 186, 190, 191
Imperial (*see also* British Empire), xiv, xv, 4, 5, 6, 7, 11, 18, 24, 25, 35, 41, 42, 48, 53, 57, 60, 64, 67, 69, 71, 76, 146, 162, 177, 210, 222, 223, 224
India, xiv, 5, 6, 7, 11, 23, 24, 25, 65, 71, 72, 95, 164, 191, 201, 222, 225, 235, 236, 242, 243
India Office, 44
Inshas (Egypt) summit of Arab leaders, 53, 229
Iran (*see also* Persia), 5, 8, 10, 17, 65, 73, 75, 76, 105, 150, 164, 169, 172, 192, 195
Iraq, xiv, xv, 5, 9, 10, 11, 12, 13, 16, 17, 18, 19, 31, 34, 41, 43, 44, 45, 46, 47, 53, 55, 56, 60, 64, 67, 70, 73, 75, 76, 79, 80, 81, 82, 83, 87, 88, 89, 90, 101, 105, 169, 172, 185–196, 198, 200, 206, 208, 210, 211, 212, 216, 221, 222, 227, 230, 233, 242; airfields, 5, 191; army, 82, 191, 196, 203, 204, 216; defence pact with Jordan, 216; Habbaniya, 191; Al-Istiqlal Party, 190, 192, 193; governments of al-Sadr and al-Pachachi, 74; National Democratic party, 192, 193; parliament, 187, 190, 191, 194, 206, 227; Iraq Petroleum Company, 65, 74, 75, 192; tribes, 185–96
Irgun Zvai Leumi (National Military Organization, Jewish Palestine), 226, 232, 238
Islam, Islamic (*see also* Muslim), 42, 46, 69, 222
Ismailiyya, Egypt, 133, 134
Israel, Israeli, xiii, xiv, xv, 16, 17, 19, 29, 30, 31, 32, 33, 42, 50, 54, 59, 74, 82, 83, 85, 87, 88, 90, 127, 168, 169, 174, 175, 176, 203, 204, 205, 207, 208, 209, 210, 211, 215, 216

Italy, Italians, 65, 96, 99, 100, 101, 149, 155, 162, 222; Fascists, 99

Jabr, Salih, Iraqi prime minister, 19, 189, 190, 191, 192
Al-Jamili, Fadhil, Iraqi prime minister, 194, 195
Japan, Japanese, 103, 163
Jericho, 29, 59, 156
Jerusalem, 44, 54, 69, 84, 85, 204, 205, 213, 231, 232, 238, 240; King David Hotel, 232
Jews, Jewish, 43, 52, 55, 56, 57, 74, 75, 126, 200, 201, 202, 203, 220, 221, 223, 224, 225, 226, 227, 228, 229, 230, 231–43; 'Black Saturday', 232; community in Palestine (Yishuv), 225, 226, 227, 231, 232, 233, 240, 243; immigration into Palestine, 16, 43, 223, 224, 225, 226, 227, 228, 229, 231, 233, 234, 235, 236, 238; state, 17, 44, 53, 54, 84, 88, 202, 204, 220, 223, 229, 232, 234, 236, 238, 240, 242
Jewish Agency, 54, 57, 58, 201, 232, 234, 240; informal understanding with King Abdallah (*see also* Abdallah), 234, 240, 246n
Jordan, Jordanian (*see also* Transjordan), xiii, xv, 12, 17, 18, 59, 60, 82, 83, 84, 85, 86, 87, 88, 175, 198–217, 240, 242; army (*see also* Arab Legion), 9, 34, 84, 87, 199, 205, 206, 214; parliament, 207, 213, 215; political opposition, 213, 216; valley, 29, 31, 209

Kirk, Alexander C., US minister to Egypt, 163
Kirkbride, Sir Alec, British ambassador to Jordan, 198, 199, 200, 201, 202, 205, 206, 207, 208, 213, 216, 217
Korean War, 30, 32, 165, 168, 169
Kurds, Kurdish, 190; Kirkuk, 74
Kuwait, 64, 73, 75, 76

Labour government, xiii, xv, 3, 4, 5, 6, 7, 9, 10, 11, 12, 13, 14, 16, 17, 18, 19, 24, 64, 67, 71, 72, 73, 76, 109, 144, 146, 164, 188, 191, 194, 196, 201, 225, 226
Labour Party, 16, 235
Lampson, Sir Miles (Lord Killearn), British ambassador to Egypt, 45, 47, 48, 49, 50, 51, 95–109, 145, 146, 147, 148

landlords, 68, 69, 72, 96, 97, 106, 187, 189, 196
landowners, 187, 193
League of Nations, 4, 50
Lebanon, Lebanese, 17, 31, 41, 43, 44, 45, 46, 49, 55, 59, 60, 79, 80, 81, 90, 107, 199, 223, 227, 233; Aleyh, 55, 57
Lehi (Lohamei Herut Israel, Israel Freedom Fighters), 226, 238
Lend-Lease, xv, 163
Levant, 47, 49
Levant–Iraq forward strategy, 34, 35
Liberal Constitutionalist Party, Egypt, 98, 100, 101, 102, 104, 105
Libya, Libyan, 28, 101
Lloyd, Selwyn, British foreign secretary, 175
Louis, Wm Roger, 3, 52

MacArthur, General Douglas, 30
McGhee, George, US assistant secretary of state, 167, 169, 170
Macmillan, Harold, British prime minister, 177, 213
Maher, Ahmad, Egyptian prime minister, 49, 97, 100, 101, 102, 108, 109
Maher, Ali, Egyptian prime minister, 50, 69, 96, 97, 98, 99, 100, 102, 103, 104, 105, 135, 136
Mahmud, Muhammad, Egyptian prime minister, 98
Al-Majali, Hazza, Jordanian prime minister, 215
'Makefast' plan, 27, 164
Makram Ebeid, William, Wafd and al-Kutla politician, 98, 106, 108, 116, 117
Mandate, see Palestine
Al-Maraghi, Murtada, Egyptian Minister of the Interior, 136
martial law (see also Egypt, état de siège), 99, 108, 114, 126, 128, 135, 136, 137
mass participation (see also disorder, and theatre of mass politics), 97, 113
Mediterranean, 24, 28, 29, 74, 95, 101, 142, 144, 146, 149, 155, 170
Middle East, Middle Eastern, xiii, xiv, 3, 5, 6, 7, 8, 9, 11, 12, 13, 15, 16, 18, 19, 23, 24, 25, 26, 27, 28, 29, 30, 31, 32, 33, 34, 35, 41, 42, 44, 49, 50, 51, 52, 56, 58, 60, 64, 65, 67, 70, 79, 80, 90, 95, 142, 143, 144, 145, 146, 147, 148,

149, 150, 151, 154, 155, 156, 157, 162, 163, 164, 165, 166, 167, 168, 169, 170, 171, 178, 185, 186, 188, 189, 191, 195, 199, 200, 201, 205, 206, 213, 216, 217, 220, 221, 222, 223, 224, 225, 226, 228, 231, 232, 233, 234, 235, 239, 241, 242; defence cooperation, pact, treaty, 16, 51, 147, 195, 196, 210, 220, 223; economic and social development (see also Bevin, partnership), xiii, 3, 6, 9, 11, 12, 14, 15, 16, 17, 18, 19, 42, 44–5, 64, 69, 71, 72, 73, 76, 109, 142, 145, 146, 188, 189, 193, 194, 196; oil, oil companies, oilfields, 18, 23, 27, 29, 35n, 64, 65, 67, 71, 72, 73, 74, 75, 76, 144, 151, 156, 157, 163, 176, 191, 192, 200, 201, 224, 230; oil embargo, 53
Middle East Command, 89, 170, 171, 172, 177
Middle East Defence Organization (MEDO), 89, 172
Middle East Supply Centre, 13, 14, 15, 45, 65
Middle East War Council, 47, 107
Al-Midfa'i, Jamil, Iraqi politician, 186
Mildenhall base, 26, 27
Morrison, Herbert, British foreign secretary, 170
Morrison–Grady Plan, 231, 232, 234, 236
Moyne, Lord, deputy minister of state in the Middle East, 107
Mufti, see Al-Husayni, Haj Amin
Al-Mufti, Said, Jordanian prime minister, 214, 215
Muslim (see also Islam, Islamic), 45, 75, 102, 221, 222, 225
Muslim Brotherhood (see also Al-Banna, Hassem), 46, 52, 69, 102, 105, 113, 114, 115, 117, 118, 119, 120, 121, 213, 122, 123, 124, 126, 127, 128, 131, 132, 133, 134, 135, 136
Mussadeq, Muhammad, Iranian prime minister, 8, 19, 73, 75, 192
Myerson (Meir), Golda, Zionist political leader, 54, 201, 240

Al-Nahas, Mustafa, Egyptian Prime Minister, 45, 46, 47, 48, 49, 51, 68, 72, 97, 98, 100, 102, 103, 104, 105, 106, 107, 108, 109, 121, 129, 135, 145, 147, 148, 169, 171

Index

Al-Nasir, Gamal Abd, Egyptian leader, 8, 80, 138, 172, 175, 210, 211, 212, 213, 214, 215, 217

nationalism, nationalists, national movements (*see also* Arab nationalism), 7, 8, 9, 10, 14, 15, 16, 19, 24, 41, 42, 46, 51, 52, 60, 64, 68, 69, 70, 76, 84, 145, 168, 199, 200, 205, 206, 222; Egyptian nationalism, nationalists, 96, 97, 107, 108, 112, 114, 120, 121, 124, 131, 132, 133, 136, 165, 166, 167, 168, 169, 170, 171, 172, 173, 177, 178, 201; Iraqi nationalism, nationalists, 185–96

NATO (North Atlantic Treaty Organization), 32, 170, 177, 211, 212

Near East (*see* Middle East), 164, 169

Negev, 88, 200, 201, 211, 231

Neguib, General Mohammed, 172, 173

Nile river, valley, 73, 107, 117, 121, 131, 153

Northern Tier, 5, 34, 89, 172, 175, 195

Al-Nuqrashi, Mahmud, Egyptian prime minister, 8, 49, 97, 102, 114, 115, 116, 117, 118, 121, 122, 123, 124, 125, 126, 127, 128, 130, 146, 147, 150, 153, 165

Nuri al-Said, Iraqi Prime Minister, 45, 46, 47, 51, 55, 75, 82, 89, 186, 187, 188, 189, 193, 194, 195, 211

oil, *see* Middle East

'Omega' plan, 175, 177

Ottoman empire, 81, 198

Palace, (*see also* Faruq, King of Egypt), 45, 47, 49, 97, 98, 100, 101, 103, 104, 106, 107, 109, 112, 117, 128, 130, 134, 137, 145

Palestine, xiv, xv, 9, 11, 16, 17, 19, 24, 25, 29, 33, 41, 42, 43, 44, 45, 47, 48, 49, 50, 51, 52, 53, 54, 55, 56, 57, 58, 59, 60, 67, 68, 72, 74, 75, 76, 80, 82, 83, 84, 85, 86, 87, 88, 89, 90, 105, 107, 114, 115, 116, 124, 126, 127, 128, 150, 154, 164, 166, 167, 188, 198, 199, 200, 201, 202, 203, 204, 206, 211, 215, 220–43; 'All-Palestine Government', 58, 59; Committees for the Defence of Palestine, 229; Higher Arab Committee, 227, 228, 229, 230, 232, 233, 235, 237, 238; *nakba* (Palestinian Arab catastrophe), 86, 242;

Palestinian, 84, 85; Palestinian Arab(s), xiii, 42, 48, 49, 51, 52, 53, 54, 55, 56, 58, 59, 60, 202, 203, 205, 206, 207, 208, 209, 212, 214, 215, 217, 220, 221, 222, 227, 228, 229, 230, 233, 236, 240, 241; Palestinian Arab refugees, 208, 210, 211, 216, 217, 241; Palestinian Arab revolt, 42, 46, 53, 200, 202, 222

partition (of Palestine), 53, 54, 56, 57, 58, 88, 200, 201, 202, 203, 221, 224, 225, 232, 233, 234, 235, 236, 238, 239, 240, 241, 242

partnership, *see* Bevin, Middle East economic and social development

pashas, xiii, 3, 9, 10, 12, 60, 70, 96, 142

patronage, 96, 116, 118, 131, 137, 138

Peel Commission plan, 200, 224, 232, 235

Pentagon, 30, 167, 170, 171, 172

Pentagon talks, 166, 167

Persia (*see also* Iran), 151, 156

Persian Gulf, 73, 75, 155, 191

Philby, H. St John, 44

Portsmouth, Treaty of, 9, 16, 19, 75, 86, 191–2, 241

Potsdam Conference, 144, 146

Qassem, Abd al-Karim, 185, 196

Al-Qudsi, Nazim, Syrian foreign minister, 87

Al-Quwwatli, Shukri, Syrian president, 81, 82

radical, radicals, 6, 7, 8, 14, 80, 84, 86, 90, 114, 185, 186, 187, 195, 196, 222, 229, 233

Ramallah line, 29, 31, 32, 156

Rashid Ali, Iraqi pro-Axis prime minister, 44, 53, 70, 101, 185, 186

Al-Rifa'i, Samir, Jordanian prime minister, 216

Robertson, General Sir Brian, 31, 208

Robertson, Sir James, 72, 73

Rommel, General Erwin, xiv, 101

Roosevelt, Franklin D., US president, xv, 163

Russia, Russian (*see also* Soviets, Soviet Union), 19, 26, 28, 30, 32, 34, 143, 148, 154, 157, 169, 201, 211, 242

Saadist Party, ministers, 97, 100, 101, 102, 104, 105, 108, 129, 130

254   *Demise of the British Empire in the Middle East*

Sabry, Hassan, Egyptian prime
minister, 100, 101
Sadat, Anwar, 105, 214
Sami, Salib, Egyptian foreign minister,
103
'Sandown' plan, 29, 30, 156, 164
Saudi Arabia, xv, 23, 41, 43, 44, 46, 52,
55, 59, 65, 74, 79, 80, 82, 83, 90, 187,
188, 190, 192, 198, 212, 214, 216, 233;
Ibn Saud, 46, 48, 51, 57, 225
Second World War, xiii, xiv, 19, 23, 24,
25, 26, 27, 30, 32, 41, 47, 53, 65, 67,
70, 72, 74, 76, 79, 89, 90, 95–109, 112,
113, 142, 147, 162, 163, 177, 185, 187,
199, 206, 220, 223, 224
Shertok, Moshe, Zionist political
leader, 232
Shi'ite(s), 187, 189
Shuckburgh, Evelyn, Foreign Office,
172, 174, 217
Sidqi, Isma'il, Egyptian prime minister,
19, 86, 114, 118, 119, 120, 121, 122,
147, 150, 153, 155, 165, 189, 235
Sirry, Husayn, Egyptian prime
minister, 101, 102, 103, 104
Slim, General, Chief of Imperial
General Staff, 33, 205
socialism, socialist(s), 4, 7, 15, 18
Soviets, Soviet Union (*see also* Russia),
xiv, 3, 4, 5, 6, 8, 9, 10, 16, 24, 25, 26,
27, 28, 29, 30, 31, 33, 34, 142, 143,
144, 150, 151, 155, 156, 162, 164, 165,
167, 168, 169, 173, 175, 176, 188, 190,
191, 195, 199, 210, 224, 225, 226, 231,
235, 237, 238, 239; Soviet bloc, 6, 65;
Soviet–Egyptian arms deal, 175,
212–13, 215
Stansgate, Lord, British secretary of
state for air, 19, 150, 151, 152, 153
State Department (US), 163, 166, 167,
168, 169, 170, 171, 177, 225, 241
Sterling Area, sterling balances, xiii, 67,
68, 76, 77, 146, 190
Stone, General R. G., Commander of
British Troops in Egypt, 105, 214
Straits, 144, 150
Strategic Air Command, 28
strategic bomber bases, forces, 151, 156
Sudan, Sudanese, 9, 19, 51, 64, 67, 71,
72–3, 74, 89, 107, 121, 127, 128, 129,
131, 151, 152, 153, 171; Gezira
scheme, 72, 73, 76
Suez Base, Suez Canal, xiv, 5, 9, 11, 23,

25, 26, 27, 28, 29, 32, 33, 35, 41–42,
51, 52, 65, 68, 76, 89, 90, 95, 124, 132,
133, 134, 135, 136, 142, 144, 145, 146,
148, 149, 154, 155, 157, 163, 164, 165,
167, 168, 169, 171, 174, 175, 176, 178,
201, 231, 239; Suez Canal
Committee, 144; Suez Canal
Company, nationalization of, 175,
176; Suez crisis, xiii, xiv, 175, 176,
177, 178
Syria, Syrian(s), 17, 18, 41, 43, 44, 45, 46,
47, 49, 50, 53, 55, 59, 79, 80, 81, 82,
83, 84, 86, 87, 90, 105, 107, 187, 188,
198, 199, 200, 203, 204, 208, 210, 213,
214, 222, 223, 227, 233, 239; Greater
Syria, 81, 82, 89, 199, 233, 239; Syrian
army, officer corps, 82, 83

Talal, Prince of Jordan, 206, 208
Tel Aviv, 29, 209
Templer, General Sir Gerald, 214, 215
theatre of mass politics (*see also*
disorder), xiv
Transjordan (*see also* Jordan), 9, 18, 41,
43, 45, 46, 49, 54, 56, 58, 59, 60, 67,
79, 80, 81, 84, 87, 88, 89, 187, 188,
190, 198, 200, 204, 222, 224, 225, 233,
234; 'Greater Transjordan' option,
201, 202, 203, 204
Treasury, xiii, 12, 13, 44, 100, 146
Tripartite Declaration of May 1950, 167,
168, 177
Troutbeck, Sir John, 3, 17, 19, 193
Truman, Harry S., US president, 53,
163, 164, 168, 220, 225, 226, 228, 232,
234, 236, 237; Truman Doctrine, 25
Tunisia, 103, 107
Turkey, Turkish, Turks, 5, 25, 29, 32, 70,
82, 96, 144, 151, 164, 170, 172, 195,
198, 211, 214

United Nations, xv, 6, 24, 30, 53, 56, 58,
60, 88, 109, 123, 124, 144, 153, 154,
168, 176, 191, 202, 203, 207, 221, 224,
226, 228, 229, 230, 234, 235, 236, 237,
238, 239, 240; General Assembly, 54,
87, 237, 239, 240, 241; Palestine
Conciliation Commission, 85;
Security Council, 52, 54, 122, 124,
165, 166, 242; UNSCOP, 238, 239, 240
United States (*see also* America, State
Department), 6, 14, 24, 26, 53, 65, 67,
71 74, 76, 87, 88, 89, 142, 145, 146,

Index   255

155, 162–78, 188, 194, 209, 220, 221, 223, 224, 225, 226n, 230, 232, 241; Defence Department, 167; Joint Chiefs of Staff, 28, 31, 164, 167; National Security Council, 168, 171, 176

Wafd party, government, xiv, 8, 45, 46, 47, 48, 68, 69, 70, 72, 96, 97, 98, 100, 102, 103–9, 115, 116, 117, 118, 120, 121, 122, 123, 124, 125, 126, 128, 129, 130, 131, 132, 134, 135, 136, 145, 146, 147, 154; Blueshirts, 97; Vanguard, 118, 119
Washington, 30, 102, 165, 167, 168, 172, 176, 177, 210, 225, 226, 231, 232
Watanists, 121, 144
Wavell, General Archibald, Commander-in-Chief, Middle East, 100, 101
Weizmann, Chaim, Zionist leader, 232
West Bank, 59, 60, 84, 85, 203, 204, 206, 207, 209, 212, 213, 216, 217
Western Desert, xiv, 45, 100, 101

White Paper on Palestine, May 1939, 43, 44, 52, 53, 223, 224, 225, 226, 227
Whitehall, 13, 17, 25, 202, 208, 220, 225, 237
Wilson, General Maitland, Commander British Troops in Egypt, 105
World Bank, 75, 76
Wright, Michael, Foreign Office, 12, 167

Yemen, Yemeni, 41, 60, 79
Yishuv (*see* Jews), 225, 226, 227, 231, 232, 233, 240, 243
Young Egypt, 102, 118, 119, 121, 122, 132, 133, 135; Husayn, Ahmad, leader, 102, 119, 132, 133, 134, 135, 136

Zaki, Salim, Commander of Cairo Police, 127
Al-Zi'am, General Husni, Syrian dictator, 18, 82
Zionist(s), 16, 44, 52, 55, 57, 58, 80, 83, 84, 88, 201, 202, 220, 221, 223, 224, 225, 226, 228, 232, 233, 237, 241

CPSIA information can be obtained
at www.ICGtesting.com
Printed in the USA
BVHW01s0855090318
510091BV00003B/16/P